THE PERSISTEN
OF HUMAN Rιᴜⁿιᴊ

The Power of Human Rights (published in 1999) was an innovative and influential contribution to the study of international human rights. At its center was a "spiral model" of human rights change which described the various socialization processes through which international norms were internalized into the domestic practices of various authoritarian states during the Cold War years. *The Persistent Power of Human Rights* builds on these insights, extending its reach and analysis. It updates our understanding of the various causal mechanisms and conditions which produce behavioral compliance, and expands the range of rights-violating actors examined to include democratic and authoritarian Great Powers, corporations, guerrilla groups, and private actors. Using a unique blend of quantitative and qualitative research and theory, this book yields not only important new academic insights but also a host of useful lessons for policy-makers and practitioners.

THOMAS RISSE is Professor of International Politics at the Freie Universität Berlin.

STEPHEN C. ROPP is Distinguished Emeritus Professor of Political Science at the University of Wyoming and an Honorary Research Fellow in the School of Political Science and International Studies (SPSIS) at the University of Queensland, Australia.

KATHRYN SIKKINK is a Regents Professor and the McKnight Presidential Chair in Political Science at the University of Minnesota.

Thomas Risse, Stephen C. Ropp and Kathryn Sikkink are the editors of *The Power of Human Rights: International Norms and Domestic Change* (Cambridge University Press, 1999).

The Persistent Power of Human Rights

Editors

Christian Reus-Smit
Nicholas J. Wheeler

Cambridge Studies in International Relations is a joint initiative of Cambridge University Press and the British International Studies Association (BISA). The series will include a wide range of material, from undergraduate textbooks and surveys to research-based monographs and collaborative volumes. The aim of the series is to publish the best new scholarship in International Studies from Europe, North America and the rest of the world.

CAMBRIDGE STUDIES IN INTERNATIONAL RELATIONS

Series list continues after index

THE PERSISTENT POWER OF HUMAN RIGHTS

From Commitment to Compliance

Edited by

THOMAS RISSE

STEPHEN C. ROPP

and

KATHRYN SIKKINK

CAMBRIDGE
UNIVERSITY PRESS

CAMBRIDGE UNIVERSITY PRESS
Cambridge, New York, Melbourne, Madrid, Cape Town,
Singapore, São Paulo, Delhi, Mexico City

Cambridge University Press
The Edinburgh Building, Cambridge CB2 8RU, UK

Published in the United States of America by Cambridge University Press, New York

www.cambridge.org
Information on this title: www.cambridge.org/9781107609365

© Cambridge University Press 2013

First published 2013

A catalogue record for this publication is available from the British Library

Library of Congress Cataloguing in Publication data
The persistent power of human rights : from commitment to compliance / Thomas Risse,
Stephen C. Ropp, and Kathryn Sikkink (eds.).
pages   cm. – (Cambridge studies in international relations ; 126)
Includes bibliographical references and index.
ISBN 978-1-107-02893-7 – ISBN 978-1-107-60936-5 (pbk.)
1. Human rights.   I. Risse-Kappen, Thomas, editor of compilation.   II. Ropp, Stephen C.,
editor of compilation.   III. Sikkink, Kathryn, 1955– editor of compilation.
JC571.P424 2013
323–dc23
2012033993

ISBN 978-1-107-02893-7 Hardback
ISBN 978-1-107-60936-5 Paperback

CONTENTS

FIGURES

TABLES

x

CONTRIBUTORS

TANJA A. BÖRZEL Professor of European Integration, Freie Universität Berlin, Berlin, Germany

KATHERINE BRYANT PhD Candidate, Department of Political Science, Texas A&M University, College Station, Texas, USA

ALISON BRYSK Mellichamp Chair in Global Governance, University of California Santa Barbara, Santa Barbara, California, USA

ANN MARIE CLARK Associate Professor of Political Science, Purdue University, West Lafayette, Indiana, USA

XINYUAN DAI Associate Professor of Political Science, University of Illinois, Urbana-Champaign, Illinois, USA

NICOLE DEITELHOFF Professor for International Relations, Goethe Universität Frankfurt, Frankfurt a. Main, Germany

RYAN GOODMAN Anne and Joel Ehrenkranz Professor of Law, New York University School of Law, New York, USA

ANJA JETSCHKE Professor of International Relations, University of Göttingen, Göttingen, Germany

DEREK JINKS Marrs McLean Professor in Law, University of Texas School of Law, Austin, Texas, USA

HYERAN JO Assistant Professor, Department of Political Science, Texas A&M University, College Station, Texas, USA

KATRIN KINZELBACH Head of Human Rights Program, Global Public Policy Institute, Berlin, Germany

ANDREA LIESE Professor of International Politics, University of Potsdam, Potsdam, Germany

WAGAKI MWANGI Public Information and Media Office, United Nations Convention to Combat Desertification Secretariat, Bonn, Germany

LOTHAR RIETH Senior Expert Corporate Responsibility and Sustainability, EnBW Energie Baden Württemberg AG, Berlin, Germany

THOMAS RISSE Professor of International Politics, Freie Universität Berlin, Berlin, Germany

STEPHEN C. ROPP Professor of Political Science (em.), University of Wyoming, Laramie, Wyoming, USA

HANS PETER SCHMITZ Associate Professor, Maxwell School of Citizenship and Public Affairs, Syracuse University, Syracuse, New York, USA

KATHRYN SIKKINK McKnight Presidential Chair in Political Science, University of Minnesota, Minneapolis, Minnesota, USA

BETH A. SIMMONS Clarence Dillon Professor of International Affairs, Harvard University, Cambridge, Massachusetts, USA

VERA VAN HÜLLEN Postdoctoral Fellow, Research Center "Governance in Areas of Limited Statehood," Freie Universität Berlin, Berlin, Germany

KLAUS DIETER WOLF Professor of International Relations, Peace Research Institute Frankfurt, Frankfurt a. Main, Germany

PREFACE

In 1999, the three of us co-edited *The Power of Human Rights: International Norms and Domestic Change* (PoHR; Cambridge University Press). In that volume, we proposed a spiral model of human rights change based on the "boomerang effect" which one of us had developed earlier with Margaret Keck (Keck and Sikkink 1998). Ten years later in 2009, we decided that it was time for some additional stock-taking. How had our original spiral model held up after a decade of much more intensive research on the issue of actual compliance with human rights norms? What new developments had there been in the human rights area and what did they say about the strengths and weaknesses of our initial work?

With questions such as these in mind, the three of us decided to reconvene parts of the old PoHR research team and to invite some other eminent scholars from Germany and the United States who were also doing important work on human rights. As was the case with our original volume, we kicked things off with a workshop held in Laramie at the University of Wyoming (August 27–29, 2009). During a coffee break there, we decided that we should get back into business and start working on a new book on human rights change. The result was a second workshop that took place in Berlin at the Freie Universität Berlin (June 3–5, 2010).

This second volume is not just about stock-taking concerning human rights change in general, but also more specifically about the scope conditions and processes leading from commitment to human rights norms to actual compliance with them. So, in addition to stock-taking (see Chapter 2), we initiated several dialogues during our two workshops. The first of these was between scholars doing comparative case studies and those using quantitative and statistical methods (see Chapters 3, 5, 7 and 13). And the second was with legal scholars working on human rights (see Chapter 6).

In addition to the need for stock-taking and dialogue, various events in the real world required that we expand our workshop agenda. A particular US administration's resort to torture in the post-9/11 world, China's continuing non-compliance with human rights norms, and the so-called "Arab Spring" strongly suggested that we revisit the central issue treated in PoHR – sustainable state compliance (see Chapters 8, 9 and 10). Other real-world events such as the disastrous effects of many states' limited capacity to enforce the rules (e.g. Sudan), as well as the human rights behavior of a wide range of non-state actors, needed additional attention (see Chapters 4, 11, 12, 13 and 14).

This book would not have been possible without generous financial support from several sources. First and foremost, the Research Center "Governance in Areas of Limited Statehood" (www.sfb-governance.de) funded by the German Research Foundation (*Deutsche Forschungsgemeinschaft*) provided most of the financing for the two workshops in Wyoming and in Berlin. In addition, we are very grateful to the University of Wyoming's International Studies Program and its director, Jean Garrison, for both financial and intellectual support.

Many other scholars also accompanied us along the way. Arie Kacowicz from Hebrew University in Jerusalem participated in both workshops and commented in detail on various chapters and on the project as a whole. We also thank Stephanie Anderson, Martha Finnemore, Beate Rudolf, Eric Voeten, and the three anonymous reviewers of Cambridge University Press for their useful critical input.

Last not least, we wish to thank Dan dePeyer for his assistance during the Wyoming workshop, the SFB team for organizing the Berlin workshop, and Janine Pietsch for research assistance. Brooke Coe put together the bibliography for the volume. We also thank John Haslam and Carrie Parkinson from Cambridge University Press as well as Chris Reus-Smit for their continuous encouragement of and support for this project. Last not least, we are grateful to Brooke Coe, Alexandra Kuhles, Gail Welsh, and Rob Wilkinson for their help at various stages of the production process.

PART I

Introduction and stock-taking

1

Introduction and overview

THOMAS RISSE AND STEPHEN C. ROPP

More than ten years ago, Thomas Risse, Stephen Ropp, and Kathryn Sikkink co-edited *The Power of Human Rights: International Norms and Domestic Change*, a volume whose centerpiece was a spiral model of human rights change (PoHR in the following, see Risse *et al.* 1999). PoHR was published on the occasion of the fiftieth anniversary of the Universal Declaration of Human Rights and ten years after the peaceful revolutions in Central Eastern Europe which then ended the Cold War. More than a decade later, dictators are on the run in the Middle East. These political changes in Tunisia, Egypt, Libya, and elsewhere are having profound effects on this region of the world, including the human rights situation there (see Chapter 10).

Over the past ten years, human rights policies have also changed considerably: First, we witness the gradual emergence of a new model of criminal accountability used by states acting collectively through the International Criminal Court (ICC) to hold individuals responsible for human rights violations (Deitelhoff 2006; Sikkink 2011). And a new international norm has emerged, the Responsibility to Protect (R2P), referring to the responsibility of the international community to intervene – by military means, if necessary – if state rulers are unwilling or incapable of protecting their citizens from gross human rights violations (Evans 2008; Weiss 2005). R2P was recently put to a test with the Western intervention in Libya which had been endorsed by the United Nations Security Council and backed by the Arab League as well as the domestic opposition in Libya.

Second, we see an increasing recognition by states and other actors in the human rights field that weak or limited statehood has become a major obstacle with regard to domestic implementation and compliance. Limited statehood refers to parts of a country's territory or policy areas where central state authorities cannot effectively implement or enforce central decisions or even lack the monopoly over the means of violence (Risse 2011b; see Chapter 4).

We thank the participants of the two workshops in Wyoming in August 2009 and in Berlin in June 2010 for their detailed comments on the draft of this chapter. We are particularly grateful to Arie Kacowicz, Kathryn Sikkink, and three anonymous reviewers of Cambridge University Press.

Third, private actors such as firms and rebel groups are increasingly committed to complying with international human rights standards in a direct way rather than through the mechanisms of domestic law. Within companies, for example, we can observe an emerging international norm of corporate social responsibility that embeds human rights standards in corporate doctrine (e.g. Prakash and Potoski 2007; see Chapters 11 and 12; regarding rebel groups see Chapter 13). Moreover, other private actors, such as families and religious communities, are increasingly recognized as violators and subject to international campaigns – but not yet to consistent governance (Brysk 2005; see Chapter 14).

Last but not least, human rights scholarship has evolved considerably. Human rights research of the 1990s was characterized by comparative case studies as the dominant approach (e.g. Brysk 1994; Clark 2001; Hawkins 2002; Keck and Sikkink 1998; Risse *et al.* 2002). This has changed in that researchers using quantitative methods have begun to investigate the processes and mechanisms by which international human rights norms spread (particularly Hafner-Burton 2008; Simmons 2009). At the same time, international lawyers have become aware of the increasing social science scholarship on human rights, while political scientists started to take the particular characteristics of law seriously (see e.g. Alston and Crawford 2000; Goodman and Jinks 2003; in general Goldstein *et al.* 2000).

This combination of political and academic developments strongly suggests that we take a fresh look at the past twenty years of human rights research. On the one hand, the socialization mechanisms identified in the original PoHR for turning international law into domestic practices have generally held up well in the "laboratory" of subsequent empirical testing. More specifically, we see that much of the recent quantitative work seems to support our earlier largely qualitative findings (see Chapter 3). These mechanisms of change can also be applied to the new human rights agenda, particularly with regard to private actors and their compliance with international norms.

On the other hand, we recognize that our original work on human rights had several weaknesses. First, we under-specified the processes and scope conditions by which and under which states as well as private actors could be moved from commitment to human rights norms to actual compliance with them. Second, our earlier work assumed the presence of fully functioning states, suggesting in turn that compliance with human rights norms was a matter of state commitment and willingness rather than of institutional capacity. "Limited statehood" challenges this assumption and forces us to take a fresh look at the compliance *problématique*. Finally, we did not look at compliance with human rights norms by powerful states like the United States or the People's Republic of China (see Chapters 8 and 9). This would seem to be a particularly important task in light of post-9/11 US non-compliance during the George W. Bush administration with the anti-torture norm and China's continuing resistance to human rights pressures.

In this volume, we concentrate on the following research question: *Under what conditions and by which mechanisms will actors – states, transnational corporations, other private actors – make the move from commitment to compliance?*

This chapter proceeds in five steps. First, we recapitulate the spiral model of human rights change as developed in PoHR. Second, we introduce this volume's own unique focus on the processes leading from commitment to compliance, define the respective terms, and discuss the book's expanded focus – not only on a much broader range of actors but also on a more inclusive set of human rights. Third, we take a closer look at the mechanisms and modes of social action that we believe can move these various targeted actors from commitment to compliance; here, we build upon and further specify the mechanisms described in the original spiral model. Fourth, and most important, we introduce the centerpiece of this book's theoretical argument – namely the impact of a set of scope conditions under which movement by state and non-state actors from commitment to compliance is more or less likely to occur. These scope conditions are then evaluated in subsequent empirical chapters. We conclude with a short description of the plan of the book.

The "spiral model" of human rights change revisited

We begin with a brief description of the spiral model of human rights change originally developed in PoHR. The key questions we wished to ask in PoHR were whether it was possible to model the various processes involved in the movement from norm expectation to real country-level results; and, if so, could we document the existence of these processes empirically through the use of country case studies of change in state human rights practices?

In attempting to answer these questions, our theoretical point of departure was the work of a well-known group of social constructivists who had been looking at the relationship between ideas and social processes in a number of diverse issue areas (Adler, 1997; Checkel 1998; Katzenstein 1996; Kratochwil 1989; Wendt 1992). The actual "spiral model" of human rights change that we developed in PoHR built upon work on the "boomerang effect" that had previously been done by Margaret Keck and Kathryn Sikkink (Keck and Sikkink 1998). Incorporating some of their insights about the causal relationships between various state and non-state actors and associated processes, we sought to come up with a more specified conceptualization of these relationships and processes that could be graphically represented.

The eventual result of these efforts was the "spiral model" of human rights change, for which we sought empirical evidence using a comparative case study approach. In our model, we identified three distinct types of socialization processes (instrumental adaptation, argumentation, and habitualization) that appeared to work together to socialize non-compliant states to human rights norms during a series of five distinct phases (see Figure 1.1):

(1) *Repression*: there was an initial phase during which the leaders of authoritarian regimes engaged in repression. While the degree of repression that the various regimes in our case studies engaged in varied widely from the quasi-genocidal behavior found in Guatemala (Ropp and Sikkink 1999) to Tunisia's "softer" neo-patrimonialist variant (Gränzer 1999; see Chapter 10), the resulting informational vacuum made it extremely difficult for opposition groups to convince authoritarian leaders that they had anything to deny. As a result, this initial phase tended to be a long drawn-out affair during which none of our three socialization mechanisms worked particularly well.

(2) *Denial*: if transnational groups eventually succeeded in gathering sufficient information on human rights violations to initiate the advocacy process, our spiral model posited and our case studies documented a second phase that we labeled denial. While the domestic opposition usually remained too weak during this phase to mount a serious challenge to the regime, the increased lobbying of international human rights organizations and of sympathetic democratic states by advocate groups often evoked outraged "How dare you!" denials from officials in repressive states. Such denials reflected a continuing refusal to recognize the validity of international human rights norms and thus an unwillingness to submit themselves to international jurisdiction in such matters. However, we also found this denial phase to be of critical importance in that discursive engagement in any form and no matter what the nature of the "conversation" opened the door to the process of international socialization.

(3) *Tactical concessions*: we found the third phase of our spiral model to be a particularly precarious one, characterized by a repressive state's use of tactical concessions in order to get the international human rights community "off their backs." These concessions normally included measures such as releasing a few political prisoners, showing greater tolerance for mass public demonstrations, and/or signing up to international treaties. We found that their use of this instrumental logic and subsequent making of what they believe to be "low cost" tactical concessions had an important secondary effect in that it facilitated the rapid mobilization and further normative empowerment of domestic advocacy groups. We found this phase of tactical concessions to be particularly precarious because the government could react to this rapid increase in mobilization either by engaging in unrelenting repression or by making even more generous tactical concessions.

(4) *Prescriptive status*: while the tactical concessions phase tended to be dominated by a state logic of instrumentality, we found that the "terrain of contestation" shifted radically during phase 4 when states granted human rights

norms prescriptive status (see chapters on Eastern Europe and South Africa, Black 1999; Thomas 1999). The "prescriptive status" phase was characterized by a well-defined set of state actions and associated practices such as ratifying relevant international treaties and their optional protocols, changing related domestic laws, setting up new domestic human rights institutions, and regularly referring to human rights norms in state administrative and bureaucratic discourse.

(5) *Rule-consistent behavior*: we called the fifth and final phase of our model "rule-consistent behavior," i.e. behavioral change and sustained compliance with international human rights. In hindsight, we view this phase as involving a set of sub-processes that were somewhat under-specified. To the extent that we did specify these sub-processes in PoHR, we viewed them as consisting of a two-level game at both the domestic and international level that pitted proponents of actual implementation of now prescriptively validated human rights norms against their opponents. From this perspective, sustainable change in actual behavior that was consistent with these norms was viewed as the result of local pro-change groups being able to leverage international support in such a way as to eventually triumph over their domestic opponents.

As mentioned above, we sought empirical evidence for the general validity of our model by using the comparative case study method. Our initial operating assumption was that, by selecting paired country cases of human rights "success" and "failure" in a number of different world regions, we would be able to tease out the various factors that made a difference as they related to the five phases of our model. For "success stories" during the 1980s, we chose Chile, South Africa, the Philippines, Poland, and the former Czechoslovakia. The more difficult cases included Guatemala, Kenya, Uganda, Morocco, Tunisia, and Indonesia. In the meantime, scholars have extended the analysis to China, Egypt, Turkey, and Israel (see Chapter 2).

After examining the evidence gathered from country-level field research that was conducted by our team of German and American scholars, we concluded that the socializing mechanisms of change that we had built into our spiral model had a good deal of explanatory power for most of the individual cases. More importantly, the phased processes of human rights change specified by the model appeared to be generalizable across different types of political regimes, socio-economic systems, and cultural regions. While human rights progress was often uneven and our various phases occurred asynchronously in different countries over time, there was a clearly identifiable pattern of human rights progress that we could also model as a larger norms cascade (Finnemore and Sikkink 1998; see also Haglund and Aggarwal 2011 for a discussion of economic and social rights). Over three decades from the 1960s until the 1990s, the various phases during which human rights change occurred grew progressively

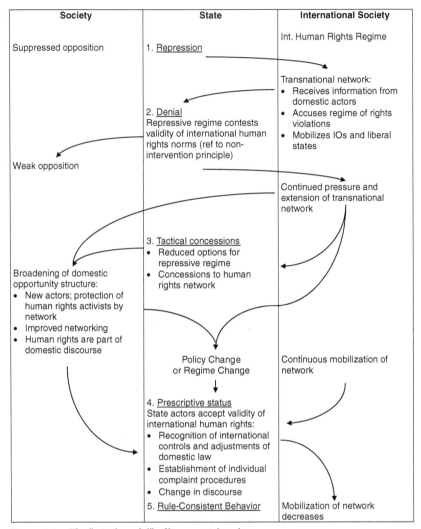

Figure 1.1   The "spiral model" of human rights change

shorter, leading to a "speeding up" of improvement in the overall global human rights situation.

Because we chose to model these causal processes, we opened ourselves up to both praise and criticism within the community of scholars working on human rights issues. Some of our scholarly critics emphasized certain sins of commission such as the fact that the spiral model seemed to "smuggle in" a hidden ideological agenda and that there was an associated linear teleological bent to the analysis. Additional alleged sins of commission included problems with the measurement and operationalization of key variables, cases where the author's application of the model to a particular country did not seem to square with the empirical evidence, and inadequate treatment of human rights situations where competing norms were involved (see Chapter 2).

Other scholars emphasized various sins of omission, sins that in retrospect were often the result of the time period when our model was developed (during the 1990s and dealing with cases from the 1980s). For example, the spiral model of human rights assumed the existence of a core group of developed democracies that adhered to human rights norms and could thus legitimately socialize norm-violating regimes to "proper" behavior. It did not seriously take into account the fact that these core states could become norm-violators themselves (see Chapter 8 on the United States). Additional sins of omission that have subsequently been recognized include the absence of attention to human rights violations in areas of limited statehood (see Chapter 4), and to the growing importance of non-state actors such as multinational corporations in the human rights field (see Chapters 11 and 12).

From commitment to compliance

The original spiral model dealt with the entire process relating to the human rights socialization of state actors – from repression and initial denial that international human rights law applied to them at all, to their eventual sustained compliance with these norms. More than a decade later, explaining state commitment to international human rights does not seem to be particularly interesting. In the twenty-first century, there is not a single state left in the international system that has not ratified at least one international human rights treaty (the Convention on the Rights of the Child topping all other global human rights treaties, see Liese 2006). Moreover, there is universal agreement that fundamental human rights constitute *ius cogens*, i.e. that part of international law to which states commit irrespective of whether or not they are party to individual treaties.

What does remain interesting is the fact that various actors other than states (e.g. NGOs, multinational corporations and rebel groups) increasingly commit themselves to basic human rights (see Part IV of this volume). As sociological institutionalists argue, the norm-guided logic of appropriateness now requires both governments *and* non-state actors in world society to at least pay lip service to the idea that there are such things as fundamental human rights (Meyer *et al.* 1997).

This book then focuses on the processes leading from commitment to compliance. By "commitment," we mean that *actors accept international human rights as valid and binding for themselves*. In the case of states and apart from *ius cogens*, this usually requires signing up to and/or ratifying international human rights treaties. With regard to non-state actors such as firms, NGOs, or rebel

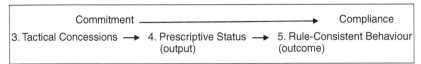

Figure 1.2   Commitment, compliance, and the spiral model

groups, commitment implies at a minimum some sort of statement that the respective actors intend to accept at least voluntary codes of conduct as obligatory (from self-regulation to multi-party "soft law" such as the Global Compact, see Chapter 11). "Compliance" is defined as *sustained behavior and domestic practices that conform to the international human rights norms*, or what we called "rule-consistent behavior" in the original spiral model. The authors of the various individual chapters in this volume specify in more detail what they mean by commitment and compliance.

We see commitment and compliance as two ends of a continuum (see Figure 1.2). The spiral model assumed that a government's commitment to international human rights takes place initially as part of the "tactical concessions" phase. PoHR did not suggest that ratification of international human rights treaties automatically translates into compliance. Rather, we claimed that encouraging governments to move from commitment to compliance involves the application of continuous pressures "from above" and "from below" (Brysk 1993). Moreover, PoHR defined "prescriptive status" (phase 4 of the model) as the point in time when governments had not only ratified international treaties, but had also transposed them into domestic law, had created the necessary institutions to enforce these laws (e.g. human rights commissions), and had fully acknowledged the validity of international human rights in their official public discourse. In the language of research on compliance (e.g. Raustiala and Slaughter 2002), "prescriptive status" equals the output dimension of compliance while "rule-consistent behavior" (phase 5) refers to the outcome dimension.

Over the past decade, quantitative research on human rights has confirmed that ratification of international treaties does not lead to compliance per se (e.g. Hafner-Burton and Tsutsui 2005; Hathaway 2002; Keith 1999). Some authors have even gone so far as to suggest that rights violations became more severe after treaty ratification. This in turn led others to argue that qualitative and quantitative studies on human rights change were reaching different conclusions, with the authors of small-N case studies reaching more optimistic conclusions than those of large-N studies (Hafner-Burton and Ron 2009).

We disagree with the view that qualitative and quantitative methodologies are yielding strikingly different results (see particularly Chapters 3 and 5). The various chapters in this volume show a growing convergence between quantitative and qualitative findings on human rights compliance, especially when the quantitative researchers consider the impact of intervening variables such as regime type when attempting to explain the movement (or lack thereof) from treaty ratification to compliance. For example, in the most sophisticated quantitative and qualitative study on the subject to date, Beth Simmons confirms the importance of some of the causal mechanisms that we originally proposed in PoHR. *Mobilizing for Human Rights* (Simmons 2009) looks at a wide range of human rights issues and demonstrates that three processes – elite-initiated agendas, litigation and political mobilization – do the explanatory work between commitment (e.g. treaty ratification by a given state) and compliance. At least two of these processes – judicial action enabled by human rights treaties and popular mobilization in favour of compliance – are consistent with the spiral model. In addition, Clark's chapter in this volume (Chapter 7) shows that public shaming of norm-violating governments through action by the UN Human Rights Commission matters for producing compliance once states have made a commitment. Murdie and Davis (2012) demonstrate similar effects with regard to human rights INGOs.

Yet, in PoHR, we under-theorized the process leading from commitment all the way to sustained rule-consistent behavior (see Chapter 2 on this point). We simply assumed, but did not explicitly specify, that the same causal mechanisms that worked to move the process along in the earliest phases would also be at work later on. We also thought that the social mechanisms to promote human rights would all be complementary and that there were no contradictions between them (see Chapter 6).

Furthermore, while the original spiral model was never meant to present a fair-weather picture of human rights change, we did not pay sufficient attention to instances in which states got "stuck" somewhere in the process or even experienced backlash. Two prominent cases come to mind: the People's Republic of China is often cited as a case in which external pressure, applied in an effort to improve human rights performance, did not produce results. However, Kinzelbach's chapter (Chapter 9) shows that the spiral model is indeed applicable to China, even though progress has been slow because the regime is much less vulnerable (in both material and ideational terms) to network pressure than are the regimes in many other countries.

An even more important case – both for academics and in terms of its political consequences – is US human rights performance during the administration of George W. Bush (2001–2009). The United States had been instrumental in bringing about the international Convention against Torture (CAT) and in creating an international normative taboo against torture and the use of other means of cruel and unusual punishment (except for the death penalty; see Sikkink 2004; Thimm 2009). The CAT received full bipartisan support in the US Senate after then-President George H.W. Bush submitted it for ratification in 1990. Yet, in the aftermath of the terrorist attack on the World Trade Center in New York City in September 2001, the US administration authorized special forms of treatment for those suspected of terrorism which both the previous Clinton administration and the subsequent Obama administration had called by their real name – torture. How is it to be explained that a US president and a vice president could publicly defend the use of waterboarding without being faced with public outrage and being forced to resign? In more academic terms, the US case begs the question of whether the spiral model is suitable to deal with countries that experience such backlash against the domestic legitimacy of human rights norms. Sikkink's chapter (Chapter 8) tackles these issues.

As mentioned above, some of the most notable shortcomings of PoHR were sins of omission that resulted from the time period from which our cases were selected and during which we developed the spiral model (the 1980s and early 1990s). Although sophisticated theoretical accounts of the relationship between state and non-state actors in world politics had existed in the academic literature for a long time (Keohane and Nye 1971), the focus when it came to understanding human rights violators was still on states (primarily authoritarian ones) and their behavior in the late Cold War environment. As a result, PoHR emphasized a narrow set of "freedom from" rights (torture, disappearance, etc.) as well as the types of civil rights (freedom of expression, assembly, etc.) that are associated with established liberal democracies.

The more ambitious task that we set for ourselves in this volume on commitment/compliance mechanisms is to move beyond an exclusive concern with (authoritarian) states as principal human rights violators. We broaden the scope of this study to include non-state rule targets such as corporations and rebel groups (Part IV of the volume). Additionally, we expand the range of human rights that our chapter authors subject to case study analysis to include gender rights (Chapter 14) and labor rights (Chapter 11).

Mechanisms and modes of social action

This brings us back to one of the fundamental concerns of PoHR: how do the various socialization mechanisms that move the human rights process along go together and hang together (see also Chapter 6)? In that previous volume, we identified three such mechanisms (instrumental adaptation, argumentation and habitualization) that were in turn grounded in different logics of action. For example, we believed that the logic of consequences, which posits that leaders of authoritarian states will act rationally in order to balance the costs and benefits of external sanctions and rewards offered for "good" human rights behavior, explained some developments during early stages of the socialization process (e.g. the tactical concession phase). However, we devoted the majority of our attention to the impact of the logics of appropriateness and persuasion, in the sense that state actors were viewed as heavily influenced by human rights norms that suggested appropriate patterns of behavior within the international community of "liberal states."

The first theoretical contribution of this book is to further tease out these relationships between various socializing mechanisms and to examine their impact. Our central point is that the logic of consequences and the cost-benefit calculations of utility-maximizing egoistic actors are often embedded in a more encompassing logic of appropriateness of norm-guided behavior as institutionalized in the contemporary international human rights regime. For example, firms committing to human rights might initially do so for purely instrumental reasons. They might have been subjected to consumer boycotts, and, thus, market pressures might have forced them to commit (see Chapter 12). However, these market pressures eventually lead to the incorporation of norms of appropriate human rights behavior into the cost-benefit calculations of firms. As a result, it no longer makes sense to test hypotheses derived from rational choice theory against those theories that stress norm-guided behavior. Rather, we aim at systematically examining the mechanisms and sequences (as well as their internal contradictions) by which the various modes of social action interact to bring about human rights change.

Scholars studying compliance have identified four such mechanisms based on different modes of social (inter-)action, two of which were already included in PoHR (e.g. Börzel *et al.* 2010; Checkel, 2001; Hurd 1999; Simmons 2009: ch. 4; Tallberg 2002).

(1)   Coercion: use of force and legal enforcement

State and non-state actors can be *coerced* to comply with costly rules. Coercion does not leave them much choice but to abide by the norms. Two cases need to be distinguished here, though. On the one hand, compliance with human rights norms can be imposed through the use of force by external actors. The emerging norm of the "responsibility to protect" ultimately aims at legitimizing such use of force to establish basic human rights standards.

On the other hand, while legal enforcement mechanisms often include coercive measures such as sanctions, they are seldom imposed on actors against their will. This is the case because states that have committed, for example, to the Rome Statute of the International Criminal Court (ICC) have voluntarily agreed to accept its provisions and to enforce them through domestic law as well. Thus, a Security Council referral to the ICC of a case like Sudan, which has not ratified the Rome Statute, can be seen as coercion. But a self-referral case brought to the ICC by a state actor that has ratified the Rome Statute (such as in the case of Uganda), should not be seen as coercion. Rather, it should be viewed as the legal enforcement of an agreed-upon prior commitment. The more human rights standards are subjected to international and regional judicialization and thus increasingly involve domestic, regional, or international courts, the more legal enforcement mechanisms come into play as a substitute for the use of force (see Sikkink 2011).

(2)   Changing incentives: sanctions and rewards

Coercion, whether applied directly and against a recalcitrant actor's will or as part of a legal enforcement mechanism, undoubtedly needs to be recognized as playing a role in the overall change process. However, we believe that incentive structures play an even more important role in moving state and non-state actors from commitment to compliance. Utility calculations can be changed by raising the costs of non-compliance. This is the rational choice mechanism par excellence insofar as it is up to the respective targeted actor to decide whether or not to change her behavior in response to the changed incentives. Once again, we can distinguish two cases here. Sanctions are negative incentives often used by the international community to punish non-compliance.[1] The same holds true for positive incentives (e.g. foreign aid) to enhance compliance with international human rights. The portfolio of most international organizations as well as individual states contains strategies and instruments to induce compliance through incentives (for a discussion with regard to democracy assistance see Magen *et al.* 2009). The effectiveness of such sanctions and rewards will depend in part on the material and social vulnerability of the target actors, as we discuss below.

(3)   Persuasion and discourse

PoHR heavily emphasized arguing, persuasion, and learning. If persuasion works, it has an advantage over either coercion or the manipulation of incentive structures in that it induces actors into voluntary compliance with costly rules (see e.g. Deitelhoff 2006; Müller 2004; Risse 2000). Persuasion is also more long-lasting as a socialization mechanism than manipulating incentive structures, since the latter leave actors' interests untouched. However, the successful use of pure persuasion through recourse to nothing but the "better argument" is extremely rare in international affairs. In reality, we mostly observe the use of a combination of arguing and incentive-based mechanisms, particularly when external actors try to induce rule targets – whether states or non-state actors – into compliance with human rights (for a general discussion see Deitelhoff and Müller 2005; Ulbert and Risse 2005).

But even if we do not observe processes of persuasion, discourse matters enormously as a mechanism leading to compliance. It is true that naming and shaming can only be successful if either the target actors or an audience central to the change process actually believe in the social validity of the norm. Once human rights have become a dominant discourse, however, this

---

[1] In some borderline cases, sanctions amount to coercion if they leave the target virtually no choice other than to comply.

discourse exerts structural power on actors. As a result, they are more likely to comply.

In addition to heavily emphasizing persuasion, we assumed in PoHR that arguing and discursive interactions had a "unidirectional" impact in that human rights advocates would always have the better arguments and that these arguments would eventually carry the day. In the meantime, and particularly in the post-9/11 environment, we have witnessed the emergence of powerful regime-based counter-discourses and narratives (see Chapters 2, 8 and 9). The existence of such discourses and narratives, together with the associated deterioration in the human rights behavior of the countries from which they emanate, obviously undermines our initial assumption regarding "unidirectionality."

(4) Capacity building

There is a fourth mechanism leading to sustained compliance with international norms which we did not discuss in the original spiral model. Compliance research, however, has always emphasized capacity-building as a pathway to compliance. The "management" approach to compliance points out that involuntary non-compliance with costly rules is at least as important as non-compliance that results from the unwillingness of actors to abide by them (see Chayes and Chayes 1991, 1993, 1995). So, if human rights norms are violated in areas of limited statehood because of a lack of state capacity to enforce them, the three other mechanisms discussed will not do the trick. PoHR did not pay attention to this mechanism and to the fact that commitment might not lead to compliance when central state authorities lack the institutional and administrative capacity to enforce decisions including human rights standards. In other words, PoHR assumed that governments were primarily unwilling rather than unable to comply, thus implicitly taking consolidated statehood for granted.

However, "limited statehood" is much more widespread in the contemporary international system than is usually acknowledged (see Chapter 4). Most important, areas of limited statehood are not confined to fragile or even failed states, but constitute a common phenomenon among developing countries. As a result, research on human rights has to take the management approach to compliance more seriously than has been the case so far. Capacity-building, as we understand it in this volume, refers to a highly institutionalized process of social interaction aiming toward education, training and the building up of administrative capacities to implement and enforce human rights law.

In sum, we believe that the four processes identified here capture the main social mechanisms which induce or prevent compliance with international human rights norms (see Table 1.1). These mechanisms rely on different modes of social action. The first and foremost theoretical task ahead is to specify the ways in which the four mechanisms relate to one another. They can be

Table 1.1. *Social mechanisms to induce compliance*

Mechanisms	Modes of social (inter-) action	Underlying logic of action
Coercion	Use of force Legal enforcement	Hierarchical authority (*Herrschaft*)
Incentives	Sanctions Rewards	Logic of consequences
Persuasion	Arguing Naming/shaming Discursive power	Logic of arguing and/or logic of appropriateness
Capacity-building	Institution-building, education, training	Creating the preconditions so that logics of consequences or of appropriateness can apply

complementary, additive or sequential. But they can also lack complementarity, operate haphazardly and even be substractive (see Chapter 6).

Scope conditions for compliance

The second contribution of this book is to specify more clearly the scope conditions under which we would expect these four social mechanisms to induce compliance by both state and non-state actors with international human rights law. We have identified five such factors related to different types of states, regimes, and to the degree of vulnerability of states and other such rule targets to external and domestic pressures. The first two scope conditions apply only to states, while the remaining ones apply to any type of rule target.

(1) Democratic vs. authoritarian regimes

The original spiral model was developed and applied only to states with authoritarian and repressive regimes. We asked under which conditions a combination of external and internal mobilization of advocacy networks would bring about liberalization and human rights change within these regimes. The empirical case studies then showed that improvements of human rights almost always resulted from regime change and democratization processes (Morocco being the one exception, Gränzer 1999; see Chapter 10). Subsequent quantitative research also demonstrated that countries with democratic regimes are more likely to comply with human rights norms than authoritarian ones (for details see Chapter 3; also Simmons 2009). In other words, regime type seems to matter.

However, we need to specify here what we mean by "democracy" in order to avoid an endogeneity problem. Sophisticated conceptualizations of democratic rule usually include participatory and electoral institutions, the rule of law and – indeed – respect for human rights (e.g. Merkel and Croissant 2000; Merkel *et al.* 2003–2004). Datasets such as the Freedom House Index or the Bertelsmann Transformation Index (BTI) also include political and civil rights as indicators to measure regime type. But since human rights behavior is our dependent variable, rule of law and respect for human rights cannot also be part of the definition of democracy we use. To avoid these methodological problems and the subsequent tautological arguments, one should, therefore, use minimalist concepts of democracy focusing on the degree of competition for executive office and the degree of participation by citizens in electing their governments.

We assume that regime type as a scope condition not only affects the general propensity to move from commitment to compliance but also makes a difference with regard to the various social mechanisms specified above. In particular, one would expect that legal enforcement of human rights through domestic, foreign or international courts would bring democracies back into compliance (see Chapter 8 on the United States). Moreover, one would also assume that mechanisms of persuasion, naming and shaming are particularly effective with regard to stable democratic regimes given that respect for human rights constitutes an institutionalized logic of appropriateness in such systems. In contrast, using incentives – whether sanctions or rewards – to induce democracies into compliance might be counter-productive, because it might be perceived as insulting (see Chapter 6). The opposite might be true for autocratic regimes, since there is no institutionally embedded logic of appropriateness which could shame them into compliance.

(2)   Consolidated vs. limited statehood

As already mentioned, the original spiral model assumed that states are unwilling rather than incapable of complying with human rights norms. We did not take into account the fact that some states lack the kinds of efficient and effective administrative structures and institutions that would allow them to enforce and implement central decisions. We took consolidated statehood for granted, implicitly assuming a full monopoly over the means of violence and the capacity to implement and enforce rules. However, as the literature on weak, fragile and even failed states reminds us, the institutional capacity of states should be treated as a variable rather than as a constant (see e.g. Rotberg 2003, 2004; Schneckener 2004).

"Limited statehood" as a major obstacle to compliance is not confined to fragile or failed states (see Chapter 4; also Risse 2011b). Many states contain political and administrative institutions which are too weak to enforce the law on the whole territory, in some issue-areas (such as human rights), and/or with regard to particular parts of the population. Related to this, many states of the Global South do not hold a monopoly over the means of violence in parts of their territory.

However, there is no straightforward relationship between state strength and consolidated statehood, on the one hand, and compliance with human rights norms, on the other. As a result, we need to combine the two institutional characteristics – state strength and regime type (see Figure 4.2). Different social mechanisms should be expected to facilitate the move from commitment to compliance. In the cases of consolidated autocratic or democratic regimes, non-compliance results primarily from state actors being unwilling to implement human rights norms. Therefore, three of the four social mechanisms discussed above – coercion/legal enforcement, positive and negative incentives, and persuasion/shaming – are expected to be applicable. In the case of consolidated democracies, legal enforcement as well as "naming and shaming" by transnational advocacy networks should be particularly effective. With regard to consolidated autocratic regimes, the original assumptions of the spiral model should hold and all three mechanisms might work in principle, even though persuasion could prove to be ineffective.

If limited statehood and lack of political and administrative capacity to enforce decisions is the main problem, however, "involuntary non-compliance" should result. Therefore, capacity-building as prescribed by the "management school" of compliance research (see above) should be the primary mechanism to move a state from commitment to compliance. This is particularly relevant for democratic regimes with weak institutions and low administrative capacity which is characteristic for many new democracies in the Global South. In the case of autocratic regimes in weak states, however, it is very hard to specify the root cause of compliance problems. Capacity-building as such, for example, could result in making a repressive regime more effective in carrying out human rights violations. Coercion, incentivizing and persuasion mechanisms, however, might be equally irrelevant if the regime is unable to enforce the law. In this case, one should think of functional equivalents to consolidated statehood as a remedy for the compliance problems in autocratic regimes within weak states.

(3) Centralized vs. decentralized rule implementation

Our third scope condition has to do with the degree of centralized or decentralized rule implementation in a given situation and with regard to any targeted actor (e.g. states, rebel groups or corporations). The original spiral model in PoHR treated states as unitary actors with regard to compliance. However, the degree to which decision making is centralized with regard to norm compliance makes a difference (Lutz and Sikkink 2000). Simmons, for example, argues that there has been greater compliance with the norm against the death penalty in countries that have abolished it because the sanction associated with the norm is centrally carried out by public authorities, and thus easy to monitor (Simmons 2009: 200). Compliance is also more likely if those actors who are committed to human rights norms are also those who comply with them directly. However, compliance is more difficult to achieve if it has to result from collaborative or conflict-ridden negotiations between different decentralized actors. In other words, a situation of decentralized rule implementation means that rule addressees (those who commit to human rights) are not exclusively the rule targets who have to comply (see Börzel 2002).

Take the case of torture: central state authorities (in consolidated states, see below) usually have direct control over their military via a clear line of command and should, therefore, be able to enforce the prohibition against torture committed by members of their armed forces. In the case of the United States and the George W. Bush administration, for example, it was not the military per se that undermined the taboo against torture, but rather officials at the highest levels of the Executive Branch of government (see Chapter 8). At the same time, and given the competencies of communal authorities in most countries, central governments have much less control over the local police forces. As a result, we would expect that it is more difficult to implement the prohibition against torture with regard to the police as compared to the military (e.g. the case of Turkey, Chapter 2, also Liese 2006).

Things become more complex if states, for example, commit to international human rights norms, but firms or even private citizens are the rule targets that are expected to comply (see Chapter 14 on gender rights). In such cases, the implementation process can be extremely decentralized, since states are legally responsible for compliance, but private citizens have to change their behavior, which often includes abandoning or transforming long-standing cultural practices. The problem is exacerbated, of course, in cases where such behavioral change is being encouraged in areas of limited statehood (see above).

Organizational centralization or decentralization also affects the behavior of nonstate actors. For example, as Hyeran Jo and Katherine Bryant show in Chapter 13, rebel groups with more hierarchical organizational structures are more likely to comply with humanitarian norms than loosely organized groups. As to business firms, compliance with regard to things such as social rights should become more problematic, the longer the supply chain (see Chapter 12).

With regard to this particular scope condition, as long as rule implementation is highly centralized, it should not matter much whether coercion, incentives or persuasion is used in efforts to induce compliance. However, since involuntary non-compliance is the main problem in highly decentralized "implementation systems," capacity-building constitutes a major remedy for tackling the problem in such cases.

(4)   Material vulnerability

Our two final scope conditions affecting the movement from commitment to compliance relate to any given rule target's vulnerability to external (as well as to internal domestic) pressure. It makes a difference, of course, whether China, Russia or the United States is accused of human rights violations as compared to the Philippines, Guatemala or Kenya (on the latter see Jetschke 1999; Ropp and Sikkink 1999; Schmitz 1999; on the United States and China see Chapters 8 and 9). The same should hold true for non-state actors commanding different types and levels of resources.

On average, rule targets commanding powerful economic and/or military resources are expected to be less vulnerable to external pressures to comply with human rights norms than are materially weak targets. This "realist" assumption is straightforward and does not require further specification. Everything else being equal, great powers can "fight off" external network mobilization more easily than can weak states. The same should hold true for non-state actors such as companies. If a Small or Medium-Sized Enterprise (SME) is subjected to a consumer boycott because of its violations of social rights in some country where it invests, the costs incurred are much higher than, say, in the case of a big oil company being subjected to a similar campaign.

Note that we do not assume that materially powerful actors are immune from external pressures or transnational mobilization. We only expect that mechanisms based on material coercion and/or negative incentives such as sanctions are less likely to yield results when used against materially powerful actors than against weak ones. Even if China or Russia were to be exposed to material sanctions by Western states or the international community as a whole, such sanctions alone would probably not be able to move their governments from commitment to compliance. Materially powerful actors are by definition less vulnerable to external economic or military pressures than are weak actors. However, as the case of Tunisia shows (see Chapter 10), even materially weak states can reduce their vulnerability toward external pressure by pursuing a strategy of economic inclusion so as to silence domestic opposition.

(5)   Social vulnerability

A more interesting proposition concerns a target's vulnerability to social pressures. As we argued in PoHR, the more states and other actors care about their social reputation and thus want to be members of the international community "in good standing," the more vulnerable they are to external naming and shaming and, thus, to social mechanisms relying on the logics of arguing and of appropriateness. Social vulnerability refers to a particular actor's desire to be an accepted member of a social group or a particular community. Constructivists argue that a state's identity may influence its vulnerability to social pressure.

States with insecure identities or those that aspire to improve their standing in the international community may be more vulnerable to pressures (Gurowitz 1999). Sociological institutionalists would argue that the logic of appropriateness comes into play here, while rational choice scholars refer to "reputational concerns." In any event, the application of social pressure works, because actors care about their standing in a social group. And the more the relevant community cares about human rights, the more the target is vulnerable to external (and internal) pressures to comply with these norms.

In the case of states, these concerns are mostly about international legitimacy (see Hurd 1999; see e.g. the case of Morocco's king, Chapter 10). With regard to non-state actors, things are a bit more complex. As Jo and Bryant show in Chapter 13, rebel groups that are likely to win civil wars and to take over the national government tend to start complying with international humanitarian law precisely because of an expected gain in international legitimacy. In the case of transnational companies, particularly those with a brand name to defend, social vulnerability is often intimately associated with material vulnerability. In the case of Shell and its rights violations in Nigeria, for example, transnational advocacy networks were able to organize consumer boycotts which then resulted in a serious loss of revenue for the company (Chapter 12; see also Chapter 11). In this case, consumers cared about human rights which made even a materially powerful corporation vulnerable to external pressures.

However, we can neither assume that any particular norm target is socially vulnerable, nor that the application of social pressure (e.g. naming and shaming) will have a favorable and unidirectional impact. This is where we have to correct the original spiral model. Some rule targets command powerful social resources which allow them to fight off external pressures. "Soft power," as Joseph Nye put it (Nye 2004), is not the sole domain of the "good guys" in world politics. The Asian values debate demonstrates, for example, that some states command sufficient international legitimacy to establish a counter-discourse to the Western-led human rights arguments (see Chapter 2). This also happened in the West itself, where the George W. Bush administration in the post-9/11 environment was able to establish a counter-discourse against the universal applicability of the prohibition against torture – at least temporarily (see Chapter 8). In other words, human rights are not the only discourse in town – and some actors command enough social legitimacy to be able to establish persuasive counter-narratives which then reduce their social vulnerability.

In sum, our authors evaluate the impact on human rights change of five scope conditions in the empirical chapters that follow. These scope conditions are (1) regime type (democracy vs. autocracy), (2) state capacity (consolidated vs. limited), (3) rule implementation (centralized vs. decentralized), (4) material vulnerability (substantial vs. limited), and (5) social vulnerability (substantial vs. limited). We believe that the existence of these scope conditions not only affects the overall process moving actors from commitment to compliance directly but also by influencing the effectiveness of the four different social mechanisms described above.

Plan of the book

Part I of the book is devoted to stock-taking. Chapters 2 and 3 evaluate the original spiral model proposed in PoHR from different perspectives. In Chapter 2, Jetschke and Liese review the literature on the spiral model that has referenced and used it over the past decade. They are particularly interested in determining whether the major assumptions of the model and its causal mechanisms are still viewed as valid. Chapter 3 by Simmons builds upon the considerable quantitative work on human rights that has been done over the past decade and evaluates the spiral model from the perspective of large-N statistical analyses. The chapter compares quantitative findings about the ability of international norms to influence domestic politics, social movements, and practices to findings from the earlier qualitative literature.

Part II is devoted to conceptual and methodological issues. Börzel and Risse argue in Chapter 4 that the original PoHR was based on some implicit assumptions that do not fit states containing "areas of limited statehood." Such areas can be defined as territorial or functional spaces in which national governments do not control the means of violence and/or are incapable of implementing and enforcing central decisions, including those in the area of human rights. If we take limited statehood seriously, we have to re-formulate and re-conceptualize the human rights agenda, both in terms of research and policies.

Dai takes issue in Chapter 5 with the findings of some recent – mostly quantitative – studies of human rights treaties. The authors of these studies claim that, while states increasingly endorse human rights norms, their actual behavior often does not comport with them. To many, this "compliance gap" calls into question the efficacy of international law. Challenging such an inference, Dai argues that the compliance gap, as it is typically depicted and measured in the literature, does not capture and in fact overemphasizes both the magnitude and the significance of the disparity between commitment and compliance.

Chapter 6 by Goodman and Jinks challenges the view developed in PoHR that "all good things go together," i.e. that the various compliance mechanisms and logics of social action and interaction reinforce each other and that there are no trade-offs between them. Their starting point is the increased attention being devoted in the literature on human rights to discrete mechanisms of social influence. Goodman and Jinks focus primarily on what they call "negative interaction effects," that is, cases in which the operation of one mechanism of influence (e.g. material inducement) might crowd out the operation of another (e.g. moral suasion). They argue that combining mechanisms in such a way will, under certain conditions, reduce the overall social effect to levels below what any individual mechanism could have achieved on its own.

Part III of our volume revisits the issue of how state actors behave from the time that they ratify human rights treaties to the point at which they actually comply with these new legally-embedded normative structures. Clark relies on quantitative methods in Chapter 7 to evaluate whether human rights treaty ratification followed by international criticism of human rights behavior has any impact on compliance. She uses dynamic panel data analysis to test the effect of states' exposure to UN human rights criticism when they have or have not ratified two major human rights treaties: the International Covenant on Civil and Political Rights (ICCPR) and the Convention against Torture and Other Cruel, Inhuman, or Degrading Treatment or Punishment (CAT). Her statistical findings suggest that once a treaty has been ratified, the likelihood rises significantly that additional criticism from the international community will cause a state to improve its human rights performance.

Chapter 8 focuses on US non-compliance with the prohibition against torture and cruel and degrading treatment during the administration of George W. Bush. Sikkink argues that US policy-makers were intensely aware of domestic and international pressures to comply with the norm, and of the possibility of domestic prosecution under US statutes implementing international human rights law. But such awareness did not lead to greater compliance. The US case shows that a country which had already ratified and implemented international treaties on a core human rights norm could nevertheless experience a profound backlash, resulting in the de facto abnegation and "reversal" of these commitments.

The People's Republic of China provides us with another example of a very powerful state which might conceivably be able to "fight off" transnational pressure for human rights compliance. Chapter 9 examines the extent to which the spiral model applies in this case. The Tiananmen Square massacre in 1989 gave rise to a transnational network focused on improving China's human rights situation. International governmental and non-governmental criticism of China's human rights practice continued to be pronounced throughout the two decades that followed. Through a comparison of the impact of the EU and US strategies to influence China's human rights performance, Kinzelbach reaches some interesting conclusions. From her perspective, Beijing's continued non-compliance on core civil and political rights is best explained by a combination of the weakness of domestic change agents attempting to apply pressure "from below" and the absence of sustained pressure from above.

One of the most important recent developments in the human rights field has been the uprisings in the Arab world. PoHR contained a case study on Morocco and Tunisia (Gränzer 1999) – two countries that have followed very different paths during the recent rebellions. In Chapter 10, van Hüllen revisits the two cases in light of recent events. While Morocco remained vulnerable to domestic and external demands and embarked on a cautious process of liberalization, Tunisia was able to shield itself off to outside pressures due to economic development. When this strategy failed to calm the opposition during the economic crisis, the regime collapsed.

Part IV of the book deals with a major portion of the new agenda in human rights research – the compliance behavior of non-state actors. In Chapter 11, Mwangi, Rieth and Schmitz focus on the UN Global Compact (GC) and related efforts to align economic interests with universally recognized principles. Unlike many skeptics of such efforts to "sign up" corporations to the observance of human rights norms, Mwangi *et al.* find that membership in the GC moves companies towards greater compliance if certain scope conditions are in place. First, the firm has to participate actively in a regional or local GC network where corporate incentives, human rights discourse and capacity-building resources are more highly developed than at the global level. And, second, additional steps must have been taken toward integrating the ten principles into the managerial and strategic culture of a company.

Chapter 12 by Deitelhoff and Wolf also assesses the status of business and human rights in general, and in zones of conflict in particular. The authors argue that the business sector is experiencing a socialization process similar to that specified in the original spiral model of human rights. They further argue that applying the spiral model to business corporations triggers interesting extensions of this model regarding its phases and causal mechanisms. During the socialization process, and under certain conditions, corporations can undergo a transformation from norm consumers to norm entrepreneurs. This transformation occurs not only because of the principled beliefs that these corporations have come to subscribe to but also out of simple cost-benefit calculations with regard to their business models within socially embedded markets.

In Chapter 13 Jo and Bryant deal with rebel groups and warlords whose human rights violations are usually deemed beyond the reach of international law and transnational pressures. Rebel groups in civil wars often commit heinous acts of violence such as killing innocent civilians. However, all rebel groups are not the same. Jo and Bryant argue that reputational concerns and organizational capacity that is adequate to enforce adherence to human rights standards are key conditions for rebel groups to move from commitment to compliance. Additionally, they suggest that rewards and persuasion are the main mechanisms that induce such compliance. By analyzing quantitative data on humanitarian access to conflict zones in civil wars fought between 1991 and 2006, the authors show that some classes of rebel groups with reputational concerns and strong organizational capacity are more likely to grant access to the ICRC than others.

In Chapter 14 Brysk pushes the envelope even further with regard to how we can best explain the compliance behavior of non-state actors. She investigates the conditions under which private individuals can be brought into compliance with international norms related to sexual politics and gender. Private actors such as families, employers and religious communities are increasingly recognized as potential human rights violators and subject to international campaigns – but not yet to consistent governance. As a constructivist perspective suggests, transnational campaigns against private wrongs (such as violence against women) rely on the use of a combination of the mechanisms of persuasion and capacity-building rather than on coercion and incentives. The chapter analyzes a strikingly similar pattern of norm change through socialization in states and international organizations in the "hard case" of sexual politics, where male elites and social institutions face few incentives or disincentives to change gendered patterns of subjugation.

The concluding chapter by Sikkink and Risse (Chapter 15) revisits the arguments of this introduction, in particular with regard to mechanisms and scope conditions. In addition, the chapter discusses some new developments in the enforcement of human rights norms, namely the emerging international norms of "Responsibility to Protect" (R2P) and of individual criminal responsibility. With regard to the scope conditions discussed above, Sikkink and Risse argue that they can be grouped together for analytical purposes in another alternative way. While regime type and social/material vulnerability concern the *willingness* of actors to move from commitment to compliance, degrees of (limited) statehood and of the centralization of compliance decisions affect actors' *ability* to comply. The chapter concludes by discussing some policy implications of this volume.

2

The power of human rights a decade after: from euphoria to contestation?

ANJA JETSCHKE AND ANDREA LIESE

When *The Power of Human Rights: International Norms and Domestic Change* (PoHR) was published, practitioners, state governments and human rights scholars around the world celebrated the fiftieth anniversary of the Universal Declaration of Human Rights (1948) and the tenth anniversary of the fall of the Iron Curtain. A series of important developments in the world, including rapid ratification of human rights treaties, the incorporation of human rights criteria in foreign policy, and humanitarian interventions justified by human rights concerns, had fueled the perception that nothing could stop the progression of human rights norms. This collective euphoria of a sea change in international relations provided the international context for the "spiral model," as an explanation for human rights change introduced in PoHR.

The PoHR was part of and further propelled constructivist research in international relations, especially in research on socialization by international institutions and norms, on regime effectiveness and compliance, on arguing and persuasion, and on "soft" compliance mechanisms, such as social sanctions ("shaming") and supervision (Checkel 1998; Finnemore and Sikkink 1998; Simmons 2009).

The book signified a "transformationalist" possibility: the emergence of a global political arena that reshapes the conditions and dynamics of both domestic and international politics without the corresponding emergence of an international state (Barnett and Sikkink 2008; Lynch 2000: 93). The spiral model provided the lenses through which domestic political activists could reconsider the strategic options vis-à-vis their government. Domestic groups were no longer seen as victims but could actively shape the context in which they were operating by transnationalizing domestic issues.

We are indebted to the anonymous reviewers and to all participants of the authors' workshops in Wyoming (2009) and Berlin (2010), in particular Arie Kacowicz and the editors, Thomas Risse, Kathryn Sikkink and Steve Ropp, for their very valuable comments and suggestions. For helpful research assistance we thank Philip Schleifer, Jessica Bither and Gerrit Kurtz.

Much has changed since PoHR was first published in 1999. Qualitative and quantitative studies on commitment – understood as formal acceptance of international (human rights) norms (usually by ratification) – and compliance – understood as behavior in conformity with norms – have tested constructivist and rationalist assumptions about the domestic impact of international norms. Furthermore, international human rights norms have been challenged and violated by a number of countries, including the United States, in their struggles against transnational terrorism (see Chapter 8) and China (see Chapter 9). These contestations challenge implicit assumptions of the spiral model: that human rights violations are primarily a problem of authoritarian countries and that, therefore, a democratic regime type, the existence of transnational advocacy actors, and public debate are sufficient conditions for human rights compliance.

This chapter reflects upon the basic assumptions of the spiral model more than a decade after it was originally developed.

- Do the major assumptions of the model and its causal mechanisms still hold?
- Have actors made the move from commitment to compliance, then assumed by the spiral model?
- What have subsequent studies found to be the strengths and shortcomings of the model?

The chapter proceeds in three steps. A first section reviews more recent case studies using the spiral model as theory explaining progress toward human rights compliance: to what extent do these new case studies confirm the theory? Here, we ask whether the causal mechanisms and the sequencing of the spiral model are confirmed. We identify the transition from phases four (prescriptive status) to five (rule-consistent behavior) as a bottleneck that only few states pass, and address two commonly discussed explanatory factors: variation of domestic mobilization and democratic regime type. We then suggest to add a third, discursive explanation for the backlash or continuing practice of human rights violations in some states. We develop the notion of normative counter-frames to human rights norms and contestation in the second section. The concluding section summarizes the crucial contributions and limitations of the spiral model and points to the need to adapt the model to a new world time.

Our review reveals that the spiral model still remains valid for the universe of cases for which it was designed, i.e. the impact of personal integrity rights in authoritarian, repressive states with little political legitimacy but considerable state authority, hardly any experience of transnational advocacy, and with material and social vulnerability (see the introduction to this volume). Specifically, it can still claim to explain the process of human rights change for the first three stages of the model. Why? In our view, this is so because these are the conditions under which we would expect transnational advocacy and framing strategies to be effective: states are perceived to be capable and can be made accountable for human rights violations. Because they are authoritarian, they can be strategically framed as illegitimate (Keck and Sikkink 1998). However, few states with a previous record of gross and systematic human rights violations have transgressed through stages four and five of the model, raising the question of model specification. Moreover, the model has not fully lived up to its general claim to be "generalizable across cases irrespective of cultural, political, or economic differences among countries" (Risse and Sikkink 1999: 6).

Most importantly, it leaves a range of important cases unexplained, such as (1) the ineffectiveness of human rights advocacy in areas of limited statehood, where states lack the capacity to fully enforce rule-consistent behavior (see Chapter 4, this volume), and (2) the failure to comprehensively mobilize against human rights violations in democratic states (see Chapter 8, this volume). Moreover, it does not expect norm-violating governments to provide good reasons for human rights violations that are accepted by audiences to a large extent. We dedicate a full section to such contestations of the applicability of human rights under all circumstances.

Testing the spiral model: evidence from single and comparative case studies

A key strength of single case studies is the detailed exploration of hypothesized causal mechanisms in the context of particular cases (George and Bennett 2005: 8 n5). Case studies that have applied the spiral model therefore provide an ideal testing ground for the mechanisms identified in the model. They also differ in their scope of analysis from the quantitative studies as discussed in this book (Chapter 3).

The spiral model has now been tested for over twenty countries: in addition to the original set of eleven cases, we find case studies on Algeria (Schwarz 2004a), Bangladesh (Schapper 2010), China (Fleay 2005), Colombia (Brysk 2009b), Egypt (Liese 2006; Stachursky 2010), Iran (Stachursky 2010), Israel (Laursen 2000; Liese 2006; Shor 2008), Mexico (Muñoz 2009), Saudi Arabia (Alhargan 2011), Turkey (Cizre 2001; Liese 2006) and Yemen (Chase 2003). Furthermore, we find new literature on Indonesia (Hosen 2002; Jetschke 2010) and the Philippines after 1999 (Jetschke 2010) – countries that were already covered by PoHR but were updated. We generally find that the spiral model travels quite well to other countries and even issue areas, such as corporate responsibility or climate change (Kollman 2008; Schroeder 2008). In the following, we review only the literature on human rights norms related to personal integrity rights and state actors, as these speak more directly to the model.

We find that many studies especially confirm the sequencing and the causal mechanisms of the first three phases, in particular the differential empowerment of supporters of human rights norms, rhetorical entrapment and the unintended effects of tactical concessions. At the same time, case studies converge on a few important findings: *first*, domestic mobilization is a key variable explaining further progress toward phase 4. However, this domestic mobilization is hard to come by and sustain, especially in cases of state security, giving state governments maneuver to repress domestic NGOs. Related to that, international and domestic mobilization is difficult to sustain after a change of government has occurred. *Second*, the dynamics between democratic regime type and transnational advocacy remain unexplored. These findings offer an opportunity to delve deeper into the mechanism of normative persuasion to account for the idiosyncrasies of transnational mobilization in the next section.

Many studies confirm the spiral model, notably its first phases, which emphasize the interaction of transnational and domestic actors in information exchange, mobilizing international criticism, and naming and shaming activities as an important condition for human rights change. At the same time, there is considerable variation in the level of domestic mobilization which consecutively explains varying progress toward later stages of the model.

Alejandro Anaya Muñoz (2009) applies the model to Mexico under the Zedillo administration (1996 to 2000) and the Fox presidency. In line with the spiral model's expectations, he observes the activation and – after the 1994 uprising of the Zapatista Army of National Liberalization in Chiapas – enlargement of a transnational network in the late 1980s. Consequently, several UN human rights bodies and the OAS began targeting the Mexican government culminating in public statements by the UN Human Rights Commission, the Special Rapporteur on Torture and the Inter-American Commission (Muñoz 2009: 45–49). The Zedillo government tactically responded by allowing a limited degree of involvement of intergovernmental bodies and mechanisms in its human rights affairs (Muñoz 2009: 49). The Fox administration introduced a human rights unit in its Ministry of the Interior in 2001, led the initiative for constitutional reform on human rights and instituted the National Human Rights Program in 2004. These measures can be traced to "the pressure exerted by international and human rights groups" (Muñoz 2009: 51). Mexico reached prescriptive status (see Muñoz 2009: 58).

Andreas Laursen (2000) applies the model to Israel's human rights policy towards the Palestinians from the West Bank to the Gaza Strip, in particular to the process leading to the ambiguous 1999 High Court judgment on the question of the use of "moderate physical pressure" – a practice the UN Committee against Torture identified as breach of Articles 1, 2 and 16 of the UN Convention against Torture. The erosion of Israel's international standing precipitated the transition from denial to tactical concessions (Laursen 2000: 439–440): Israel's policy of answering the Intifada (December 1987) with "force, might and beating" led to international pressure and shaming and contributed at least partially to "the ratification of a number of human rights treaties in 1991 and the promulgation of two human rights related Basic Laws in 1992" – classified as tactical concession (Laursen 2000: 449).

In the case of Turkey, Umit Cizre (2001) reports that the country entered the phase of tactical concessions in the second half of the 1990s: the Çiller government no longer denied human rights violations, such as torture, even as it denied their widespread and systematic nature. The Turkish government increasingly entrapped itself in human rights rhetoric, culminating in a series of legal and structural reforms and public promises to effectively prevent torture, e.g. by Premier Ecevit in 1999 (Liese 2006: 161–162). It established a human rights coordination council and signed the International Covenant on Civil and Political Rights in 2000. Liese (2006: 118, 123) observes a growth of domestic human rights NGOs after the commitment to European human rights instruments had increased (in 1987, 1988, 1992) and thus confirms the model's assumption about the empowerment of domestic human rights defenders (Risse and Ropp 1999: 246).

Variation according to domestic mobilization

Not all studies confirm the model and a common theme running through many studies is that many countries do not reach phase 5 of the model, where we expect rule-consistent behavior as a habitual practice. Quite frequently, we therefore encounter attempts to refine the mechanisms in the latter stages of the spiral model of human rights change or to further explore its scope conditions. We will briefly summarize the main empirical findings, before we further systematize their critique in the third section of the chapter.

The more recent studies emphasize counter-strategies of *target governments to minimize the pressure of human rights networks*. For instance, Fleay argues that China successfully managed multilateral pressures and was able to channel international moral pressures into "China's preferred approach to human rights in international relations, the bilateral dialogue." By 1998 there was hardly any support for resolutions on China at the UNCHR (Fleay 2005: 319): moreover, she argues that China – a state with much more power than the states examined in PoHR – has had an impact on international human rights debates in general and on the mechanisms for their enforcement, in particular (Fleay 2005: 41, 320f.; Kent 1999; see also Chapter 9, this volume).

Many authoritarian governments quite successfully limit the activities of NGOs and prevent the domestic network from expanding. This explains, according to Ann Kent (1999: 328), the stagnation of human rights reform in China between 1989 and 2003 and the fact that China has not moved to stage three of the model. In the case of Colombia, Alison Brysk (2009b: 38) points out that although Colombia "possesses all of the ingredients for change predicated by comparative study of human rights reform" human rights mobilization has been less effective than in peer states. Governments "have learned to semantically manipulate and diminish human rights accountability" (Brysk 2009b: 42). As a result, the struggle for human rights in Colombia appears to have reached a "glass ceiling" (Brysk 2009b: 41). In Egypt, during the height of transnational mobilization (1993–2000) the government also found ways to suppress the opposition of domestic NGOs, for example by forbidding them from receiving foreign funds, confiscating material, closing offices and bringing charges against human rights defenders (Liese 2006: 171–176, 268). This strategy was frequently reported between 1993 and 2000, when mobilization had reached a peak. In general, human rights advocacy NGOs which criticize governments face suspicion, harassment and intimidation (see Stachursky 2010: 322–323).

Laursen (2000: 443) argues that Israel's wider public supports measures that amount to human rights violations. Pointing at the multiplicity of actors and of respective positions in Iran and Egypt, Stachursky (2010) criticizes the spiral model for failing to recognize divisions within civil society, especially between human rights NGOs and other civil society groups such as religious organizations, and between NGOs operating on a national level and those located at the grassroots level (see also Laursen 2000: 443). And Landman correctly points out that the model misses a more complex argument about the "uneven, fragmented and contradictory" relationship between social mobilization and the protection of human rights (Landman 2005b: 563).

To sum up: the studies discussed above show that many countries fit into phases one to three (Repression, Denial and Tactical Concessions) of the spiral model, but that the model is less useful in explaining the move from commitment to compliance. It appears to be of less utility in explaining the behavior of democracies. Most studies expand the debate on blocking factors as discussed in PoHR (Risse and Ropp 1999: 260–261) and summarized in Table 2.1.

A central variable that might impede further progress in the phases is the lack of domestic mobilization. Here, the model might have overestimated the domestic effects of transnational advocacy. Until recently, scholars assumed that domestic groups that supported human rights groups would gain domestic support once external actors support their case. The studies reviewed here looking closely at subsequent patterns of *domestic mobilization of civil society* portray a more nuanced picture. For example, with regard to Turkey, a major obstacle in the transition from "prescriptive status" to "rule-consistent behavior" is the lack of political and societal support for local human rights organizations, which depend mostly on foreign funding, are regarded as associated with the Kurdish question, and have a leftist ideological orientation (Cizre 2001: 73–74; Liese 2006).

A second impeding factor concerns the optimistic evaluation of the ability and capacity of states to safeguard human rights during and after democratic transitions. The authors of the spiral model did not consider that effective advocacy might lead to the dissolution or weakening of states (see Chapter 4, this volume) and thus to significant compliance problems.

The empirical results of the cases reported here overlap in a central finding with quantitative studies (see Chapter 3, this volume): treaty ratification

Table 2.1. *Blocking factors as identified in selected qualitative case studies*

Country	Phase	Problem/blocking factors	Source
China		China's lack of social and material vulnerability, China as norm shaper	Fleay (2005)
Colombia	4	Delegitimization of human rights defenders and persecution of journalists diminish civil society's impact and state responsiveness	Brysk (2009b)
Indonesia	4	Domestic human rights NGOs lack backing (are seen as separatist) and lack domestic connections	Jetschke (2010)
Israel	3–4	Public is largely supportive of the governments' measures against suspected terrorists Perceived and real threats of terrorism and national insecurity	Laursen (2000) Liese (2006)
Mexico	4	Difficulty to pressure a government whose human rights reputation has improved	Muñoz (2009)
Turkey	(3–)4	Turkish NGOs lack support by political parties, intellectuals, media, and grassroots Climate of impunity and difficulty of enforcing human rights protection (problem of decentralization)	Cizre (2001) Liese (2006)

(commitment) does not unconditionally lead to rule-consistent behavior (compliance). PoHR would not reject the findings of these studies. "Prescriptive status," as operationalized by PoHR, was much more demanding than mere ratification, it also included institutionalizing norms in domestic law, engaging in a dialogue with their critics and arguing consistently (Risse and Sikkink 1999: 29). The full transition to the final fifth phase of the socialization process (rule-consistent behavior) depended on continued domestic and international mobilization (Risse and Ropp 1999: 248–250; Risse and Sikkink 1999: 33). Only then does the model expect that "international human rights norms are fully institutionalized domestically and norm compliance becomes a habitual practice of actors and is enforced by the rule of law" (Risse and Sikkink 1999: 33). Yet, the model did not specify how much pressure it would take to move from phase 4's commitment to phase 5's compliance. Neither did it specify the conditions under which continued mobilization would occur.

We would not go as far, however, as to reject the central mechanisms and stages of the model, as some authors suggest. Some studies have concluded that the model was teleological, "deterministic" and overly "optimistic" in character (see Chase 2003: 218; Landman 2005b: 563–564; Shor 2008: 122) or that "the Risse and Sikkink model is very linear, even tautological: it has an ultimate destination and there are no points along the way marking possible detours or obstacles to derail movement in the planned direction" (Marsh and Payne 2007: 668). Reviewers also point out that positive human rights changes have historically come about without the intervention of transnational human rights networks, and thus could continue to do so (Chase 2003: 217). In our view, the authors of PoHR repeatedly made the point that they "do not assume evolutionary progress" but "identify those stages in the model where governments might return to repressive practices" (Risse and Sikkink 1999: 18, 23, 35). And they never claimed that transnational advocacy was the only causal pathway to a sustained human rights improvement.

At the same time, the model certainly can be criticized for its "idealism" and perhaps apolitical perspective in phases four and five: once the promotion of human rights had become official state policy, the model did not expect political conflicts over human rights to occur. Counter-strategies and contestation were predicted to occur in the early phases of the model, not in the later ones. This idealism slipped into the model primarily through the mis-specifications listed above and the assumptions that domestic political elites would internalize human rights norms and that compliance would therefore mostly occur voluntarily. Overall then, one might argue that the transition from phase 4 to 5 was under-specified by the spiral model (see Schapper 2010: 9), most likely because of case selection in PoHR. Of the eleven cases, only four (Chile, Poland, Czechoslovakia, South Africa) had reached rule-consistent behavior (Risse and Sikkink 1999: 240). The fourth phase, in which governments argue with their critics and address standards of appropriateness, was reached by seven of the eleven cases in PoHR.

Variation according to target state's regime type

A consistent finding of quantitative studies is the positive relationship between democratic regime type and respect for human rights (Davenport 2007; Hafner-Burton and Tsutsui 2005; Hathaway 2005; Poe and Tate 1994; Simmons 2009). But only full democracy significantly lowers human rights violations in the long term (Bueno de Mesquita *et al.* 2005). While we have a much better understanding of the relationship between democracy and respect for human rights, we know little about how to get there.

Here, an important finding concerns deviation from the spiral model's sequencing in the case of democracies that violate human rights. Authors have struggled with the question whether the behavior of human rights violating democracies can be adequately captured by the model's phases. Here, Israel and the United States are primary examples which only partially confirm the model (e.g. Ron 1997; Shor 2008). All studies basically argue that various Israeli governments have been subjected to intense international pressures, undertaken tactical concessions, and partially show a pattern of behavior that the authors of PoHR would associate with "prescriptive status." However, Israel skipped the denial phase, i.e. never resorted to invoking its right to non-interference. Instead it referred to other forms of denials that justify repression by the exceptional necessity to counter threats to a state's stability. While Israel's status of ratification would place it in phase 4 of the model, it (and some other democracies in this category) adopts rhetorical strategies that are typical for autocratic governments and earlier phases: we find various forms of denial and contestation (nothing has happened or what happened is something different, i.e. not a human rights violation but a necessary defense of state security) and justification (Cohen 2001; Jetschke 2010).

We have only little empirical knowledge on the question whether mobilization against human rights violating democratic states is easier as compared to autocratic ones. Quantitative studies find that democracies are the easier cases for transnational pressure (Neumayer 2005: 17), because of their higher social vulnerability and sense of belonging to the international community of "civilized states." This requires at least a façade of moral sensitivity and adherence to international norms, which make democracies more likely to refrain from rejecting international jurisdiction (Shor 2008: 124). From a liberal perspective, one could argue that politicians in democracies depend on public approval, and that institutions (independent courts) and legal rights, such as freedom of speech, are in place, which force governments into a public dialogue and argumentation process with their critics. These two factors are missing in more authoritarian states, as a result of which governments can afford to deny: as long as domestic mobilization does not reach a specific level, governments face few restraints when they attack domestic human rights organizations and thus interrupt the ties between the transnational and the domestic pressure groups. Yet, argumentation processes in democracies do not only draw upon democratic norms, "good" transnational human rights norms and identities as members of the international community, but also on unique national identities (Israel) or on norms such as state security, which may be put in juxtaposition. The interaction of perceived threats (communism, fundamentalism and terrorism) and democratic regime type then undermine transnational advocacy by reducing social vulnerability. Furthermore, a common argument put forward by democratic leaders is that due to their democratic nature they are at the spearhead of human rights implementation and thus should not be criticized (see Chapter 8). Consequently, democracies which justify the curtailing of human rights may also be "hard cases" for transnational pressure. Their policies are legitimized by voter approval even if these policies result in human rights violations.

The challenge of counter-frames and normative contestation

Several empirical studies refer to competing norms or to legal contestation to explain why human rights ultimately do not "make it" in some states. First, state sovereignty was regarded as a crucial blocking factor (Schwarz 2004b), while, recently, several studies also refer to national security as a competing frame (Cardenas 2007; Liese 2009: 42). The authors of the spiral model recognized the power of argumentative counter-challenges to human rights advocacy, but they did not theorize it: in the concluding chapter to PoHR, Thomas Risse and Steve Ropp (1999: 262) claimed that the arguments governments use to justify their behavior might constitute "blocking factors" that cannot always be treated as quasi-objective conditions which are necessarily preventing domestic human rights improvements: "[r]ather, they can also be viewed as arguments put forward by norm-violating governments in a public discourse with their critics." This was quite an intriguing observation, which however went against the assumptions of the spiral model. It suggested that there was also a persuasive logic available for use by norm-violators (Jetschke 2010: 34). The specific approach that the authors of the spiral model adopted viewed state actors as norm addressees and targets of pressure. Given PoHR's focus on authoritarian regimes, it appeared quite natural to assume that their governments had a fixed preference to stay in power, that they would thus use arguments instrumentally, and that their arguments would quickly be unmasked and invalidated. None of the case studies in PoHR seriously questioned this assumption. All states had overcome the denial stage (phase 2) in which governments deny that human rights norms are applicable to their situation. As such, the model did not allow for conceptualizing mutual persuasion or the interactive construction of the meaning of norms (Jetschke 2010; Wiener 2009) and it did not fully specify the scope conditions under which governments would themselves manage to persuade audiences of the need to curtail specific human rights. Before 9/11 and Western experience with terrorist attacks, it was simply not considered that – given the right conditions, most importantly within a democratic space – human rights would not win out in public discourse.

The spiral model not only failed to take note of the dialogical character of the logic of persuasion, but lacked a concept of persuasion allowing for the possibility that various domestic and international audiences might actually accept the arguments of norm-violating governments (Fierke 1996; Krebs and Jackson 2007; Payne 2001). As soon as governments invoked the principle of sovereignty, they were said to be "not seriously interested in a dialogue with their critics" (Risse and Sikkink 1999: 20). The model thus lost important information on how exactly human rights violations were justified.

This, precisely, is the focus of more recent work in this field (Brysk 2009b; Jetschke 2010; Liese 2009). These studies argue that if governments manage to get approval for their justifications, this reveals an important "counter-symbolic social structure" to human rights, pointing us to collective understandings about appropriate behavior in given situations that effectively legitimate some human rights violations in specific situations. And, they study when justifications or state accounts for human rights violations are effective, in the sense that they either silence domestic critics or weaken transnational advocacy. How do states justify, or "frame," human rights violations if they occur? Most studies focus on two aspects: cultural values or the imprecision of normative rules.

(1) Constructivist scholarship usually refers to clashes between internationally codified norms and norms in the domestic legal structure (Checkel 2001; Cortell and Davis 2000) or local norms and practices (Acharya 2004: 248, 251). Anthropologists, sociologists and critical legal scholars view human rights, as codified by international law, as not reflecting universally shared norms and values, but as reflecting particularistic values, an ideological bias, or the cultural and "ideological" supremacy of the West (Marsh and Payne 2007: 684; Wa Mutua 2000). The authors of the spiral model could counter that they only focused on those human rights norms which were considered universally acknowledged, such as personal integrity norms.

(2) Legal scholars point at the imprecision of international norms, allowing state actors some interpretative discretion (Steyn 2008). Because international law relies on state consensus, legal definitions are frequently left vague and flexible to maintain the broadest possible consensus while allowing for subsequent developments. For example, the UN Committee against Torture stated that the "definitional threshold between ill-treatment and torture is often not clear" (United Nations 2008), implying that states have some interpretative space for the provisions of the Convention against Torture.

While we do not deny that a lack of normative fit or imprecision play a role, we focus on political conflicts over norms embedded in the social structure of international relations, especially those relating to state sovereignty and state security. Normative conflict or contestation is not only the most interesting but also the least understood factor in research on international human rights impact. If we do not simply assume that norms are ineffective because material or strategic interests are at stake (as is presumably the case in countries such as China, Pakistan or Russia), then we must assume that there is also a normative structure on an international level that lends itself to the denial or contestation of human rights norms and to the justification of associated violations. So what makes for an effective justification or state account for human rights violations?

There are essentially only two responses to allegations of human rights violations available to governments: justifications and excuses (Cardenas 2007; Cohen 2001; Scott and Lyman 1968). "Justifications" are effective counter-frames. In the case of justifications, actors accept their responsibility for a particular act that is labeled as "wrongdoing" but reject the evaluation that the act itself was wrong. Governments admit, for example, that the military has shot individuals, but they deny that these individuals have been innocent citizens ("civilians"). Instead they claim that the victims have been members of a terrorist organization or a self-determination movement challenging state security ("enemy combatants"). The construction of victims as non-civilians allows portraying the action as lawful (Venzke 2009; Heller et al. 2012).

"Excuses" denote a different type of response: here, a government accepts the description of a particular situation as the occurrence of a violation. But it denies its responsibility for this particular violation (e.g. because violations were carried out by non-state actors).

In the category of "justifications" state sovereignty is perhaps the most important (Jetschke 2010). To understand how state sovereignty is being played out in discourses about human rights violations, we have to reconsider its broader meaning. Sovereignty constitutes states as rights holders that have exclusive control over a delimited territorial space and a right to territorial integrity, have authority over a people, and exercise effective control and jurisdiction over their population and territory. States have the (only) legal monopoly over organized violence,[1] in exchange for the duty to protect their citizens and ensure their welfare.[2] Being a legitimate state – in our view – includes notions of the state as a legal-rational state bureaucracy as this ensures that governments act in a predictable way (Barnett and Finnemore 2005; Meyer et al. 1987). While we admit that this understanding of state sovereignty is an ideal-typical one, that for many states "limited statehood" is the reality, and that globalization transforms this understanding of the state even in the industrialized world (e.g. Leibfried and Zürn 2005), this ideal-typical definition of the state in international relations sets the model to which states aspire. Human rights challenge the exclusive authority of a state over its citizens (a state's authority can be disputed if its agents commit gross and systematic human rights violations) and they constrain the means to exercise the monopoly over organized violence (not all measures are allowed).

As we note that human rights have been strengthened in international law – most recently through the Responsibility to Protect (R2P) – we also observe that along with human rights guarantees, legal regimes securing the state as an organizational unit have been strengthened. This has occurred not as an end in itself but rather as a way to strengthen the organization most capable of guaranteeing human rights and a stable (inter)national order: for example, the territorial integrity of states has been continually strengthened to the extent that today, international law forbids the forceful change of state boundaries (Barkin

---

[1] The international legal definition of a state goes back to a German international lawyer, Georg Jellinek. This legal definition became institutionalized in the Montevideo Convention of December 26, 1933 (Hobe 2008: 68f.).

[2] This is also how state functions have now been defined by the International Commission on Intervention and State Sovereignty (International Commission on Intervention and State Sovereignty 2001).

and Cronin 1994; Zacher 2001). To that end, the right to self-determination – a key human right itself – has been continually delimited (Cassese 1995: 112) to a right that must be exercised peacefully.

We believe that state sovereignty confers specific rights upon states, even as states are at the same time obliged to respect the life and well-being of their citizens. These rights sometimes compete with human rights, for example, in situations in which the freedom of speech and freedom of assembly allow groups to gather support for their self-determination cause and are perceived to threaten territorial integrity.

The R2P of 2001 redefines state sovereignty as entailing state sovereignty as well as rights but it does not necessarily provide a solution to the dilemma facing states. R2P emphasizes a state's responsibility to protect the lives of citizens inside a state's sovereign territorial jurisdiction, and holds that if a state fails to meet its responsibility because of incapacity, unwillingness or complicity, then this responsibility "trips upwards to the international community" (Thakur 2011: 1). At the same time as the international community reaffirms its human rights commitment, it also affirms states' territorial jurisdiction and ultimate responsibility for the lives of its citizens. For example, the international community only assumes responsibility if violations exceed a so-called "just cause threshold" (Bellamy 2011: 21). R2P also becomes ambiguous when we consider transnational terrorism. Here, states are ultimately responsible for protecting their citizens against terrorist threats, but these sometimes do so by severely curtailing and grossly violating several rights of suspected terrorist or even the wider public in the name of protection.

As these examples demonstrate, conflicting norms not only raise the question of which norm is applicable in a specific situation, they also raise the question of who decides when such a specific situation exists. These questions are unavoidably political and they are likely to engender political struggles. Because the spiral model assumed that because human rights were inherently universal and good, these struggles tended to be won by groups acting in the name of human rights. As demonstrated above, however, sovereignty continues to challenge human rights.

We expect that a specific configuration of challenges to the state and specific state characteristics will block the mobilizing attempts of transnational human rights networks (see Table 2.2). This configuration consists, most importantly, of (a) armed challenges to state authority, that (b) threaten the territorial integrity of states or their secular character and that (c) constitute unconstitutional challenges to a democratic type of regime. These factors do not prevent, but they condition, human rights progress and they are at least partly discursively constructed. We contend that in these types of cases, governments are likely to win over a significant share of the population to support policies that repress specific groups within the state. Once specific curtailments of human rights are in place and domestic NGOs are being restrained in their activities, human

Table 2.2. *Sovereignty and potential challenges*

Norms defining state sovereignty/ responsibility	Actors and groups potentially challenging sovereignty
Territorial integrity	Self-determination movements
Authority	Armed (terrorist) movements
Monopoly over violence	Militia
Legal rationality	Religious or "primordial" groups

rights violations in the categories of torture or disappearances become more likely as domestic monitoring becomes more difficult. In this manner, effective counter-frames can work to reverse the logic of the spiral model: they legitimize repressions against those NGOs that constitute effective bulwarks against human rights violations.

The Arab Spring (see Chapter 10) seems to be a good example of such conditional effects: all Arab Spring states were authoritarian and therefore relatively easy targets for domestic mobilization (condition (c) non-existent). In all Arab Spring cases, public discourses demonstrated a preoccupation with the question of whether these states would remain stable and secular after democratization (discursive construction of condition (c)). In Egypt, for example, the opposition was only accepted as legitimate once a public debate about the relative political power of the Muslim Brotherhood revealed that Egypt has a chance to remain secular (Esposito 2011). While the opposition in the case of Libya was an armed rebellion – a fact that challenges our proposition on the necessity of opposition being unarmed – it was supported by the West because the government of Muammar al-Gaddafi used disproportional force against the domestic opposition, thereby violating the norm that a state should protect its citizens. Syria has so far successfully escaped a human rights transition because here the issue of territorial disintegration came immediately to the fore (Sly 2011).

In her examination of the campaigns of transnational human rights networks, Jetschke (2010) likewise shows that the effects of these campaigns vary systematically with the nature and intensity of threats to national security. Only where activists revealed that an accepted justification for violations was lacking, did they achieve significant mobilization. Accepted justifications often related to the threats posed by Islamist groups against the secular state (as in Indonesia) and/ or threats to the state's territorial integrity. Under such circumstances, there was a higher chance that rights-violating governments would not be pressured (see also: Cardenas 2007).

Turkey (with regard to the activities of the Partiya Karkerên Kurdistan), equally comes to mind. This case demonstrates quite clearly the intricacies involved in human rights promotion. The prominent role of the military was long justified by the claim that it constituted an effective bulwark against the possible emergence of an Islamist state (Rumford 2001) and against territorial disintegration. Alignment with the European Union led to the introduction of political reforms that drastically diminished its political role (Engert 2010). But the military's willingness to tolerate these reforms was heavily dependent on the commitment of Islamic parties to maintain a secular constitution (Insel 2003). Human rights advocacy was also impeded by the Turkish movement's identification with the Kurdish self-determination cause (Cizre 2001), an issue that clashes with territorial integrity.

One might even argue that, today, threats to democracy constitute a legitimate justification for some forms of human rights violations. Thus, while Simmons (2009) convincingly argues that individuals in states undergoing the transition to democracy may be the ones profiting the most from international human rights treaties, there are numerous empirical examples that show how – on a discursive and political level – democracy and human rights can be played out against one another. For example, the Aquino government in the Philippines (1986–1992) quite successfully securitized a fledgling democracy and thereby justified human rights violations: it argued that the new democratic system needed to be defended against a Communist insurgency, and that repression against activists and journalists needed to be regarded as collateral damage (Hedman 2000; Jetschke 2010: ch. 6).

The other type of state responses, excuses, is also observed elsewhere in this volume and in this chapter (see above): a government using such "evasions" effectively draws on a common understanding that only those actors should be held responsible who possess all of the attributes associated with sovereign states, i.e. authority over its population, control over the territory within which this population resides, and control over the means of organized violence. For example, the Colombian government not only denies that human rights violations take place and reframes "evidence" about human rights violations as propaganda by organizations that have been effectively undermined by armed groups (Brysk 2009b), it also excuses "violations" by blaming paramilitary organizations that the government itself cannot control. The observation that other governments accept these justifications and excuses provides evidence for the existence of a logic of appropriateness according to which human rights are not unconditionally accepted.

In sum, justifications and excuses can be quite effective in undermining the strength of transnational advocacy, because two central scope conditions for effective framing are absent (Snow and Benford 1988): in the absence of a responsible state government, transnational network actors will be impeded in their efforts to construct a causal chain explaining human rights violations; and in the presence of threats to state security, networks will be unable to prove that a human rights violating government acts out of self-interest and is not interested in a greater public good.

Our concept of normative contestation suggests that a core of norms relating to state security is obstructing the full implementation of international human rights norms. Human rights campaigns as they are currently conducted are likely to affect this core only when it does not concern the issue of state security, for example, when self-determination movements are unarmed and pursue their goals peacefully or when religious groups do not threaten the secular character of the state. Again, both quantitative and qualitative studies support our concept about the nature of normative contestation. First, statistical studies on human rights consistently find a strong correlation between armed conflicts and violations of human rights (Davenport 2000; Neumayer 2005; Simmons 2009). According to these findings, states that are threatened by armed rebellions are much less likely to live up to their human rights commitment. Consequently, we can expect that the dynamic of the spiral model is blocked by threats to national security, as has been argued, among many others, in the case of Israel: "The perceived and real threats of terrorism and general insecurity are clearly 'blocking factors' in the 'spiral model'" (Laursen 2000: 444).

Second, governments can develop a counter-frame very easily if human rights violations occur against groups that are themselves "perpetrators." Keck and Sikkink (1998) were among the first to argue that human rights campaigns are more effective when the violations are targeted against innocent citizens and, hence, the public fears that anyone could become the next victim. If the victims belong to a specific group that can be seen as "evil," i.e. can be portrayed as "terrorists," as "traitors" that threaten territorial integrity or as Islamists, and when even human rights NGOs can be portrayed as extensions of these movements, then human rights advocacy will surely be less persuasive.

Conclusion: strengths and limitations of the spiral model

In light of more than a decade's application of the spiral model to additional cases, and in spite of the numerous critiques that can be made of it, two crucial contributions can now be identified: PoHR provided a clear-cut model of the stages and mechanisms explaining the diffusion of international human rights norms and domestic human rights change. Such a model was unprecedented, despite some previous very influential work in this area, including the "boomerang model." To date, the spiral model remains the reference for most studies on multi-level human rights politics and compliance with human rights norms. As a medium-range theory it has been largely accepted. The majority of criticisms stem from the empirical observation that many states never reached phase 5, that rhetorical entrapment has its limits, and that human rights norms do not always "trump" other norms which guide (and legitimize) state action. We have argued that the original euphoria overlooked the possibility of domestic support for certain human rights violations, even in democracies and the existence of competing global (not national) norms, such as the maintenance of security, secularity or public order.

In this regard the spiral model has to be adapted to a new world time, a time which the Western world would term "post-9/11" and which reflects the Western experience with threats to security and stability, an "era" that other states have known before. When PoHR was published in 1999, a decade after the fall of the Berlin Wall, the focus of many human rights advocates was still on how to achieve prescriptive status for relevant norms. Twelve years, and a decade after 9/11, later, the "bottleneck" is clearly the transition to the final phase of the socialization process (rule-consistent behavior). As a result, scholarly attention has already shifted from a concern with compliance mechanisms and transnational actors to issues such as legal plurality, local customs and norms and (slowly) to the role of domestic courts. To this end, and in line with emerging research, we suggest focusing on normative conflicts and effective counter-frames to human rights. Sovereignty with all its connotations of legitimate authority over a territorially defined space and a rational bureaucratic and secular state character still poses a potent protection against challengers of state authority. As our review of qualitative case studies and our brief discussion of the recent Arab rebellions have demonstrated, how these norms are played out in public discourses impacts on how much and what kind of (external) support domestic opposition groups can expect. From the perspective presented here, R2P does not present new arguments facilitating decisions on when to intervene in countries where gross and systematic human rights violations occur. It evidences a reframing of the debate without effectively solving the conflict between human rights protection and state sovereignty.

3

From ratification to compliance: quantitative evidence on the spiral model

BETH A. SIMMONS

Human rights researchers have discovered quantitative indicators and methods. As a result, for better or for worse, human rights research has joined the mainstream approach to social science research in the past decade. The systematic comparison of specific hypotheses, followed by controlled hypothesis testing using a range of indicators of rights now easily accessible in carefully constructed, well-vetted, widely and freely available datasets, is becoming an important mode for studying human rights. This has allowed both rights advocates as well as rights skeptics to plumb their conceptions of the causes and consequences of the international human rights regime.

The dedicated efforts of scholars, organizations and rights advocates to produce comparable, consistent and carefully constructed indicators for various aspects of human rights realizations has been a boon to research. Used carefully, critically and with an appreciation for its inherent limits,[1] quantitative research has the potential to check whether understandings generated from case studies can be generalized. It can also suggest systematic ways in which our "theories" might be amended or conditioned. The purpose of this chapter is to review the relatively recent (and mostly quantitative) research in precisely this spirit. My focus is primarily on the arguments advanced over a decade ago in what at that time was one of the most carefully executed and theoretically motivated explorations of the relationship between international human rights norms and actual practices: the "spiral model" developed by Thomas Risse, Stephen Ropp and Kathryn Sikkink in *The Power of Human Rights* (1999; PoHR in the following). The first section sets out in brief the original elements of PoHR's theory of how international human rights norms have practical effects on human rights practices. The second section compares the theoretical assumptions and causal claims of the spiral model with the last decade's cascade of quantitative research. PoHR was fairly explicit about the conditions under which they expected human rights norms to influence outcomes, and the specific mechanisms through which normative change could take place.

---

[1] See the discussion of limitations in Simmons (2009).

The chapter concludes by assessing the extent to which on the whole qualitative and quantitative research findings are mutually reinforcing. In contrast to claims that methodological differences have driven a wedge between researchers from varying methodological traditions, I find that the combination of qualitative and quantitative research has greatly improved our parallax on human rights. Indeed, there is just as much if not more cacophony *within* the quantitative school and *among* qualitative researchers than there is *across* approaches. I also find that while no one has been able (or motivated) to test quantitatively the spiral model in its entirety, a good deal of quantitative research is consistent with what we might have expected to observe if the major claims of the model do indeed capture certain aspects of reality. However, parts of the original model are quite indeterminate and therefore consistent with a broad range of possible tests and outcomes. Nonetheless, I argue that the way forward is not to construct unnecessary methodological divisions among social scientists, but rather to develop and refine our research using the best tools available and appropriate for the research question. For the most part, this means using mixed methods and developing partnerships to refine and test theories that are not only innovative, but that explain a lot of what appears at first to be confusing about the world in which we live.

The power of empirical research

Necessary conditions: political liberalization and domestic structural reform

The spiral model attempts to explain how international human rights norms come to influence actual human rights practices domestically. No one – PoHR included – has ever proposed a single statistical test of the spiral in its entirety. Yet there is a growing body of research that addresses at least parts of the model PoHR proposed over a decade ago. Some of the relationships documented in the quantitative scholarship are at least partially consistent with PoHR's theoretical expectations. The unique contribution of the model was the series of dynamics it proposed. Quantitative research has shed light on a few static relationships, capturing one or two "phases" of the model at best. This is hardly surprising, since quantitative researchers never set out explicitly to test for the model PoHR proposed.

PoHR began with one huge caveat: "Stable improvements in human rights conditions usually require some measure of political transformation and can be regarded as one aspect of [the political] liberalization process" (PoHR: 4). Rights cannot be expected to improve much – much less become "habitual" – in the absence of broader political liberalization. External norms and even external political pressure cannot be expected to sustain significant rights improvements unless there are fundamental changes in the domestic institutions of accountability and governance. If there is one clear message from the quantitative literature, it is that this basic assumption is largely warranted. Practically every regression that has ever been run finds a strong and convincing positive correlation between human rights – or more specifically, broadly accepted measures of physical integrity and political repression, the rights outcomes with which PoHR were primarily concerned – and various measures of political liberalization (typically the polity scale, which largely gauges institutions of participatory democracy; see Apodaca 2001; Landman 2005a; Neumayer 2005; Poe *et al.* 1999). Below a certain level, however, small improvements in democracy indicators have little to no influence on repressive human rights (Bueno de Mesquita *et al.* 2005; Davenport and Armstrong 2004).[2] "Show-case" democracies tend to experience only brief and reversible improvements in the basic human rights of their opponents (Cingranelli and Richards 1999). Clearly, these are not the regimes for which respect for human rights norms are likely to become "habitual."

PoHR also acknowledged the related idea that sustained improvements in human rights practices were conditioned by the broader legal and judicial capacities of the country in question: "We argue that the enduring implementation of human rights norms requires political systems to establish the rule of law" (PoHR: 3). The spiral could launch, but would sputter and eventually fail if other institutional changes did not take place in which norms could find domestic traction and eventually enforceability. Quantitative researchers have found some evidence for the proposition that countries with more highly developed legal institutions, and in particular independent judiciaries, do tend to have better civil rights protections, for example guarantees against unreasonable search and seizure (Cross 1999) and better access to fair trials (Simmons 2009). As will be discussed below, domestic legal and institutional mechanisms that are able independently to check government policies are increasingly proposed and tested in the quantitative literature as a mechanism through which international human rights norms eventually gain sufficient domestic traction to change rights practices overall.

It is not surprising, given their skepticism for long-term normative "internalization" in the absence of deeper governing and institutional changes, that PoHR did not have especially high hopes for international human rights norms in the context of the countries in their edited volume. None of the countries in their volume were stable democracies over the course of the past fifty years. Uganda, Tunisia and Morocco were never governed as democracies by

---

[2] Simmons (2009) found a similar result for a related right: the right to a fair trial. "Democratization" – or incremental yearly movements on the polity scale – was only associated with improvements in the provision of a fair trial among the subset of countries that were basically already decades-long stable democracies, but not stable autocracies or transitioning regimes (Table 5.3, p. 184).

traditional standards. South Africa, Kenya, Chile, Guatemala, the Philippines and Indonesia can be considered "transitional," "transitioned" or "partial" democracies, but they vary considerably in terms of the strength of their traditions of governing by the rule of law, with Chile at the strong end of the spectrum (also to a certain extent Morocco) and Guatemala at the weak end.[3] From the outset, PoHR considered all of these countries to varying degrees "hard cases" and expected international norms to fare differentially across them (PoHR: 2). In the end, they professed a degree of "surprise" with the power of human rights ideas in some cases (in Chile, Guatemala and Indonesia) but were also dismayed in others (Tunisia and Kenya; PoHR: 3). Could these differences be explained by broader trends in democratization and judicial and legal reform, or the specific mechanisms of the spiral model itself?

Phase 1: repression activates transnational civil society groups

Non-governmental organizations have been at the heart of understanding how and why human rights values became salient internationally in the twentieth century. Human rights have been championed by civil society actors, and embraced by most governments far more grudgingly. This is the natural consequence of the content of these rights; they tend to empower individuals and civil society groups vis-à-vis their governments. The qualitative literature has been dominated by studies of the importance of civil society groups, non-governmental organizations, and transnational advocacy networks in moving the human rights agenda forward (Korey 1998) and contributing to the "legalization" of these norms in international law (Breen 2003; Clark 2001; Cohen 1990; Dezalay and Garth 2006). NGOs are now said to constitute "external legitimating audiences" that keep the unlimited exercise of state sovereignty to some degree in check (Friedman *et al.* 2005).

PoHR made fairly specific claims about the role of NGOs. They put most of their emphasis on the mobilization of *transnational* human rights organizations and networks in the *early* stages of the spiral. They highlighted the informational as well as the advocacy roles of these groups, with a special focus on their linkages to the West (PoHR: 5). External pressure generated and sustained by these groups is central in the spiral model to "remind liberal states of their own identity," protect domestic groups by giving external legitimacy to their claims, and to keep up the pressure "from above," crucially supplementing that "from below" (PoHR: 5). Transnational human rights networks are therefore hypothesized to be crucial actors in the process of state socialization.

Quantitative research has a tough time convincingly distinguishing the mechanisms of persuasion, bargaining, incentive, manipulation and shaming

---

[3] In order to avoid an extended debate and justification for these categories, I have simply used the categorization presented in Simmons (2009: Appendix 2).

that have become central to socialization theory. This reflects the broader difficulties the diffusion literature has in distinguishing mechanisms of coercion from adaptation, emulation or internalization (Simmons *et al.* 2008): it is hard to infer motives from statistical correlations. One cut at this problem is simply to use statistical methods to test the proposition that the density of NGO networks is at least loosely associated with observable indicators that governments might be becoming "socialized." Global statistical data on the nature and strength of these networks is not especially nuanced. Several quantitative researchers have used "the number of international NGOs with domestic participation," which they "interpret as a measure of civil society strength" to try to capture this argument. While it does not prove the dynamics of the spiral model as a whole, most studies find what PoHR would expect: there is a correlation between local memberships in international non-governmental organizations and better rights practices, where the dependent variable is Freedom House's measure of civil and political rights, the Political Terror Scale (Neumayer 2005) or personal integrity rights (Hafner-Burton and Tsutsui 2005). Such findings of course do not confirm the spiral model *in toto*, but they are *roughly* consistent with its expectations. Since PoHR claims that domestic civil society actors are more important *later* in the cycle, the *domestic* memberships in INGOs used in the studies above should intensify when denial subsides and tactical concessions are on the rise. Few quantitative tests that are sensitive to such timing have been done, but according to one study there appears to be spikes in local ties to INGOs *after treaty ratification* (which one might think of as either a tactical concession or possibly prescriptive behavior, depending on whether one views such moves as strategic or sincere (Simmons 2009)). Again, while these tests were not designed to test PoHR's spiral, they do suggest a rough correspondence with the qualitative story told by their research.

Governments make tactical concessions

The spiral model is intriguing because in some sense it appears to rest on irrational logic. Governments take what they think will be inconsequential policy actions that they think may mollify their international and external critics. In PoHR's account, these actions often end up entrapping repressive governments (PoHR: 16). This is a core point on which PoHR diverges sharply with realist accounts of human rights. Many quantitative as well as qualitative scholars simply refuse to accept the PoHR premise – that tactical concessions matter to the big picture of human rights politics or practices. What matters is *enforcement* of norms, and this is what they all tend to assume is radically AWOL in the area of international human rights. Talking the talk is just that. Walking the walk, PoHR's theoretical opponents believe, requires much more forceful action (Downs *et al.* 1996; Goldsmith and Posner 2005; Hafner-Burton 2005; Krasner 1999), in the absence of which governments might even commit worse abuses

behind the shield of their concession (Hafner-Burton 2008). Tactical concessions such as treaty ratification have been characterized variously as an exercise in "public relations" (Keith 1999), "window-dressing" (Hafner-Burton and
Tsutsui 2005), or a (mere) "expressive" gesture (Hathaway 2002) that brings no
consequences in practice. Ultimately, these authors all stress, tactical ratification
does not matter to rights practices because treaties are not enforced. "As long as
enforcement of a human rights treaty remains relatively weak, countries with
egregious human rights records will join it purely for the symbolic benefits that
ratification confers" (Cole 2005: 492).

If PoHR's rhetorical entrapment argument is correct, it does raise a tough
question: why can't repressive governments foresee the communicative quick-
sand they are about to wade into and steer clear of it in the first place? PoHR
has three answers. First, governments miscalculate, and they do so *systematically*: "When they make these minor concessions, states almost uniformly over-
estimate their own support among their population" (PoHR: 27). Somewhat
mysteriously, governments apparently don't learn, either over time or from the
experiences of other governments, that minor concessions can lead to a real
political quagmire. Second, they may be bribed. Third, governments might be
in the early throes of socialization. Saying (or better yet, doing) is believing. A
certain amount of self-persuasion may very well be underway.

Miscalculation is a possibility, but it is likely only under a narrow set of
circumstances. Not all governments are equally likely to miscalculate. Stable
governments presiding over stable regimes in particular are likely to be able to
make good predictions about the likely outcome of their tactical concessions.
Repressive governments might decide to make a tactical concession to their political opposition, and if they encounter hopeful expectations of liberalization
respond with further repression. Some will be able to forecast quite well their
ability to "manage expectations," even if they need to use more repression to do
so (Vreeland 2008).

Where conditions are in flux, however, such estimations have much greater
confidence intervals around them. Tactical concessions could lead to "unexpected consequences" under conditions of turmoil and change. This argument
is consistent with the results of some quantitative research that suggests that the
ratification of international treaties (very likely tactical in some cases) tends to
be most positive and significantly correlated with improved rights practices in
neither stable democracies nor stable autocracies (where their consequences are
relatively predictable) but in countries undergoing various degrees of regime
transition, where it is much harder for a government to foresee the social and
political consequences of its actions (Simmons 2009).

We can also hypothesize that miscalculation is more likely where information is very thin, and then test for a relationship between the information
environment and the tendency to make tactical concessions. States are more
likely to bend to international pressures when they cannot forecast very well the

consequences predicted by the spiral model. Quantitative tests are few, but one study found "emulative" treaty ratification behavior to be strongest where the information environment was most thin: in regions of the world where information was stifled by government controlled media and earlier when the record of the consequences of tactical ratification was still sparse (Simmons 2009). This could mean that poor information accounts for some of the miscalculation associated with cynically adopting international norms.

But even with poor information, why should we expect governments to "uniformly" underestimate the pressure they will face to further liberalize? One possibility is that forecasts are only relevant in the short run. Some quantitative evidence suggests the shorter a repressive government's time horizon, the more likely it is to make a human rights concession; if its discount rate is high enough the immediate praise for doing may simply outweigh the longer term consequences in terms of galvanizing political demands for further rights guarantees (Simmons 2009). The short-term benefits may exceed the (high discounted) future costs.

The second possibility – external bribery – has been the subject of some quantitative empirical investigation. It is relatively straightforward to analyze whether governments make tactical human rights concessions in response to various material or even non-material inducements offered by outsiders. The most straightforward case can be made for aid: it is relatively easy for donor governments to manipulate aid to reward concessions they believe to be important. But quantitative research does not unambiguously support the proposition that aid responds to human rights policies – tactical or genuine. A study of the UK aid policies found that aid responded to human rights if at all when important foreign or economic policy interests were not at stake (Barratt 2004). Studies of European aid conclude that despite attention to "soft power," the human rights situation in developing countries does not consistently shape European aid commitments (Carey 2007). The United States' aid policy has also been constrained by broader foreign policy concerns. During the Cold War, aid went to repressive and non-repressive governments alike, although in the 1990s military aid did tend to flow less readily to the more repressive regimes (Blanton 2005). The United States seems somewhat more willing to use aid to encourage rights improvements when they have a significant potential to impact the United States, as in the area of human trafficking (Chuang 2005–2006), but otherwise the response of US aid to rights concessions of any kind is weak. It is hard to see how aid might be used in a targeted way to encourage human rights concessions, especially ones that are merely tactical.

The responsiveness of multilateral aid to human rights policies is similarly inconclusive. On the one hand, some studies have concluded that countries that receive loans from the World Bank are likely to have better workers' rights than those who do not (Abouharb and Cingranelli 2004), which appears consistent with the use of aid as a reward for human rights practices. On the other hand, other studies have emphasized that the austerity implied by multilateral loan conditions actually makes the realization of a range of rights less likely (Fields 2003; Franklin 1997). If this is the case, it is not very likely that these organizations care enough about tactical concessions to target their aid contingent upon it. More likely, they are simply not paying attention. If the rights abuse is significant enough to be investigated and censured by the UN Human Rights Commission, multilateral lenders may take more note (Lebovic and Voeten 2009). But this finding does not support the claim that *tactical concessions* are bought and paid for through international foreign aid. (I return to this point when discussing the role of external pressure in encouraging *real* human rights improvements, below).

Even more strained are arguments (and evidence) that tactical concessions are made to attract trade or investment. Such arguments have a series of high hurdles to overcome: to explain why economic agents might care about human rights practices; to explain why governments would be willing to interfere with private investment decisions that do not involve serious national interests, and to explain why either public or private actors would take a tactical concession seriously. Political economists have put forward the idea that certain human rights policies that we may think of as tactical serve as a signal of a government's willingness to accept principle limits on its exercise of power. A government willing to commit to respect human rights is also likely to respect property rights, the argument goes (Farber 2002; Moore 2003). There is some evidence that suggests that countries with less repressive rights practices tend to attract more foreign capital (Blanton and Blanton 2007), but surely this is only the case when rights are a part of a deep commitment to stable institutions, transparency in governance and the rule of law. If one could achieve all of the above and yet cut costs by repressing labor, it is not likely that traders or investors would mind all that much.[4]

As a global matter, however, the evidence for rewarding tactical concessions appears weak. Despite claims that governments ratify treaties, for example, for tangible economic benefits such as aid, trade or investment (Hathaway 2004; Hawkins and Goodliffe 2006), researchers have found relatively little empirical evidence that any of these increases significantly when governments ratify major human rights treaties (Nielsen and Simmons 2009). While much more work should be done on how international and domestic actors respond to a range of tactical concessions, the evidence to date hardly suggests that actors are satisfied with and thus reward in any material way these mere gestures. And why should

---

[4] New research suggests that there may indeed be competitive pressures generated through trade with countries with high labor standards. If firm X wants to sell its goods in high labor standard Country A they will be pressured to improve labor practices at home and in third countries where they produce their goods. As a result, countries tend to adopt labor practices that are similar to the countries to which they export. See for example Greenhill *et al.* (2009).

they? Only an irrational or uninformed actor would reward a government for an insincere policy concession (Goodman and Jinks 2004).

There remains the possibility – the one most theoretically central to the case that PoHR wishes to make about socialization – that tactical concessions are expected and believed to be appropriate measures given the growing significance of external norms, the increasing domestic hope for rights recognition, and the density of transnational connections that link the two. PoHR makes frequent appeals to the concept of "world time" – the global social context in which communicative action takes place. Some quantitative research supports the idea that tactical human rights concessions respond at least in part to the global social context. Sociologists have gathered evidence that the ratification of some human rights treaties (the Convention on the Elimination of Discrimination Against Women, for example) is associated with major global socializing events that promote rights, such as international conferences and meetings. They also adduce evidence that the more states are "embedded" in international institutions, the more likely they are to ratify international human rights agreements (Wotipka and Ramirez 2008). Similar evidence about the importance of international socializing events has been advanced for what may be the "tactical" adoption of national human rights institutions (Koo and Ramirez 2009). These could be the kinds of persuasive opportunities that PoHR believes encourage states to take at least small steps toward addressing the abuses exposed by their critics.

The quantitative evidence overall suggests that there are both internal and external influences on tactical treaty ratification. While concessions in some areas, such as women's rights, seem to be closely connected with all-out socialization efforts by the international community, in other areas, such as torture and civil and political rights, external pressures may exist but governments have to be exceptionally attuned to the domestic political situation. The quantitative evidence linking ratification of the torture convention to the existence of opposition political parties in repressive regimes supplies some support for the making of tactical concessions, as described in the spiral model (Vreeland 2008). So too does the finding that non-democracies with poor human rights records are more likely to ratify the torture convention than are democracies with poor human rights records (Hathaway 2007) – the former do not foresee the real probability of enforcement, at least in the short run. The finding that ratification of the International Covenant on Civil and Political Rights tends to be later rather than earlier in the term of a repressive government (Simmons 2009) suggests that short time horizons may have something to do with these choices. Most quantitative researchers are likely to agree with PoHR that *some* governments make *some* tactical concessions.[5] There is disagreement on *why*

---

[5] Note, however, that many quantitative as well as qualitative studies suggest that the same "concessions" are not always tactical across countries. One of the strongest predictors of

(internal dynamics versus external material or social pressures; socialization versus cynical calculations). But on this point PoHR was ambiguous as well. Suffice it to say that influences "from above" as well as "from below" have been at work in various regions of the world, at different points in time, and with respect to different aspects of the international human rights regime, to create a certain number of tactical concessions to rights norms. The central issue is: do these concessions matter for the practice of human rights around the world?

The consequences of tactical concessions

The central contribution of PoHR was the idea that even small concessions to rights principles had potentially powerful impacts. International human rights norms were seen as so powerful that action or even talk meant simply to appease domestic critics, external peers or transnational "norm entrepreneurs" could actually unleash political and social forces that governments did not expect to face when the concession was made. Moreover, as discussed above, PoHR thought that speech acts which might initially have been primarily tactical eventually convince governments themselves that certain rights are desirable and appropriate behavior. This combination of influences, PoHR proposed, could improve the chances that human rights would be respected by that state.

One difficulty of testing this argument empirically is that it is hard to prove definitively which concessions to human rights are tactical and which are genuine. If qualitative researchers have had some difficulty establishing exactly why governments make minor adjustments to their rights policies, quantitative researchers working with global data have an even more difficult time. It is difficult to establish with any precision exactly which moves are "tactical." Another reason for this gap in the spiral model's DNA is that empirical researchers have tended to skip phase 4 of the spiral model ("prescriptive status") in their impatience to get right to the punch line: behavioral change. But this means that a central claim of the spiral model has gone completely untested: no one has demonstrated the link between tactical concessions and the increased propensity for governments to actually begin to "talk the talk."

Testing this central claim would require a kind of quantitative research that so far has been rare in the literature surveyed in this chapter: actual textual analysis of a relevant corpus of government statements, press releases, documents,

the ratification of human rights treaties is the democratic nature of the regime, which is consistent with an argument that countries are sincere ratifiers of these treaties (for the most part, Simmons 2009). Ratification to lock in democratic gains in recently transitioned democracies is also a variation on sincere ratification (Moravcsik 2000). Sometimes there is genuine persuasion: "States are likely to be persuaded by arguments that draw on widespread taken-for-granted norms, in particular, prohibitions on bodily harm, the importance of precedent in decision making, and the link between cooperation and progress" (Hawkins 2004). See also Goodliffe and Hawkins (2006).

speeches and debates that would demonstrate a change in the language governments use when discussing policies related to rights practices. PoHR should expect (but to my knowledge no researchers have produced) evidence that the quality as well as the quantity of references to human rights increases over time once tactical concessions have been made. In fact, if the spiral model has some purchase on reality, it should be possible to produce statistical evidence of a growing correlation between indicators of the activation of domestic groups and the incidence of increasingly compelling "speech acts" as reflected in official documents such as those listed above. Better still, it should be possible to find a correlation between these speech acts and rights improvements (with some lag). Such an analysis would bolster the claim of the importance of consistently acknowledging the legitimacy of international human rights norms on actual outcomes. It would provide critical evidence about the importance of rhetorical entrapment in explaining eventual rule-consistent behavior.

The most studied "tactical concession," as discussed above, has been the ratification of international treaties, although it is quite clear that most governments are sincere when they ratify (or sincerely refrain from doing so), while only a fraction appear to ratify without any intention to significantly change rights practices.[6] Other less studied but possible tactical concessions might include institutional changes, such as the creation of national human rights institutions, the release of political prisoners, or the use of trials to prosecute egregious individual rights abusers. Very little research has been done on the effects of tactical concessions, outside of treaty ratification.[7] It is standard to skip any attention to rhetoric and jump straight to the behavioral outcomes – dependent variables indicative of improved rights practices. The modal research of the 2000s looks directly for correlations between treaty ratification and improvements in rights behavior, not pausing for a moment to examine and attempt to verify the claims for the power of argumentation advanced by PoHR.

The findings of researchers who have examined this relationship between tactical concessions and actual improvements in human rights practice have been all over the map. This is true even though they use very similar data and related methodologies. The big difference is in how they choose to set expectations, the conditions (of lack thereof) they place on their arguments, and how exactly they measure outcomes. The first generation of quantitative research took a homogenous approach to treaty ratification. All states were assumed to be alike – or sufficiently similar – such that the early quantitative researchers saw no need to develop conditional arguments about how they thought ratification might work

---

[6] Another relatively small set of countries maintain or improve their rights practices, but do not ratify international treaties, which raises another set of puzzles dealt with elsewhere (Simmons 2009).

[7] The quantitative research on national human rights institutions focuses primarily on their creation and not, thus far, on their effects. See for example Koo and Ramirez (2009).

in various contexts. "Country-years" were simply pooled in a big regression, from which researchers tried to draw general inferences. Proceeding in this way, Linda Camp-Keith found no statistically significant impact to ratification of the International Covenant on Civil and Political Rights (ICCPR) on Freedom House's measure of civil and political rights, or Gibney and Stohl's personal integrity index (Keith 1999). Oona Hathaway found no positive impact to ratification of the Convention Against Torture (CAT) on her carefully constructed torture scale when pooling all states unconditionally into a single regression (Hathaway 2002). Emilie Hafner-Burton and Kiyoteru Tsutsui regressed the total number of major human rights treaties ratified on the political terror scale and found no relationship, again across all countries (Hafner-Burton and Tsutsui 2005). All of these scholars concluded that the ratification of human rights treaties did not matter. In fact, they argued that, in sharp contrast to the spiral model, such a tactical concession could even be deleterious. Ratification would *satisfy* critics, *deflect* criticism, *legitimate* repressive regimes, and allow them to continue or maybe even to worsen their repressive practices (Hafner-Burton *et al.* 2008; Hathaway 2002). Many concluded there was a growing "compliance gap," although exactly what this meant in practice was somewhat unclear (see Chapter 5, this volume).

Why might these findings appear to be so pessimistic? It might very well be that this first generation of researchers was not specific enough about the conditions under which they expected the ratification of treaties to matter for rights practices. They may not have completely thought through the political and social mechanisms that would link a tactical concession such as treaty ratification to the possibility of an improved rights outcome. If they had, would they not have seen the obvious explanatory limits that the ratification of the Convention Against Torture would have in Norway, a country with a perfect score on Hathaway's scale for the history of the index? Did they realistically expect North Korea's 1981 ratification of the ICCPR[8] to matter much in that country?

It is critical to understand, as PoHR clarified in their description of the spiral model, that tactical concessions *alone* do not improve the practice of human rights. Treaties are legal agreements written down on pieces of paper (or posted on the Internet) and they don't have arms, legs, brains or iPhones. They can't *do* anything. They must be used by purposive agents that have the motivation to leverage them to achieve their goals. Releasing a few political prisoners does not fundamentally improve rights, unless people are encouraged to demand broader changes in civil and political rights. Setting up national institutions can be a meaningless isomorphism unless bureaus have a certain degree of independence and sufficient resources to get started on serious work.

---

[8] See www1.umn.edu/humanrts/research/ratification-korea.html (accessed June 1, 2010).

As PoHR was careful to spell out, non-governmental actors residing locally and also operating transnationally have an essential role to play in pressuring and persuading a government to follow up their symbolic gestures with real action. It does not make sense to argue that non-governmental organizations are "more important" than ratification, trials, institutions or the release of prisoners. Domestic actors with a huge and ongoing stake in the outcome use these tactical moves to focus their efforts, build political support and legitimate their demands for human rights.

One insight of PoHR's spiral model was that under specific circumstances tactical concessions would culminate with what they termed "prescriptive status" or better yet "rule-consistent behavior." This was likely where domestic civil society could become activated: "*Only when and if* the domestic opposition fully mobilizes and supplements the pressure 'from above' by pressure 'from below' can the transition toward prescriptive status and sustained improvement of human rights conditions be achieved" (PoHR: 34; emphasis added). PoHR was not very specific about the conditions under which it expected such mobilization to take place, but one approach is to think in terms of the expected value of mobilization. People will not mobilize when they do not expect much of a pay-off from doing so; after all mobilization against the government in many cases is costly and even dangerous. We can think of the *expected value of mobilization* as the product of two factors: the *value* people put on succeeding in achieving their goals and the *likelihood* of success. In other words, in order to really mobilize, people need a *motive* to organize and a *means* through which they might be able to influence their government to change its practices. In highly repressive regimes, the value placed on succeeding in securing a right is extremely high. It is a huge improvement in rights well-being to be free from arbitrary arrest for political reasons and to be guaranteed reasonably humane treatment while in government custody. In highly repressive regimes, people are highly motivated to organize to take advantage of a tactical concession and call for even more concessions in order to publicize the principles to which the government has rendered lip-service. The only problem is that they are likely to pay an extremely high price. Highly repressive regimes are likely to meet such demands by crushing them and making life very difficult for the leaders of the mobilization.

In other cases, governments can be expected to be relatively responsive to the demands of political opponents. In fact they may have such a long history of such responsiveness that there is very little "rights space" that the public does not freely and regularly enjoy. In these cases, people have the means to effectively put demands to the government, but they are not nearly so motivated. And because social mobilization and political organization require effort, few will have the motivation to organize to work for even better rights, which they experience as having diminishing marginal utility. So whereas the first few rights are extraordinarily highly valued, the 99th might not be worth taking to the streets. When allegations of torture were revealed at Abu Ghraib and elsewhere, for example, they scarcely became part of the national electoral debate in 2004; Americans generally were content that in most cases their rights were well-protected and were not politically mobilized on this issue. This was an instance in which people had the means, but not especially the motivation, to demand compliance with the Torture Convention.

Thought of in terms of the expected value of mobilization, then, we should expect pressure "from below" in countries ruled by neither stable, repressive autocracies (where people are deterred from mobilizing for fear of getting crushed) nor in stable democracies (where decades of responsive government has supplied already a full range of rights – hence the motive to organize is weak). Tactical concessions should be expected to have their most profound impact where people anticipate they have some chance of successfully realizing their demands at reasonable cost. This implies that the spiral is most likely to work its way to a positive conclusion in neither stable autocracies (where domestic groups risk being crushed), nor stable democracies (where phase 1 repression is extraordinarily rare to begin with), but rather in countries that are transitioning to, backsliding from or in a state of partial democracy (Simmons 2009). In those cases the pressure "from below" is most likely to become activated.

The quantitative research is now beginning to reflect this and other more conditional arguments about the relationship between tactical concessions and improved rights. Recent research is beginning to demonstrate for example that treaty ratification in countries whose regimes are in flux (neither stable autocracies nor stable democracies) does indeed have some important influence on rights practices. "Transition countries" that have ratified the CAT are much more likely to make improvements along Oona Hathaway's torture scale than are transition countries that have not ratified the CAT. "Transition countries" that have ratified the ICCPR are more likely to provide fair trials and are more likely to respect freedom of religion than are those transition countries that have not ratified. And in all of these cases, the positive consequences of ratification are concentrated in this category of countries; no effect could be found in either stable democracies or stable autocracies, *which is consistent with the spiral model and what might have been expected from the outset*. Tactical concessions matter tremendously, but only where domestic groups have the motive and the means to demand more meaningful change.

Recent quantitative work increasingly suggests that various other kinds of tactical concessions have a conditional impact on broader human rights practices. For example, Chapter 7 in this volume demonstrates that once a treaty has been ratified by a country subsequently investigated for widespread human rights abuses by the United Nations Human Rights Commission, human rights performance improves.

Another example of the importance of conditionality in explaining patterns of change relates to the presence or absence of trials for human rights violations.

In some cases, human rights trials might qualify as a "tactical concession." Certainly, it is not obvious that a few trials will lead to any fundamental changes in human rights practices. New research suggests that *at least in transition countries*, such trials have had important rights consequences generally. Hunjoon Kim and Kathryn Sikkink argue that human rights trials work to some extent through their ability to deter future abuses, by reducing the probability that the crime will go unpunished (Kim and Sikkink 2007).

While Kim and Sikkink emphasize the deterrent effect of criminal trials, their work complements a large literature on the additional leverage litigation (whether successful or not) can give to broader social rights movements. "Cause lawyering" (Ellmann 1998) describes the strategic use of legal resources, such as treaties, constitutional provisions and the local penal code, to bolster claims in local courts that governments or, in the case of torture, specific government officials have broken the law by which they are bound.

The quantitative scholarship does reveal conditional but strong consequences that result from government actions that might correctly be termed "tactical." The strongest findings are consistent with the idea that mobilization of domestic groups and the establishment and strengthening of the rule of law contribute to positive outcomes. Much more quantitative work could be done to explore the conditions under which strategic prisoner releases or the establishment of national human rights institutions or even constitutional innovations to incorporate rights might contribute to longer run rights improvements, but the data collection efforts are significant and research is just getting underway.

Conclusions

The pathway from commitment to compliance with international human rights norms has been highly varied across time and space. It has also been quite contingent, and fraught with setbacks as well as noteworthy successes. Almost every study of this pathway has emphasized the ways in which purposive actors have used international human rights norms to persuade, cajole, pressure and shame governments to live up to the commitments they have made to respect the rights of their own people. The spiral model was a succinct description of an ideal type of progression from commitment to compliance with human rights norms. Only a weak logic connected the stages of the model; the fulfillment of one stage presented the possibility – hardly the inevitability – of movement to the "next" stage. More than a decade of research has now accumulated in support of at least one conclusion: tactical concessions often have important human rights consequences. At least where agents with the motive and the means to organize domestically and transnationally, and where organizational pressures can be sustained, commitments have been associated with better human rights outcomes than one might have anticipated in their absence.

PoHR got at an essential truth: emboldening individuals and groups to view themselves as rights holders "triggers" a new politics based on altered expectations and new political alliances. Not everywhere and at all times; in fact, one weakness of the spiral model was its imprecision on scope conditions. PoHR perhaps was not clear enough on this issue in trying to explain why so many countries seem to get stuck at the point of making tactical concessions without ever coming close to rule-consistent behavior. Subsequent quantitative research suggests that one important scope condition is enough of a liberalizing opening to make domestic mobilization possible. Tactical commitments – especially legal ones like treaty ratification – also are likely to have much more traction where independent foci of authority (e.g. the courts) can independently support rights claims vis-à-vis the government. At the same time, some studies discussed above have supported the notion that external sources of material pressure, social shaming and group enforcement push the spiral along.

But it is hardly the case that methodological differences have dictated the answers to the question about what drives compliance with international human rights norms. Emilie Hafner-Burton and James Ron have written, provocatively, that "to date, assessments of efforts at protecting human rights have been shaped in large part by choice of research method" (Hafner-Burton and Ron 2009). They developed a detailed argument as to why qualitative researchers have been optimists, while quantitative researchers have come to much more pessimistic findings.

Why these findings should vary by research methodology is not quite clear, but in any case there is scarcely any systematic variance to explain between the findings of qualitative and quantitative researchers. As their own article notes, findings generally converge when investigators agree upon scope conditions.[9] No researcher – quantitative or qualitative – has advanced the argument that international treaty norms have a radical effect on human rights in countries where domestic opposition is immediately and brutally put down, just as no researcher of any methodological persuasion has argued that international norms and treaties operate independently of purposive actors and domestic or transnational politics. The most interesting research to date has been precisely on the specification of the mechanisms linking domestic and transnational politics, and using multiple methods to elucidate these connections (see Chapter 5, this volume).

---

[9] See Hafner-Burton and Ron (2009: 368 and 371). First, somewhat cautious qualitative findings are attributed to scope conditions: "many qualitative studies noted important *scope conditions* for their claims, and many explicitly recognized that human rights progress is often partial ... not inevitable" (p. 368); three pages later, somewhat optimistic quantitative findings are attributed to scope conditions as well: "Second-generation statistical researchers have discovered some good news but attribute most of it to particular *scope conditions* and domestic factors" (p. 371; emphasis added).

This is not to say a good deal more could not be done in this regard. As quantitative researchers move away from their obsession with global trends, more quantitative data on more detailed domestic mechanisms can be collected within smaller groups of countries or regions. The research to date has been dominated by a few crucial human rights, such as repression, civil rights, torture and physical integrity. These are of central importance, but there is almost as much to be gained by comparing whether and how international norms such as the death penalty, women's rights and children's rights also impact local practices. And as PoHR's original volume stresses, there are many possible kinds of tactical concessions that could be explored. While current research has focused on treaty ratification, it would also be useful to find out if other kinds of tactical responses – from the release of prisoners to the payment of compensation to victims – have the effect of stimulating more demands and ever higher expectations from domestic and transnational audiences.

Finally, there is much to do quantitatively on the new research agenda that Thomas Risse and Stephen Ropp set out in the introductory chapter of this volume. The conditions under which non-governmental actors comply with international human rights norms remains hugely understudied by quantitative researchers (but see Greenhill *et al.* 2009). This is of course partly an artifact of the way data have been collected for decades: by and about *states*. Several of the contributions to this volume point to progress on moving away from an exclusive focus on *state* compliance. Firms are increasingly crucial actors both in terms of their direct impact on human rights as well as their status as civil society actors that can support or oppose demands for rights protections (see Chapters 11, 12 and 13, this volume). The problems associated with sampling cases and collecting data on such varied, secretive and ephemeral entities as firms in an unbiased way is truly daunting. But until more work can be done to disaggregate the nature of the political actors with important influences over human rights outcomes, we will be missing a significant part of the dynamics that explain or impede the move from accepting principles to changing actual rights practices.

PART II

Conceptual and methodological issues

4

Human rights in areas of limited statehood: the new agenda

TANJA A. BÖRZEL AND THOMAS RISSE

The Power of Human Rights (PoHR; Risse *et al.* 1999) developed a spiral model of human rights change that started from four implicit and interrelated assumptions:

(1) Human rights-violating states are consolidated states that enjoy both the monopoly over the means of violence and the ability to make and fully implement central political decisions.
(2) Illiberal regimes violate human rights intentionally, that is, because they want to, not because they lack the capacity to comply with international norms.
(3) Rights-violating perpetrators are state actors for the most part.
(4) (Transnational) non-state actors promote compliance with international human rights by pressuring state actors towards norm adoption and implementation and by socializing them into the new norms, respectively.

These assumptions are valid for the cases discussed in PoHR and beyond (see Chapter 2). But they do not fit "areas of limited statehood," i.e. territorial or functional spaces in which national governments do not control the means of violence and/or are incapable to implement or enforce central decisions including the law. We argue in the following that consolidated statehood forms the exception rather than the rule in the contemporary international system and that "areas of limited statehood" are more widespread than is commonly assumed (see Risse 2011b; Risse and Lehmkuhl 2007). In particular, areas of limited statehood are not confined to fragile, failing or failed states, but characterize most developing countries in the current world system.

If we take limited statehood as a scope condition "from commitment to compliance" seriously (see introduction to this volume), we have to re-formulate

We thank the participants of the two workshops at the University of Wyoming in August 2009 and in Berlin in June 2010 for their critical comments, in particular Arie Kacowicz, Steve Ropp and Kathryn Sikkink. Research for this chapter has been funded by the German Research Foundation (*Deutsche Forschungsgemeinschaft*) in the framework of the Research Center 700 "Governance in Areas of Limited Statehood" which is gratefully acknowledged.

and re-conceptualize the human rights agenda, both in terms of research and policies. Naming and shaming, the "boomerang effect," and the other mechanisms developed in PoHR and the broader literature on transnational advocacy networks (Keck and Sikkink 1998) primarily target governments that are unwilling rather than incapable to comply with international norms. However, human rights violations in areas of limited statehood are often committed because of two interconnected phenomena:

(1) Central governments do not enforce the law, because they not only lack the willingness but also the means to control their own enforcement agencies, e.g. the police.
(2) Non-state actors or "state" actors uncontrolled by central authorities are primary perpetrators of human rights violations in areas of limited statehood – be it warlords, private militias, (multinational) companies or transnational criminal organizations (see also Chapters 12 and 13, this volume).

This chapter discusses the conceptual-analytical as well as the political consequences of these insights. We begin by defining our understanding of "limited statehood" and map the phenomenon and its relevance for human rights. We then show how limited statehood significantly mitigates the well-known positive effect of democracy on human rights, another scope condition identified in the introduction to this volume (Moravcsik 2000; Simmons 2009: 82; see Chapter 3, this volume). Many transition countries on a path to democratization have committed themselves to international human rights and have ratified the respective treaties. But human rights are nevertheless violated because of limited statehood. At the same time, we find a number of countries whose domestic institutions lack both democratic quality and effective statehood and which nevertheless are *not* human rights violators. These double findings of norms-violating democratic transition countries, on the one hand, and norms-respecting weak states, on the other, suggest that consolidated statehood is not a necessary condition for compliance with human rights.

We then compare two transition countries that score relatively high on democracy but suffer from limited statehood. Guatemala's compliance with human rights is rather low which is largely related to a lacking capacity of central state authorities to enforce human rights against decentralized state agents and non-state actors. Georgia used to suffer from similar problems but has improved its human rights record over recent years. We argue that this is due to an internal and external strengthening of state institutions through domestic reforms and international capacity-building since the Rose Revolution in 2003.

Finally, we discuss the consequences for the spiral model as developed in PoHR when applied to areas of limited statehood. We conclude with implications for the promotion of human rights in areas of limited statehood.

Conceptualizing limited statehood

The spiral model as developed in PoHR implicitly assumed that states are fully capable of complying with international human rights norms if they only want to or are forced to by transnational mobilization through mechanisms such as the "boomerang effect."[1] In other words, the original spiral model took it for granted that states would be able to enforce the law. The underlying theory of compliance was one of deliberate or voluntary non-compliance (Raustiala and Slaughter 2002). Autocratic regimes violate human rights because, for example, they want to stay in power. The spiral model and the built-in boomerang effect are then meant to pressure norm-violating states "from above and from below" (Brysk 1993) and, thus, raise the costs of non-compliance for them. But, as most scholars have noted, commitment as such does not lead to compliance in the human rights area (Hafner-Burton and Tsutsui 2005; Keith 1999; see Chapter 1, this volume). Some have taken this as an indication of a cynical attitude adopted by leaders of authoritarian regimes (particularly Hathaway 2002, for a critique see Simmons 2009; see also Chapters 3 and 5, this volume).

But what if governments commit to international human rights through rati-fication of the relevant treaties, appear willing to comply, but cannot do so for a variety of reasons? The literature calls this "involuntary defection" (Putnam 1988) or "involuntary non-compliance" (Chayes and Chayes 1993, 1995). What if governments do not have sufficient capacity to enforce the law to which they have committed? What if central decision-making authorities lack the insti-tutional means to control, e.g., their military or their police forces, let alone non-state actors violating human rights? These considerations lead us to the discussion of "limited statehood." We suggest that scholarship on human rights ought to take limited statehood more seriously as a significant obstacle for mov-ing from commitment to compliance.

What constitutes "limited statehood"? We start with Max Weber's conceptu-alization of statehood as an institutionalized authority structure with the abil-ity to steer hierarchically (*Herrschaftsverband*) and to legitimately control the means of violence (see Weber 1921/1980). While no state governs hierarchic-ally all the time, consolidated states at least possess the ability to authoritatively make, implement and enforce central decisions for a collectivity. In other words, they command what Stephen Krasner calls "domestic sovereignty," i.e. "the for-mal organization of political authority within the state and the ability of public authorities to exercise effective control within the borders of their own polity" (Krasner 1999: 4). This understanding allows us to distinguish between *statehood* as an institutional structure of authority, on the one hand, and the kind of *govern-ance* services it provides, on the other hand. The latter is an empirical not a defin-itional question. The ability to effectively make, implement or enforce decisions

---

[1] See Risse (2011a) for the following.

constitutes statehood. Whether this enforcement capacity is exercised within the boundaries of the rule of law and through the respect for basic human rights or not, concerns the quality of governance, but not the definition of statehood.

We can now define more precisely the concept of "areas of limited statehood." While areas of limited statehood belong to internationally recognized states, it is their domestic sovereignty which is severely circumscribed. Areas of limited statehood concern those parts of a country in which central authorities (usually governments) lack the ability to implement and/or enforce rules and decisions and/or in which the legitimate monopoly over the means of violence is lacking. The ability to enforce rules or to control the means of violence can be restricted along various dimensions: (1) territorial, i.e. concerning parts of the territory; (2) sectoral, that is, with regard to specific policy areas; and (3) social, i.e. with regard to specific parts of the population. As a result, we can distinguish different configurations of limited statehood.

Areas of limited statehood are an almost ubiquitous phenomenon in the contemporary international system, but also in historical comparison. After all, the state monopoly over the means of violence has only been around for a little more than 200 years. Most states in the contemporary international system contain "areas of limited statehood" in the sense that central authorities do not control the entire territory, do not completely enjoy the monopoly over the means of violence, and/or have limited capacities to enforce and implement decisions, at least in some policy areas or with regard to large parts of the population.

The concept of "limited statehood" needs to be distinguished from "failing" and "failed" statehood. Most typologies in the literature and datasets on fragile states, "states at risk," etc. reveal a normative orientation toward highly developed and democratic statehood and, thus, toward the Western model (see e.g. Rotberg 2003, 2004). The benchmark is usually the democratic and capitalist state governed by the rule of law. This is problematic on both normative and analytical grounds. It is normatively questionable, because it reveals a bias toward Western statehood and Euro-centrism. It is analytically problematic, because it tends to confuse definitional issues and research questions. If we define states as political entities that provide certain services and public goods, such as security, the rule of law and welfare, many "states" in the international system will not qualify as such.

Moreover, failed and failing states comprise only a small percentage of the world's areas of limited statehood (see Figure 4.1). Most developing and transition countries, for example, contain areas of limited statehood insofar as they only partially control the means of force and are often unable to enforce collectively binding decisions, mainly for reasons of insufficient political and administrative capacities.[2] Brazil and Mexico, on the one hand, and Somalia and Sudan, on the other,

---

[2] This is not to argue that limited statehood is confined to developing countries. Southern Italy, for example, contains areas of limited statehood insofar as the Italian central state authorities are incapable of enforcing the law vis-à-vis those parts of the population who are

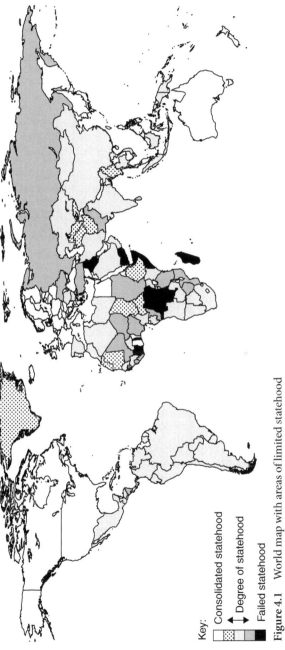

Figure 4.1 World map with areas of limited statehood

Key:

Consolidated statehood

Degree of statehood

Failed statehood

constitute the opposite ends of a continuum of states containing areas of limited statehood. Moreover, we do not talk about "states of limited statehood," but areas, i.e. territorial or functional spaces within otherwise functioning states in which the latter have lost their ability to govern. While the Pakistan state enjoys a monopoly over the use of force in many parts of its territory, the so-called tribal areas in the country's northeast are beyond the control of the central government.

Unfortunately, we do not have good (and quantifiable) data on the nature of the phenomenon of limited statehood, for three reasons. First, existing databases on failing and fragile states, on (good) governance, and on development tend to conflate the degree of statehood, on the one hand, with the governance services provided in a country, on the other. If weak statehood, for example, is defined as a lack of public services, this tends to confuse at least three things: weak state capacity to govern, unwillingness of state actors to provide services, and – last but not least – provision of governance (or lack thereof) by other than state actors. Second, most databases aggregate their findings on the national level, i.e. they suffer from what has been called "methodological nationalism" (Zürn 2002). As a result, the degree of statehood may be overrated in countries, such as Kenya, where the government controls the heartlands but does not reach into parts of the periphery, or underestimated, as in case of Somalia where remote provinces have developed some effective governance capacity. Finally, a major conceptual issue involves differentiating between lack of willingness to implement policies, on the one hand, and lack of capacity, on the other. The police forces of Mexico City, for example, do not enforce public security in most of the poorer quarters of the metropolitan area (Braig and Stanley 2007). But it remains unclear whether the city government is unwilling or incapable of doing so, since the law is well-enforced in the wealthy quarters of the city. To what extent non-compliance is a problem of willingness or capacity is an empirical question, which is not always easy to answer, not least because human rights violations are also reported at the national level. We come back to this issue in our two illustrative case studies on Georgia and Guatemala.

Despite these conceptual and methodological issues, a look at a world map shows the scope of limited statehood. The shades of grey signify degrees of statehood with "white" countries representing consolidated statehood and "black" countries (such as Somalia) representing failed states (see Figure 4.1). The degrees of statehood are derived from three indicators: "failure of state authority" and "portion of country affected by fighting"[3] (measuring the state monopoly over the means of violence), as well as "bureaucratic quality"[4] (see Lee *et al.*

---

directly or indirectly involved with the mafia. The same holds true for the drug business in many parts of the world's major cities including New York, London, Paris or Berlin.

[3] Source: Political Instability Task Force (PITF), Center for Global Policy, George Mason University, Washington, DC.

[4] Source: International Country Risk Guide (ICRG), Political Risk Services, Syracuse, New York.

Table 4.1. *Human rights by regime type and degree of statehood*

Configuration of statehood Regime type	*Consolidated statehood*	*Limited statehood*
Authoritarian regimes	Human rights violations due to lack of willingness (as in PoHR)	Human rights violations due to lack of willingness *and* capacity
Democratic regimes	Mostly human rights compliance	Human rights violations due to lack of capacity

forthcoming, for details). These indicators roughly correspond to our definition of (limited) statehood. They are conservative and partly even misleading figures, since the index only measures entire countries and not areas of limited statehood. But they do show that the phenomenon of limited statehood is real and not to be underestimated.

In other words, only few countries such as Somalia, Haiti or the Democratic Republic of Congo (DRC) fall in the category of failed, failing or fragile states. The vast majority of states – democracies such as Argentina, South Africa or Mozambique, but also authoritarian states such as Zimbabwe or semi-authoritarian countries such as Russia – fall in the middle category in that they are neither failed nor consolidated states, but contain areas of limited statehood in the sense defined above. We focus on these types of states in the following.

Limited statehood, human rights and the spiral model

The spiral model developed in PoHR implicitly assumed consolidated statehood. It focuses on authoritarian regimes (the northwestern cell of Table 4.1) and describes various mechanisms and stages by which such governments can be brought into compliance with international human rights norms through pressures "from above and from below" (see Chapters 1 and 2, this volume). The spiral model also assumed that authoritarian regimes are unwilling to rather than incapable of protecting basic human rights. It maintained that such regimes – once pressured and/or persuaded into compliance – would have no problem in implementing basic human rights standards through various enforcement mechanisms. To put it in terms of the various compliance theories (Börzel *et al.* 2010; Hurd 1999; Raustiala and Slaughter 2002), the spiral model incorporated compliance mechanisms theorized by enforcement and legitimacy approaches. Enforcement approaches focus on sanctions as well as positive incentives to change the cost-benefit calculations of actors thereby inducing compliance. The legitimacy school concentrates on persuasion and learning to induce actors "to do the right thing" and thereby comply with costly rules. Each of these approaches ultimately assumes a functioning state that is in principle capable of enforcing central decisions and the law. The compliance problem is lack of willingness rather than state capacity.

The spiral model also assumed that democratic and consolidated states (the southwestern cell in Table 4.1) are mostly good compliers with human rights norms, an assumption which quantitative work has corroborated in the meantime (Simmons 2009; but see Chapter 8 in this volume). In this sense, PoHR took regime type into account as a scope condition, but only implicitly. This volume explicitly problematizes both the democracy vs. autocracy as well as the consolidated vs. limited statehood dimensions (see Chapter 1, this volume).

The world is full of authoritarian as well as democratic regimes that try to govern areas of limited statehood. Many African states fall in the northeastern cell of Table 4.1. This also holds true for Russia, a semi-authoritarian regime, which does not fully control its territory. These authoritarian and semi-authoritarian regimes violate human rights, since they lack the willingness *and* the capacity to comply. Finally, the southeastern cell of Table 4.1 is populated by democratic regimes with areas of limited statehood. For example, India, the world's largest democracy, belongs in this category. If we assume that democracies are willing to commit to and to comply with human rights at least in principle, rights violations in countries populating the southeastern cell of Table 4.1 occur mainly because a state is not in full control of parts of its territory or with regard to parts of the police force or the military. In other words, the compliance problem is a capacity issue in these cases.

Figure 4.2 uses Bertelsmann Transformation Index data to map the 129 transition and developing countries according to their degree of statehood and their degree of democracy.[5] The figure yields the following picture: first, as is to be expected, most consolidated democracies are also consolidated states (the upper right corner of Figure 4.2; exceptions are, for example, India and Jamaica). At the same time, we do not find any consolidated democracy among failed, failing and fragile states.

Second, the lower right corner of Figure 4.2 is populated by authoritarian and consolidated states, such as Vietnam and Cuba. Third, the most interesting

---

[5] To measure the degree of democracy, we use the composite "political participation" scale which is the mean of the following indicators: free and fair elections; effective power to govern; association and assembly rights; freedom of expression. To measure the degree of statehood, we combined the values for "monopoly over the means of violence" and "basic administrative capacities." Data are calculated from "Detaillierte_Werte_BTI2010.xls," downloaded from www.bertelsmann-transformation-index.de/bti/ranking, last accessed October 30, 2010.

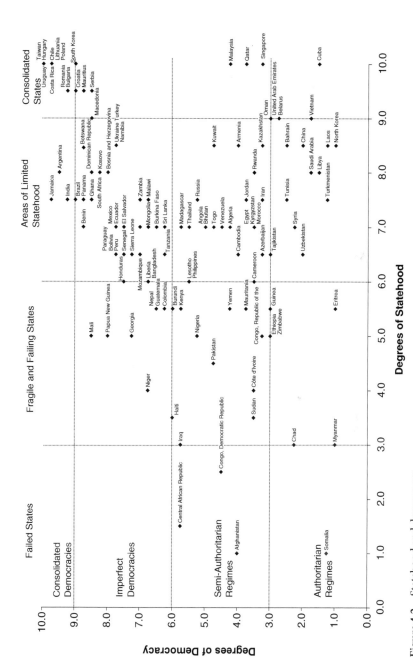

Figure 4.2   Statehood and democracy

picture can be found among failing and fragile states, on the one hand, and countries containing areas of limited statehood, on the other. Among them, we find both authoritarian and semi-authoritarian regimes (Uzbekistan, Syria, China, Russia, etc.), but also many imperfect democracies scoring way above average on the participation scale of BTI 2010 (such as Georgia, Mozambique, South Africa or Guatemala). If we use the categories introduced in Table 4.1 and take democracy as an indicator for the degree of willingness to comply with human rights, while statehood indicates the degree of capacity to comply, we derive the following assumption:

> *The more fragile, failing, or limited in statehood a particular state is, and the more authoritarian its regime, the more human rights compliance will result from a combination of inadequate capacity and unwillingness to act.*

In other words, the further we move down in the middle categories of Figure 4.2 (failing/fragile states as well as areas of limited statehood), the more compliance with human rights is a question of both lack of willingness and lack of capacity. The more we move up in these middle categories, the more compliance with human rights becomes a question of capacity rather than willingness. Below, we evaluate this assumption with regard to Georgia and Guatemala as two imperfect democracies whose statehood is severely limited (Georgia is even coded as a fragile state in the BTI 2010).

Let us now look at the human rights performance of areas of limited statehood. Figure 4.3 depicts the above-average human rights performers ("rights protecting states"; using civil rights performance as the indicator), while Figure 4.4 shows the below-average performers ("rights violating states").

A comparison of Figures 4.3 and 4.4 yields the following insights: first, we find most rights-protecting states in the upper right corner of Figure 4.3. Semi-authoritarian regimes and imperfect democracies tend to show a higher respect for human rights, the more consolidated their statehood is. This suggests a positive interaction effect between democracy and statehood. Or to put it differently, the negative effect of authoritarianism on human rights violations is mitigated by statehood in regimes that are neither clearly autocratic nor democratic. However, a number of countries are quite advanced in their democratization process and suffer from problems of limited statehood, but do not systematically violate human rights (Georgia, Haiti, Niger, Mali, Papua New Guinea, Lebanon). We illustrate this point with our case study of Georgia below.

Second, most of the rights-violating states can be found among (semi-) authoritarian states that are fragile, failing or contain areas of limited statehood. This confirms, of course, the well-known correlation between (semi-)authoritarianism and rights violations, even though there are quite a few imperfect democracies, too, that also violate civil rights (Nepal, Bangladesh, Guatemala and Sri Lanka, among others). Lack of domestic sovereignty or limited statehood

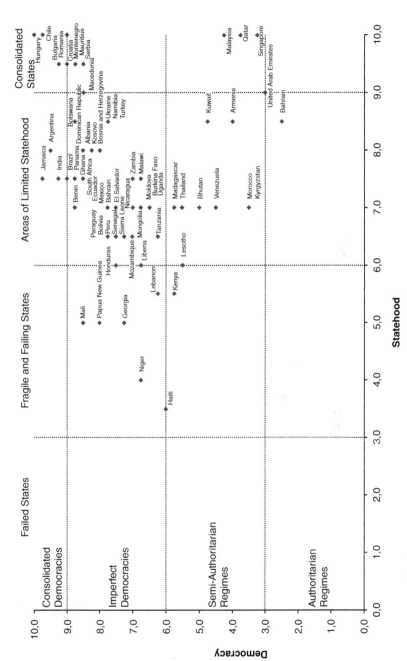

Figure 4.3 Civil rights protecting states

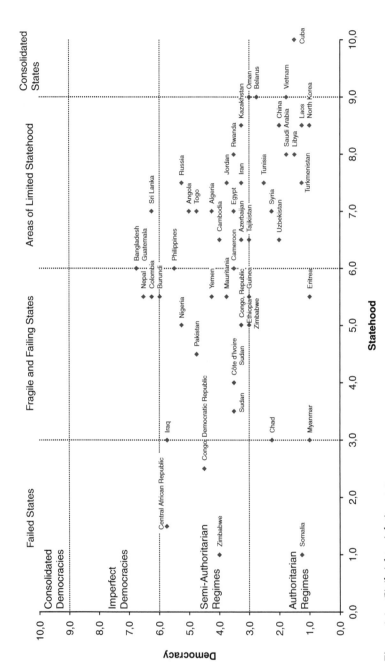

Figure 4.4 Civil rights violating states

significantly contributes to the violation of human rights. Or, to use the categories in Table 4.1 again, most rights-violating states in the international system suffer from both a lack of willingness *and* a lack of capacity to comply with these norms. To illustrate our argument empirically, we seek to isolate the capacity issue by discussing two countries that are above average on the democracy scale (suggesting willingness), but severely suffer from limited statehood.

Guatemala and Georgia rank comparatively high on the democracy scale (see Figure 4.2), which we take as indicating both a commitment to human rights and the willingness to comply. At the same time, both countries contain areas of limited statehood with Georgia even falling in the category of fragile states (Figure 4.2). Both countries are, therefore, located in the southeastern cell of Table 4.1 combining democratic regimes and limited statehood. As a result, we expect possible human rights violations to result primarily from a lack of capacity rather than a lack of willingness to comply. Thus, we have selected the two countries because of shared characteristics on both the democracy and the statehood scores. Yet, Guatemala which has already been covered in the original PoHR (Ropp and Sikkink 1999) continues to be a rights-violating country, while Georgia has made quite a few improvements. How can we account for the variation?

Guatemala: erosion of the state and rights violations by non-state actors

As Ropp and Sikkink argued in PoHR, the end of the civil war in Guatemala initially led to considerable improvements of the human rights situation in the country which was substantially fostered by both transnational campaigns and by domestic pressures as theorized by the spiral model (Ropp and Sikkink 1999). Yet, the human rights situation deteriorated again over the past decade and progress has been slow to non-existent in Guatemala.[6] This increase in rights abuses is no longer caused primarily by an oppressive regime, but by violent non-state actors and the lack of domestic sovereignty of the state in combating non-state violence. In fact, the security situation has deteriorated significantly in recent years (violent death rates have risen close to the levels of the civil war). Impunity is rampant (up to 90 percent of violent crimes are never prosecuted) and human rights violations against vulnerable groups (women, children, indigenous communities) also continue to be high, in particular in rural areas: "Since the close of its civil war in 1996, rampant criminal activity has made Guatemala arguably the most dangerous country in Latin America. Murders increased by more than 120 percent from 1999 to 2006, with the murder rate in Guatemala City reaching

---

[6] The following is largely based on an unpublished memorandum by Uwe Gneiting whom we thank for his tremendous help and assistance in researching this case.

an astounding 108 per 100,000 inhabitants (compared to a world average of less than 9 per 100,000)" (Brands 2010: 9–10; see also Deibert 2008–2009: 167–168). The patterns of human rights violations have changed in the Guatemalan context from state-sponsored violence during the Civil War to human rights violations committed by non-state actors, in particular urban gangs and new "transnational threats," such as organized crime groups (i.e. narco-traffickers) and (to a lesser degree) transnational corporations.

The increase in violent crime committed by non-state actors has shifted the center of human rights violations with regard to physical integrity rights from rural areas (where the military committed most of its human rights violations during the Civil War) to the metropolitan area of Guatemala City where criminal groups have gained a stronghold over the past decade. In rural areas, new human rights threats have also appeared. For instance, in the not very densely populated north of Guatemala, narco-trafficking groups that have been pushed south from Mexico are slowly establishing a form of parallel authority structure, promising security and resources to cooperating communities, building checkpoints and private roads. In other rural areas, the entrance of transnational mining companies is increasingly affecting the human rights situation of rural communities (Fulmer et al. 2008).

As a result of these changes in patterns and perpetrators of human rights violations, the Guatemalan state is mainly criticized for its inaction to combat human rights violations committed by non-state actors within its territory. The developments in Guatemala over the past decade, in particular the emergence of new transnational security threats, have put the issue of state capacity (i.e. particular weak institutions, lack of resources and reach, and high government turnover) to the forefront.

First, the lack of state capacity is evident (i.e. limited geographical reach of state institutions, weakly trained police forces) and actually results in part from the horrible human rights abuses committed by the military, paramilitary forces and the police during the 1980s (Ropp and Sikkink 1999).[7] This has made subsequent US administrations, European states and the European Union extremely unwilling to build state capacity in terms of defense and security aid (at least as compared to other Central and South American countries). Moreover, the government is reluctant to put more security forces on the streets. When, as a last resort, the left-leaning government placed military forces on the streets in order to improve security in the capital, it was confronted with significant backlash due to the historical role the military has played in the country.

The result has been limited statehood. As Hal Brands points out:

> From Petén in the north, to Huehuetenango in the west, to parts of Guatemala City itself, as much as 40 percent of Guatemalan territory is

---

[7] We owe the following point to Steve Ropp.

> either subject to dispute or effectively beyond the control of the police and the central government ... In 2007, then-Vice President Eduardo Stein acknowledged that criminal elements controlled six of Guatemala's 22 departments (the largest geographical and political subdivisions of the country) and had a strong presence in a least three others.
>
> (Brands 2010: 10)

Furthermore, the topic of violence and security dominates the political debate. As a result, improving the security situation would be in the utmost interest of the government to remain in power. The lack of progress in this area thus points to a lack of means to protect human rights rather than an unwillingness to do so. Improvements in security conditions and the rights situation in the wealthier parts of the capital are mostly due to the widespread emergence of private security forces employed by companies and rich citizens.

With regard to impunity, the evidence on the willingness side is more mixed. On the one hand, the Guatemalan government has voluntarily allowed the UN Commission against Impunity in Guatemala (CICIG) to work in the country in order to investigate cases and make recommendations on the improvement of the justice system (a risky move considering the high visibility and perceived authority of the commission). In other words, Guatemala has been prepared to accept intrusions in its "Westphalian" sovereignty in order to combat human rights violations. On the other hand, the government and the Guatemalan Supreme Court have continuously refused to persecute or extradite persons responsible for human rights violations during the Civil War (appealing to sovereignty arguments), which continues to be seen as one of the most striking cases of impunity in the country. As a result, the commitment of the government to combat impunity in a rigorous manner has to be seen with skepticism. Nevertheless, the justice system also faces clear institutional limitations and access to a fair trial is hindered by an inefficient and corrupt bureaucracy.

A combination of willingness and capacity is also valid when it comes to human rights violations committed by transnational corporations (Fulmer *et al.* 2008). With regard to transnational mining companies, the state has the capacity to punish well-documented acts of human rights violations, but is very slow in doing so. This leads to the conclusion that economic policy objectives appear to trump human rights concerns since the best solution would be to revoke the exploitation license for the mining operations in question. In other areas, such as labor rights, a lack of state capacity to monitor compliance plays a greater role. As a case in point, there is a clear difference between compliance in urban vs. rural industries, which in part can be traced back to capacity constraints of the labor inspectorate to monitor compliance in remote areas.

In sum, Guatemala is a case in which most rights violations are committed by non-state actors, in particular transnational criminal networks as well as "private armies" associated with wealthy landowners, but also by transnational corporations, especially mining companies. State institutions are generally too weak to enforce human rights effectively and to improve domestic sovereignty with regard to public security in vast parts of the country. However, and particularly with regard to transnational corporations, the government is also unwilling to enforce its own standards, e.g. with regard to labor rights (see e.g. CALDH and The International Labor Rights Fund 2004).

Georgia: strengthening statehood and reducing rights violations

Since gaining independence after the demise of the Soviet Union, Georgia's statehood has been severely limited. Its monopoly of force has been challenged in the two regions of South Ossetia and Abkhazia, where separatists supported by North Caucasian volunteers and later also by Russian troops have been fighting for secession. In the Georgian "heartland," economic collapse, civil war and pervasive corruption have seriously crippled the capacity of the state to set and enforce laws (Börzel et al. 2008).[8] While its democratic quality subsequently improved, the human rights situation remained poor, particularly in the two separatist regions, which have increasingly escaped the control of the central government in Tbilisi.[9] While the central government sought to suppress the separatist movements in Abkhazia and South Ossetia, Abkhazian and Ossetian authorities have committed serious human rights violations against the Georgian minority since the 1990s. Ethnic Georgians have long been suffering from discrimination in public life and enduring attack. Their situations worsened during and as a result of the war with Russia in 2008 by which Abkhazia and Southern Ossetia gained de facto independence (Office for Democratic Institutions and Human Rights 2008a). With the support of Russian troops, separatists have burned Georgian villages, destroyed property and forced families out of the territories (Human Rights Watch 2009a: 90, 130). The de facto authorities of South Ossetia and Abkhazia did not fulfill their obligations under international human rights law to ensure conditions for the displaced persons to return to their homes. The Georgian government, in turn, was unable to stop these developments. It refused to be held accountable for the rights violations and was overwhelmed by the flow of internally displaced people who had to

---

[8] We thank Wiebke Wemheuer, Bidzina Lebanidze and Esther Ademmer for their helpful comments and assistance on the Georgian case as well as Sven Hilgers for his general research assistance.

[9] Human Rights Watch World Report 1998 (www.hrw.org/legacy/worldreport/Helsinki-13. htm – P660_161190 (accessed October 30, 2010)).

live under partly inhuman conditions, could not return to their homes and still do not enjoy full civil and political rights (Office for Democratic Institutions and Human Rights 2008a: 17). Corruption of local enforcement authorities provided fertile ground for (transnational) crime, including trafficking in women, abductions of foreigners and Georgian citizens for ransom, and violent robberies of businesses (Nodia 1995). The collusion of criminal gangs with corrupt police officers also undermined efforts to effectively control Georgia's "borders" with the two separatist regions, turning Abkhazia and South Ossetia into safe havens for criminal networks (Bertelsmann Stiftung 2007: 6).

While its monopoly of force has been and remains contested in the separatist territories, the capacity of the Georgian state to set and enforce collectively binding rules in its "heartland" has improved. The Rose Revolution of 2003 disposed of the post-communist government under Shevardnadze. The new president, Mikheil Saakashvili, pledged to fight corruption and restore Georgia's territorial integrity (Boda and Kakachia 2005). The war against Russia ended rather than re-established control over Abkhazia and South Ossetia. But the new government successfully launched a series of reforms to strengthen the political, administrative and economic capacities of the central state. It immediately took action against corruption within law enforcement agencies, which resulted in the complete dismantling of the traffic police. Some 15,000 officers lost their jobs practically overnight. In addition, a special force of 30,000 men and women attached to the Ministry of Interior was dissolved and all members fired. Reforms of the police forces continued with investments in modern equipment, the creation of a new Police Academy, mandatory exams and training for police officers, and considerable increases in the salaries (Hiscock 2006). While petty corruption has been effectively fought, political corruption is as pervasive as during the Shevardnadze era. Yet, the incumbent elites have managed to centralize the control over the flow of revenues, cutting into the power base of political opponents (Börzel and Pamuk 2012). Moreover, constitutional reforms increasingly concentrated political power in the executive. The less than perfect separation of power remains an ongoing concern in Georgia's transition to full democracy.

Besides strengthening state capacities, liberalization and deregulation have boosted economic growth and helped to attract direct foreign investments and external financial assistance. The United States, the EU and other international actors have significantly stepped up their support for Saakashvili's reforms helping to strengthen the capacity of state institutions to set and enforce domestic regulation. In 2008, for example, the two Western donors gave five (US) and 20 (EU) times more financial aid to Georgia than to Guatemala[10] (see Börzel et al. 2009).

---

[10]   www.aiddata.org (accessed September 21, 2011).

Since the Rose Revolution in 2003, Georgian statehood has become more limited because it lost de facto control over the two separatist regions where human rights abuses continue but are committed by Abkhazian and South Ossetian authorities and Russian troops. At the same time, statehood has been consolidated on the territory controlled by the Georgian government where the human rights situation improved until 2008. Yet, with the strengthening of the state, the Saakashvili regime has also tightened its grip on political power, particularly since the war against Russia. Opposition parties as well as external observers criticized the elections of 2008 as flawed (Office for Democratic Institutions and Human Rights 2008b: 1). Freedom of media, speech and assembly have been increasingly restricted (Bertelsmann Stiftung 2009a: 7–8), and the fight against corruption is used to eliminate political opponents (Börzel and Pamuk 2012). While political opposition has not been openly prosecuted, the ill-treatment of (political) prisoners by law enforcement agents is still an issue of concern in Georgia (Human Rights Watch 2005b: 4–5; UNCCPR 2007: 3–4). The broadcasting of video footage of prisoners being beaten and sexually abused resulted in massive street protests two weeks before the parliamentary elections in 2012, and contributed to the defeat of Saakashvili's ruling party.

Thus, Georgia faced similar problems in compliance with human rights as did Guatemala. Its state institutions have been too weak to prevent violations committed by decentralized authorities, particularly in the two separatist regions, where its monopoly of force has been increasingly contested. In the Georgian "heartland," the corruption of local law enforcement agents crippled the capacity of the state to stop human rights violations by criminal networks. While the Saakashvili government failed to restore control over Abkhazia and South Ossetia where human rights violations continue, it has managed to strengthen state capacities by fighting corruption and liberalizing the economy with the help of international donors.

As a result, human rights violations by decentralized state agents have decreased on the territory still controlled by the Georgian government, and the overall human rights record of Georgia has improved. Recently, however, we observe a deterioration again due to active restrictions of political and civil rights by central state agents in the aftermath of the war against Russia. Strengthening the state alone does not guarantee compliance with human rights, since there are authoritarian tendencies in the Saakashvili government. Whether these tendencies carry the day in the end depends on the continued strength of civil society connected to transnational (and Western) advocacy networks and pressure by international organizations, the EU and Western states. Moreover, as Georgia has firmly committed itself to international human rights and is dependent on the political and financial support of the international community, the mechanisms of the spiral model should prevent a relapse of Georgia into authoritarianism. The parliamentary elections of 2012 give some reason for optimism: President Saakashvili accepted the defeat of his ruling party resulting in the first peaceful transition of power in the history of Georgia.

In sum, the main difference accounting for the variation between Guatemala (worsening human rights record) and Georgia (improving, at least until recently) seems to be the greater embeddedness in the international (particularly Western) community. The United States and the EU invested many more resources in capacity-building (and, thus, strengthening the state) in Georgia as compared to Guatemala. The Georgian government strives to become part of "the West" and is also under a lot of international scrutiny given its past human rights performance. Finally, civil society organizations are stronger in Georgia than in Guatemala. In other words, if we compare two countries on similar levels of democracies and (weak) statehood (southeastern corner of Table 4.1), the mechanisms identified by the spiral model in PoHR in conjunction with sustained efforts at capacity-building seem to make the difference.

Conclusions

This chapter has taken a closer look at two of the scope conditions emphasized in the introduction to this volume, namely regime type and degrees of statehood. We have argued that the human rights *problématique* in areas of limited statehood differs from the one envisaged by PoHR, since the original spiral model assumed consolidated statehood in terms of state institutions capable of effectively implementing and enforcing human rights standards. Consolidated statehood is indeed important to prevent human rights violations by state and non-state actors. In addition, the spiral model also presumed that authoritarian regimes are unwilling rather than incapable of enforcing these standards. This is different with regard to areas of limited statehood, where central governments are as incapable as they may be unwilling to enforce human rights, and where human rights violations are often committed by non-state actors, be it companies, rebel groups or even NGOs. The two cases of Guatemala and Georgia served to illustrate this point. In both countries, non-state actors as well as state agents beyond the control of the central governments commit most of the rights violations. As a result, it is lack of capacity rather than lack of willingness which prevented both countries to move from commitment to compliance. The difference between the two countries can be explained by the variation in exposure to the international (Western) community as well as by the fact that Western organizations have invested many more resources in capacity-building in Georgia than in Guatemala.

Emphasizing limited statehood and its interaction with democracy has significant consequences for the ways in which we analyze human rights policies as well as make policy recommendations. First, limited statehood directs attention toward an alternative explanation for human rights violations which has not yet been theorized sufficiently. Guaranteeing even basic human rights and establishing the rule of law require strong state capacities which are missing in areas of limited statehood by definition. National governments might be fully willing to enforce human rights and might be signing up to the whole range of international legal instruments. Yet, many governments do not have sufficient means to implement the law domestically. This lack of capacity could explain to some extent the observed discrepancy between the ratification of international human rights treaties, on the one hand, and continuing human rights violations in many countries, on the other (e.g. Hafner-Burton 2008; Hathaway 2002; see Chapter 5, this volume). Rather than postulating an alleged divide between quantitative pessimists and qualitative optimists in the study of human rights (Hafner-Burton and Ron 2009), the continuing discrepancy between prescriptive status of human rights and rule-consistent behavior in a country might point to areas of limited statehood.

Second, focusing on areas of limited statehood allows for disaggregating the state rather than treating it as a unitary actor. A national government might be able to control the national capital and its surroundings, but lacks the capacity to enforce the law in some of the provinces. The Georgian government has been able to reduce human rights violations in its "heartland" but still lacks control over the two separatist regions where the rights of ethnic Georgians continue to be abused. Or the other way round: Somalia has been a failed state for more than fifteen years. Mogadishu, the capital, and the access routes have suffered from civil war and sustained violence through much of this period. In contrast, Somaliland – one of the provinces – has been relatively calm and has maintained a degree of order including the provision of some basic human rights (Debiel *et al.* 2010; Menkhaus 2006/2007). Likewise, a government might be able to introduce comprehensive human rights legislation but is unable to control or sufficiently equip its enforcement authorities, particularly if police and courts operate in remote parts of the country (Hönke 2008; Liese 2006). Thinking in terms of areas of limited statehood then allows for much more precise measurements where the real human rights problems are.

Third, an emphasis on human rights violations resulting from limited statehood directs our attention toward the "management school" in compliance research (particularly Chayes and Chayes 1993, 1995). This group has always argued that non-compliance with international regulations results from weak institutions, lack of resources and resulting problems of involuntary defection rather than lack of willingness by governments. A comprehensive quantitative study of compliance with EU law and regulations demonstrates that variation in state capacities offers a powerful explanation for variation in compliance, alongside more traditional factors such as power (Börzel *et al.* 2010). Interestingly enough, many international organizations have long understood that capacity-building and assistance in building up sustainable institutions goes a long way in the promotion of human rights and democracy and have acted accordingly (Magen *et al.* 2009). Most of the resources spent on democracy promotion by donors such as the United States and the EU focus on capacity-building through financial and technical assistance.

It follows that the spiral model developed in PoHR and its various mechanisms have to be complemented in areas of limited statehood. If the primary cause for rights violations is limited statehood and lack of capacity to enforce the law, positive incentives, sanctions or persuasion will not do the trick, but have to be matched by institution- and capacity-building. In such cases, transnational campaigns and mobilization alone are unlikely to achieve results.

This does not mean, however, that the spiral model is irrelevant under conditions of limited statehood. Rather, its mechanisms have to be directed toward actors other than the state or the national government. If non-state actors such as companies or rebel groups are primarily responsible for human rights violations, the mechanisms of the spiral model including transnational pressure can be directed against them (see Chapters 12 and 13, this volume). Moreover, as Kathryn Sikkink has recently argued, the emerging norm of individual criminal responsibility might be used to hold non-state actors (or state actors behaving as criminals) accountable for human rights abuse thus providing a powerful deterrence effect. Her data suggest that prosecutions after transition to democracy lead to improved human rights which is significant in our context, since democratization processes often go hand-in-hand with weakening state capacities to enforce the law (Kim and Sikkink 2010; Sikkink 2011; see also Chapter 15, this volume). Last but not least, the emerging international norm of the "responsibility to protect" (R2P) might mitigate gross human rights abuses in failing and failed states. If national governments are either unwilling or incapable of protecting their citizens, the international community has to assume the responsibility to step in, if need be militarily (Bellamy 2011; Evans 2008; Finnemore 2003). While R2P has been invoked recently in the cases of Libya and the Ivory Coast, only the latter case might qualify as a fragile or failing state.

In sum, focusing on areas of limited statehood alerts scholars and practitioners to the fact that capacity issues have to be taken at least as seriously in strategies to promote human rights compliance as the mechanisms theorized by the spiral model which target unwillingness to comply. Moving states from commitment to compliance then requires us to take limited statehood as a structural condition of most countries in the contemporary international system more seriously. Capacity-building – be it through strengthening central state institutions, be it through using functional equivalents – must complement the socialization mechanisms proposed in PoHR.

5

The "compliance gap" and the efficacy
of international human rights institutions

XINYUAN DAI

A central question in International Relations is how international institutions influence sovereign behavior. *The Power of Human Rights* (PoHR), edited by Thomas Risse, Stephen Ropp and Kathryn Sikkink (1999), has helped shape this research agenda by highlighting the mechanisms by which *international* institutions generate *domestic* effects. Together with a number of other contributions in the literature, it has refreshed our thinking on how international instruments can be useful tools not just for states but also (under certain circumstances) for non-state actors – domestic or transnational – that wish to influence governments. Indeed, study of the domestic effects of international institutions has been one of the most active areas of research in the past ten years.

While much of this scholarship has focused primarily on *how* international institutions matter, the realist challenge persists: despite an increasing number of ways in which international institutions can influence states' behavior, do international institutions really matter? Do international institutions – particularly those that lack enforcement power in the areas of environmental and human rights politics – really alter states' behavior? In the area of human rights policies, recent empirical studies suggest that international human rights treaties are often too weak to induce states' compliance (Hafner-Burton and Tsutsui 2007; Hathaway 2002; Keith 1999). More strikingly, they suggest that, while states increasingly endorse international norms, their actual behavior by and large does not conform to these norms. They further argue that the compliance gap has persisted and, in some cases, even widened over the past thirty years (Hafner-Burton and Ron 2009). To many people, this persistent and possibly

For helpful comments, I thank the editors, Thomas Risse, Steve Ropp and Kathryn Sikkink, as well as other participants at the Wyoming workshop and the Berlin workshop, particularly Ann Marie Clark and Arie Kacowicz. For comments on related projects, I'd like to thank Alex Thompson and seminar participants at Duke University, Northwestern University, Wissenschaftszentrum Berlin, Free University Berlin, Hertie School of Governance in Berlin, as well as Rice University. I gratefully acknowledge a Special Research Fellowship from the Alexander von Humboldt Foundation, which facilitated my initial research on this project.

growing gap between commitment and compliance calls into question the efficacy of international human rights law and institutions. The resulting policy proposals tend to emphasize enforcement and coercion rather than the "toothless" international law.

In this chapter, I discuss these important challenges in assessing the domestic effects of international human rights institutions. While the empirical findings about the compliance gap are important and interesting, many of the inferences drawn from them are plagued with conceptual and methodological problems. I shall argue that we need to pay careful attention to the process through which international norms lead to domestic political change (as exemplified in PoHR). International human rights institutions rarely enforce states' compliance directly through the use of carrots or sticks. Rather, they typically influence states by empowering human rights victims and activists. To the extent that international institutions can enable and further facilitate non-state actors in their efforts to change governmental behavior, even seemingly weak international institutions – those that lack direct enforcement power – can have powerful effects. This line of reasoning in turn has important implications for the evaluation and the design of international institutions.

Commitment and compliance

To address how international institutions influence sovereign behavior, scholars often look into states' compliance with international agreements. In this volume, as articulated by Thomas Risse and Stephen Ropp in the introduction, we focus on the final stages of the spiral model. We are interested in how and under what conditions actors move from commitment to compliance. This requires us to be clear what we mean by commitment and compliance so as to better understand the causal links between these two stages.

In the literature, the definition of commitment varies. Typically, commitment refers to the acceptance of international human rights norms. Because many scholars focus on norms as expressed in treaties and accords, the signing or the ratification of the international agreement is often taken as the indication of commitment (Simmons 2009). Of course, one may wonder to what extent a government's signature or ratification reflects its genuine commitment. In the language of the spiral model in PoHR, does the signing or the ratification of an international human rights agreement constitute a tactical concession (phase 3 of the spiral model) or the awarding of prescriptive status (phase 4 of the spiral model), indicating genuine endorsement? Beth Simmons' (2009) study of human rights treaty ratification suggests that there exists a continuum of commitment that links tactical concessions and prescriptive status.

Similarly, the definition of compliance also varies. There are several dimensions of compliance: compliance with procedural obligations, such as the requirement to report; compliance with substantive obligations stipulated in the treaty; and compliance with the spirit of the treaty (Weiss and Jacobson 1998). Typically though, compliance refers to the degree to which a country's behavior actually conforms to an explicit provision in an international agreement (Fisher 1981; Mitchell 1994; Young 1979). Thus, it seems more appropriate to view it as a continuum (Simmons 1998). Linking this latter view of compliance to the spiral model, there would thus seem to be a continuum of compliance between prescriptive status (phase 4 of the spiral model) and rule-consistent behavior (phase 5 of the spiral model).

Depending on where on its respective continuum commitment or compliance occurs, different mechanisms are likely at work in the move from commitment to compliance. For instance, when commitment is not much more than a tactical concession, the mechanisms to move actors towards compliance would tend to be external incentives such as the use of "carrots or sticks." In contrast, when commitment is closer to a genuine endorsement of the norms such as at the stage of prescriptive status, the mechanisms to move actors towards compliance are likely to be argumentation or capacity-building. Of course, as one's definition of commitment gets closer and closer to a genuine endorsement of international norms, one has to confront the issue of endogeniety. That is, if commitment indicates genuine endorsement of international norms, compliance is more likely to follow. In other words, the incentive of states to comply may be predetermined by the decision to commit, even though the capacity of these states to comply depends on many different factors including, for instance, how centralized the compliance decision is. This may complicate, to some extent, the assessment of the independent effect of commitment on compliance.

In this chapter, I view both commitment and compliance as continuous variables. Although I take the signing of an accord or ratification of a treaty as an indication of commitment, I leave it open as to whether this act constitutes the genuine endorsement of international norms. This allows me to view multiple causal mechanisms as potential "drivers" of human rights change. Regarding compliance, I view it as a continuous variable reflecting the degree of conformity with international norms. I am interested in finding out exactly what drives compliance and accordingly how it reflects the effects of international institutions.

Conceptual and methodological issues with the compliance gap

Empirical findings differ regarding the effects of international human rights treaties. In important ways, this reveals some confusion over key conceptual questions: how do we expect international human rights treaties to influence states' policy behavior? Should we expect them to have a direct effect on abusive governments? Should we expect them to have a universal and uniform effect on all of the governments in the world? In the end, just what are the criteria by which human rights institutions should be evaluated? Clarifying these issues is important to appropriately assessing the effects of international human rights treaties. It will further help to provide a reliable base from which we can derive policy implications for the design and reform of international human rights institutions.

To confront this confusion, I start with an important recent finding about the compliance gap. Large-N statistical works have suggested that, although states increasingly endorse human rights norms, their behavior does not always (or even usually) conform to these norms. More alarmingly, this compliance gap, even if not growing, has persisted over the past thirty years (Hafner-Burton and Ron 2009; Hafner-Burton and Tsutsui 2005). To many, this indicates the failure of international human rights institutions to influence states' behavior. I revisit this inference. I discuss both conceptual and methodological problems and how they might prevent us from drawing reliable inferences from the compliance gap for the effects of international human rights treaties.

Empirical depictions of the compliance gap

What does the compliance gap mean? Intuitively, it refers to the extent to which deeds lag behind words, or compliance falls short of commitment. In the area of international human rights politics, there have been a number of ways to depict this gap.

One way to think about the compliance gap may be to contrast states' formal commitment to a specific treaty with their subsequent compliance. The compliance gap emerges whenever countries commit to an international human rights agreement but their subsequent behavior falls short of the standards embodied in the agreement. Although this may sound straightforward, conceptual pitfalls abound in this measurement of the compliance gap, as I illustrate below.

To capture states' commitment to international human rights norms, scholars typically use the number of international human rights treaties that those states have endorsed. There have been a growing number of global human rights treaties,[1] as well as numerous regional human rights agreements. The number of countries that have ratified each of the major international human rights treaties has also been rising over time.

To measure states' compliance with a multitude of human rights agreements on the other hand, scholars face daunting challenges. In part due to data

---

[1] One can access these documents at www.unhchr.ch/tbs/doc.nsf. The major global human rights treaties include the International Covenant on Civil and Political Rights, the International Covenant on Economic, Social and Cultural Rights, the Convention against Torture and Other Cruel, Inhuman or Degrading Treatment or Punishment, the Convention on the Elimination of All Forms of Discrimination against Women, the International Convention on the Elimination of All Forms of Racial Discrimination, the International Convention on the Protection of the Rights of All Migrant Workers and Members of Their Families, and the Convention on the Rights of the Child.

limitations, much of the recent quantitative research focuses on a narrow set of human rights such as personal or physical integrity rights. This category of human rights violations refers to abuses such as extrajudicial killing, torture or similar physical abuse, disappearances, and political imprisonment. The datasets that are most often used to gauge the protection of personal integrity rights are the Political Terror Scale (PTS)[2] and the Cingranelli and Richards Human Rights Data Project (CIRI).[3] Both of these datasets use annual country reports by the US State Department and Amnesty International, but they categorize the same set of human rights violations into different levels. The data in both datasets seem to suggest that the global average of states' respect for personal integrity rights improves slightly by Amnesty International coding and worsens slightly by the State Department coding.

Accordingly, analyses based on these datasets typically find that personal integrity rights are hardly improving, if not worsening, over the past few decades. One can reasonably ask questions about the coding. For instance, has the coding of states' practice been consistent over such a long time span of several decades? Ann Marie Clark and Kathryn Sikkink (2010) have recently suggested that increasingly better information about states' behavior and greater attention to the full range of human rights – perhaps along with analysts' reduced tolerance of human rights abuses – may have contributed to the possibility that the data coding becomes more demanding over time, in the sense that it becomes less likely to register all behavioral improvements.

If we bracket away the issue of data reliability, the contrast between the rising trend of broad human rights endorsements and the rather flat trend of personal integrity rights improvement seems to suggest a growing gap between words and deeds. However, contrasting personal integrity rights practice with the number of human rights treaties that states sign that may or may not regulate personal integrity rights would be inappropriate because of the inflated indicator of commitment.

Perhaps a more reasonable comparison is between the protection of personal integrity rights and states' commitments to the specific treaties that govern over these rights. Indeed, Hafner-Burton and Tsutsui (2007) report the bad news about compliance concerning personal integrity rights as contrasted to the good news about commitment with the International Covenant on Civil and Political Rights (CCPR) and the Convention against Torture and Other Cruel, Inhuman or Degrading Treatment or Punishment (CAT). Regarding commitment, they find that countries are much more likely to sign onto the CCPR and the CAT over time. In fact, during the time period from 1976 to 2003, the likelihood that a country signed onto the CCPR and the CAT rose from 0.2 to 0.9. Regarding compliance, however, they find that neither the CCPR nor the CAT had any

---

[2] www.politicalterrorscale.org/about.html.
[3] http://ciri.binghamton.edu/.

systematic effect on the personal integrity rights in repressive states even a decade and a half after their commitments.

Indeed, if one compares the growing trend of treaty ratification and the stagnant – or at least not impressive, given the usual data – trend of behavioral change concerning personal integrity rights, one finds that the gap between commitment and compliance grows over time. Yet, does this really refute the efficacy of international human rights institutions? I now discuss three sets of conceptual and methodological concerns that problematize such an inference.

Problem 1: indicators and data sources

To date, no comprehensive dataset exists to capture states' compliance with all human rights treaties or all rights covered in any particular treaty. The personal integrity rights that much quantitative human rights research focuses on provide an approximate indicator for a narrow subset of the human rights covered in global treaties. Even when we focus specifically on political rights, the question remains regarding the appropriate indicators and the data sources. Two other data collection projects on aspects of political rights paint a somewhat different picture.

Freedom House provides an annual evaluation of global freedom based on political and civil rights.[4] The former refers to participatory rights in the political process, including the right to vote freely for distinct alternatives in legitimate elections, to compete for public office, to join political parties and organizations, and to elect representatives who have a decisive impact on public policies and are accountable to the electorate. The latter refers to the freedoms of expression and belief, associational and organizational rights, rule of law, and personal autonomy without interference from the state. Each country is assigned a numerical rating – from 1 indicating the highest degree of freedom to 7 indicating the lowest level of freedom – for political rights and civil liberties respectively. Each pair of political rights and civil liberties ratings is then averaged to determine an overall status.

Although data from Freedom House do not paint a rosy picture of behavioral improvements, they do give a somewhat different impression than do other datasets discussed earlier. The comparison of political rights and civil liberties against the growing endorsement by states of the CCPR suggests a number of things. First, political rights and civil liberties have visibly improved over the past years. The global average of political rights and civil liberties has improved from around 4.45 to 3.26 and it represents a 20 percent positive movement on the 1 to 7 scale. If the world could hypothetically be perfectly free and thus the freedom average could theoretically reach absolute freedom, the progress over the past thirty years would represent 35 percent of that potential move towards

---

[4] www.freedomhouse.org/template.cfm?page=351&ana_page=341&year=2008.

absolute freedom. Second, despite this progress, the compliance gap – contrasting the rate of endorsement of the CCPR with the average freedom score – persists and is arguably getting larger, because the number of countries that endorse human rights norms simply increases at a greater rate than does their average behavioral improvement. Thus, the choice of indicators and data sources matter, not so much for the existence of a compliance gap, but rather for its magnitude. This is because they provide a different picture of the average progress that the world is making in political and civil rights.

The Polity IV data project[5] is another often used dataset that sheds light on some aspects of political rights. It captures the quality of governing institutions over a spectrum ranging from fully institutionalized autocracies through mixed regimes to fully institutionalized democracies. The polity score captures political regimes on a 21-point scale ranging from -10 (hereditary monarchy) to +10 (consolidated democracy). Like all other indicators, the polity score does not accurately capture compliance with the CCPR. It at best serves as an approximation for some political rights endorsed in the CCPR.

If one compares the rate at which states ratify the CCPR and the rate at which governmental institutions shift from autocracy to democracy, the choice of indicator and data source, again, affect how much of a compliance gap we observe. Alongside the growing endorsement of the CCPR, countries have become increasingly more democratic. The global average in governing characteristics shifted from –2.57 in 1976 (leaning toward autocracy) to 3.69 in 2007 (leaning toward democracy). This represents a 31 percent improvement over the 21-point scale. Again hypothetically, if all the countries in the world uniformly aspired toward having democratic institutions and thus the polity score average could theoretically reach 10, the progress over the past thirty years would represent 50 percent of that potential move toward uniformly democratic regimes. Yet, even this positive trend still cannot "match up" with the greater rate of the CCPR ratification. However, the magnitude of the gap is smaller here than that based on the Political Terror Scale.

In sum, the improvement in human rights practice concerning political rights is more visible in some areas using some indicators, than in other areas with different indicators. It seems that human rights practice across the globe does not improve as fast as global acceptance of human rights treaties, as indicated by the number of countries endorsing these treaties. However, the magnitude of such a gap varies depending on the aspects of political rights under examination, their indicators and the sources of data. Furthermore, given that political rights endorsed by global human rights treaties are substantially broader than physical integrity rights, we need to look beyond personal integrity rights before we can draw reliable inferences concerning the relationship between levels of commitment and compliance.

---

[5] www.systemicpeace.org/polity/polity4.htm.

Problem 2: broader types of human rights

Global treaties govern a diverse set of human rights, ranging from political and civil rights to economic and social ones. There are human rights treaties against racial discrimination, gender discrimination and political oppression, among many others. The magnitude of the compliance gap is not only affected by the choice of indicators and data sources, but also by the types of human rights under examination.

One of the two flagship UN human rights treaties is the International Covenant on Economic, Social and Cultural Rights (CESCR). While data availability and reliability is perhaps more of an issue here than usual, scholars have used the Human Development Index to approximate the behavioral outcome. This index is calculated on the basis of data on life expectancy, adult literacy rates, combined gross enrollment ratios, GDP per capita, etc. The comparison between the global average of the Human Development Index and the rising number of the CESCR ratifiers paints a different picture about the compliance gap than the analysis based only on the personal integrity rights. Although the global average of the Human Development Index has not risen as fast as the number of the CESCR ratifiers, the global development index has been steadily improving from 0.6 to over 0.7 in a forty-year period. That represents about 20 percent improvement of human development globally compared to the status in the year of 1975.

Another important global human rights treaty is the Convention on the Elimination of All Forms of Discrimination against Women (CEDAW). As with the CCPR and the CESCR, the CEDAW also contains indicators of broad government obligations that are difficult to capture. One measure of behavioral improvement with regard to the CEDAW is women's participation in governments. Again, the comparison between women's share in parliamentary politics against the rising number of the CEDAW ratifiers presents a less alarming picture about the compliance gap than the analysis based on personal integrity rights. Another measure of behavioral improvement with regard to the CEDAW is girls' education. Beth Simmons (2009) finds that the ratio of girls to boys in basic education has been rising steadily. In addition, the average literacy gap of women trailing men has been consistently shrinking.

In sum, the compliance gap varies substantially from case to case. However, in addition to the issues concerning indicators and types of human rights, the more serious problems with the compliance gap are conceptual. The compliance gap, as it is typically depicted and measured in the literature, does not capture what we intuitively understand as the discrepancy between commitment and compliance. In fact, as I illustrate next, it exaggerates this discrepancy in a fundamentally flawed fashion.

Problem 3: conceptual problems

Conceptually, the compliance gap denotes the discrepancy between what one has agreed to do and what one is currently doing. In other words, it refers to the extent to which one's behavior falls short of one's commitment. Yet, the picture of the compliance gap painted in the empirical human rights research does not capture this concept.

A symptomatic problem of the conventional measurement of the compliance gap is that, in situations where the average compliance is improving over time, the average compliance gap nevertheless enlarges. This is puzzling. As we know, commitment in international human rights treaties is typically binary. That is, a country either signs onto a human rights treaty or does not and, then, either ratifies it or does not. Thus, once a country ratifies a human rights treaty, the benchmark of commitment which that country's compliance is evaluated against is fixed. As such, so long as states' behavior improves on average, the extent to which behavior lags behind what is required of signatory countries should be shrinking. In other words, if we faithfully compare states' behavior to what they have agreed to do in treaties, then better compliance should indicate a smaller compliance gap over time.

Yet, many empirical studies in the area of human rights claim to discover just the opposite: in spite of behavioral improvement, the "compliance gap" is found to be persisting or even enlarging over time. This perplexing finding, however, is due to the fact that what is used in these studies as a benchmark for evaluation is not the fixed content of states' commitment, but rather the ever rising number of states that endorse a particular human rights treaty.

It is misleading to depict the compliance gap this way. This depiction does not capture the discrepancy between what one is doing and what one has agreed to do. Furthermore, it is arbitrary as it contrasts the *average* behavior with the *accumulative* number of ratifiers of a treaty. While behavioral improvement is averaged across countries and is capped by the content of the commitment,[6] the benchmark of evaluation as the number of ratifiers is accumulative and ever increasing. The compliance gap, measured this way, grows over time – not because behavior has by and large worsened, but rather because it reflects a built-in artifact: despite behavioral improvement, such a "compliance gap" is doomed to enlarge over time so long as the *average* behavioral improvement rises at a lower rate than the accumulative number of ratifiers of a treaty.

Thus, although the empirical findings on the compliance gap in international human rights research are interesting, they tell us little about the actual discrepancy between commitment and compliance, nor whether and how international human rights institutions impact states' behavior.

---

[6] In reality, states' compliance with human rights agreements can rarely be perfect. While states can commit to reduce 30%, 50% or even 90% of their harmful emissions in environmental agreements, it will be outlandish if states committed in human rights agreements that would reduce the extrajudicial killings from 10,000 to 1,000, even though that represented a 90% reduction. Typically, states accept the principles in human rights treaties in their entirety. Thus, human rights agreements are demanding in the sense that, while it is possible to over-comply with environmental agreements, it is difficult to be in full compliance with human rights agreements.

How do we learn more about the effects of international human rights institutions? And, what are the appropriate criteria by which we should evaluate their effects? I address these questions in the following section.

Domestic effects of international human rights institutions

In assessing international human rights institutions, scholars increasingly emphasize the need to be systematic. However, "being systematic" is often taken to mean increasing the sample size to cover more countries in the world. What is often not taken as seriously is the other equally, if not more, important aspect of systematic research. That is, we need to design empirical tests that are more systematically guided by our theoretical expectations.

To properly evaluate the effect of international institutions and international law on domestic human rights practices, we need to better appreciate the ways in which such instruments work. As Risse *et al.* emphasize in PoHR, international human rights norms do not automatically lead to behavioral change. We thus need to pay careful attention to the processes leading from commitment to compliance.

Furthermore, we need to confront the fact that carrots and sticks at the international level – even those facilitated by international institutions, such as the World Trade Organization (WTO) or the International Monetary Fund (IMF) – are unlikely to be the driving force behind states' compliance with human rights institutions (Dai 2007). States are typically unwilling to spend their resources systematically to enforce human rights. Thus, it is doubtful whether conventional theories of inter-state politics greatly increase our understanding of international human rights compliance (Simmons 2009). This means that we need to ask not just how international human rights institutions directly influence states, i.e. through mechanisms such as coercion, sanctions and rewards, or capacity-building. More importantly, we need to ask how international human rights institutions influence states indirectly through non-state stakeholders and domestic mechanisms (Dai 2007; Simmons 2009). As Beth Simmons emphasizes, concerning the effects of international human rights institutions, "[t]he real politics of change is likely to occur at the domestic level" (2009: 126).

In this section, I examine the channel of influence through which international human rights institutions facilitate and empower domestic human rights activists, who in turn (and under certain conditions) may successfully influence governmental policy. I first discuss why this indirect channel of influence is particularly important for international human rights institutions. I then focus on the specific ways in which international human rights institutions work in the process. Finally, I highlight key characteristics of this indirect channel of influence and the conditions that facilitate it.

International human rights institutions as "weak" instruments

While virtually all international institutions and international law can mobilize non-state actors and work through domestic mechanisms, this channel is particularly crucial for weak international institutions such as international human rights law. Human rights institutions are relatively weak. For example, in contrast to the IMF with its instrument of conditionality or the WTO with its instrument of dispute settlement, international human rights institutions typically do not have the authority to directly enforce states' compliance. Neither do they have the resources to directly enhance states' capacity to comply, as some of the international environmental institutions have with their ability to grant financial assistance. This is not to say that international human rights institutions do not have powerful effects. They do, as I shall argue. This is merely to say that human rights institutions are in comparison more limited in their ability to impact states directly through the use of carrots and sticks.

To begin to understand why the indirect channel of influence through non-state actors and domestic processes can be feasible and important for international human rights institutions, we need to first understand why international human rights institutions are weak in the first place. Many factors may render an international institution weak and hence ineffective. But weak international institutions tend to share something in common that makes them weak by design. One way to sort out their commonality is to look deeply into the nature of these institutions to examine who benefits from compliance and how the beneficiaries are related to governments. Although all international agreements regulate states' behavior directly or indirectly, the beneficiaries of compliance or the victims of non-compliance differ across different international agreements. Typically, potential victims of a country's non-compliance can be other states (as in many security regimes), non-state actors in other states (as in trade regimes) or non-state actors in that same country (as in most human rights regimes).

Since the beneficiaries of compliance are related to governments in different ways, states' incentives to comply differ with regards to different international institutions. At one end of the spectrum, as in many security institutions, states have strong incentives to either enforce compliance individually or to delegate resources to an international regime to carry out collective enforcement. Here, we tend to see strong institutions in terms of enforcement and resources. At the other end of the spectrum, as in human rights institutions, the targets of regulations are governments and the beneficiaries of compliance are domestic actors. Here, we tend to see non-binding declarations and accords or institutions that are delegated limited authority and provided with sparse resources.[7]

---

[7] For how various incentive structures give rise to diverse institutional arrangements in treaty regimes, see Dai (2002).

For this latter type of weak international institution, the indirect channel of influence through non-state actors is both a feasible and an important channel for bringing about change. First of all, it is feasible because the stakeholders with the most profound interest in compliance are domestic non-state actors who are victims of their own governments' non-compliance. They have the incentive to utilize whatever instruments are at their disposal – including international human rights institutions, weak as they may be. Such international institutions can thus work through the domestic stakeholders, who have a genuine stake in the issue.

Second, this indirect channel of influence is important both to weak international institutions and to domestic stakeholders. To weak international institutions, which lack resources and the enforcement power, the indirect channel of influence exercised through domestic stakeholders is perhaps the most important among the limited number of instruments available to them. To domestic non-state stakeholders who have little protection at home, international institutions – even weak ones – can be important sources of support. Accordingly, both international institutions and domestic pro-compliance stakeholders have incentives to utilize each other. To the extent that they can do so, such weak institutions may nevertheless empower domestic stakeholders, who in turn can influence domestic policies and practice under certain circumstances.

From this perspective, the primary effect of international human rights institutions lies in their ability to empower domestic stakeholders. To understand and properly evaluate the effect of international human rights institutions, therefore, one must pay attention to the particular ways they work.

Indirect effects and power of weak international human rights institutions

Although lacking direct enforcement power, weak international human rights institutions may nevertheless have powerful effects. In fact, a central insight in PoHR is that international human rights agreements – whether states concede to them only as a tactical concession or whether states sincerely give validity to them – can have powerful domestic effects on governmental human rights policy and practice once they are in place. Generally, sustainable improvements in domestic human rights policy and practice may be viewed as a result of a combination of pressure "from above" and pressure "from below" (PoHR: 33) Specifically, they may be viewed as a result of local pro-change groups successfully leveraging international norms and institutions to triumph over their domestic opponents (Keck and Sikkink 1998; see also PoHR).

How do international human rights institutions empower domestic non-state stakeholders in order to generate such domestic effects? While articulating the domestic constituency mechanism, I highlight two important channels through which international institutions can empower domestic constituents

(Dai 2005). International human rights institutions, even though seemingly weak, can increase the political leverage and improve the informational status of pro-compliance constituencies. For example, the Helsinki Process (Thomas 1999) clearly reflected the value of both channels of influence, in that the Helsinki Final Act increased the amount of information available to domestic human rights activists and strengthened their leverage over the Communist governments. Besides providing human rights activists and the public with vital information, the Helsinki Final Act strengthened the leverage of human rights activists in specific ways: it legitimized human rights initiatives, enabled them to make strategic use of the Final Act, and suggested a focal point for various opposition movements. Furthermore, through follow-up meetings, the Conference on Security and Cooperation in Europe (CSCE) provided a forum for continuing mobilization of human rights activism (Dai 2007).

Of course, the mere existence of such channels of influence does not in-and-of-itself result in domestic change. First of all, while virtually all international institutions have the potential to influence states' behavior through the channels that link them to domestic constituencies, not all of them realize such potential. For this to happen, domestic constituencies have to exist that have incentives to respond to these external institutions and to leverage them internally. In the case of the Helsinki Final Act, human rights movements existed throughout the Soviet Bloc in different forms and with different focuses even before the Helsinki Summit. The Helsinki Final Act thus did not create dissent or dissidents, but simply turned existing human rights victims and activists into stakeholders and exercised its influence indirectly through the empowerment of domestic human rights activists. In contrast to the Helsinki Accords, earlier UN human rights accords had not played into domestic politics, in part because domestic human rights activism had not reached a significant level to react to and further utilize these accords.

Second, even when international institutions play into domestic mechanisms of compliance, the effect of international institutions on states' policies depends on the relative strength of domestic pro-compliance constituencies. In other words, the effect of international institutions through domestic mechanisms of compliance is translated into policy by domestic constituencies.[8] It follows then that the specific characteristics of domestic pro-compliance constituencies

---

[8] However, even when domestic constituencies fail to translate the impact of international institutions effectively into policy, international institutions are not irrelevant. Although stronger pro-compliance activism can translate the impact of international institutions more effectively into policy, it is to the weaker pro-compliance activism that additional instruments from international institutions are particularly valuable. For instance, the informational function of international institutions is particularly important for pro-compliance activists in countries where states monopolize information. This is the case even if pro-compliance activism in these countries can not yet generate substantial influence on states.

themselves constitute a crucial scope condition for the domestic effect of inter-national human rights institutions.

This emphasis on domestic constituencies in my account of institutional effects contributes to one of the central tasks in this volume. Namely, what are the scope conditions under which international human rights institutions impact states' policy and behavior? I argue that the existence of domestic stake-holders and their mobilization are crucial conditions for the domestic effects of human rights norms (Hafner-Burton and Tsutsui 2005; Neumayer 2005; Simmons 2009; see also Chapter 7 in this volume).

This emphasis on domestic constituencies also speaks to two other scope conditions under investigation in this volume. First, the effect of international human rights institutions depends on the domestic interest and/or norms com-petition, and particularly the relative position and strength of domestic stake-holders in such competition. Second, the effect of international human rights institutions depends on domestic political institutions – but only jointly with characteristics of domestic stakeholders. In liberal democracies, domestic stake-holders may not resort to international human rights norms in order to affect change. In such cases, it is hard to say that domestic human rights improve-ments are induced by international human rights institutions. In contrast, in repressive states, domestic stakeholders have limited resources and thus may have a greater incentive to resort to supportive international norms. In such cases, international human rights institutions may prove more consequential. More broadly, I would argue that political institutions alone do not account for the domestic effect of international human rights institutions. As Chapter 8 on the United States by Kathryn Sikkink in this volume demonstrates, democracy is an insufficient condition for compliance with international norms. In gen-eral, although democratic institutions intensify politicians' accountability to their domestic constituents, whether that induces higher or lower compliance is determined by the political attributes of domestic competing interests (Dai 2006).

Relatively speaking, this account of the indirect effects of international insti-tutions is less specific regarding the importance of the various characteristics of international institutions. For instance, international institutions that have potential domestic effects can take the form of legally binding human rights treaties, but they can also be non-binding accords. What determines whether they can generate domestic effects is not entirely their legality nor how many resources states are willing to delegate to them. Although legal enforcement is important (Chapter 8, this volume), it is not a necessary condition for bet-ter human rights behavior (Finnemore and Sikkink 1998). Furthermore, as Goodman and Jinks (Chapter 6, this volume) caution, greater legalization – par-ticularly related to the enforcement aspect of change – may have a "crowding-out" effect in relationship to other causal logics. Similarly, international agreements that highlight legal enforcement may potentially deter states from participating in such agreements in the first place (Dai 2007). Instead, what matters just as much, if not more, is how domestic stakeholders utilize them and thereby turn their potential into real effects. For example, although there has been persisting reluctance among states and corporations to accept legally binding initiatives on the responsibilities of transnational corporations, non-binding instruments such as the Global Compact can have genuine effects on the practice of the business community (Chapter 12, this volume).

Obviously, international human rights institutions can generate domestic effects through more channels and in many more ways than discussed so far. For example, Beth Simmons (2009) examines the effect of international human rights law – i.e. legally binding treaties that states formally ratify – in three domestic processes: elite-initiated agenda setting, litigation, as well as political mobilization. According to her theory of political mobilization, the existence of international human rights treaties may raise the expected value of mobilization and thus enhance the probability of successful mobilization. In so doing, "treaties change the complexion of domestic politics in ways that make a net positive contribution to rights practices in many – though not all – countries around the world" (Simmons 2009: 138). Here, the effects of treaties are not directly on states but rather operate indirectly through the empowerment of domestic stakeholders. Similarly, Ann Marie Clark (Chapter 7, this volume) focuses on the indirect effects of international human rights institutions by examining the ways in which they "provide a backdrop for further engagement and argument about facts and accountability."

Key characteristics of indirect effects

In this account of indirect channels of influence by international human rights institutions, two characteristics are particularly worth noting. One key characteristic is that the compliance gap – understood as the discrepancy between words and deeds, or between the normative benchmark and actual behavior – is often a natural and indeed useful component of the process by which international human rights institutions work. Typically, domestic mobilization starts with the recognition of a compliance gap. That is, stakeholders – domestic or international, driven to change states' practices – identify problematic areas of governmental policy or behavior and use instruments including international institutions to articulate the imperative for change. The very existence of this compliance gap, along with the effective articulation of its existence, provides decentralized enforcers with the normative and/or material tools that they need in order to persuade and/or pressure governments to improve their behavior or policy more in line with their commitments. As suggested in the spiral model of PoHR, the recognition and particularly the successful framing by human rights supporters of a gap between words and deeds is often the starting point for political mobilization.

It may seem intuitive that, if states' behavior improves, it must mean that the discrepancy between commitment and compliance is shrinking and therefore that the compliance gap can be a good indicator of behavioral change and/or of the effects of international human rights institutions. I argue, however, that the compliance gap – either the static "snapshot" or a temporal measure of it – is not a reliable indicator of states' behavior or of the effects of international human rights institutions. Rather than solely reflecting objective behavioral change, the compliance gap also reflects the subjective benchmark by which behavior ought to be evaluated.

Indeed, the articulation of the compliance gap, especially when used as a tool for political mobilization, is an intensely political and strategic process. In some cases, human rights practice may actually have been the same or improving; but the gap "emerges" because a new benchmark is articulated by which practice should then be evaluated. As Alison Brysk discusses in this volume (Chapter 14), the international benchmark concerning the practice of female genital mutilation (FGM) emerged over several decades. When FGM was first recognized to be a violation of the rights of women and girls to health in the late 1990s, the resulting "gap" between the usual practice and a new legitimate criterion could only be thought of as a step forward in changing states' behavior. To some extent, the "compliance gap" is in part a result of the human rights movement, which does not focus solely on enforcing the existing norms, but stresses the creation of new norms and the extension of existing norms to new issues.

Similarly, as Nicole Deitelhoff and Klaus Dieter Wolf demonstrate in Chapter 12, a gap between benchmark and practice often reflects the evolutionary understanding of the benchmark guiding behavior. As they show in their chapter, human rights norms were increasingly perceived as offering guidance not only to states but also to the business community. As a consequence, the campaign by non-government organizations targeting transnational companies came to focus on the complicity of these companies in the human rights violations of governments in their zones of operation. Indeed, as Ann Marie Clark shows in Chapter 7, human rights norms may be created by some actors in one context and used by different actors in another context. The resulting gap between behavior and a new criterion, rather than indicate the failure of international human rights institutions, helps initiate a discursive socialization process (Chapter 7, this volume).

The other key characteristic of these channels is that, because international human rights institutions typically influence states indirectly through diverse non-state actors and various domestic mechanisms, its effect is path dependent and conditional. A simple correlation between treaty ratification and sustained policy change is likely to miss its incremental effects at multiple junctures in the long process leading from commitment to compliance.

While states' ratification of a human rights treaty creates a visible and often salient opportunity for domestic mobilization, ratification does not uniformly lead to behavioral change. In fact, a long chain of events lies between the two. Depending on the nature of actual human rights practice, as well as the abilities and the limitations of human rights advocates, domestic stakeholders may or may not be able to successfully frame the existence of a compliance gap. And in cases where they do, mobilization may or may not succeed in altering states' policy and behavior. Even when mobilization is effective, it may or may not translate into sustained behavioral improvement in a linear fashion.

This path-dependent and conditional nature is fundamentally important in our accounts of human rights institutions' effects. In PoHR, for instance, the spiral model suggests that the process leading from the articulation and institutionalization of international human rights norms to actual human rights progress among states is not inevitable. In fact, each stage only leads to the next one under certain conditions. Similarly, according to Simmons (2009), none of the effects of international human rights law are inevitable. Rather, they are likely to materialize only where domestic stakeholders have both the motive and the means to mobilize. As I have argued elsewhere (Dai 2007), weak international human rights institutions may alter a government's strategic environment by increasing the political leverage and improving the informational status of pro-compliance constituencies. Yet such international instruments do not themselves create human rights activists. Rather, for such instruments to be consequential, one precondition is the existence of human rights activists who have an intrinsic interest in utilizing these instruments. Thus, while international human rights institutions have positive effects when they lend moral and strategic support to domestic stakeholders who seek such support, not all such effects eventually lead to states' behavioral change.

While the path-dependent and conditional nature of human rights institutions' effects is no news for scholars who have been pondering how international institutions and law matter, it has not always been appreciated in the empirical human rights research. This may have been one of the primary reasons accounting for the divergent findings concerning the existence and the implications of the compliance gap. Indeed, I suggest that such divergence has much to do with one's theoretical expectations about how international institutions and law are supposed to work. Interestingly, quantitative research that takes the conditional effects of international human rights institutions seriously does find international human rights law works under specific conditions. For instance, Emilie Hafner-Burton and Kiyoteru Tsutsui (2005) and Eric Neumayer (2005) find international human rights treaties influence states' practice under the condition of international or domestic human rights mobilization. Beth Simmons (2009), in one of the most comprehensive empirical studies of international human rights law, finds that international human rights law works most in transitional democracies where domestic stakeholders have both motive and means to mobilize.

To properly account for the effect of international institutions and international law, we cannot simply link international treaties directly to sustained policy change. Rather, we need to investigate how these international instruments play into the complex and multistage process of decentralized enforcement. Future work to test the effects of international law must take causal mechanisms and scope conditions seriously. This is particularly important when studying weak international institutions, which tend to influence states only indirectly through domestic politics and only under certain conditions.

Conclusion

How should we understand the effects of international human rights institutions? What are the appropriate standards of evaluation? For instance, does compliance indicate the effect of international human rights law? Do international human rights institutions matter only when ratification of human rights treaties leads to sustained policy change? Does such a change have to occur in 200 countries worldwide for us to say that international human rights norms really matter? If policy change is desirable and possible only in a subset of countries, does the policy change in these countries have to be so great as to pull higher the global average of change? Furthermore, does such policy change have to pull up the global average more than events such as war and regime change do, for us to conclude that international human rights law matters?

It is crucial that we pay careful attention to the criteria by which we evaluate human rights treaties. Compared to international institutions in other issue areas, human rights treaties are weaker instruments by design. Compared to military interventions and imposed regime changes, human rights treaties are also less costly. The fact that human rights treaties can have and have had powerful effects on political mobilization under certain conditions should not lead us to expect unreasonably and unrealistically that they should have powerful effects uniformly in all circumstances. To deny the efficacy of international human rights institutions because they do not have universal and direct effect on states is to miss vital opportunities enabled by cost-effective instruments to push for positive, if incremental, change.

6

Social mechanisms to promote international human rights: complementary or contradictory?

RYAN GOODMAN AND DEREK JINKS

The study of the international human rights regime has increasingly emphasized *how* this regime matters rather than *if* it matters. An especially productive turn focuses on integrated conceptual models, which accept the importance of multiple forms of influence on state behavior. *The Power of Human Rights* (PoHR) provided a foundation for such studies by bringing attention to the significance of different logics of interaction at different points in the socialization process of states (Risse *et al.* 1999). That leading work and allied scholarship recognize the complexity of actor motivation, human and organizational behavior, and the global-level social environment.[1] What is needed now is a social theory that accounts for why human rights abuses occur and how the international community does or might influence rights abusers to alter their behavior. The objective is to explain how changes in the relevant social environment – namely the existence, and ultimately the formal acceptance, of international human rights – affect the behavior of individuals, governments and non-governmental organizations.

The "spiral model" of human rights change developed in PoHR – and further elaborated in this volume – is an important step in developing such a theory. At a high level of generality, the model provides a conceptually and empirically compelling account of the relationship between national policies and formal international human rights regimes. On this model, various socialization processes work together to influence non-compliant states to accept and ultimately comply with human rights norms through a five-stage process: repression, denial, tactical concessions, prescriptive status, and rule-consistent behavior. The model emphasizes how instrumental adaptation, argumentation and habitualization impel states first to commit formally to human rights regimes and thereafter, under certain conditions, to internalize human rights norms. Four

---

[1] In our own work, we have endeavored to develop a descriptively adequate inventory of mechanisms of global social influence – including material incentivization, persuasion and acculturation – and we have described, in some detail, the micro-processes of each mechanism. We also demonstrate how international human rights regimes might be designed to trigger and sustain these modes of influence (Goodman and Jinks 2004, in press).

mechanisms of social influence are identified by the authors as crucial to modeling the domestic political consequences of the human rights regime: coercion;
incentivization; persuasion/learning; and capacity-building. Relevant actors
move from conduct indicative of the "repression" phase to conduct indicative
of the "rule-consistent behavior" phase because they are forced, encouraged
by material incentive, convinced by persuasive argument, or enabled to do so.
These mechanisms might work directly on governmental officials or they might
work indirectly by mobilizing other relevant actors to influence government
officials. The point is that international human rights norms – under certain
conditions, through these socialization processes – prompt some relevant actors
to change their behavior and/or their views.

The strengths of this approach are considerable. The interaction between various relevant actors is conceptualized as a dynamic social encounter, triggering
a range of socialization processes. The theoretical account is mechanism-based,
identifying the processes whereby certain social predicates cause certain outcomes. The inventory of mechanisms is comprehensive – and ontologically
eclectic. The model, as a consequence, yields clear, testable predictions about the
nature of human rights change. Empirical work relying at least in part on this
model has, and will continue to, provide subtle refinements.

One important, but correctable, weakness of this approach is the way in
which it conceptualizes (or fails to conceptualize) the relationship *between* the
various mechanisms of social influence. According to the "spiral model," international human rights norms, through various agents and in various ways, often
mobilize each mode of influence. The assumption is that these mechanisms are
broadly, if not completely, complementary. This assumption of complementarity, we will argue, is empirically suspect; and it inhibits refinement of the model
along several axes.

The next phase of research on human rights should include two related ambi-
tions. First, it should systematically account for potential negative interactions
between mechanisms of influence. Second, it should specifically consider how
regime design might accentuate or mitigate such interactions. This is not to
say that such considerations were entirely absent from PoHR. That work, and
much of the work inspired by it, does reference "backlash" effects. Those references admit to the importance of accounting for negative as well as positive
feedback effects. However, such effects are not conceived explicitly and studied
systematically as positive or negative interactions between social mechanisms.
Also, such "backlash effects" are only a small subset, and perhaps the most
obvious form of counter-productive external pressures on state actors. What
is needed, in our view, is analysis of a broad range of interactive, sequencing
and condition-dependent effects. These should include subtle effects – which
are not necessarily recognized by the actors themselves, which do not necessarily involve instrumental calculation, and which may nevertheless produce more
durable social change. In short, we need better answers to some core questions:

are social mechanisms complementary or contradictory? In what ways are they compatible or incompatible? And what difference do these considerations make for modeling the influence of global norms? This chapter offers reflections on these questions. We first identify and discuss various interaction effects between social mechanisms – emphasizing several crowding-out and crowding-in effects. We then identify and discuss various sequencing effects. Finally, we offer some reflections on whether and how these developments in the behavioral sciences ought to influence the modeling of human rights change.

Crowding-out effects

One important consideration is whether the operation of one mechanism of influence might undercut the operation of another. Put more provocatively, combining mechanisms will, under certain conditions, reduce the over-all social effect to levels below what any individual mechanism could have achieved in isolation. Understanding these interactions helps to expose two fallacies: a "separability fallacy" and a related "additive fallacy." The separability fallacy, which has long held prominence in economics, maintains that material incentives do not undermine the effectiveness of other mechanisms of social influence (Bowles 2008). According to the additive fallacy, simultaneously employing more than one mechanism (or as many as possible) to achieve a desired end increases the probability of obtaining it. These fallacies plague much mechanism-based international law and international relations scholarship. Even cutting-edge statistical research that thoughtfully isolates the effects of each mechanism overlooks potential negative interactions between the mechanisms (Henisz and Zelner 2005; Polillo and Guillén 2005). Leading qualitative analyses often combine mechanisms of influence – suggesting, for example, that transnational groups and international organizations succeed by bringing multiple pressures – material, social, moral, cognitive and persuasive – to bear on deviant states (Johnston 2008: 198; Sikkink 1993: 437; Chapter 9, this volume). Other studies point to the ineffectiveness of persuasion in global affairs but do not consider whether strategies based on material inducement may have hobbled those attempts. For example, researchers may have overlooked that a cause of non-compliance with "soft law" could be due to the (simultaneous or prior) existence of hard law or materially-oriented enforcement strategies. Lastly, policy recommendations often involve a kitchen-sink approach. Advocates call for almost every conceivable form of pressure and inducement to be exploited in dealing with human rights violators without contemplating negative interactions between mechanisms that undergird those multiple tactics. In short, potential interaction effects are often not considered from a theoretical or empirical point of view. In this section, we highlight several such effects which, we contend, should inform the empirical study of international human rights regimes.

Under many circumstances, strategies based on material inducement are incompatible with other socialization strategies. According to the processes of socialization, under certain conditions actors partially or completely internalize a social or cognitive script. Over time, such behavior may be described as "intrinsically motivated" (Frey and Jegen 2001: 589; Deci *et al.* 1999; Ostrom 2005: 253). Substantial empirical evidence demonstrates, however, that material rewards or punishments often "crowd out" intrinsic motivation for engaging in prescribed behavior (Bowles 2008; Ostrom 2005: 253). This evidence suggests that actors are often sufficiently motivated to conform to social norms for nonmaterial reasons. Where this condition obtains, an explicit incentive-based policy is often bound to fail or backfire – producing higher rates of norm violations due to the introduction of material incentives. For example, an explicit incentive-based policy can suggest that the preferred behavior (expanding voting rights, protecting indigenous peoples, etc.) is not self-evidently appropriate or that the broader social environment does not adequately value self-motivated rule adherence (Frey and Jegen 2001: 594, 602–605). Accordingly, strategies that focus on the use of material punishments and rewards – such as smart sanctions, criminal prosecution or restrictions on financial investment – will at times increase non-compliance with the promoted behavior. In short, the employment of material incentives is often incompatible with the employment of social and cognitive "incentives."

We discuss five specific types of negative interactions, and how each could affect the movement of states from commitment to compliance with human rights norms. The discussion provides examples of human rights applications for illustrative purposes – to better convey and describe the concepts. On some occasions, we use stylized examples; and on other occasions, we draw from historical accounts. These examples are not meant to prove the existence of the relevant negative interaction. The examples are simply to illustrate how the negative interactions might work in practice.

Category 1: conveyance of prevalence information

Negative interactions between material inducement and internalization may occur due to implicit information conveyed through the operation of material incentives. That is, an instrument that employs material inducement can suggest that the proscribed practice is widespread. And information about the prevalence of a practice influences the behavior of target actors in several ways.

Such information might increase non-compliance where other-regarding preferences are conditioned on notions of reciprocity and fairness. If target actors are "conditional reciprocators," they may abandon their other-regarding preferences when a material inducement cues them to believe that other actors are defectors. Substantial empirical evidence documents that many pro-social actors are "conditional reciprocators" and that prevalence information weakens their otherwise robust commitment to pro-social behavior (Bowles and Gintis 2004: 17–28; Falk *et al.* 2008: 151, 172, 176; Fehr and Gintis 2007). These ground-breaking empirical studies have informed analyses of domestic law and public policies where regulatory schemes have conveyed prevalence information indirectly or unintentionally – from tax enforcement to environmental protection to crime control and public order maintenance (Frey 1997a; Frey and Stutzer 2008; Kahan 2005).

Prevalence information might also increase non-compliance by affirmatively promoting a social norm supporting the proscribed behavior. Because actors often emulate orthodox or widespread social practices, the instrument might cue actors to form beliefs about the characteristics and behavior of other group members and, in turn, to adopt those practices for themselves (Sliwka 2003, 2007). That is, "conformists" alter their own practices when a regulatory instrument signals that a significantly high fraction of other actors behave in a particular way (Sliwka 2007). Interestingly, some research also suggests that persuasion-based interventions trigger the same effect. For example, Deborah Prentice's work demonstrates that overt efforts to persuade actors to discontinue a behavior can result in a "blowback" effect. The persuasive effort itself suggests to members of the target audience that the behavior is common and presumably embraced by other relevant members of the social environment (Prentice 2012).

The effect of prevalence information also operates at a higher level of generality. That is, material inducement-based approaches convey information about how actors are motivated and how actors order their preferences. An emphasis on material inducements, therefore, fosters a cultural environment in which members are expected to behave according to a particular behavioral logic – the lesson conveyed is that actors (do and should) rationally calculate whether to eschew specific social norms based on their material self-interest (see Wendt 2001: 1047 and 1034). As Bruno Frey has warned, a legal regime designed for knaves may produce knaves (Bowles 2008: 1605; Frey 1997a). And, in an important study of the design of international organizations (Koremenos *et al.* 2001), Alexander Wendt explains in a similar vein, "if instrumental rationality instantiates an individualistic view of the Self, then by acting on that basis institutional designers may unintentionally reproduce that mode of subjectivity and thereby make it more difficult to create a genuine sense of community" (Wendt 2001: 1047, 1034).

These interactions could undermine the movement of a state from commitment to compliance. There is ample evidence that information about the prevalence of human rights practices, in a region or across the globe, creates a social environment that influences the practices of other states (Goodman and Jinks 2004, in press; Simmons 2009). One would, therefore, worry that a perverse effect of human rights awareness campaigns by NGOs or monitoring and reporting by international bodies could produce the very type of prevalence information that diffuses undesirable practices. Increasing the effectiveness of monitoring and documentation of regional or worldwide violations of a particular norm could, for example, have the unintended consequence of delaying or impeding greater levels of compliance within states. One problem for regime design is the differential effect on states that are generally compliant, states that are non-compliant, and states on the margin between the two. Monitoring and bringing attention to human rights abuses is presumably most vital to improve conditions in the first set of countries (where political change is difficult) but may have the most destabilizing effects on compliant countries (especially those where success is fragile) and on marginal countries (where conditions are most unsettled).

Category 2: overjustification and social signaling

Material inducement can crowd out socially motivated adherence to a norm through an "overjustification" effect (Bénabou and Tirole 2006). Overjustification occurs any time a particular course of action is justified by both normative sentiments and material incentives. In other words, compliance with a social norm or rule is overjustified if actors have multiple, ontologically discrete reasons to observe the norm or rule. Substantial empirical evidence demonstrates that overjustification adversely influences levels of norm compliance in several ways. We mention three: social signaling, self-perception and self-determination. First consider the social signaling effect.

Many actors, motivated by concern about their status in a community, will adopt pro-social behaviors to signal their moral character. The introduction of a material incentive, however, overjustifies compliance and thus degrades its value as a social signal (Ariely *et al.* 2009; Bénabou and Tirole 2006; Fehr and Falk 2002: 710). That is, "the presence of incentives may ... reduce the value of generous or civic-minded acts as a signal of one's moral character" (Bowles and Hwang 2008: 1813) and the actor may find that "even a small material reward over-justifies his good deed" (Bowles 2008: 1609). As a consequence, material incentives weaken the commitment of these actors to the pro-social norm.

We would expect two extensions of this overjustification effect. First, the effect should apply to material penalties as well as material rewards. That is, a material penalty can also crowd out beneficent behavior if the actor does not want to be perceived as motivated by material pay-offs. Second, the effect should apply to nonmaterial incentives as well. That is, actors may want to signal that their behavior is directly attributable to their own principled beliefs about right conduct, and not to gain social recognition or avoid censure. In all these cases, the presence of multiple incentives may degrade the value and clarity of the signal. Actors are thus less likely to adopt the desirable behavior.

How might such an overjustification effect hinder efforts to get states to commit and to comply with international human rights? First, various scholars posit "signaling theories" of international human rights law. On this view, states make costly human rights commitments to demonstrate to the international community that they are genuinely committed to humane treatment of their citizenry. The model of negative interactions, however, suggests that material rewards for protecting human rights (e.g. through foreign investment or Millennium Challenge awards) might erode the value of such a signal. There is accordingly less reason for a state to make such commitments in the first place. This overjustification effect can also persist at subsequent stages in the move from commitment to compliance. In general, the value of a particular signal often degrades over time. As observers learn to discount signals that are not followed by meaningful change, increasingly costly signals (including both acts of commitment and compliance) are required. The overjustification effect should lower the utility of the signals at these subsequent points as well.

As another example, consider a state that would be willing to improve its compliance with human rights but does not want to be perceived as having done so in response to material or other external threats. A state, for example, may not want to be considered weak, that is, by appearing to succumb to international coercion. Daniel Thomas's study of the Helsinki regime alludes to such a potential overjustification effect:

> Less than a year after the Helsinki Final Act, the combination of domestic mobilization and transnational networking had rendered the international normative environment inhospitable to the political status quo in Eastern Europe ... The Soviet Union and its allies were thus caught between trying to create the impression of compliance with Helsinki norms and denying the legitimacy of Western pressure for human rights improvements.
>
> (Thomas 1999: 205, 214)

Kinzelbach (Chapter 9, this volume) alludes to existing research showing that China was less likely to make accommodations when faced with foreign economic pressures. That research suggests the Chinese authorities did not want domestic human rights improvements to be perceived as publicly bowing to US pressure (Li and Drury 2004: 391; Li and Drury 2006: 321). An interest in not being perceived to bend to international pressure may more generally impede strategies to effectuate compliance through incentivization. Margaret Doxey explains in the context of sanctions and international conflict: "There is a danger, too, that a defiant reaction may mean less readiness to compromise than before sanctions were imposed ... [T]he target government cannot adopt a more conciliatory attitude without loss of face and apparent betrayal of what have been presented as national values" (Doxey 1996: 104). Thomas's and Kinzelbach's empirical claims, and to a lesser extent Doxey's too, do not explore the causal mechanisms in these particular episodes. We draw liberally from these examples simply to illustrate the potential significance of the overjustification effect, and how it might explain observed behavior with respect to international pressure.

This overjustification effect could also impede signals sent in the other direction – from the social group to the individual actor. Overjustification compromises the ability of actors to identify and interpret signals from the social environment about appropriate conduct. That is, it would be difficult for actors to draw important inferences from the behavioral patterns of states – to discern, for example, whether governments with good human rights records are acting out of a principled belief concerning how states ought to behave or out of an instrumental calculation of material pay-offs. For instance, such noise would make it difficult for the group to signal that a true consensus exists that modern states reject torture as normatively abhorrent. An alternative message is that self-regarding states are inspired to avoid material penalties for engaging in torture or inspired to obtain material rewards for eschewing the practice.

Of course, the very existence of an instrument employing material inducements sends a signal that the community condemns the proscribed behavior and is willing to expend resources and exert force against bad actors. Hence, the instrument and each instance of material inducement can signal strong social support for the (human rights) norm. And, the *absence* of a material inducement-based strategy might send the opposite signal – that the community lacks strong social support for the norm. This "expressive function" of a material inducement-based strategy is an important countervailing effect, to be sure (Sunstein 1996).

Our point is not to deny or in any way discredit that bit of conventional wisdom, but rather to underscore several important ways in which it must be qualified. Most importantly, our analysis suggests that overjustification weakens social system-actor signals as well as actor-actor signals – which cautions against jointly employing material and social incentive strategies. Whether the "expressive function" of punishment swamps this overjustification effect will turn on numerous considerations. For example, the expressive function is compromised if penalties and rewards issue from actors who have insufficient social standing vis-à-vis the signaled actors – a narrow band of donor countries, a remote foreign court, unrepresentative segments of civil society, a hostile country. The expressive function is also diminished or lost if material pay-offs result simply from structural conditions rather than from a purposefully directed (and publicly endorsed) system of incentives. More fundamentally, the expressive function of punishment might work only when the proscribed behavior is broadly, unequivocally and manifestly understood as inappropriate. In other words, the expressive function of employing material inducements might predominate only when there is little risk of overjustification given the well understood status of the norm in question.

Category 3: overjustification and self-perception

Overjustification triggered by the provision of material incentives might also adversely affect target actors' self-perception. First, material inducements can interfere with the very cognitive processes that lead to internalization of a norm. Overjustification causes some actors to lose cognitive track of their motives for abiding by a norm and to attribute their actions to material incentives: "Individuals sometimes do not understand their own motives perfectly … If monetary incentives are set for an activity, then an individual concludes that it performs this activity because of those incentives. If the incentives are abandoned, motivation is reduced as compared to a situation where there never have been extrinsic incentives" (Sliwka 2003: 2–3; also Lepper *et al.* 1996: 24–25; Lepper and Greene 1978). Under certain conditions when material incentives are interrupted, norm compliance will fall *below* the level that would have existed had those incentives never been introduced. The strength of intrinsic motivations for observing a social norm will have been (cognitively) lost. Similarly, actors otherwise inclined to observe a social norm because they consider observance an extension of their identity or required by their internal value system, might instead perform the act only when the balance of material incentives weighs in favor of compliance.

We should also note a second form of overjustification and self-perception. The psychological processes just described also help explain why actors who have already internalized a pro-social norm will not act on it once material incentives are introduced. Actors motivated by concerns about their self-worth "consider themselves as less praise-worthy when they collect money [for engaging in moral behavior], which reduces the psychological incentive to perform the activity" (Fehr and Falk 2002: 710).

How might these interactions undermine the movement from commitment to compliance with international human rights norms? As a stylized example, consider access to the EU economic market as a motivation for candidate countries to adopt particular human rights policies. For instance, after Croatia is admitted to the EU, domestic actors may reflect back and find it difficult to determine whether human rights changes were inspired by intrinsic commitments to such values or the considerable external material incentives. Similar effects may result from economic inducements and targeted sanctions to get specific individuals to comply with human rights. Those instruments are designed to operate on motivations at the individual level, and may relatively quickly improve performance. Yet the instruments may also undermine long-term compliance by crowding out the cognitive link between behavioral changes and personally held humanistic values.

Any model of human rights change should take account of these legacy effects. That is, if the historical progression toward human rights compliance involves certain combinations of influence strategies, the "final" stage of rule-consistent behavior may be less obtainable and, if reached, may be more shallow and more difficult to sustain.

Another consequence of the overjustification effect involves the intensification of human rights violations when international pressure lapses. That is, in some cases the targeted state actors may focus on international pressure – trade and economic sanctions and other forms of coercion – and away from normative reasons for respecting human rights. Interruptions in the external pressure might lead to norm compliance falling *below* the level that would have existed had those external measures never been introduced. Studies suggest that a lapse in economic sanctions sometimes bolsters targeted actors to engage in undesirable behavior. More specifically, Daniel Thomas's study of the Helsinki process suggests such effects might have resulted from the interruption of foreign pressure on Czechoslovakia (Thomas 1999: 226). Thomas does not explore mechanisms for the observed behavior. The Czechoslovakian reaction, however, is suggestive of the overjustification effect, and the episode illustrates the type of interactions in which the effect might take place.

Category 4: overjustification and self-determination

Finally, overjustification reduces the perception of self-determination in target actors – decreasing long-term compliance with the overjustified norm. Much empirical evidence suggests that the provision of material incentives often compromises individuals' sense of self-determination and thus degrades their intrinsic motivations for engaging in a behavior (Bowles 2008).

> When people perceive an external intervention as a restriction to act autonomously, intrinsic motivation is substituted by this external intervention. The locus of control shifts from inside to outside the person. The person in question no longer feels responsible but makes the outside intervention responsible instead. However, this shift in the locus of control only takes place when the intervention is considered to be controlling.
>
> (Frey and Stutzer 2008: 412)

This crowding-out effect can be dramatic. Several studies demonstrate that when actors would otherwise seek to engage in a practice "in the absence of other rewards, the introduction of explicit incentives may 'overjustify' the activity and reduce the individual's sense of autonomy" (Bowles 2008: 1607) thus driving down the aggregate levels of pro-social behavior (Frey and Jegen 2001: 594; Frey and Stutzer 2008).

Although this research clearly demonstrates that the provision of extrinsic incentives decreases intrinsic motivation, the relevance of this finding for our project is less clear. The complication is that, as a conceptual matter, neither moving part in the self-determination research program maps perfectly onto material and non-material mechanisms discussed in the human rights literature. The concept of "intrinsic motivation" includes socialized end states generated by both persuasion and some other shaming- or acculturation-based strategies – namely, those that involve cognitive pressure. Hence, the crowding-out effects identified in the self-determination studies trade-off with intrinsic motivations brought about by either persuasion or deep acculturation. The notion of "extrinsic incentives," however, includes both material inducement and some shaming- or acculturation-based strategies – those that involve social punishments and rewards of various forms. Indeed, self-determination research finds that social and symbolic rewards are often perceived by actors as controlling and thus degrade their intrinsic motivation in some circumstances (Deci *et al.* 1999). This is a terrifically important point because it suggests that some forms of discursive socialization (partially internalized, social pressures) may crowd out other forms of discursive socialization (completely internalized, cognitive scripts). Hence, discursive socialization may not always be a step along an evolutionary path to complete internalization.

Nevertheless, there is strong evidence to suggest that social pressure is superior to material pressure in promoting or preserving intrinsic motivation. Indeed, some important studies directly comparing the effects of material and non-material incentives conclude that material pressure generally crowds out intrinsic motivation to a greater degree than social pressure (Deci and Ryan 1985, 2002; Ryan and Deci 2000). Additionally, other research suggests that the difference is not one of degree, but of direction. In those studies, the data suggest that material sanctions negatively interact with intrinsic motivation, but social pressures that individuals partially internalize – through feelings of guilt, shame, social esteem and general concern for others' regard – actually "crowd in" intrinsic motivation. Across all these studies, social inducements are, when compared with material inducement, generally superior: social pressure either does less damage to intrinsic motivation or reinforces it.

Consider two ways in which these crowding-out effects might undermine human rights compliance. First, actors may stiffen their resistance to human rights norms when international coercion is considered controlling. Importantly, resistance in such cases is not due to the content of the norm, but rather to the form of influence. Indeed, empirical studies show that actors' resistance – even to a normative practice that they would otherwise agree with – can increase when material pay-offs are presented (Frey and Jegen 2001; Oberholzer-Gee and Kunreuther 2005). One study of apartheid South Africa suggests a form of domestic resistance in response to external material inducements: "The expected pressure by business on government as a result of sanctions has not occurred. In fact, sanctions brought business and government closer together in the patriotic cause of circumventing foreign interference" (Adam and Moodley 1993: 57). Notably, another study on the South African nuclear program indicated a similar effect in that arena: "Even intensified sanctions ... were ineffective in halting the program. Nuclear scientists justified their work in terms of sanction-busting and chauvinistic ideology. 'The camaraderie was amazing,' a former technician was later to admit, 'We were proud that our efforts were beating the sanctions'" (Fig 1999: 95). Other studies suggest that Prime Minister P.W. Botha, in particular, increased internal repression after his regime made a (self-perceived) commitment to reform that was followed by an intensification of international sanctions:

> [Economic sanctions] contributed significantly to the assault on the psyche of white South Africans. Botha, predictably, reacted to the measures with pure belligerence. Genuinely mystified by what he considered the perverse refusal of foreigners to credit his good intentions, he gave up reform to concentrate on repression. He lost the will to change.
>
> (Waldmeir 1998: 57)

Second, external material inducements can become a locus of control that over time shift actors away from self-determined reasons for promoting human rights. Accordingly, communicative exchanges within a domestic setting might shift toward the more limited agenda of powerful international institutions when those institutions promote human rights through material inducements. One concern is that, in those cases, had the domestic actors been left to their own devices, a broader and stronger human rights agenda might have emerged. The implications for human rights change are obvious. In concrete terms, one might speculate whether these causal mechanisms help explain some of the limits of human rights change in South Africa. Although economic sanctions may have rallied international attention and otherwise bolstered domestic anti-apartheid activists, the sanctions regime may have also weakened support for deeper structural reform. David Black's study of South Africa describes the moderating effect of international sanctions:

> [O]fficial sanctions helped to structure a moderate and limited transition in which, in important respects, there was no "radical rupture with the past." This is most obvious in relation to the structure of the economy and the steps a new government might take to redress South Africa's deep historic inequalities ... International emphasis on political, rather than economic, transformation reflect the dominant global perspective on human rights generally, however, and therefore is not surprising even in the South African situation.
>
> (Black 1999: 78)

Another study suggests a related concern when the domestic anti-apartheid movement directed its attention toward international support:

> A firmly held belief among the black opposition is that the South African government is basically kept in power by its Western allies. Hence, sufficient external pressure – the withdrawal of international support – would force Pretoria to relinquish its exclusive political control ...
>
> Such an assessment, however ... has also contributed to a widespread view of liberation as something of a cargo cult, a commodity to be delivered by outsiders. Unfortunately, inasmuch as it has geared protest toward triggering outside pressure rather than challenging the domestic power equation directly, this attitude has reinforced domestic political paralysis.
>
> (Adam and Moodley 1993)

SOCIAL MECHANISMS TO PROMOTE HUMAN RIGHTS   115

These descriptions may explicitly reflect a political, rather than a cognitive, model of trade-offs – although the first study alludes to legitimating and communicative effects, and the latter study references attitudinal motivations. The important point for our present purposes is simply that the cognitive model of negative interactions can also potentially help explain such results, and the South African case indicates the nature of the model's potential importance.

Category 5: "a fine is a price"

A related research program shows how fines often release actors from concerns about social disapproval thereby increasing non-compliance with the relevant social norm. Conventional wisdom, of course, suggests that fines deter infractions; fines are also thought to signify the social unacceptability of a behavior – thus reinforcing the societal pressure to abide by the norm. Substantial empirical evidence, however, documents the opposite behavioral effects. In certain circumstances, actors perceive "a fine is a price" simply to be paid in exchange for engaging in a proscribed behavior (Fehr and Falk 2002: 711; Gneezy and Rustichini 2000a). In field studies, subsequent to the introduction of a fine, the rate of misbehavior increased and stabilized well above pre-fine levels (Gneezy and Rustichini 2000a: 3, 8). One explanation of this result attributes the behavioral change to information conveyance.[2] That theoretical account, however, requires perfectly rational, perfectly self-interested actors (Gneezy and Rustichini 2000a: 13); and, even if accurate, would support an important point – rational actors are willing to violate a social norm by purchasing the prerogative to do so. Another explanation of this finding is that fines change the social meaning of norm violations. If actors experience discomfort in violating a norm, the fine releases them from such pressure (Fehr and Falk 2002: 709; Gneezy and Rustichini 2000a: 14). The fine essentially changes actors' perception of the nature of the obligation (Gneezy and Rustichini 2000a: 14; Fehr and Falk 2002: 711 (explaining that "the introduction of the fine not only reduces the disapproval for being late but parents also no longer consider being late as blame-worthy")). The latter explanation is consistent with other studies demonstrating that monetary incentives encourage actors to feel justified in violating a social obligation.

How might these crowding-out effects impede human rights compliance in different settings? State actors might be more likely to disregard procedural obligations (e.g. the obligation to report to human rights treaty bodies) if the price of non-compliance is a fine. And, states may be more willing to abridge some substantive norms (e.g. labor standards) if the international penalty involves fines or economic countermeasures. Within domestic legal systems, monetary

---

[2] The fine provides new information that misbehavior will not result in more severe penalties; actors are no longer deterred by the uncertain threat of worse sanctions (Gneezy and Rustichini 2000b).

compensation may also change the social meaning of rights infringements and accordingly degrade compliance. Consider, for example, a commentator's concerns about the potential effect of monetary compensation on the rights of indigenous peoples: "Incorporating 'just compensation' as a liability constraint on government limitations of aboriginal rights could create a risk that 'justice' will be equated with compensation. Once compensation is provided, it may lead to a practical extinguishment of aboriginal claims in the minds of regulators and the public" (Metcalf 2008: 446 (citing Gneezy and Rustichini 2000a)). Finally, if the worst sanction that US officials will face for committing torture is a stunted career and the ability to travel abroad (Chapter 8, this volume), they may be more willing to engage in such acts considering that society has priced the violation of the norm so moderately.

Sequencing effects

Modeling the domestic effects of international human rights norms should also consider various "sequencing" effects. That is, the interaction of mechanisms will vary depending on the sequence of their employment. A fully articulated model must account for the effects of different mechanisms at different stages in the institutionalization of a norm. Of course, there are no universal rules to apply across contexts. We can, nevertheless, derive lessons about general tendencies that should subsequently be considered in individual cases. Those context-specific decisions will be better informed by understanding factors such as the potential detrimental social effects of various sequencing choices, opportunities for mutually reinforcing mechanism interactions at different points in time, and the distinct functions that each mechanism can perform during different periods in the development of a human rights regime.

One general lesson involves the systematic changes in preferences that actors experience by their very participation in and exposure to an institutional environment. Because persuasion, learning and other forms of discursive socialization alter state preferences over time, international organizations could incorporate more flexible administrative devices such as renegotiation clauses or encourage sunset provisions on treaty reservations – essentially devices that recognize that the preferences of states are endogenously formed by their interactions within the regime. A human rights regime could also enhance its effectiveness by demanding modest initial commitments and ratcheting up obligations over time. Strategies could include allowing supervisory organs to expand their authority incrementally and creating opportunities for optional protocols only after an organization has existed for an extended time period. Voting rules within IGOs might also anticipate greater consensus on issues over time. Regime architects could, for example, appease hesitant states by requiring larger supermajorities to bind member states later in the life of the institution. In short, mechanisms that are ineffective at one stage can be effective at another due to preference changes within institutional settings. Regime architects should build more flexible structures in anticipation of those cultural shifts.

When, for example, should material inducement precede or follow discourse-centered approaches? One important factor is the existing strength of social expectations and cognitive beliefs supporting the normative ends sought by the material inducement. In global affairs, reliance on material force is generally risky because it is prematurely, haphazardly or seldom employed. One precondition for effective material inducements is strongly motivated enforcers. As studies of strong reciprocity suggest, material sanctions without the prior social and cognitive alignment of important actors (especially third-party punishers) will be employed inconsistently, if employed at all. Premature punishment – prior to the institutionalization of a norm – can also result in a (greater) backlash by deviants who feel unjustly penalized. In addition, as the crowding-out literature suggests, attempting and then removing material incentives can undercut other socialization strategies. Indeed, some evidence suggests an "afterglow effect" (Irlenbusch and Sliwka 2005) whereby the crowding out of intrinsic motivations endures long after the removal of material incentives.

On the other hand, employing material inducements at an earlier stage can accrue specific benefits. When long-term political and economic support for administering material force is lacking, punishments and rewards may be best reserved for limited circumstances such as: an initial phase in the development of a human rights regime or the initial point at which states join or begin to participate in an organization. For example, material costs and benefits could incentivize states to join organizations in which they are later subject to measures that rely on persuasive and other discursive forms of influence. As recent scholarship on China suggests, once (even powerful) states join multilateral organizations, path dependency may lead to greater levels of socialization (Johnston 2008). An additional reason to emphasize material inducement early on involves other crowding-out effects. Negative interactions – Category 3 (*overjustification – self-perception*) and Category 4 (*overjustification – self-determination*) – occur when actors are already intrinsically motivated prior to the introduction of material incentives. Similarly, other negative interactions – Category 2 (*overjustification – social signaling*) and Category 5 (*fine is a price*) – occur when actors have begun to internalize societal pressures prior to the introduction of material incentives. Accordingly, foregrounding material inducements before actors have traversed down the road of socialization may be more effective. That suggestion does not contradict other designs that we just discussed, but it does make their application more complicated. Awaiting the institutionalization of a norm is advisable if one is trying to minimize retaliation by actors who are punished for violating human rights, but waiting can amplify the crowding-out effects among actors who would otherwise respect human rights.

As a final example of social effects of sequencing, consider benefits to emphasizing discursive forms of socialization prior to other mechanisms. First, certain social and discursive structures could enhance the effectiveness of material inducements. In particular, instruments utilizing material inducements can have a "crowding-in" effect when monitoring and enforcement is conducted by a peer group. Of course, the existence of a peer group may be an antecedent condition for some forms of socialization such as acculturation (rather than a product of acculturation). However, discursive socialization such as acculturative processes, through the communication and sharing of common practices, can help reinforce the sense of a community. A more fully acculturated group would accordingly enhance the positive effects of peer enforcement. Moreover, discursive socialization can help develop community-wide schema – for evaluating human rights standards, the definition of violations, and acceptable justifications – thus sharpening the framework that a system of material incentives needs to operate most efficiently. Notably, these forms and benefits of delayed onset of material inducement reflect, in many respects, the evolutionary path of the European Convention on Human Rights and its member states (see Helfer and Slaughter 1997: 314–317). This account is also consistent with Ann Marie Clark's work on compliance with the International Covenant on Civil and Political Rights and the Convention Against Torture. Clark found that naming and shaming strategies improve human rights conditions when they are directed against states that have formally joined these treaty regimes – and such strategies are associated with deteriorated human rights conditions when employed against non-parties to the treaties (Chapter 7, this volume).

Implications and conclusions

We anticipate that some readers will doubt the relevance of the research on negative interactions for state behavior. Indeed, the bulk of research involves individual psychological phenomena, including notions of personal identity and individual-level internalization of norms. It is a fair question how these individual-level dynamics might translate into actions on the part of the state. Do citizens internalize the identity of the nation state and personally feel shame when the state suffers a blow? Is such an indirect and collective form of shame the same as personal shame for one's own wrongdoing in terms of content, duration and interaction with other psychological motivations? Perhaps individuals do not personally internalize the identity of the state. In that case, do policy-makers act "as if" the state is motivated by its honor and notions of self-respect; and in making decisions "for the state" do material inducements that target the state trade-off with honor-based and intrinsically driven motives?

These types of inquiries reflect some of the unanswered questions involving links between motivations for human behavior that have been studied at the individual level and macro-level state practices. Therein lies the challenge. The extent to which the research on negative interactions appears inapplicable to state-level behavior should challenge human rights scholars to develop a better account of the connections and disconnections between micro-level motivations and macro-level changes in state practice. The important point, albeit a modest one here, is that scholars who doubt the applicability of this research yet accept conventional theories of human motivation in global affairs carry the burden of explaining how and when human motivations are relevant to influencing the behavior of states.

To the extent that the study of human rights change depends on conventional theories of human motivation, the psychological research we discuss calls into question those foundations. PoHR and its progeny (including chapters in the present volume) invoke – implicitly or explicitly – conventional theories of individual psychology in considering how to influence state behavior. They rely, for example, on motivations of human behavior such as shame, social status and material reward. At a general level, such methodological commitments are widely shared in international relations scholarship. Hans Morgenthau, for instance, derived his theory of global affairs from notions of human nature emphasizing selfishness and an innate human urge for power. Alexander Wendt predicated his account of state behavior on symbolic interactionism, a theory developed through the empirical study of individual psychology (Wendt 1999). In this chapter, we focus on individual-level mechanisms that appear most prominently in human rights studies – such as the "spiral model" – that involve processes which lead states to change their behavior.

We do not defend (at least, not here) the methodological reliance on individual psychological factors. Rather, to the extent to which descriptive and explanatory accounts depend on those factors, researchers should develop a more sophisticated assessment of how these mechanisms operate and interact. Recent studies on human cognition and decision-making have produced counterintuitive and provocative findings about the relationships between different motivations for human behavior. One of the most important discoveries involves negative interactions and trade-offs between different forms of motivation. Researchers who engage in mechanism-based analysis of human rights should integrate those findings into their own research. Moreover, we do not claim that these interaction effects always or even typically occur in the institutional contexts most relevant to human rights change. Mechanisms of social influence are additive, or at least broadly consistent, in many circumstances, we suspect. The point is that the findings documented here suggest that modes of social influence will at times conflict – and will, at times, work well when optimally sequenced.

In other words, the crowding-out and sequencing effects do not recommend abandoning the "spiral model" – or the prevailing conventional wisdom on human rights change. These interaction effects, instead, suggest several refinements to the model and other accounts of human rights change. First, this research suggests further refinement of the typology of mechanisms. The conceptualization of mechanisms must not obscure important, and potentially conflicting, differences between the micro-processes of various socialization strategies. These distinctions require further disaggregation of various mechanisms along a few lines. Incentivization strategies, for example, should not be conflated. The research on crowding out suggests that distinctions should be maintained between material and nonmaterial incentives. Within the category of material incentives, research also suggests the importance of the distinction between implicit and explicit incentives – implicit incentives might include, for example, the provision of economic support for a good human rights record without any attempt to condition the support on compliance with human rights norms. In addition, incentivization strategies – the classic method of mobilizing extrinsic motivation – should be distinguished from strategies designed to mobilize intrinsic motivation. The "spiral model," for example, accounts for the distinction between material and nonmaterial incentives, but it inadequately conceptualizes the provision of social incentives as an incentivization strategy – importantly different from a persuasion-based approach. And, it does not anticipate potential negative interactions between material and nonmaterial-based influence strategies.

Second, the research that we have highlighted underscores the importance of precision in the mapping of causal pathways. Because the social encounters underlying models of human rights change are both complex and dynamic, it is important to identify clearly who is influenced by whom via what mechanism. Mechanism-based theorizing generally and the tracing of interaction effects specifically require that the identity of influence agents, influence targets and influence strategy are all made theoretically explicit.

Third, a better understanding of interaction effects makes clear the importance of specifying various theoretically crucial baselines. Most obvious is the degree to which the target shares some relevant aspect of the normative vision undergirding the international human rights scheme. This is important, for instance, because trade-offs with intrinsic motivation ought to be irrelevant as a causal matter where there is no intrinsic motivation. In addition, the baseline level of extant influence strategies should be assessed. Putative trade-offs between material and nonmaterial incentivization are potentially more important where monetary incentives are introduced into an environment with substantial extant social pressure. What is needed, in other words, is something more than general descriptions of the vulnerability of specific actors to material or social pressures. Finally, the baseline vulnerabilities of targets to particular influence strategies or particular influence agents should be assessed.

These refinements would, in our view, facilitate: (1) the identification and explanation of interaction effects (including positive interactions); (2) more highly specified causal pathways that involve micro-level, mechanism-based accounts; (3) greater specification of the conditions under which commitment will lead to compliance; and (4) a more satisfactory theoretical account of "backlash," backsliding, and other cases where commitment does not result in compliance.

PART III

From ratification to compliance:
states revisited

7

The normative context of human rights criticism: treaty ratification and UN mechanisms

ANN MARIE CLARK

How do human rights norms condition states' responses to international criticism? As noted in the introductory chapters, the spiral model outlines a process in which focused communication, argument and, in some cases, persuasion can take place once a state recognizes human rights norms' prescriptive status. A regularized, some might say stylized, version of human rights communication takes place both when states accede to global human rights treaties and when governments are addressed under the procedures that have evolved for consideration of countries' human rights records at the United Nations (UN). If international norms, rules and principles provide a backdrop for further engagement and argument about facts and accountability, we might expect to see differing levels of change in a country's human rights record depending on how deeply, and under what circumstances, it engages with the international human rights framework. This chapter applies a form of dynamic time series analysis, a statistical technique, along with a short case study of UN action on Indonesia, to consider the effects of the discursive engagement represented by treaty commitment and whether human rights treaty compliance varies when a state receives additional international attention.

Commitment in the analysis below is indicated by the ratification of one or two major human rights treaties, the International Covenant on Civil and Political Rights (ICCPR, UN 1966), which entered into force in 1976, and the Convention against Torture and Other Cruel, Inhuman, or Degrading Treatment or Punishment (CAT, UN 1984), which entered into force in 1987. *Compliance* with human rights norms is based on a measure of the level of respect for basic physical integrity rights, described below. In addition to the expectations brought into relief when a state ratifies a human rights treaty, procedures

For comments, I am grateful to fellow authors in this volume, as well as Aaron Hoffman, Sidney Jones, Arie Kacowicz, James A. McCann and Nicole Simonelli. Thanks also to Judith Kelley, Tim Büthe and the 2007 Seminar on International Relations at Duke University. The Woodrow Wilson International Center for Scholars and Purdue University provided fellowship support. Katherine Appleton, Lisa Carroll, Marian Cash and Kali Wright-Smith provided research assistance.

within the UN framework can also be invoked to raise concerns about a country's human rights record. Resolutions adopted by the UN Economic and Social Council (ECOSOC) in 1967 and 1970, known by their numbers as Resolutions 1235 (UN ECOSOC 1967) and 1503 (UN ECOSOC 1970), allow the UN to highlight the gap between international human rights standards and a country's behavior, whether or not it is party to a human rights treaty. The procedures under the resolutions are institutionalized examples of human rights criticism, which is often referred to as "naming and shaming."

Theory informed by the spiral model and elaborated by Chapters 3 and 5 in this volume suggests that, as a form of prescriptive status that states grant to human rights norms, treaty ratification may not produce immediate effects but should condition states' responses to more pointed criticism by external actors. The findings in this chapter suggest that once a treaty has been ratified, the potential beneficial effect of further criticism rises. I find that naming and shaming, as represented by action under the UN Human Rights Commission from 1981 to 2005, prompted better human rights compliance among states that had ratified CAT, when compared with the effects on non-ratifiers or the effects of ratification or criticism alone. In other words, commitment to CAT seems to enable the international community's focused action on human rights to elicit greater compliance. A similar effect is not observable at statistically significant levels for the ICCPR, although the dynamic is observed at non-significant levels. This general effect, and the better effects for deeper and more targeted criticism, is predicted by the discursive dynamic of the spiral model.

Naming and shaming

"Naming and shaming" is shorthand for the act of framing and publicizing human rights information in order to pressure states to comply with human rights standards. It echoes the phrase, "mobilization of shame," used by Alfred Zimmern to refer to the resolute work of "defenders of good causes, with the public opinion of the world at their back" who could expose the gap between idealistic rhetoric and reality through the use of facts (Zimmern 1939: 470; see also Clark 2009). First writing in 1935, Zimmern was referring to the importance of public observation of meetings of the League of Nations. Joyce (1978: 80) later used "mobilization of shame" to refer to NGO tactics for promoting human rights. This chapter's inquiry into the impact of human rights treaty ratification when coupled with the special human rights procedures at the UN – procedures which depend in large part on information provided by NGOs, as "defenders of good causes" – is consistent with the spirits of Zimmern and Joyce in its focus on the hypothesized power of information when placed in the international limelight.

If ratification and norm-based targeting of states are social processes, as suggested by the very use of the word "shaming," we might expect human rights norms to act as reference points for reasoning and argument about political action (Kratochwil 1989, 2000; Risse 2000). In line with the spiral model, treaties (and the opportunity for ratification) can be conceived as points in the articulation and mutual understanding of international human rights norms over time. "Shaming," or criticism, as represented by the use of additional UN procedures, might be expected to intensify treaties' effects by highlighting the compliance gap discussed by Xinyuan Dai. In line with the spiral model, states may be more susceptible to argumentation and change if they have already acknowledged the legitimacy of human rights norms.

Treaty ratification and UN targeting

In order to frame the analysis presented below, it is first important to offer some details about UN treaty ratification and the Commission procedures. Both treaties included in this study, the ICCPR, which entered into force in 1976, and CAT, which entered into force in 1987, commit states to honor human rights pertaining to civil liberties and rights to physical integrity. Treaty ratification, acceptance of a treaty as legally binding, is an expression both of a state's commitment to human rights and an explicit acknowledgment of a norm's prescriptive status, as noted in Chapter 3 of this volume.

Procedurally, ratification opens a state to further scrutiny by the official committee established to monitor each treaty: countries that ratify each treaty are required to submit an initial report on compliance in the first year, and regular periodic reports. After a government submits its report, a representative of the country appears before the treaty body to respond to questions and concerns. Members of the treaty body can question state representatives about the content of the report and compare the states' reports with information received from independent sources such as non-governmental human rights organizations. Each treaty body issues written "concluding observations" in response to the government's report. Becoming a party to either of the two treaties, therefore, requires a government to offer at least minimal documentation and justification of its practices in the context of prevailing human rights norms. CAT's requirements are more focused and specific than those of the ICCPR, being limited to one general category of abuses and vesting the treaty body with some independent investigative power. CAT imposes individual accountability for acts of torture by requiring states to make torture an offense under domestic law (Sikkink 2011: 103). CAT's treaty body also has the power to investigate allegations of torture.

Weaknesses of the reporting process include the reality that states may submit reports late, and the treaty bodies are chronically overloaded with reports to consider. Although efforts at follow-up to states' reports have increased with time (Schmidt 2003), the treaty bodies' follow-up capacities are limited. The level of direct and immediate responsiveness to the treaty bodies tends to be up to the state. Still, ratification sets in motion a "dialogue with the international community on how key values are faring within the country" (Ramcharan 2009: 42). In the language of the spiral model, ratification represents an explicit acknowledgment of a norm's prescriptive status.

The treaty committees mentioned above serve only to examine states that have ratified or acceded to their respective treaties. A second way that states become participants in the global human rights conversation is involuntary and more critical: under Resolution 1235 and 1503, the UN Human Rights Commission (now Human Rights Council)[1] has singled out states with poor human rights performance each year. The workings of the procedures under Resolutions 1503 and 1235 are well documented elsewhere (e.g. Bossuyt 1985; Kamminga 1992; Nifosi 2005); I describe them briefly below.

Public consideration

With ECOSOC Resolution 1235, the Commission and its Sub-Commission on Prevention of Discrimination and Protection of Minorities, referred to below as the Sub-Commission,[2] were authorized to "examine information relevant to gross violations of human rights" in particular countries (UN ECOSOC 1967). Resolution 1235 provides the procedural basis for annual debates on specific human rights situations at the sessions of the Commission (Weissbrodt et al. 2001: 237). It became known as "public consideration," in contrast with the "confidential" procedure associated with Resolution 1503, because it enabled the Commission to discuss states' human rights violations on the record. Possible actions include adopting a resolution or appointing individual experts to investigate human rights concerns in the country. These persons have usually been named either as Special Rapporteurs or as Independent Experts, and have typically held a one-year mandate that can be renewed. Thematic procedures were also developed under the aegis of the public procedure (see Kamminga 1987; Weissbrodt 1986).[3] The public procedure, whatever its limitations, puts pressure on states "to show that their ... records are good or that at least they are taking measures to improve," which Nifosi cites as an indication of the seriousness with which countries treat public consideration (Nifosi 2005: 40). A country

---

[1] The Human Rights Commission was reorganized as the Human Rights Council in 2006. The study presented here covers 1981–2005, so the material below refers to actions of the Commission.

[2] In 1999 the Sub-Commission was renamed the "Sub-Commission on the Promotion and Protection of Human Rights"; after the Human Rights Commission was dissolved in 2006, so was the Sub-Commission. A replacement for the Sub-Commission has operated since 2008 as the UN Human Rights Council Advisory Committee.

[3] Mentions of states when grouped under these thematic procedures are not included in this analysis.

resolution is usually couched in understated wording but some countries have gone to great lengths to avoid such mention (see Guest 1992).

Private consideration

A second procedure was introduced with ECOSOC Resolution 1503, which enabled the Sub-Commission to receive and consider information about human rights, and government responses, in a confidential, "private" procedure (UN ECOSOC 1970). Communication with a government under Resolution 1503 is initiated based on allegations of abuses coming from various sources. As provided for by the procedure, individuals, NGOs and states submit information to a working group set up to screen the information and decide whether to pass the information to the Sub-Commission or its current equivalent (UN ECOSOC, Sub-Commission 1971). This Sub-Commission refers the matter to the Commission, based on whether a "consistent pattern of gross and reliably attested" human rights violations presents itself, according to the language of the resolution (Bossuyt 1985: 181). The Commission then chooses whether to implement private consultation under Resolution 1503. If the country has already been the subject of 1503 proceedings in the previous year, the Commission also decides whether to continue consideration, end it, or transfer the matter to consideration under the public procedure. In practice the private and public procedures have often been applied in sequence (Nifosi 2005: 36); for example, in early use of the procedures, between 1978 and 1985, Equatorial Guinea, Bolivia, El Salvador, Guatemala, Iran, Afghanistan and Haiti were all considered first under 1503 and then under 1235 (Bossuyt 1985: 203). Early on, governments tried to use 1503 strategically to put off public consideration, but rules have evolved to prevent one procedure from undermining the other (Nifosi 2005: 37–39). The threat of transfer from private to public procedure has more recently been described by Nifosi as an incentive for cooperation under the private procedure (2005).

Although the 1503 procedure is nominally a confidential process, participants across the UN human rights apparatus are aware of the information being reviewed, and when governments are asked to explain themselves under Resolution 1503, it can be "quite embarrassing to the governments concerned" (Bossuyt 1985: 184). The 1235 process includes more potential for NGO attendance at meetings, as well as the possibility of putting states under the more intense monitoring by establishing the country-oriented special rapporteurs and independent experts (Nifosi 2005: 401). Countries considered under the private procedures have been announced to the public yearly since 1978 (UN OHCHR n.d.).

To summarize, the measures above do not exhaust the possible ways that the UN can target states that are violating human rights, but they represent a repertoire of comparable UN procedures that have been employed to deal with governments' violations. The outcomes may include a resolution of concern, assignment of an individual investigator, or some other form of mandated attention. Each of these actions indicates substantive censure on human rights, or a form of "social punishment" (Lebovic and Voeten 2006); for a full list of countries considered, see International Service for Human Rights and Abraham June 2006). Although Commission politics have been widely criticized, most recently in the lead-up to its 2006 reorganization, Lebovic and Voeten (2006) found that Commission action was generally consistent with the severity of violations from 1978 to 2001, particularly after the late 1980s. As for the diplomatic effects of the procedures, Bossuyt asserted in 1985 that "there is no doubt that a continuous review of the human rights situation in a country progressively erodes its human rights reputation at the United Nations" (Bossuyt 1985: 184).

Ratification and the special procedures: some illustrations

Treaty ratification should be expected to initiate positive change, but there may be a number of reasons for an apparent lack of consistent positive effects associated with treaty ratification, as discussed in Chapter 3 of this volume. The logic of cheap talk is one possibility. In other words, states may ratify expecting an uptick in perceptions of legitimacy (or some other symbolic benefit) but also expecting little follow-up from the international community. Ratifying states may seek to use treaty ratification as a chit to trade for "wiggle room" on further violations. Kent's study of China's engagement with the UN on human rights mentions such a strategy in passing, as employed by China in the late 1990s. China had already ratified seven conventions and one protocol in the 1980s, including CAT, with reservations (Kent 1999: 44, 44n.103). When, in 1997, China sought to avoid confrontation with the UN Human Rights Commission, it engaged in diplomatic delaying tactics that held out "the promise of future dialogue" and "the renewed possibility that China might sign the International Covenants," along with threats to limit trade with its Western partners (Kent 1999: 76–77).

Gränzer's study of Tunisia from the original PoHR volume suggests that treaty ratification may enable a state to avoid contestation with external critics and stanch domestic protest, at least for a time (Gränzer 1999: 132). Tunisia showed rhetorical commitment to human rights with its early ratification of the ICCPR, but Gränzer concludes that the move actually deprived critics of "argumentative substance" and enabled further human rights violations after some progress had been made (1999). Effects of ratification may also be complicated by differences in domestic regime type and institutional capacity, as suggested in Chapter 4 in this volume.

The options available in the UN have also depended to some degree on the political will of the international community. As noted by Bayefsky, many human rights violators have not been targeted under Resolution 1235 or 1503

(2001: 54). Dialogue under the Commission resolutions, however, can continue from year to year, depending on the mechanisms that are invoked. This means it is possible to trace the procedures' application over time to a single country. The case of Indonesia can be used as an illustration.

The case of Indonesia

The findings presented later in this chapter suggest that, on average, international attention as embodied in the Human Rights Commission procedures produced human rights gains when a country had ratified CAT, but not in the absence of treaty commitment. Indonesia was targeted under Commission procedures both before and after it ratified CAT, so the Indonesian case provides an opportunity to trace a single country's experience over time. The UN was an early critic of Indonesia, as shown in Ramcharan's (2009) rare account of discussion at the first meeting of the UN's 1503-procedure working group. He reports that Indonesia was one of eleven countries discussed at the January 1975 meeting. At that time many thousands of prisoners had been held in Indonesia for almost a decade as a result of the 1965 coup attempt against President Sukarno, followed by General Suharto's rise to power. At the meeting, the discussion exhibited the tension between countries' representations of their security concerns and concern for human rights principles. According to Ramcharan, then-member Theo van Boven of the Netherlands remarked that

> "tens of thousands of prisoners are now for eight or more years in detention. The machinery of justice is working so slowly. This is not satisfactory." The Yugoslav member ... noted: "A government is entitled to take security measures. Some of the facts complained of are admitted by Indonesia. What is worrisome is the slow pace of bringing people to the Courts. Secondly, are we sure that the wish to protect the security of the State is well-founded?" ... The Chairman ... noted, "none of us would want to deny that Indonesia ... has a right to protect its interests. We are nevertheless faced with a situation which reveals that large numbers of people have been detained for long periods of time".
>
> (Ramcharan 2009: 95)

The working group reportedly urged the Commission to call for the Indonesian government either to try detainees or to release them "where no evidence appeared to exist" (Ramcharan 2009: 96). The Commission did not carry out the working group's recommendations. Instead, the Commission "regrettably ... took an almost entirely political approach" to Indonesia and the other countries under discussion (Ramcharan 2009: 97), implying that political considerations took precedence over human rights concerns. At the end of that same year, Indonesia invaded East Timor. For many more years, Indonesia's human rights practices drew attention and criticism from the international community – on

East Timor, treatment of prisoners and dissidents, and for mass killings and other human rights abuses in the regions of Aceh and West Papua.

Indonesia rejected the UN's human rights criticisms into the mid 1980s. As noted above, from 1978 to 1981 and again from 1983 to 1985, Indonesia was considered under Resolution 1503. The country was subject to further official – now public – consideration at the Human Rights Commission under Resolution 1235 in 1993 and 1997. In between, on the other hand, resolutions naming Indonesia and East Timor were considered and rejected at the Human Rights Commission in 1994 (Weissbrodt and Mahling n.d.). This period was still a time of heavy interaction between Indonesia and the UN, however. The Special Rapporteur on Extralegal, Summary, and Arbitrary Executions made a widely publicized investigatory visit to East Timor in 1994 (Agence France Presse 1994), raising awareness of UN procedures within Indonesia.[4]

The Commission on Human Rights provided a forum for NGOs to submit critical information on Indonesian violations, as did the UN Special Committee on Decolonization, where the issue of East Timor was examined yearly in the 1980s and 1990s (Robinson 2010: 85–86). Amnesty International's annual reports in this period, for example, mention its submissions to both of these parts of the UN apparatus. At the same time, however, Indonesia joined a group of governments in the 1990s that sought to challenge the universality of human rights and weaken the Human Rights Commission (Hochstetler *et al.* 2000; Human Rights Watch 1998). In the language of the spiral model, this could be seen not just as denial, but as an attempt to undermine the prescriptive status of human rights. However, the international attention mustered in UN fora "often placed Indonesia under a most unwelcome spotlight and constituted a key form of political pressure" (Robinson 2010: 86) and, as Jetschke demonstrated in the original PoHR, Indonesia's rhetoric began to signal more openness in the 1990s (Jetschke 1999: 159–161).

Important for this chapter's analysis, Indonesia had signed CAT in 1985, but had never ratified. International criticisms of Indonesia had been sustained, but Indonesia was not following through on its stated commitments and had never made the formal commitment of ratifying CAT (or, indeed, the ICCPR). In 1997, the Commission resolution on East Timor mentioned Indonesia's "lack of progress ... towards complying with commitments undertaken in statements agreed by consensus at previous sessions of the Commission" (M2 Presswire April 17, 1997). The government proceeded with ratification of CAT in 1998, as part of an announced national human rights plan after President Suharto's forced resignation in May of that year.

The Indonesia case is consistent with the hypothesis presented below that UN criticism, as a form of monitoring, is more effective in the presence of treaty commitment. After ratification, the international community heavily monitored

----

[4] Anja Jetschke, personal communication (email, December 7, 2010).

Indonesia's human rights as part of UN involvement in the independence process for East Timor and Indonesia's transition post-Suharto. In September 1999, the Commission held a special session on East Timor (see Robinson 2010: 205–211). More pointedly, at its special session, the Commission again produced a resolution on Indonesia under the 1235 procedure. This was the first action under Resolution 1235 to take place after Indonesia had ratified CAT. It was also the first after the fall of Suharto. The resolution was followed by investigation by not one, but three, of the Commission's ongoing thematic special rapporteurs – on Torture, Extrajudicial Executions and Arbitrary Detention – as well as a UN Commission of Inquiry established by the Human Rights Commission's resolution. Amnesty International organized its own campaign on Indonesia that included visits, the mobilization of members' letters, and reports issued throughout the year (Amnesty International 2000: 131–132).

The human rights focus on Indonesia by the international community after Indonesia's CAT ratification and political transition was accompanied by some significant improvements in underlying conditions after 1998. While serious human rights problems remained, a drastic decline was apparent in the secret or incommunicado detention of political prisoners, which had facilitated torture. Although counterinsurgency continued in Aceh, greater political openness was accompanied by diminished reports of torture.[5] Reported violations in the post-1998 years included government-supported militia violence leading up to the referendum on East Timor, as well as concerns about police conduct, other repressive methods, and threats to human rights activists (Beittinger-Lee 2009: 74–75). The new government of Abdurrahman Wahid, who had a short rule from October 1999 to July 2001, did not permit the UN Commission of Inquiry access to the West Timor region on its late November 1999 visit, although it was granted access to Jakarta and East Timor (Beittinger-Lee 2009: 76). In December 1999, however, Wahid freed 196 remaining Suharto-era political prisoners. In 2000 he continued deeper structural reforms that included separating the police from the military and moves to reduce the power of the military under civilian rule and improve the independence of the judiciary (Beittinger-Lee 2009: 76–77).

As a new party to CAT, Indonesia did not submit its initial report on compliance, due in 1999, until 2001. The concluding observations filed in response by the Committee Against Torture, CAT's treaty body, noted the need for more information on implementation of the convention in practice (UN OHCHR Committee against Torture 2001). Indonesia's second periodic report, due four years later in 2005, was submitted in 2008. One of its opening statements cites the very decision to submit the report as evidence of commitment to comply with the treaty (UN OHCHR Committee against Torture 2008: 3). This statement

---

[5] Personal correspondence with Sidney Jones, Senior Advisor, International Crisis Group (email, November 16, 2010).

may indicate a point at which the government chose to emphasize commitment even though compliance was clearly inadequate, in part because of some capacity issues. Accordingly, in concluding observations on Indonesia's 2008 report, the CAT committee identified a long list of contemporaneous concerns. The treaty body described itself as "deeply concerned" five times: on mention of ongoing allegations of torture in police detention, its use in military operations, impunity, on laws that permit the public use of physical punishment, and the criminal treatment of children (UN OHCHR Committee against Torture 2008). For a second time, it asked for more statistical data on several facets of law enforcement and detention practices and on implementation of laws relevant to the implementation of the CAT.

Findings from a mission to Indonesia in 2008 by Manfred Nowak, then the UN's Special Rapporteur on Torture, also hint that limited capacity may play a role in Indonesia where some commitment exists. Nowak found that police torture of criminals was a bigger problem than governmental torture of political opponents, but some serious cases targeting opponents were still attributable to police-military operations (Jones, 2010 correspondence, cited above). And, "impunity with regard to perpetrators of torture and ill-treatment in past conflicts is almost total," according to Nowak (UN Human Rights Council 10 March 2008: 24, para. 71). Beittinger-Lee, who enumerates many ongoing problems since 1998, offers a similar "reality check" on Indonesia's post-1998 human rights situation, noting that Indonesia seemed to be "on the way toward an institutionalization and protection of human rights" in national legislation, as well as more extensive ratifications of international human rights standards, but this stabilization is qualified by remaining human rights problems, particularly in the area of human trafficking (Beittinger-Lee 2009: 74–75, 86–87).

As illustrated above, the politics of the treaty ratification and UN targeting are complicated in individual cases, and the process is neither unidirectional nor monocausal. Progress has indeed been made in Indonesia since CAT ratification, but in the context of intense monitoring. The cross-national analysis presented below suggests that treaty ratification can be considered a condition that may or may not improve behavior on its own, but may enable deeper and more meaningful exchange about human rights behavior.

Data and method

Given the many factors at play in human rights change, a statistical model potentially offers a useful tool for summary analysis. In creating the statistical model I assume that ratification and UN targeting exemplify two different kinds of discursive engagement with human rights norms. Treaty ratification is a commitment states make. Becoming the target of UN criticism does not presume a prior commitment, and it is involuntary.

Based on previous studies mentioned in Chapter 3, I hold low expectations for the effects of treaty ratification per se. On the other hand, while states might use treaties as cheap ways to be seen to be supportive of human rights, advocates and agents of intergovernmental organizations do employ treaties and other human rights standards and mechanisms – when available – as reference points for more pointed criticism and argument aimed toward encouraging compliance.

As connoted by the word "shaming," targeted criticism is an undesirable event for the state in a way that treaty ratification is not. States come under UN scrutiny as a result of complaints about their behavior. These mechanisms can fall short, yet states that care what others think try very hard to avoid such condemnation. These involuntary discursive interactions concerning a state's own record enable more pointed scrutiny. If so, one would expect targeted criticism to elicit stronger and more immediate responses from states than treaty ratification.

To analyze the effects of ratification and criticism more broadly over time, I use a dynamic panel data approach. The data cover the years 1981–2005 for 145 countries, with a maximum of twenty-three country-year observations and a minimum of one. The data and method choices are described in more detail below.

Dependent variable: human rights to physical integrity

The dependent variable is a combined measure of respect for physical integrity rights, by year, for each country. Physical integrity rights include the rights to freedom from political imprisonment, torture, disappearances and extrajudicial killing. These rights cover a somewhat narrower spectrum of rights than those included in the ICCPR, and a somewhat broader group than those covered by CAT. Two approaches to measuring a country's physical integrity rights performance are available: the Political Terror Scale (PTS; Gibney *et al.* 2008) and the physical integrity index of the Cingranelli-Richards Human Rights Dataset (CIRI; Cingranelli and Richards 2008a). Both rely on the annual reports of Amnesty International (AI) and the US State Department as sources. The PTS codes AI and State Department reports separately. CIRI relies mainly on the State Department's annual reports, using AI as a second source. Its physical integrity index sums values assigned to a country each year in each of the following four categories: torture, political imprisonment, political killings, and disappearances. CIRI's coding assigns a value to the level of violations in each category mentioned in the reports: none, occasional violations, or "widespread" violations, and the investigators note that qualitative report content is considered in addition to any numeric counts of violations that might be reported by AI or the State Department (Cingranelli and Richards 2008b). The PTS applies standards-based criteria, coding the AI and the State Department reports separately for each country per year, based on the severity of political violence as threats to physical integrity rights. CIRI and PTS differ to some degree in their coverage of countries and years. Only the observations coded in all three ways, and for which the associated control variables are available, are included in this analysis.

The dependent variable, *Human Rights*, is a composite of the two separate PTS scores (coding of each year's AI report and State Department report) and the CIRI physical integrity score. The three values are highly correlated despite the different coding approaches, suggesting that both refer to essentially the same underlying process.[6] The composite is intended to increase the dependent variable's reliability by reducing random measurement error that may be associated with the stand-alone human rights indicators. To create the composite, each of the three scores for a country-year was first transformed to a common scale from zero to one, and then the three were added. Thus, *Human Rights* has a range of 0 (worst human rights score) to 3 (best).

Independent variables

Treaty ratification

Treaty ratification serves as an indicator of a basic affirmative commitment to respect human rights.[7] Both ICCPR and CAT commit states to honor human rights pertaining to physical integrity. Like other human rights treaties, both were opened for signing and ratification some years before they entered into force by passing a threshold number of ratifiers.

The ICCPR entered into force in 1976; since the data for this study start five years later, the early ratifications are not included in the data. New parties to the ICCPR must submit a report to the Human Rights Committee the year after becoming a party to the treaty, and every five years thereafter. As of the last year analyzed (2005), 159 of 191 countries were parties to the ICCPR (United Nations n.d.).

CAT was opened for signing in 1984 and entered into force in 1987, so its early ratifications are included in the data. New parties to CAT are required to submit a report to the Committee against Torture within one year of ratification and every four years thereafter. Its commitments are more focused than those of ICCPR. As of the last year analyzed (2005), 149 countries (out of 191) were parties to CAT (United Nations n.d.).

For each treaty, a country receives a 1 in the year of ratification and thereafter, 0 otherwise.[8] To test whether the treaties have an additive effect, another

---

[6] PTS and CIRI from 1981 to 2005 are correlated with one another at between 0.7520 and 0.7951, and with *Human Rights* at between 0.9156 and 0.9341.

[7] Parties to the treaties may also commit themselves to abiding by a number of optional, stronger complaint mechanisms, but those commitments are not incorporated.

[8] States that ratified ICCPR in or before 1981, when the data begin, start with a 1 in that year for the ICCPR variable.

variable, *treaties*, was created to represent the ratification of both treaties. Its range is 0 to 2.

Targeted criticism, a form of "naming and shaming"

Targeted criticism includes consideration of the country's record under the public or confidential procedures of the Human Rights Commission. This variable is called *UN_action* in the results table. As noted, countries are named under Resolution 1235 or 1503 when serious violations are alleged. Action under Resolution 1235 or 1503 is assigned a 1 in each year, and 0 otherwise. For years in which a country is passed from private to public consideration, its *UN_action* variable is 2. The maximum value of *UN_action* in any given year is 2.

The interaction of commitment and "naming and shaming"

To explore combined effects of the two kinds of discursive engagement, I use an interaction term for treaty ratification and UN targeting, represented as (*ratification* * *UN_action*). Its possible values thus range from 0 to 2, for analysis of the single treaties, and from 0 to 4, for analysis of the two treaties together.

Conceptually, the interaction term queries ratification's conditioning effect on a government's response to targeted criticism. In other words, does a country's response to "naming and shaming" vary based on whether it has committed to one of the treaties? Although the interaction term does not distinguish whether ratification preceded or followed UN action, for the great majority of observations in which the interaction term is non-zero, ratification preceded UN targeting. Thus, in large part, a non-zero interaction term represents what happens when UN targeting occurs after the country has already ratified the treaty under investigation. Indonesia, for example, experienced targeting in 1993 and 1997 when it had not ratified ICCPR or CAT, so the interaction term has a value of 0. In 1999, when it was again the target of a Commission resolution, it had ratified CAT the year before, so its interaction term is 1 in 1999.

Lagged dependent variable and control variables

A lagged dependent variable and control variables used in other studies are also incorporated here. The control variables include level of democracy (the *Polity2* variable below [Marshall and Jaggers 2009]), international war and civil war (Diehl 2009), logged population (World Bank Group 2009), and logged per capita GDP (World Bank Group 2009). Yearly dummy variables have also been included to account for any shared effects of events specific to a particular year, as is standard practice.

Method

The analysis employs the Arellano-Bond estimator, a dynamic panel data technique developed by the econometricians Manuel Arellano and Stephen R. Bond (Arellano and Bond 1991).[9] The approach can be used to address several issues that arise in testing cross-national ratification and shaming effects. First, like other dynamic panel data techniques, it analyzes within-country variation. Second, it does not require strict exogeneity of the regressors. Norms involve intentions, arguments and reasons given by actors about prospective or past action so that, as Simmons explains (2009: 215), the factors that lead a country to ratify a human rights instrument may also affect its human rights performance. If norms set a characteristic and observable process in motion, we can expect that the process will be endogenous, requiring steps to correct for possible bias in any statistical analysis. Third, the method uses past values of the differenced independent variables as instruments for later values, which is useful when another suitable instrument is not readily available, as for a global comparison of treaty ratification and UN criticism. Use of instruments is another way to increase confidence that bias resulting from correlation of the errors has been reduced. Finally, a desirable conceptual side effect to the use of differencing is that the regression coefficients represent the influence of change in the independent variable, such as change in ratification status or in the application of UN human rights procedures.[10]

Results and interpretation

The coefficients in Table 7.1 should be interpreted as estimates of the effect of *change* in the independent variable (treaty ratification or UN targeting, or their interaction) on *change* in the dependent variable (human rights behavior). The results show an interesting interaction dynamic between treaty ratification and UN criticism. Although the coefficients for treaty ratification alone and UN criticism alone are negative, suggesting a detrimental effect in the year of ratification or criticism for those countries that only ratified or only were targeted by the UN, the coefficient for the interaction between ratification and UN criticism is positive, which suggests that criticism in the context of treaty ratification produces improvement. CAT in particular seems to provide a context within which more targeted discourse can have a positive effect. The effect is also evident if

---

[9] The approach is also known as "difference GMM," and is described in Baum (2006: 232–235).

[10] See notes to Table 7.1 for more information on technical specifications. As a further technical note, the results in Table 7.1 were compared with those produced by using the extension of the Arellano-Bond technique proposed by Roodman (2009), i.e. the *collapse* option in xtabond2, which reduces the number of instruments and is a check against over-fitting. Results were little changed.

Table 7.1. *Effects of ratification and targeted criticism on respect for human rights*
Dependent variable: human rights (0–3) (combined CIRI and PTS index)

	(1)	(2)	(3)
Treaty of interest	CAT	ICCPR	ICCPR & CAT
$y_{(t-1)}$	0.3207**	0.3548**	0.3346**
	(0.0400)	(0.0420)	(0.0415)
ICCPR		−0.0997	
		(0.0926)	
CAT	−0.2288*		
	(0.0853)		
ICCPR&CAT			−0.1307*
			(0.0685)
UN action	−0.2043*	−0.1528#	−0.1883#
	(0.0827)	(0.0942)	(0.0999)
ICCPR*UN_action		0.0830	
		(0.1097)	
CAT*UN_action	0.3112**		
	(0.1075)		
ICCPR&CAT *UN_action			0.1307#
			(0.0685)
Polity2	0.0173**	0.0174**	0.0177**
	(0.0059)	(0.0060)	(0.0060)
Population (ln)	−0.3877	−0.3519	−0.3293
	(0.3813)	(0.4222)	(0.4063)
GDP per capita (ln)	0.0291	0.0227	0.0240
	(0.0482)	(0.0462)	(0.0475)
International War	−0.0450*	−0.0557**	−0.0539*
	(0.0230)	(0.0217)	(0.0213)
Civil War	−0.0847**	−0.0961**	−0.0973**
	(0.0283)	(0.0280)	(0.0281)
Constant	7.3445	6.7919	6.1577
	(6.0376)	(6.9025)	(6.5597)
Countries in sample	145	145	145
Observations in sample	2,272	2,272	2,272
# of instruments:	250	278	290
2nd order serial corr (p-value)	0.5160	0.3660	0.4203
Sargan (p-value)†	1.0	1.0	1.0

***p* values:** **= significant at $p \le .01$; *=significant at $p \le .05$; # = significant at $p \le .1$.
Method: difference-GMM, one-step with robust standard errors; three maximum
lags for exogenous instrumented variables and dependent variable. Endogenous
variables: iccpr, cat, iccpr&cat, UN_act, $y_{(t-1)}$. Other controls: year dummies.
Coefficients omitted for year dummies. †Sargan statistic for one-step model with
robust standard errors uses corresponding two-step estimate (see Bond 2002: 151).

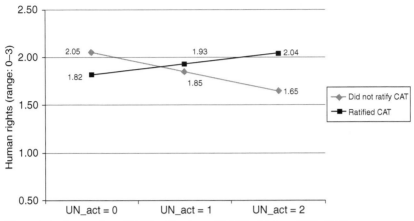

Figure 7.1 Interaction of CAT ratification with UN criticism, 1981–2005

countries have ratified both treaties. The ICCPR does not have a statistically significant effect in this model. The results are discussed in more detail below.

CAT

Table 7.1, Column 1, shows results for the Convention against Torture. Targeted criticism by the UN was associated with worsened human rights performance if the states were not parties to the treaty. A new CAT ratification, standing alone, was also associated with a worsened human rights performance. However, the most interesting result is that UN targeting resulted in statistically significant improvement when states were also parties to the CAT.

Because a coefficient for the interaction with treaty ratification is included, both the CAT ratification and the UN coefficients should be interpreted as the effect *when standing alone*. That is, the *UN_action* coefficient shows the effect of UN action if the state has not ratified CAT.[11] While the coefficients for ratification and UN action are negative, their interaction produces statistically significant, positive improvements in human rights behavior with larger coefficients (meaning a bigger effect) than those for the ICCPR model, and they are highly significant statistically. Figure 7.1 graphs the estimated effects of CAT based on the regression results. The figure suggests that targeted states' performance on average changed for the better if they had ratified CAT, but for the worse if they had not. Among the control variables, change in levels of democracy and GDP per capita were positive influences on human rights and civil war was

---

[11] See Brambor *et al.* (2006) for a helpful discussion of how to interpret the components of interaction terms.

a statistically significant negative influence. International war and population size were less strongly significant. The fact that the effect of UN action combined with ratification shows a positive effect even when controlling for democracy and the other important factors suggests that democratic transitions (as for example, Indonesia's transition that accompanied ratification) do not "wash out" the effect when considered cross-nationally, but that other factors such as civil war can be expected to limit overall positive change.

ICCPR

Table 7.1, Column 2, shows results associated with the International Covenant on Civil and Political Rights. As mentioned above, any effects on the earliest ratifiers are not included, although if any of those early ratifiers was the subject of UN human rights action in 1981 or later, its performance is included in the interaction dynamic.

Results for the ICCPR ratification, UN action, and their interaction are not nearly as clear as for the CAT model. Only the coefficient for UN action, the effect of UN targeting when the state has not ratified the ICCPR, approaches statistical significance at conventional levels. The coefficient is negative, which means that as in the CAT model, UN targeting was associated with a change for the worse for a country when it occurred in the absence of treaty ratification. While the coefficient for the treaty itself standing alone is also negative, it is not statistically significant. Neither is the combined effect of UN action and treaty ratification, although the coefficient has a positive sign. The results for the ICCPR in this model suggest, then, that on average its ratification has had neither a positive nor a negative effect, although the signs of the coefficients of interest mirror the interaction dynamic of the CAT model. The impact of changes in democracy on human rights level is still positive at a statistically significant level, and the impact of civil war is negative.

Combined influence of ratifying both treaties

To check the effect of ratifying both ICCPR and CAT, a variable with values of 0, 1, or 2, for ratifying no, one, or both treaties, is incorporated (see Column 3). The causal direction of the variables' coefficients in the model mirrors the results of Columns 1 and 2. Again, while ratification alone or UN criticism alone is associated with some degree of worsening, together they produce a positive, but not strongly statistically significant, effect. As might be expected since the results for ICCPR were not statistically significant, the coefficients in the combined model variables are smaller than those for CAT and not as statistically significant. The interaction coefficient falls only within a generous $p<0.15$ significance threshold. Control variable coefficients are similar to the other models. Given the mixed statistical significance of estimates for the ICCPR model and the treaties combined, a graph based on those estimates is not presented.

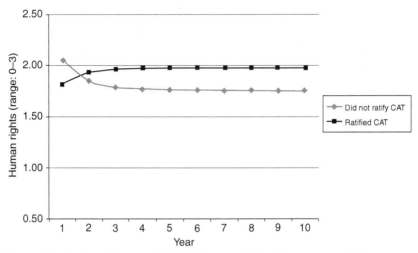

Figure 7.2 Estimated impact of UN criticism on CAT ratifiers vs. non-ratifiers, over ten years

The duration of the "naming and shaming" effect in the presence of ratification

As mentioned above, the results shown in Table 7.1 and in Figure 7.1 represent the immediate change wrought by a new ratification or shaming in a single year. Indeed, UN targeting sometimes only lasts for a year. The coefficients represent the effects of change in ratification status, in level of targeting, or in the inter-action of the two. If change does not occur, the effect will not be present. Thus, they do not suggest continued improvement for every year a country is a party to the treaty, for example, but the lagged coefficient estimates how long the impact lasts over time.

For a common sense understanding of the dynamic most strongly demon-strated for CAT, Figure 7.2 allows us to compare the duration of the first year's effects when a ratifier or non-ratifier is "named and shamed." The coefficient of the lagged dependent variable for the CAT model, at 0.3207, tells us that the effects of the specified dynamic persist at a rate of about 32 percent. As Figure 7.2 shows, based on these results, CAT ratifiers' human rights level would be predicted to rise and stabilize over time when a country has been targeted, while non-ratifiers' human rights would be projected to deteriorate further with time before stabilizing at a lower level, other things being equal.

Conclusion

The act of ratification, on its own, was associated with either no change in human rights (for the ICCPR), or a slight worsening of human rights (for CAT, or for the two treaties combined) in ratifying countries. Similarly, shaming, on its own, was always associated in this model with a slight worsening of human rights in the targeted country. The Indonesia illustration is one more example of the fact that human rights criticism, even when sustained over a long period, is an uphill battle. As noted, the negative or inconclusive solo effects of ratification shown in this model echo what other scholars have found when a simple ratification effect is tested.

If ratification and UN targeting together were confirmed as meaningless or wholly detrimental, we might have to rethink the importance of treaties to the strategies of human rights activists and international legal advocates. But in combination, CAT ratification and targeted criticism produced improvement. Notably, the results apply to human rights performance in some of the most difficult cases – those targeted by the UN for severe patterns of violations. The estimates in the model are drawn from all cases, not just cases where states are democracies or in transition to democracy, and the effect persists when controlling for changes in democracy.[12]

States have differing rationales for treaty ratification and some effects of ratification may not be observable (Simmons 2009). A related problem may be that our data are not responsive enough to assess some human rights changes (Clark and Sikkink forthcoming), or to assess what we think is beneficial in a human rights treaty. And, as Simmons discusses in this volume, paying attention to the mechanisms and conditions associated with ratification permits more nuanced conclusions. Although this chapter does not separate ratifiers based on conditions of governance, the interaction term separates targeted states based on whether they have ratified, and thus allows us to pay attention to conditions that form the discursive background for UN attention. Even with imperfect data, the present analysis suggests that, with CAT ratification as a backdrop, the international human rights regime matters in a positive way when it focuses on difficult cases. The results also suggest that, if there is little cost to having ratified – that is, no focus on holding states to account for their norm acknowledgment – improvement is less likely.

The causes of the dip in human rights performance upon ratification of CAT deserve more attention than is possible here, but the results may lend support to the idea that talk is initially cheap.[13] Alternately, the dip may be consistent with

---

[12] In a minority of cases in the sample, treaty ratification took place in a year when a country was also experiencing UN criticism. In these cases, the model would similarly predict improvement.

[13] It has been suggested that human rights reporting may become more stringent after countries ratify, producing an association between ratification and poorer performance in the data, but in a provisional study to check their results, Hafner-Burton and Tsutsui (2005: 1401) found no evidence of an information effect associated directly with treaty ratification. Clark and Sikkink (forthcoming) explore other kinds of information effects that may make it more difficult to assess human rights improvement over time.

a "crowding-out" effect (Goodman and Jinks 2008). In other words, a negative impact could be engendered by external human rights regulation if state officials substitute the act of ratification for the application of human rights remedies. A possible "substitution" of ratification reporting for substantive action was illustrated above by Indonesia's 2008 statement about having made its periodic report submission to CAT as an act of compliance (UN OHCHR Committee against Torture 2008).

The results validate the advocacy approach of applying pressure with reference to states' expressed human rights commitments. Criticism appears more likely to generate improvement when treaty ratification has occurred. Ratification seems to set up an important safety net that matters when the UN attempts to act on cases of severe human rights abuse.

The question why CAT shows such dramatic results deserves attention in future research. From a practitioner perspective, the observed effect of CAT is consistent with Rodley's observations that treaty monitoring is best complemented by other UN procedures (Rodley 2003). The difference between the effects of CAT and ICCPR may be explained partly by the fact that Committee against Torture, CAT's monitoring body, has been more focused and interactive than the ICCPR's monitoring body in cooperating with other special procedures for informal follow-up and information exchange, particularly with the UN's Special Rapporteur on Torture (Rodley 2003). Such collaboration might also counteract a crowding-out effect, if a ratifying state like Indonesia begins to interpret its obligations differently once it is scrutinized. In light of existing research it seems possible that, since ICCPR's commitments are more wide ranging and extend beyond physical integrity rights, this chapter's analysis may not capture some effects more germane to ICCPR (see Simmons 2009 and Chapter 3, this volume; Landman 2005a).

This chapter has employed the working assumption that treaty ratification and criticism of human rights behavior form part of the talk, whether cheap or costly, associated with states' human rights performance. Ratification opens a door for outsiders' efforts at criticism, making it more difficult for a state to deny the relevance of human rights norms and fostering background conditions within which other kinds of international diplomatic discourse may be more effective. This is observed most dramatically with regard to the Convention against Torture. Formal human rights commitments, by setting up a tension between compliance and commitment, enable international actors to promote human rights change more effectively.

8

The United States and torture: does the spiral model work?

KATHRYN SIKKINK

Scholars of international relations have long said that the real test of international law and new norms is their ability to influence the actions of even the most powerful states. Thus, no discussion of compliance with human rights law would be complete without a consideration of the case of the United States. In particular, I will focus on US non-compliance with the prohibition on torture and cruel and degrading treatment during the administration of George W. Bush. Did domestic and international human rights pressures have any influence on this case? In particular, in the chapter, I explore whether the "spiral model" description and explanation of human rights change in our study *The Power of Human Rights* (PoHR) is useful to understand the US move from non-compliance to greater compliance with the prohibition on torture.

At first glance, the US case would appear to confirm realist expectations that powerful states are able to disregard international rules at will without significant cost. When carefully examined, however, the US case offers a more complex but not necessarily a more optimistic story. US policy-makers were in fact intensely aware of domestic and international pressures, and in particular, the possibility of domestic prosecution under US statutes implementing international human rights law; many of their actions, including the infamous torture memos, were partially driven by this awareness. But such awareness did not lead to greater compliance until after the Bush administration left office.

The US case shows a possibility we did not consider in PoHR: that a country which had already ratified and implemented international treaties on a core human rights norm could nevertheless have a profound backlash and reversal of these commitments, even when they are deeply embedded in both international law and domestic law. The United States, having previously moved well into what we called stage four, or prescriptive status, with regard to torture, veered backwards to engage in repression, denial and backlash. Although US practices of torture and cruel, inhuman and degrading treatment were not as widespread as those used currently in Syria or in Egypt during the Mubarak

This chapter draws extensively on material from chapter seven of Sikkink (2011).

regime, they are extremely important for their human and political effects because they were carried out by a powerful democratic state with great influence on other states. In addition, the US policy of "extraordinary renditions," that is, the illegal kidnapping and transfer of suspects to other regimes, sent individuals to countries including Syria and Egypt, where torture was known to be widespread, with the express purpose of allowing these governments to interrogate them.[1]

Second, even relatively forceful pressure campaigns against these human rights violations by both domestic and international actors were mainly ineffective as long as the Bush administration was in office because it felt no moral vulnerability to the pressures. The Bush administration didn't feel morally vulnerable in large part because it used a compelling counter-norm, that of anti-terrorism, to justify the use of torture and trump the legal prohibitions on the practice. This anti-terrorism counter-norm was accepted by large parts of the US population and by some US allies abroad, lessening both domestic and international pressures for change. A powerful country like the United States has little material vulnerability to international pressures, so the combined lack of moral and material vulnerability meant that it was necessary for the Bush administration to be voted out of office before any enduring policy change could occur.

The anti-terrorism norm was not a "new norm," indeed it was present historically in the discourses of many governments including the United Kingdom in its struggle against the IRA, or authoritarian regimes in Argentina or South Africa who confronted armed opposition groups they labeled as terrorists. Like these other governments did previously, the US government justified the use of extraordinary policies, including torture, as a means of combating terrorism. In the context of this compelling anti-terrorism norm, even the threat of human rights prosecution did not have the effect of changing policy. The fear of legal punishment only led the Bush administration to attempt to find legal justifications or legal protections from prosecutions, rather than make good faith efforts at compliance. In the longer term, it is possible that the scale of the human rights violations and the high-level legal justifications paradoxically left a paper trail that will make some accountability possible in the future. I briefly consider the case of the conviction in absentia of CIA agents in Italy for kidnapping to illustrate that even the United States is not above the reach of the system of international human rights law that it helped create.

---

[1] Egypt was the most common destination for the CIA's extraordinary renditions, but the CIA transferred Maher Arar, a Canadian citizen, from Kennedy Airport in New York City to Syria on September 26, 2002 where he was incarcerated and tortured before being released without charges in 2003. See Mayer (2008: 115, 130–133).

Commitment to the prohibition against torture

The United States has ratified fewer human rights treaties than other comparable countries, but it did ratify a number of treaties that impose international legal obligations never to use torture and inhuman and degrading treatment under any circumstances, including the Geneva Conventions of 1949, the International Covenant on Civil and Political Rights, and the Convention against Torture and Other Cruel, Inhuman or Degrading Treatment or Punishment (CAT). The United States was deeply involved in drafting these treaties, and worked to make the prohibition on torture and cruel and degrading treatment more precise and enforceable. The Geneva Conventions of 1949 prohibit the use of torture of individuals detained in both international conflict *and* conflict of a non-international nature. During the drafting of CAT, the US delegation worked to make the treaty more precise and clearly supported treaty provisions on universal jurisdiction with regard to torture (Burgers and Danelius 1988). The administration of George H. Bush submitted the treaty to the Senate in 1990 and supported ratification, and a bipartisan coalition in the Senate worked to ensure that the Senate gave its advice and consent for ratification in 1994.

Increasingly, US jurists argue that international human rights treaties are not "self-enforcing" and thus must be implemented in domestic law in order to have effect in US courts. The Geneva Conventions were implemented in domestic legislation in 1996, when overwhelming majorities in the Congress passed the War Crimes Act, which makes it a criminal offense to commit grave breaches of the 1949 Geneva Conventions, including torture and cruel and degrading treatment. Congress passed the law mainly so that the United States could prosecute war criminals from other countries, especially the North Vietnamese, who had tortured US soldiers during the Vietnam War. The Pentagon recommended at the time that the legislation include breaches of humanitarian law by US soldiers as well, because it believed that the United States generally followed the Geneva Conventions and this would set a high standard for others to follow (Smith 2006).

After the Senate had ratified the CAT, in 1994 Congress also enacted a new federal anti-torture statute to implement the requirements of the Convention (*18 USC. § 2340 et seq*). It makes torture a felony and permits the criminal prosecution of alleged torturers in federal courts in specified circumstances. A person found guilty under the act can be incarcerated for up to 20 years or receive the death penalty if the torture results in the victim's death. Thus, using the categories of the spiral model, we could say that by 1998, the prohibition on torture had acquired at least prescriptive status, and was firmly embodied in US treaty commitments and in domestic law implementing those treaty commitments. Bush administration neoconservatives distrusted international law and institutions and believed that the United States as the sole superpower was not subject to international rules, but they were nonetheless particularly concerned about the possibilities of prosecution under these two statutes.

The spiral model and the United States: compliance with the prohibition on torture and cruel, inhuman and degrading treatment

The spiral model calls attention both to what actors do (rule-consistent behavior) but also what they say (prescriptive status means that actors regularly referred to the norm to describe and comment on their own behavior and that of others). What has made US practice on torture so unsettling was not only that the behavior violated the norm, but that state officials explicitly denied previously accepted norms against torture.

This explicit quality of non-compliance with the prohibition on torture is one way that US practices during the Bush administration diverged from past US practice. While there is evidence that the US condoned torture in US training programs in the past, prior to 2003, high-level policy-makers did not explicitly justify practices that can be considered torture and cruel, inhuman and degrading treatment. In the past US officials offered green lights for torture and repression, which were understood as such, for example, by the Argentine and Chilean military (Sikkink 2004). The Bush administration went beyond such green lights for repression and offered explicit justification for non-compliance with the prohibition on torture to our own military and intelligence agencies. Their memos made it clear that they no longer believed in the prescriptive status of the norm. Rather, they argued that the new context of the war on terror made such norms obsolete. The US government never actually said that it was going to torture or engage in cruel or degrading treatment. But its rhetorical positions were so extreme that they went well beyond attempts to reinterpret the norm, and can only be understood as a rejection of the norm itself. For example, on January 25, 2002, White House Counsel Alberto Gonzales sent a memo to President Bush where he argued that the Geneva Convention should not be applied to the conflict in Afghanistan in part because the new "paradigm" of the war on terror "renders obsolete Geneva's strict limitations on questioning of enemy prisoners" (Danner 2004: 84). In later memos on torture, the definitions of torture given departed so radically from past practice and interpretations of the United States as well as most other states that they can only be seen as efforts to undermine the norm, not to modify it. The loss of prescriptive status in turn fueled more widespread use of torture and cruel and degrading treatment directly by US troops and personnel. In these circumstances, what impact did domestic and international actions and pressures have on contributing to a change in US policy?

Phase 1: repression

According to the spiral model, the first phase is the appearance of repression and the activation of the network. Although the main pressure on the United States began after the publication of the photos of Abu Ghraib prison in April of 2004, the use of torture (and the justifications for the use of torture) began well before that. I will not have the space here to substantially document my claim that the United States was in violation of the prohibition on torture and inhuman treatment. I refer the reader to the large body of official reports and secondary literature that document the practices.[2] The International Committee of the Red Cross (ICRC), after visiting detention facilities in Guantanamo in June 2004, said its investigators found what it called "an intentional system of cruel, unusual and degrading treatment and a form of torture" (Lewis 2004). Reports by FBI agents also revealed ongoing use of practices that the FBI deems unacceptable, such as keeping detainees chained in uncomfortable positions for up to twenty-four hours (Zernike 2004).

By 2004, the Defense Department had identified twenty-six specific cases where detainees had died in US custody and fourteen cases where the cause of death was not "natural." These figures are supported by documents, including autopsy reports, that the Defense Department has made public (Jaffer and Singh 2007: 29). However, the US government still has not permitted a full independent investigation to establish the exact circumstances surrounding these deaths and responsibility for them. Journalists and human rights organizations have documented that in many cases these individuals died as a result of torture.[3]

There are still debates about exactly which techniques constitute torture and which constitute inhuman and degrading treatment and about what the Geneva Conventions mean when they refer to humane treatment. But I believe it has been established without doubt that the United States was not in compliance with its international and domestic legal obligations to refrain from torture and to treat detainees humanely from at least 2002 to 2008.[4]

Before 9/11 the human rights network itself was already engaged in work on the issue of human rights violations in the United States. Nevertheless, US violations of human rights in the wake of the 9/11 attacks led to a dramatic increase in the activities of the transnational human rights networks with regard to the United States. Traditional international human rights groups formed coalitions with the civil liberties groups such as the American Civil Liberties Union (ACLU) or the scores of immigration law activists, to carry forward their work.

---

[2] See "Article 15–6 Investigation of the 800th Military Police Brigade" (The Taguba Report); "Final Report of the Independent Panel to 'Review DOD Detention Operations'" (The Schlesinger Report) August 2004; "AR 15–6 Investigation of the Abu Ghraib Prison and 205th Military Intelligence Brigade," LTG Anthony R. Jones, "AR 15–6 Investigation of the Abu Ghraib Detention Facility and 205th Military Intelligence Brigade, MG George R. Fay," "Report of the International Committee of the Red Cross (ICRC) on the Treatment by the Coalition Forces of Prisoners of War and Other Protected Persons by the Geneva Convention in Iraq During Arrest, Internment and Interrogation," February 2004. All of these reports are available in the appendices to Danner (2004).

[3] For example, see Mayer (2008: 148, 224–225, 238); Horton (2010).

[4] In particular, I would argue that a case could be made that the United States violated obligations under articles 2, 3, 7, 11, 13, 14, 15, and 16 of the Torture Convention.

After the release of the Abu Ghraib photos, these networks and organizations turned their spotlight on US practices more than they ever had in the past. They did not organize major demonstrations in the streets, but mainly used information politics and lobbying to bring issues to the attention of the media and policy elites in attempts to persuade and change policy. So, for example, when some retired military lawyers became increasingly disenchanted with the Bush administration policy on interrogations and the laws of war, they collaborated with US human rights organizations on some joint activities.

Phase 2: denial

In PoHR, we found that virtually all countries initially resist and reject international and domestic criticism and pressures for change in their human rights violations. The United States clearly passed through such a denial and backlash phase. But the US case is different because it involves deep backlash and denial in a country that had already progressed well into a prescriptive status and rule-consistent behavior stage. The backlash after 2001 shows that the earlier commitment to the anti-torture norm was superficial and not internalized by many elites or by the general public. In addition, Bush administration officials used the anti-terrorism norm to trump the prior commitment against torture. In this context domestic and international pressures, including demands for prosecution, did not lead to compliance but only to a series of legal and political maneuvers to try to protect officials from prosecution.

As part of the process of denial, the Bush administration made three main arguments that were developed in a series of legal memos and reports prepared by the Department of Justice and the Defense Department between August 2002 and September 2003. Some of these arguments were also echoed in public statements. The *first* was the argument that the Geneva Conventions did not apply to the conflict in Afghanistan, and thus the detainees from that conflict would not be considered prisoners of war, but rather illegal combatants. This decision is problematic with regard to the laws of war, but it carried with it implications that opened the door to torture. The Geneva Conventions absolutely protect any detainee from torture, whether in international conflicts or conflicts of a non-international nature. Thus, a decision that the Geneva Conventions don't apply to a conflict was understood by some as implying that torture is therefore permitted.

The *second* argument was about the definition of torture: the Bush administration made strenuous efforts to reinterpret the definitions of torture and to redefine its obligations under the Geneva Conventions and the Torture Convention so that the United States could use the interrogation techniques it wanted. The Bybee memorandum of August 1, 2002, attempted to use a definition of torture that is outside the standard definition as used in the Torture Convention and in common parlance. First, it suggests that "physical pain amounting to torture must be the equivalent in intensity to the pain accompanying serious physical injury, such as organ failure, impairment of body function, or even death." Nowhere in the history of the drafting of the Torture Convention or in US legislation implementing the Convention does the idea appear that to be counted as torture, the pain must be equivalent to death or organ failure. Second, the Bybee memorandum says that in order to qualify for the definition of torture, "the infliction of such pain must be the defendant's precise objective" (US Department of Justice 2002). The memorandum attempts to create such a narrow definition of torture that only the sadist (i.e. – for whom pain is the "precise objective") that engages in a practice resulting in pain equivalent to death or organ failure is a torturer. In other words, the memo creates an absurd and unsustainable definition, a definition contrary to the language of the law and common sense.

The *third argument* relied on a controversial constitutional position about the president's role as commander in chief of the armed forces to argue that the president had the authority to supersede international and domestic law and to authorize torture. This runs contrary to the plain language of the treaty, which says that "No exceptional circumstances whatsoever, whether a state of war or a threat of war, internal political instability or any other public emergency, may be invoked as a justification of torture," and "An order from a superior officer or public authority may not be invoked as a justification for torture."

But at the same time as it was engaged in denial and backlash, Bush administration officials also showed awareness that the policies they were undertaking were illegal and that they could open state officials to the possibility of prosecutions. For example, in March of 2002, just a few months after Coalition forces occupied Afghanistan, CIA lawyers made a request to the Justice Department for something called an "advance declination" or what we might call an anticipatory "immunity" or "pardon" for interrogation practices (Sifton 2010a). The Department of Justice criminal division refused to sign any advance declinations on policy grounds; there was simply no precedent for such an action. But the fact that the CIA requested one tells us something about the state of mind in the CIA in early 2002. It contradicts Bush administration officials who assert that they believed that what they were doing was legal and instead suggests that from the beginning they sought legal tools to protect the CIA and other state officials from prosecution for acts they understood potentially to provoke criminal liability.

The failure to secure advance criminal immunity for interrogations made it more important to members of the Bush administration that the so-called torture memos also provide arguments that would make prosecution for torture more difficult. So, for example, by arguing that the Geneva Conventions didn't apply to the war on terror, the Bush administration also intended to make domestic prosecutions for torture less likely. The US War Crimes Statute of 1996 specifically criminalized under US law grave breaches of the Geneva Conventions.

One of the first confidential memos, dated January 25, 2002, cited the threat of prosecution as a reason to declare that detainees captured in Afghanistan were not eligible for Geneva Conventions protections. If the detainees were not covered by the Geneva Conventions, the memo implied but did not say, then torturing them would not be a grave breach of the Conventions, and thus the US War Crimes Statute would not apply and could not be used to prosecute US officials (Smith 2006). The memos were a direct response to requests from the CIA to get guidance about the limits to interrogation, as a form of legal cover for actions for which they knew they could be prosecuted. Similar demands for legal cover came from the US military. A commander at Guantánamo completed a twelve-page request for permission for more aggressive forms of interrogation including waterboarding. His lawyer wrote that members of the armed forces who used these techniques could be committing crimes under the Uniform Code of Military Justice, but that this might be solved with high-level legal permission or immunity (Gellman 2008: 176–180).

In the US case, the terms "denial and backlash" are too simple to characterize what was actually going on within the Bush administration. They were simultaneously engaged in denial and backlash, at the same time as they were crafting preventative strategies to protect US officials from human rights prosecutions. Thus denial and backlash are revealed to be in large part strategic maneuvers rather than firm statements of beliefs. This is probably also the case in many of the authoritarian regimes we studied in PoHR, but in the US case, the availability of extensive leaked memos and well researched books has the advantage of revealing more completely the inner workings of the government.

A second way in which denial and backlash may be too simple a characterization, is that from the very beginning of the policy, there were serious divisions within the Bush administration itself: particularly within the armed forces and between the State Department and the Defense Department. There was also eventually opposition between the Executive Branch and the Congress, including key Republicans in the Congress, and between the Executive Branch and parts of the Judicial Branch.

For example, opposition to the decision that the Geneva Conventions didn't apply in Afghanistan surfaced early within the Bush administration. One day after the memorandum by Gonzales recommending that the administration not apply POW status under the Geneva Conventions to captured Al Qaeda or Taliban fighters, Secretary of State Colin Powell wrote to Gonzales urging in the strongest terms that the policy be reconsidered. And in a memo dated January 11, 2002, State Department Legal Counsel, William Taft IV wrote that "if the US took the war on terrorism outside the Geneva Conventions, not only could US soldiers be denied the protections of the Conventions – and therefore be prosecuted for crimes, including murder – but President Bush could be accused of a 'grave breach' by other countries, and prosecuted for war crimes" (Mayer 2005: 82).

Some retired military generals and admirals were so concerned about the positions taken by Gonzales that they wrote an open letter to the Judiciary Committee considering the nomination of Gonzales for Attorney General (Brahms 2005). Individuals associated with the military accused members of the Bush administration of "endangering troops," "undermining the war effort," "encouraging reprisals," or "lowering morale," not to mention "losing the high moral ground." Military and FBI officials not only disagreed with Bush administration insiders about the legality of torture but also about the *effectiveness* of torture. The entire Bush administration strategy was premised on the idea that torture is a necessary and effective tool in the war against terrorism. Investigative journalist Jane Mayer argued that "the fiercest internal resistance to this thinking has come from people who have been directly involved in interrogation, including veteran F.B.I. and C.I.A. agents. Their concerns are practical as well as ideological. Years of experience in interrogation have led them to doubt the effectiveness of physical coercion as a means of extracting reliable information" (Mayer 2005: 108). The FBI complaints about harsh interrogation practices began in December 2002, according to released internal documents. In late 2003, an agent complained that "these tactics have produced no intelligence of threat neutralization nature to date" (FBI Criminal Justice Information Services 2003).

Phase 3: tactical concessions

In PoHR, we argued that if both external and internal pressures continue, however, most countries move beyond the denial phase to another phase that we called "tactical concessions." In this phase, the norm-violating state seeks cosmetic changes to pacify domestic and international criticism. Only with substantial continued pressure, and only if states are vulnerable in some shape or form, do we see actual behavioral change in the norm-violating state. A powerful and wealthy state like the United States is clearly less vulnerable than many other countries we have studied. Thus we would expect that human rights pressures might work more slowly and less effectively in the case of a hegemon. Nevertheless, such change is not impossible, and there are historical cases where the United States has been vulnerable to human rights pressures.

Because of the ongoing pressure the Bush administration faced and because of internal divisions, the Bush administration eventually moved in some areas from complete denial to the phase of tactical concessions. These early tactical concessions were the result of opposition to US executive policy, primarily from within the executive branch itself, as well as some opposition from Congress.

Bush had nominated White House Legal Counsel Alberto Gonzales for the position of Attorney General. But because Gonzales had solicited and approved some of the torture memos, he faced the possibility of controversy in his confirmation hearings. So, just before the hearings, in a memo prepared explicitly for public consumption, the Bush administration stated for the first time, "Torture is abhorrent both to American Law and values and to international norms" (US Department of Justice 2004).

In this sense, the first "tactical concession" of the Bush administration was to make a clearer principled condemnation of torture, and to recognize international norms on the issue. The Justice Department memo of December 30, 2004 "withdraws" and supersedes the August 2002 torture memorandum and modifies important aspects of its legal analysis, including the controversial definition of torture. Although the new memo does not reject the president's authority to order torture, it says it is "unnecessary" to consider that issue because it would be "inconsistent with the President's unequivocal directive that US personnel not engage in torture" (US Department of Justice 2004).

This memo is still problematic for a number of reasons, including because it continues to ignore the legal obligation of the United States not to engage in torture under any conditions. Nevertheless, this new memo on torture was a recognition that the administration had not been able to unilaterally redefine torture. The definitional attempts had been costly, or were going to be costly to the confirmation of the Attorney General, and thus some had to be put to rest. As Retired Rear Admiral John Hutson recognized during the Gonzalez hearing, the Justice Department memo was not an exoneration of Judge Gonzales, but an indictment. "It's an acknowledgment of error."

Hutson isn't the only individual to see the December 30, 2004 Justice Department memo as a retraction of earlier policy. A *New York Times* article on February 16, 2005, reported that CIA lawyers were "furious" about the Justice Department decision to repudiate its earlier policy on torture, because "the CIA might be left to bear sole responsibility and the brunt of criticism for the use of harsh techniques." Because in their recent testimony Gonzales and other high-level administration officials have started sidestepping responsibility for interrogation policies, the CIA is worried that it will be left "holding the bag" (Jehl 2005).

The Bush administration fought against making more substantial changes. One high-profile challenge to the Bush administration policy on torture was an amendment to the defense bill, the Detainee Treatment Act sponsored by Senator John McCain to ban cruel, inhuman or degrading treatment of prisoners. The White House fought bitterly against the legislation, and at one point Bush threatened to veto it when it arrived on his desk, which would have been the first veto of his presidency. The Senate nevertheless passed the bill by a margin of 90–9. While this development could be seen as a significant defeat for the White House's interrogation policy, the White House continued to fight aggressively to defend its interrogation policy. The White House sought to exclude the CIA from complying with the anti-torture legislation (Schmitt 2005). And the final compromise version of the bill included White House language offering explicit legislative legal protections from prosecution for US personnel who engaged in interrogations.[5] This little noticed legislative language will make prosecutions for torture much more difficult in US courts because there is statutory law saying that as long as US government officials thought they were acting according to the law they can't be convicted (Sifton 2010b).

The most serious opposition to the Bush policy came from the US Supreme Court. In a series of path-breaking decisions, the Supreme Court upheld the rights of detainees to humane treatment and to the protections offered by the rule of law, both domestic and international. In June 2006, in the case *Hamdan* v. *Rumsfeld*, the Supreme Court gave a major rebuke to the Bush administration policy and legal interpretations. The Court ruled that the military commission system set up to try accused war criminals in Guantánamo Bay violated both US laws and the Geneva Conventions. In what is now considered a landmark decision about the limits of executive power, the Court said that even during war, the president must comply not only with US laws as established by Congress but also with international law (*Hamdan* v. *Rumsfeld* 2006). The Court directly contradicted the legal theories put forward by President Bush's legal advisors that the president has broad discretion to make decisions on war-related issues, which in turn they used to claim the president could authorize torture. In this sense, although *Hamdan* did not directly address torture, it addressed the legal claims in two central ways. First, it determined that the Geneva Conventions applied to detainees in Guantánamo and, second, it undermined the claim of exclusive executive authority upon which the torture arguments had been based.

After the *Hamdan* ruling, once again, the administration didn't respond by changing its interrogation policy, but by further ramping up its efforts to provide an iron-clad legal protection from prosecution. Bush administration officials pressed Congress to pass the Military Commissions Act of 2006, which strengthened the protection against prosecution already included in the Detainee Treatment Act.

In early 2006, the administration continued to hold firmly to its interrogation policy, and to resist pressures from the Senate, the Supreme Court and civil society. International pressure had also been building and it presented an inconvenience, at a minimum, to the fulfillment of other Bush administration policy goals. A *Washington Post* article in November 2005 that the CIA was holding detainees in secret prisons in Eastern Europe led to an uproar in Europe and to an investigation by the EU of secret detention centers in Europe and cooperation of European governments with the US policy of extraordinary rendition. Despite such criticisms, Condoleezza Rice, traveling in Europe in December 2005, maintained a tone of denial, by chastising European leaders for their criticisms and claiming that interrogation of these suspects helped "save European lives" (Brinkley 2005). Rice simultaneously argued that "at no time did the US agree to inhumane acts or torture," and continued to state that "terrorists are not covered by the Geneva Conventions" (Bernstein 2005: 22). It is hard to see how

---

[5] Section 1004(b) of the Detainee Treatment Act of 2005 (42 USC. 2000dd–1(b)).

this position represents even a move beyond denial into tactical concessions. It is important to note that, just as Rice does in the quote above, administration officials usually combined denial with invocations of the anti-terrorism norm.

In February 2006, a UN appointed independent panel released a report calling on the United States to close the prison in Guantánamo, where it claimed that US personnel engaged in torture, detained people arbitrarily and denied fair trials. In May 2006, the UN Committee against Torture criticized US policy and urged the United States to close down the Guantánamo Bay prison and to end the use of secret overseas detention centers. The United States was not totally indifferent to this body, as witnessed by the size of its twenty-six-member delegation to the meeting, and the size of its 185-page supplemental report. Human Rights First International Legal Director, Gabor Rona, observing the meeting noted that this "suggests a return from the brink of international disengagement," but also noted that the US government "did not move away from its most criticized positions" (UN Convention Against Torture Observations 2006).

In sum, during the Bush administration, the US policy response stayed in the range of denial and tactical concessions on some, but not all, issues regarding torture, despite a significant increase in international and domestic pressures.

Stage 4: prescriptive status

It is at this point that the fit of the spiral model with the case of US torture breaks down. The spiral model predicts that if international and domestic pressures continue, the target government will often ratify the respective international human rights conventions, or institutionalize the relevant human rights norms in the constitution or in domestic law. But in the case of torture and the United States, the norm lost prescriptive status and did not regain it until after the Bush administration left office. "Lost" may be too passive a verb here. The Bush administration engaged in active, strategic and costly efforts to deconstruct the norm, as well as to protect its officials from the possibility of punishment for breaking the law. The Bush administration *actively undermined* the prescriptive status of the norm, and so, for this period, we have to say that the norm did not have prescriptive status for top US policy-makers in the Bush administration, a fact that profoundly influenced US behavior as well as behavior in other countries.

The situation in the Bush administration stalled at the stage of "tactical concessions" because initially the worldview of the neoconservatives in the Bush administration was confirmed. There were apparently few domestic or international political costs to their violations of domestic and international law. The large negative publicity in the release of the Abu Ghraib photos was not sufficient to end the practices. The American public did not demand more accountability for the use of torture. Despite the fact that the graphic revelations of torture came in an election year, torture did not become a campaign issue in any of the elections that followed in 2004, 2006 or in 2008.

Not only was the administration not deterred by domestic and international criticism of its practices, but it promoted many of the individuals most associated with non-compliance of the prohibition on torture. Mr. Bybee, whose name was on the first controversial "torture" memo (although it was actually written by John Yoo), was named to the Ninth Circuit Court of Appeals. White House Legal Counsel Alberto Gonzales, who solicited and approved the memos, was nominated and confirmed for the Attorney General. John C. Yoo said that President Bush's victory in the 2004 election, along with the lack of strong opposition to the Gonzales confirmation, was "proof that the debate is over." He claimed, "The issue is dying out. The public has had its referendum" (Mayer 2005: 82).

But, contrary to Yoo's prediction, the issue did not die out. The secret legal memos generated fierce opposition within the administration. When this opposition did not lead the government to make a significant change in policy, insiders leaked the memos to the press in order to keep pressure on the government to change its policy. Once the memos became public, they generated controversy and provided detailed information that fed the opposition to Bush administration policy.

Domestic and international pressures continued. One key form of pressure focused on prosecutions for torture and extraordinary rendition, often using as evidence the voluminous US documents, either those leaked to the press, or released as a result of Freedom of Information Act (FOIA) requests in the context of prosecutions. Because of the Bush administration's disdain for international law, and its belief that anti-terrorism policy required harsh interrogations, it was not open to persuasion on these issues. Thus, opponents hoped that the threat of material sanctions through prosecutions would make more of an impact.

Foreign prosecutions

In November 2009, a trial in Italy resulted in convictions of twenty-three Americans and two Italians for kidnapping an Egyptian terror suspect off the streets of Milan and sending him back to Egypt where he was tortured. An Italian judge decided that what the US government called "extraordinary rendition" fit the Italian criminal code definition of "kidnapping." Milan prosecutor Armando Spataro was the man behind the first major legal blow to the CIA's extraordinary rendition program. The victim in this case, Nasr Osama Mostafa Hassan, or Abu Omar, as he was called, was an Egyptian refugee who was already a terrorism suspect in a case carefully followed by the Milan prosecutor's office. Indeed, the reason that Spataro's office knew immediately that Abu Omar had been kidnapped was that they were tapping his phone as part of their own terrorism investigation. The prosecutor's office launched an investigation. They did not initially know about the role of the CIA, but they suspected that the Italian Secret Service was involved in some way in the kidnapping. It took years for the prosecutor's office to put the case together, using cell phone records, email messages, hotel reservations, car rentals, and other information that the CIA agents left in a relatively clear trail (Spataro, personal interview, 2008).

All of the convicted Americans are believed to be CIA agents, but Spataro was not even certain if, in all cases, they had the real names of the agents, who used assumed names as part of their covert activities in Italy. The Americans were put on trial in absentia, a type of criminal trial permitted by the Italian judicial system but not permitted in the United States. They were tried in absentia because the Italian government refused or ignored the prosecutor's extradition requests, but even if the Italian government had issued an extradition request, the United States would not have extradited the officials to stand trial abroad. It is quite possible that none of the convicted Americans will go to prison. Even if they don't serve out their sentence in prison, the process of prosecution in this case constitutes a significant form of punishment. At a minimum, these officials will have to be very careful about all travel, especially in or through Europe, since, as a former CIA official said, "the convicted spies would probably face the threat of arrest anywhere outside the US for the rest of their lives" (Donadio 2009). Second, we presume the prosecution has dramatically complicated the careers of the CIA officers. It is difficult to be an undercover agent when you have been the subject of a very public prosecution and you can't easily travel abroad. A number of the accused and convicted officials have since retired from the CIA.

Other foreign human rights prosecutions against US officials for torture have been presented, including cases against Donald Rumsfeld for torture in France and Germany, but they have not yet prospered. A US group, the Center for Constitutional Rights, and its German ally, the European Center for Constitutional and Human Rights, filed the complaints in Germany under a special law Germany enacted to bring it into compliance with the Rome Statute of the International Criminal Court (ICC). The law provides for universal jurisdiction for war crimes, crimes of genocide and crimes against humanity, allowing the German Federal Prosecutor to investigate and prosecute such crimes irrespective of the location or nationality of the defendant or plaintiff. In the first ruling in the German case, the judge determined that it was first up to the United States to investigate the issue, and that the plaintiffs had not exhausted their remedies there. When the United States failed to act, the plaintiffs filed a motion for reconsideration, but in 2007, the judge decided that the case could not be effectively tried in Germany because they needed access to documents that they didn't have (Kalleck, personal interview, 2010). Besides Rumsfeld, the defendants in the German complaint also included former CIA Director George Tenet and other high-level US officials, as well as some of the lawyers who wrote the memos justifying torture.

Two foreign cases against US officials are now moving ahead in Spanish courts, against the six Bush administration lawyers who wrote the memos providing the legal justification for the use of torture: Alberto Gonzales, John Yoo, Jay Bybee, David S. Addington, William Haynes, and Douglas Feith, and a second case against CIA officials for extraordinary rendition, similar to the case in Italy. While many of these judicial processes will eventually stall or lead to dismissals or acquittals for political or legal reasons, at a minimum, they can endanger the peace of mind, financial security, or reputation of suspected perpetrators. In the next few decades, if little else, former Secretary of Defense Donald Rumsfeld, John Yoo, and others who advocated the policy of explicit non-compliance with the Geneva Conventions and the Torture Convention at a minimum may find themselves in a difficult position when they travel abroad. Before they initiate any international trip they may need to make inquiries about the state of prosecutions in any country where they intend to travel.

Domestic prosecutions

Early in the process, US-based NGOs called for accountability for Bush administration officials who condoned or engaged in torture. While the mainstream human rights organization stressed accountability, two domestic civil rights organizations with long experience litigating in US courts took the lead in the domestic human rights lawsuits: the American Civil Liberties Union (ACLU) and the Center for Constitutional Rights (CCR). These lawsuits were civil suits for damages, not criminal cases, because US law does not permit private prosecution of criminal cases. As of 2010, none of the cases had prospered, as judges used a variety of justifications to dismiss the cases (Ratner, personal interview, 2010). In August 2011, however, two US courts, the 7th Circuit Court of Appeals and District Court in Washington, DC allowed US citizens to proceed with civil suits against Donald Rumsfeld for torture. Both courts rejected claims that Rumsfeld should enjoy immunity and that the plaintiffs were not entitled to compensation because the violations took place in a war zone (Lithwick 2011). Although it is unclear how the cases will be eventually decided, it is significant that cases against high-level US officials for torture are finally being allowed to move ahead in US courts.

In addition, the US military has continued to prosecute a series of cases involving the abuse of detainees. As of 2006, Human Rights Watch found that US authorities have opened investigations into about 65 percent of the cases of the over 600 US personnel implicated in approximately 330 cases of detainee abuse in Iraq, Afghanistan and Guantánamo Bay. Of seventy-nine courts-martial, fifty-four resulted in convictions or a guilty plea. Another fifty-seven people faced non-judicial proceedings involving punishments of no or minimal prison time (Detainee Abuse and Accountability Project 2006: 3, 7). Although many cases were not investigated and no senior officers have been held accountable, this is not an insignificant amount of accountability and punishment.

To date, US sanctions have focused only on torture committed "by" public officials, and have disregarded the issues of instigation, consent or acquiescence of other higher-level public officials. Almost all (95 percent) of the military personnel who have been investigated are enlisted soldiers, not officers. Three officers were convicted by court-martial for directly participating in detainee abuse, but no US military officer has been held accountable for criminal acts committed by subordinates (Detainee Abuse and Accountability Project 2006: 7).

Phase 5: rule-consistent behavior

During the Bush administration, there was very little change in the direction of genuine rule-consistent behavior with the prohibition on torture and inhuman and degrading treatment. The Pentagon created a new Office of Detainee Affairs, "charged with correcting basic problems in the handling and treatment of detainees, and with helping to ensure that senior Defense Department Officials are alerted to concerns about detention operations raised by the Red Cross," and completed a series of investigations into abuses in detention centers and identified some of the possible causes of such abuses, including the failure to give meaningful guidance to soldiers in the field about rules that governed the treatment of detainees (Pearlstein and Patel 2005). Congress enacted various important pieces of legislation, including the Detainee Treatment Act, discussed above, and the requirement that the Secretary of Defense report to Congress on the number and nationality of detainees in military custody.

Despite some of these positive developments, during the Bush administration there was no clear evidence that true behavioral change has occurred in the US case with regard to torture. In the cases of more authoritarian countries, regime change, i.e. the transition from an authoritarian to a democratic government, is often a necessary but not sufficient condition for sustained behavioral change. Of course, regime change did not occur in the United States because it continued to be a democracy throughout this period. But it may be possible to adapting this finding to a more democratic setting. In the case of the Bush administration, many of the memos and policy decisions made regarding torture and cruel and degrading treatment were made in small enclaves of hardliners, led by Vice-President Cheney, deliberately insulated not only from public opinion, by also from the Congress and the judicial branch. Not only were the other branches of the government excluded from decision-making, but in many cases, significant high-level members of the executive branch itself, including key individuals in the State Department, the Justice Department, and the Judge Advocates General of the military were also deliberately cut out of the decision making process because the hardliners feared that they would raise objections based on domestic and international law.[6] In this sense, the least democratic practices within a formally democratic regime contributed to the worst human

---

[6] This interpretation of the inside workings of the Bush administration with regard to interrogation policy is consistent with that of Mayer (2008); Goldsmith (2007); Gellman (2008).

rights practices. More sustained behavioral change did not take place as long as the Bush administration was still in power.

On his second day in office, President Barack Obama ordered the CIA to close down secret overseas prisons and called on the Pentagon to close the Guantánamo prison within a year. The president also revoked the previous Bush administration executive orders and regulations on interrogation that were contrary to US treaty obligations and US law. In April 2009, the Obama administration released four secret memos detailing legal justification for the Bush-era CIA interrogation program. But at the same time as he released the memos, the president also issued a statement guaranteeing that no US officials would be prosecuted for their role in the interrogation program. The Obama administration has also failed to end the practice of indefinite detention without trial, finally close the military detention facility at Guantánamo Bay, and end rendition of detainees to countries that practice torture.

The Obama administration reversed US policy on torture. In this sense, the Obama administration has moved the United States back to both prescriptive status and rule-consistent behavior with regard to torture, but has not renounced extraordinary rendition nor ended arbitrary detention without trial for the prisoners still held in Guantánamo and Bagram air base in Afghanistan. The Obama administration has also been unwilling to pursue any accountability for past human rights violations. President Obama has said that he wishes to look forward, not backward. The Obama administration Justice Department conducted an investigation of John Yoo and the other lawyers who gave legal justification to the Bush administration's brutal interrogation practices, but it concluded that they used flawed legal reasoning but were not guilty of professional or criminal misconduct. The United States has now entered into the debate that has been going on throughout the world for the last thirty years about the desirability of accountability. But because US actions involved citizens from many countries and took place on a global scale, the debate about accountability is a global debate.

Conclusions

The spiral model is a relevant, if not a hopeful, way of understanding the US response to pressures. It highlights that in some ways, the United States has responded very much like other states and societies faced with accusations and pressures of rights violations. The Bush administration, and the US public more generally, responded with some of the same kinds of denial and backlash that we have seen in more authoritarian regimes confronted with human rights pressures. But the more democratic nature of the US regime also led to differences. Once evidence of torture appeared, the US human rights and civil liberties NGO sector responded rapidly and forcefully to the appearance of human rights violations. They have continued to work on and press for accountability, both through civil and criminal cases. One key and unique feature of the US case was the response from within the military and intelligence communities themselves, where prominent members of the FBI as well as groups within the military, especially the legal groups within the military, provided significant opposition to human rights violations and to the arguments that facilitated such abuses. All these forms of opposition, from the media, NGOs, and from within the government itself, was possible because these groups operated within a more democratic setting.

The spiral model suggested that in order for domestic and international pressures to have an impact, governments must have some form of vulnerability to internal and external pressures. Hegemons, because of their wealth and power, are less materially vulnerable than most other countries. But moral vulnerability requires that governments must be sensitive to the pressures, and that they care about their image. The Bush administration, because of its attitude toward international law and its anti-terrorist discourse, has been particularly insensitive to both domestic and international pressures. The Obama administration was more sensitive to such domestic and international opinion, and took early efforts to reverse Bush administration policy. It has not been willing to pursue accountability for past violations, and some of its initial efforts, for example, to close the detention center at Guantánamo, have failed.

There were other ways in which the spiral model does not fit the US case. In particular, the spiral model suggests that a prescriptive status phase of treaty ratification usually follows the state of tactical concessions. In this case, the prescriptive status phase pre-dated the repression by almost a decade, and the Bush administration actively undermined and denied the prescriptive status of the anti-torture norm. However, the fact that the norm had prior prescriptive status, and the United States had ratified the relevant treaties and implemented them in domestic law before committing human rights violations, creates a much more complicated legal situation for those implicated in torture.

For the purposes of this volume on the factors that lead from commitment to compliance, this chapter is a cautionary tale. First, it suggests that even a quite firm commitment to international law, signaled by ratification and implementation in strong domestic statutes, can be undermined by a relatively small group of powerful political operators in the context of a security threat, a compelling anti-terrorism discourse, and domestic indifference to the rights of others. The Bush administration was able to successfully deflect criticism and pressures against it on this issue. It was not able, however, to make the issue go away, nor could it establish its new norms and definitions as standards within the international system.

The combination of prior commitment and the possibility of enforcement or punishment through prosecution was not sufficient to sustain compliance with the law. Commitment, punishment and enforcement are important steps toward compliance, and should be part of the compliance toolkit, but it would be erroneous to rely primarily or solely on punishment rather than norm internalization as a mechanism for bringing about human rights change. It illustrates a point that Ryan Goodman and Derek Jinks make elsewhere in this volume (Chapter 6); material incentives like punishment can sometimes have negative or unintended effects on behavioral change. I do not believe that the fear of punishment led to increased non-compliance – that is, to increased torture and ill treatment – just to an increase in policies designed to justify such behavior and provide legal cover against prosecution. It is not at all clear that the threat of punishment "crowded out" other more positive processes of normative change in the United States. Indeed, the leaked torture memos became evidence of high-level Bush administration complicity with torture, and a focal point for heated public debate and condemnation of the practices they justified.

US torture policy was opposed, both internally and externally, by a coalition of actors who had internalized the norm, including human rights organizations, like-minded governments, Supreme Court judges, and, perhaps most surprisingly, individuals within the FBI and the US military. Such opposition was unable to reverse the practices until after the election of the Obama administration. The Obama administration has reversed interrogation policy but blocked processes of accountability for past human rights violations. It is likely that just in the case of the other countries considered in this volume and the previous one, strong and sustained domestic and international pressures, innovative legal and political strategies, fortuitous circumstances, and the passage of time will be necessary to establish some accountability for the past.

9

Resisting the power of human rights: the People's Republic of China

KATRIN KINZELBACH

Probably more than any other event in the last decade, the 2010 Nobel Peace Prize for human rights and democracy activist Liu Xiaobo confirmed to a global audience that the Chinese party state does not shy away from silencing its critics. The winner of the prestigious award sits in prison with hardly any chance for an early release despite numerous international calls for leniency. His wife was placed under house arrest, thereby cutting Liu's only channel for communication with the outside world. China protested ferociously against Liu Xiaobo's selection, and was the first country ever in the history of the prize that announced diplomatic and economic threats to prevent international diplomats from attending the award ceremony. Is this episode symptomatic for the power of human rights or, rather, for China's power to resist human rights?

Considering the scope conditions developed for this volume, China must be viewed as a particularly hard case for the power of human rights to triumph over its opponents. As China emerges as a great power, her material vulnerability to external pressure continues to decline. With the growing importance in global affairs, notably in the aftermath of the 2008 financial crisis and the more recent European sovereign debt crisis, China's social vulnerability to external pressure is also falling: rather than seeking to demonstrate compliance, Beijing rebukes its international critics with increasing confidence. At the United Nations, China continues to express commitment to human rights, but it simultaneously challenges core implications that derive from these norms (Kinzelbach 2012). Domestically, the Communist Party's grip on power is firm. The total number of human rights activists in China is uncertain, and they are only loosely organized.

China is not only an authoritarian state, it also faces critical governance challenges. The severe urban–rural divide, a rapid economic growth that disproportionally benefits the eastern parts of the country, and rampant corruption present serious obstacles to a consistent implementation of policies adopted by central state authorities. Following Risse and Börzel, the inability of the center to enforce policies equally across the whole country is understood as a distinctive feature of limited statehood (see Chapter 4 in this volume). One example in point is the implementation of China's family planning policy. The blind lawyer Chen Guangcheng reached international fame for documenting abuses by municipal authorities in Linyi, Shandong province, notably the use of physical violence to intimidate pregnant women and their families, as well as the execution of involuntary sterilizations and abortions. Such enforcement measures are illegal in China but nonetheless recurrent in rural areas. Particularly in the case of decentralized rule implementation it is in practice very difficult to understand whether human rights violations result from an unwillingness or an inability to comply. This was also pointed out by Chen Guangcheng himself who, after years of prison detention and house arrest, sought refuge in the US embassy in Beijing, and subsequently left China in May 2012. From New York, he called on Chinese leaders to address "crucial differences between the law on the books and the law in practice" (Chen 2012).

China's authoritarian regime, which contains features of limited statehood, thus fits in the upper right-hand box of Table 4.1, this volume.

With respect to the pathway from commitment to compliance, the crucial question is: are there any mechanisms that push China toward compliance? To answer this question, I start the chapter with a discussion on how the spiral model relates to the case of China. I proceed with an overview of domestic and international responses. Third, I take a closer look at the track record of external attempts to influence China's human rights situation, notably of engagement policies that use capacity-building, incentives and persuasion, with a focus on the policies of the United States and of the European Union. The chapter concludes by reflecting on the options available to international actors when addressing human rights violations in countries that not only suppress domestic activists but that also command significant international power.

China, the spiral model and counter-discourse

China is a significantly more influential player than the countries that were examined in the original *Power of Human Rights* (PoHR) research. It is therefore not at all evident that the model provides a valid explanatory framework. However, several China scholars have described dynamics that are in line with the causal explanations put forward by the spiral model. For example, Michael Davis wrote as early as 1995, "While continuing to crack down hard on dissidents and labour activists, as well as journalists, the government has demonstrated an increasing tendency to attempt to justify its policies in human rights terms. In doing so it has embraced *de facto* the standards it often rejects on policy grounds" (Davis 1995: 11–12; see also Svensson 2002: 308).

Caroline Fleay analyzed explicitly whether the case of China confirms or challenges the spiral model, looking at the period from 1957 to 2003 (Fleay 2005).

She concluded that the model provided a valid explanatory framework. At the same time, Fleay stressed that China did not only engage with her critics but Beijing also tried to alter the international human rights system in such a way that an effective monitoring of China's human rights practice was undermined. Prior to Fleay, Ann Kent had already documented in her authoritative work *China, the United Nations, and Human Rights* how Beijing managed to avoid UN scrutiny through tactical manoeuvring (Kent 1999).

From the aftermath of the Tiananmen massacre in 1989 up until today, China is most adequately situated in phase 3 of the spiral model, the precarious stage of tactical concessions (see Fleay 2005: 310; Lempinen 2005: 329; Kinzelbach 2010: 270). According to the spiral model, this is the phase in which the boomerang pattern, i.e. the combination of pressure from below and pressure from above, starts to work. More optimistically, Rosemary Foot suggested in the year 2000 that China could be situated between phases three and four (Foot 2000: 256). While China outperforms the average country in its income class on economic, social and cultural rights, this is not the case with regard to civil and political rights (Peerenboom 2007: 20). China does not currently satisfy the key indicators for phase 4,[1] nor is there evidence that China is firmly en route to prescriptive status.

Nonetheless it must be recognized that the People's Republic participates actively in the international human rights regime. China has ratified six of the nine core international human rights treaties. It has also signed, but not ratified, the International Covenant on Civil and Political Rights (ICCPR). China has issued a series of governmental white papers on human rights and two national human rights action plans (Information Office of the State Council of the People's Republic of China 2009, 2012). China files reports to treaty bodies, has invited UN special procedures and participated in 2009 in a public review of its human rights situation under the Human Rights Council's new Universal Periodic Review mechanism. China also criticizes other countries for their human rights violations. As Marina Svensson pointed out a decade ago, this shows that China "has come to accept the international regime on human rights and the universal application of these conventions, at least when it serves its own purposes, which once again undermines its relativistic position" (Svensson 2002: 273).

After the Tiananmen massacre, Beijing adopted a relativistic approach by speaking of "Chinese human rights" or "human rights with Chinese characteristics." According to the government's first white paper on human rights issued

---

[1] These include: the ratification of international human rights conventions; institutionalization of human rights norms in the constitution and/or national law; the existence of domestic human rights institutions; and a discursive practice of the government that acknowledges not only the validity of human rights norms irrespective of the audience but also refrains from denouncing criticism as "interference in internal affairs."

in 1991, "Chinese human rights" had three salient characteristics: extensiveness, equality and authenticity (Information Office of the State Council of the People's Republic of China 1991). Apart from this sweeping statement, the white paper said little to clarify what differentiates "Chinese human rights" from universal human rights. Robert Weatherley pointed out in 1999 that Beijing had failed to define what it meant by a uniquely Chinese concept of rights (Weatherley 1999: 2). Despite such criticism, the concept has not been dropped entirely from Chinese communications targeted at an international audience. For example, in September 2011, the director of the Human Rights Studies Centre of the Party School of the Communist Party's Central Committee, Zhang Xiaoling, stressed at the Fourth Beijing Forum on Human Rights, an international conference, that China was developing "a socialist theoretical system for human rights with Chinese characteristics."[2]

Ahead of the 1993 World Conference on Human Rights, China also supported the concept of Asian values, juxtaposing "Western individualism" with "Asian communitarianism." Advocating for cultural exception and prominence of economic and social rights, the Chinese Ambassador and later Deputy Foreign Minister Liu Huaqiu stated in Vienna, "The concept of human rights is a product of historical development. It is closely associated with specific social, political and economic conditions and the specific history, culture and values of a particular country. Different historical development stages have different human rights requirements" (Davis 1998: 112). According to Mark Thompson, the "Asian values" discourse initially appeared persuasive because impressive economic results matched the rejection of liberal democracy. But the 1997 Asian financial crisis undermined the international prestige of "Asian values" (Thompson 2001: 154).

In the mid 1990s Beijing also resurrected the non-interference argument which had previously almost disappeared from China's self-defense in multilateral human rights forums (Kent 1999: 72). The notion of absolute sovereignty continues to be a dominant trend in China's human rights diplomacy today. Internationally, China thus combines attempts to redefine human rights with the propagation of sovereignty as a competing frame (on competing frames see Chapter 2 in this volume). Domestically, the notion of human rights gained ever-increasing acceptance. In a remarkable departure from previous policy, China's constitution was amended in 2004 to include the sentence "The State respects and preserves human rights" (People's Republic of China 2004: art. 33.3). The new provision contains no qualification, be it on the type of rights (economic, social and cultural rights versus civil and political rights) or with regard to any particularistic characteristics. It was the result of domestic activism, chiefly by Cao Siyuan, a legal expert and political activist who organized a

---

[2] See press release at: www.chinahumanrights.org/Messages/Focus/59/2/t20110926_799516. htm (accessed September 29, 2011).

conference in Qingdao in June 2003 to propose changes to China's constitution. Cao was harassed and put under surveillance but his conference nonetheless influenced and accelerated official consultations on the constitution (Goldman 2005: 2–3).

The significance of the 2004 constitutional amendment should, however, not be overrated. Neither the constitutional provision nor international treaties of which China is a party are directly enforced by domestic courts. And many of China's national laws, for example the Criminal Law, the Criminal Procedure Law and the new Law on Lawyers, continue to contain provisions that violate basic human rights, such as the freedom from arbitrary detention and the right to a fair trial. Even a relatively recent proposal for a national Human Rights Law, developed with external funding by a group of academics around Mo Jihong at the Chinese Academy of Social Sciences, is not free from such contradictions (for a detailed analysis see Ahl 2010). What is more, the significant evolution that could be observed in China's official human rights rhetoric is being undermined by a new discourse on harmony, initiated by the Party in 2006. As Eva Pils has argued, the propagation of concepts such as "harmonious society," "harmonious adjudication" and "harmony rights" represents a targeted effort by the Party to dilute the concept of rights as well as the increasingly pervasive rights consciousness. It appears that the rhetorical attack on the rule of law has even encouraged state security organs to revert back to an unconcealed exercise of power when intimidating human rights activists, instead of more concealed tactics such as hiring thugs or using plainclothes police officers (Pils 2009: 153).

International and domestic responses to human rights violations in China

Immediately after the Tiananmen massacre a series of diplomatic and economic sanctions were imposed, marking the beginning of international concern over human rights in China. Most of the sanctions were short-lived and Western countries quickly focused on China's social vulnerability by tabling resolutions at the UN Commission on Human Rights. Prior to the 1991 Commission on Human Rights, however, China successfully dissuaded the two co-sponsors, the United States and the EU, by offering not to veto a Security Council resolution on the Iraqi invasion of Kuwait if they dropped the human rights resolution (for details see Wan 2001: 111–113). In the following years, the resolution proposal was again tabled but the vote on the resolution was each time prevented through a no-action motion. US lobbying for the resolution intensified after the Clinton administration de-linked the renewal of China's Most Favoured Nation (MFN) status from human rights concerns in 1994. Partly in order to counter domestic criticism of the decision, the United States shifted its attention to the multilateral level and China lost the no-action motion for the first time in 1995. Nonetheless, Beijing managed to avert condemnation by the UN: in the second vote on the resolution proper, twenty-one countries voted against, twenty in favor and twelve abstained. The decisive vote was cast by Russia, which switched sides and voted against the resolution after initially objecting to the no-action motion. One explanation on the change in Russia's decision holds that China offered to make concessions in a border dispute between the two countries (Baker 2002: 53).

Seeking to reduce negative publicity, China then offered to hold regular human rights dialogues with its critics behind closed doors. Because of their co-sponsorship of the China resolution, the position of the United States and the EU were of primary importance to Beijing. In 1997 the EU cast a split vote when France, Germany, Italy, Spain and Greece (the so-called Airbus Club) withdrew their backing for the resolution. China punished those EU members that voted for the resolution by canceling diplomatic visits and trade contracts. The success of this tactic gave rise to the bullying strategy that Beijing continues to use up until today. In 1998, neither the EU nor the United States sponsored a resolution on China and decided to focus on the confidential dialogues instead, as well as on bilateral aid projects to assist China in developing capacity in the area of governance and rule of law.

Given that the implementation of capacity-building programs is subject to approval by both the donor and the beneficiary country, they have not only been tailored to what is palatable for the Chinese authorities; they have also been started, interrupted or discontinued according to the political winds of the day. For example, in 2006, China called off the Sino-Swiss human rights dialogue as well as Swiss-funded development projects in protest at the Swiss sponsorship of the so-called Berne Process, a series of informal consultations between Western governments who engage in bilateral human rights dialogues with China. The Chinese Ministry of Foreign Affairs (MFA) viewed the initiative as hostile to China and pressured Switzerland into giving up the sponsorship of the Berne Process. This significantly weakened Western countries' coordination on their human rights policies vis-à-vis China. After Switzerland caved in, Swiss-funded cooperation projects were allowed to resume.

US-funded programs are possibly the most affected by the politicization of aid, and that not only due to actions on the Chinese side. When the Clinton administration first offered China assistance on rule of law in 1997–1998, the implementation of the proposed programs proved to be far from straightforward, because the US Congress initially blocked many of the proposals made by the State Department. Starting as late as 2002/2003, the United States launched substantial assistance programs focusing on the promotion of democracy and rule of law (Stephenson 2006).

As hypothesized by the spiral model, the process of human rights change rests chiefly on the interaction between international and domestic actors and must, indeed, be kick-started by domestic efforts. Roberta Cohen pointed out that human rights violations committed in the People's Republic were first addressed by means of an elite-driven, domestic agenda: in the late 1970s, after Mao Zedong's death and the arrest of the Gang of Four, China's new leaders publicly commented on the horrifying excesses of the Cultural Revolution and of the Anti-rightist Campaign (Cohen 1987: 449). Also Chen Dingding emphasizes the domestic and elite-driven nature of China's policy changes in the area of human rights (Chen 2005). Wan Ming cites elite interests in social order and self-preservation as the two main drivers that helped to adopt human rights norms in China (Wan 2007: 752). Margaret K. Lewis makes a similar argument in explaining the 2010 Evidence Rules, which seek to control abuse by the police in investigating criminal cases. According to Lewis, the new rules were adopted to boost government legitimacy rather than judicial integrity (Lewis 2011). In the absence of genuine political reform, such legal improvements remain severely limited as drivers of human rights compliance. Wan thus recommends focusing on "upstream deliberations rather than downstream behaviour" when analyzing domestic political dynamics (Wan 2007: 729).

According to Marina Svensson, the human rights debate within China is shaped by three main groups, namely the government and its spokesmen, the establishment intellectuals, and dissidents (Svensson 2002: 16). Merle Goldman also highlights the fact that, by the turn of the twentieth century, a growing consciousness of political rights had spread from intellectuals to a much larger part of the population, including workers, peasants, the growing middle class and religious believers. As a concrete manifestation of this "rights consciousness," she cites the fact that the number of group petitions grew dramatically in the mid 1990s (Goldman 2005: 90–91).

From 1998 to 2000 there was also an attempt to organize a political opposition, the China Democracy Party (CDP). This initiative represented the most direct challenge to China's party state system since the 1949 revolution (Goldman 2005: 169–180). When the CDP leaders decided to register the new party, transnational network pressure was mobilized. However, the boomerang effect only lasted for a short time. The registration of the CDP was timed to coincide with a state visit by US President Bill Clinton. During his visit, the Chinese government exercised restraint. This validates that international attention can provide protection for domestic human rights activists. But soon after the American president's departure, the CDP leadership was arrested. And despite international protests, CDP activists were punished with extraordinarily long prison sentences, ranging from eleven to thirteen years. The Chinese authorities reacted to their critics by stating that the CDP was a threat to state security, i.e. with an argument that was identified by Jetschke and Liese as a common counter-frame to human rights (see Chapter 2, this volume). In fact, Chinese human rights defenders are frequently committed for a crime under the State Security Law, not least because this limits the defendant's procedural rights of defence. In addition, court hearings are conducted behind closed doors, thereby also hampering public and international scrutiny.

Despite such restrictions, domestic actors have sought to use legal procedures as a means to advance the cause of civil and political rights in China. Lawyers, journalists and activists joined forces in the so-called *weiquan* (rights defence) movement. The rights defenders operate in a narrow space and are threatened by arrests (for example of Chen Guangcheng, see above), disappearances (for example of Gao Zhisheng, who worked as a defence lawyer for Falun Gong practitioners), and by the government's refusal to renew the annual lawyer's license (for example Teng Biao and Jiang Tianyong lost their licenses after offering free legal services to Tibetans following the March 2008 protests in Lhasa). According to Fu Hualing and Richard Cullen, *weiquan* lawyers "advance and retreat in response to the changing macro-political-legal environment, but there is no sight that they are giving up their legal struggles" (Fu and Cullen 2011: 40) Eva Pils, on the other hand, speaks of a dislocation of the Chinese human rights movement, with rights-based protest shifting away from institutional channels to more subversive forms of expression on the streets, in art, and on the Internet (Pils 2009: 159).

The strategic timing of public appeals has been used on several occasions, but peaked in the year 2008: several domestic activists drew a link between the Olympic Games and human rights in a series of open letters and petitions.[3] And on the occasion of the sixtieth anniversary of the Universal Declaration of Human Rights, celebrated on December 10, 2008, Nobel Peace Prize winner Liu Xiaobo and other democracy activists published the Charter 08. This is a manifesto which (in the spirit of the Czechoslovakian Charter 77) urges the Chinese government to press ahead with political reform. The Charter 08 initiative gathered significant momentum and several thousand people are said to have signed up. But Liu was detained even before the manifesto was publicly circulated. Also he was convicted for a state security crime: "inciting subversion."

Not only formal arrests and convictions, also residential surveillance is used by China's state security organs to silence critics, intimidate sympathizers and decapitate nascent movements that organize in the name of human rights. Control and repression intensified in the first half of 2011 ahead of the party's ninetieth anniversary and in response to several small-scale Jasmine demonstrations that took place in the wake of the Arab Spring. According to a Beijing-based human rights establishment intellectual, the heightened control measures were

---

[3] Examples include the June 2007 petition "We Want Human Rights, Not the Olympics" released in Shanghai, documented in China Rights Forum (2007) 3, pp. 69–72; a letter by Gao Zhisheng in September 2007 to the US Congress calling for a boycott of the Olympics (documented at http://en.epochtimes.com/news/7-9-27/60173.html (accessed November 25, 2008)); an open letter entitled "Real China and the Olympics" issued by Teng Biao and Hu Jia in September 2007 (available at: http://china.hrw.org/press/news_release/the_real_china_and_the_olympics (accessed November 25, 2008)); and an open letter by the Tiananmen Mothers in February 2008 (available at www.hrichina.org/public/contents/press?revision%5fid=47515&item%5fid=47439 (accessed November 25, 2008)).

less caused by a concern that the Jasmine Revolution could spill over, but rather by a more general fear that the revolutionary dynamics and forms of organization observed in Egypt and Tunisia could equally surface in China.[4]

Thus far, the combination of repression and counter-discourse has hindered the strengthening of domestic human rights groups, a key requisite identified in the spiral model for progress toward prescriptive status. In addition to repression and counter-discourse, another reason for the weakness of domestic human rights groups appears to be that Chinese citizens nowadays enjoy a level of freedom that was simply unthinkable only one generation ago – and domestic demands for human rights have consequently become less pronounced than was still the case in the 1980s and 1990s. Bruce Bueno de Mesquita and George Downs have argued that the process of liberalization in China is only restricted with regard to what they call "coordination goods," i.e. rights that are critical to political coordination but less critical for economic cooperation, for example freedom of assembly and freedom of speech. As a result, any form of independent organization in China is systematically suppressed, while the legitimacy derived by the regime from economic growth is maintained (Bueno de Mesquita and Downs 2005).

The track record of capacity-building, incentives and persuasion

International human rights policies vis-à-vis China coincide, by and large, with the mechanisms that are presented in Chapter 1 of this volume. Only coercion is not an option, because China's material power is too great. I therefore focus the following analysis on the three remaining mechanisms, namely capacity-building, incentives and persuasion.

Capacity-building

Have institution-building, education and training programs impacted positively on human rights in China? As already mentioned above, many Western states have funded technical cooperation programs to increase the capacity of the justice and security sector to comply with human rights norms. They have also funded human rights education programs in the academic sector. Sophia Woodman studied the aid programs of nine countries (Australia, Canada, Denmark, France, Germany, the Netherlands, Norway, Sweden, the United Kingdom) as well as those funded by the European Union (EU). Her research points to a lack of a distinctive human rights dimension in the aid provided, which is due to China's objection to a rights-focus. Woodman also found that the programs suffer from weak foundations, insufficient needs assessments and a lack of China-specific knowledge in the Western aid industry. She concludes

---

[4] Confidential communication, July 2011.

with the rather hazy finding that some of the projects were beneficial, but "some probably are not, and a few may even be harmful" (Woodman 2007: 148).

With reference to US-funded legal reform programs, Matthew Stephenson comes to a similarly pessimistic conclusion. He asserts that China's willingness to engage in such programs is driven primarily by economic interests. This has led the United States to adopt what Stephenson calls a "Trojan horse strategy." Cooperation in the field of commercial law and attempts to control administrative discretion and corruption in the name of economics is expected to spill over to other areas, leading to stronger legal controls of government discretion at all levels. Stephenson discusses three possible routes by which such diffusion could happen, focusing on the interdependence of the legal system, the change of China's legal culture and the building of a constituency for reform. He questions the assumption that such projects may "trickle down" to induce broader and deeper reforms that run against the wishes of the Chinese authorities and concludes that "given the state of existing theory and empirical evidence, such a conviction seems unfounded" (Stephenson 2006: 214).

Considering the lack of a specific human rights dimension in many of the externally funded technical cooperation programs that are being implemented in China (in addition to Woodman 2007 also see Oud 2009), an optimistic conclusion about their positive impact on human rights compliance would appear to be tenuous. The sheer size of China limits the impact that a relatively small portfolio of aid programs may have. The impact potential of rule of law programs would seem to be further limited in situations where litigation on behalf of human rights is challenged by a politicized and controlled legal apparatus. If designed well, externally funded rule of law programs can decrease violations that result from the lack of capacity. Such programs may also support individual change agents within the legal system. But they inevitably have little influence on the political struggle over reforms. Strikingly, the Chinese expression for rule of law is *fazhi*, a term which is more adequately rendered in English as "rule by law," not "rule of law." Rather than giving law the primacy over government power, a key function fulfilled by the ongoing legalization drive in China is to funnel and moderate discontent, thereby legitimizing rather than de-legitimizing the one-party state (see Diamant *et al.* 2005: 6–7 and Fu and Cullen 2011: 40–41).

Capacity-building programs are most likely to be successful in facilitating China's move from commitment to compliance with norms that are not a threat to the regime's ability to exercise control – for example the prohibition of torture. On the other hand, rights such as the freedom from arbitrary detention or freedom of expression will hardly be improved through technical cooperation.

Incentives

Can incentives promote human rights compliance in China? Incentives are based on the logic of consequences: sanctions are threatened and awards are offered to manipulate the target state's cost-benefit calculations, thereby compelling it into changing its behavior (see Chapter 1, this volume). Vis-à-vis China, this strategy has primarily been used by the United States.

Analyzing the linkage between human rights and the renewal of China's MFN status, A. Cooper Drury and Li Yitan suggested that strategic bargaining in the period 1989–1995 was ineffective in terms of systemic changes and even counter-productive with regard to tactical accommodations (Drury and Li 2004, 2006). Also Alan Wachman argued that issue-linking between MFN status and human rights only had a marginal influence on China (Wachman 2001: 274). Wachman further warned that "well intended efforts to shame on behalf of a moral objective may have counterproductive effects that actually impede those who might, otherwise, be able to take positive measures to improve human rights" (Wachman 2001: 277). Ann Kent comes to the opposite conclusion, finding that Beijing ceased to make tactical concessions after the Clinton administration de-linked China's MFN status from human rights considerations (Kent 1999: 79).

Even after de-linking China's MFN status from human rights considerations, the United States continued to use positive and negative incentives, notably ahead of important bilateral summits, to negotiate concessions from China. One such case is the release of prominent Uyghur businesswoman and political figure Rebiya Kadeer in March 2005. Her release came just ahead of a visit by US Secretary of State Condoleezza Rice to China. According to confidential interviews, the US government agreed not to sponsor a resolution at the 2005 Commission on Human Rights in return for letting Rebiya Kadeer fly out to the United States. Similar deals were struck for a number of other political prisoners: for example Ngawang Choephel, a Tibetan musicologist imprisoned for espionage, was released in the run-up to a summit between Chinese President Jiang Zemin and US President George W. Bush in February 2002; CDP activist Wang Youcai was released in March 2004 in response to an appeal for medical parole issued by Congressman Jim Leach and Senator Chuck Hagel. And one of the so-called singing nuns, Phuntsog Nyidron, departed to the United States in advance of a summit between Hu Jintao and President Bush in April 2006.

By the end of the decade, such high-profile, publicly conducted releases to the United States no longer occurred. One possible explanation is that the Chinese government ceased to view them as cheap bargaining chips. Instead, China increasingly appears to conclude that the benefits of such concessions do not outweigh the costs. After China became the largest foreign holder of US treasury bonds in late 2008, it has evidently become less important for Beijing to worry about what US officials and the US public think about China's lack of compliance with human rights. At the same time, the US government has become progressively more hesitant to raise human rights concerns with China.

Within China, not only elite opposition but also public opinion increasingly reject American human rights pressure. As Wan Ming pointed out, this was not the case for most of the 1990s. At that time US human rights efforts were still "well received by large segments of Chinese society" (Wan 2001: 61). China's social vulnerability to external human rights criticism was, therefore, significantly higher when the memories of the Tiananmen massacre were still fresh. Today, most criticism concerns the civil and political rights of rather exceptional and domestically not well-known human rights defenders, as well as the treatment of Tibetans and Uyghurs, or members of the Falun Gong movement. Unlike in the case of the Tiananmen protesters, few Chinese identify with the aforementioned groups.

Because of the shift in public sentiment vis-à-vis external human rights criticism, it has become easier for Beijing to employ not only state security but also nationalism and sovereignty as effective counter-discourses. By protesting against interference in China's domestic affairs, Beijing not only invokes the sovereignty norm as a competing frame; Beijing also regularly dismisses external criticism as a pretext, arguing that the West and particularly the United States were wary of China's rise and thus sought to damage it. It is true that the US policy on human rights in China has oscillated between confrontation and engagement. Indeed, any human rights policy that is based on strategic bargaining shows inconsistencies over time because the specific incentives to be offered (or threatened to be withdrawn) at any given moment ultimately depend on domestic politics. It is therefore relatively easy for a target government to discredit the criticizing actor as being driven not by the noble concern over human rights but by a hidden agenda. In the case of China, this counter-discourse seems particularly effective because it strongly resonates with a key component of the historiography of the Party, namely that the foundation of the People's Republic re-established China's dignity after the subjugation to imperial rule, bringing an end to the "century of humiliation." In the view of many Chinese, the government is right in protesting ferociously against humiliation.

The harsh criticism against Liu Xiaobo's Nobel Peace Prize, which was generally viewed as a sign of weakness and lack of judgement in Western media, may alternatively be read as a calculated message to a domestic audience. There is an ongoing debate within the political establishment about the desirability of political reforms, especially in view of the 18th National Congress of the Communist Party in 2012, at which China's next top leaders will be confirmed. Beijing's harsh and unsubtly nationalistic reaction to the praise for Liu Xiaobo can be explained as an attempt to discredit reformers as puppets of foreign enemies. The negative reception of Beijing's response in Western media is only a small risk. Indeed, most international articles on Liu Xiaobo are not even censored in China but are readily available on the Internet. This is so because such articles are only read by a small portion of the Chinese population; they simply lack the necessary reach to cause concern in Beijing.

Given that incentives operate with the logic of consequences, they can only be successful if the target country is materially or socially vulnerable. Due to

China's decreasing material vulnerability coupled with decreasing social vulnerability caused by foreign governments' reluctance to bargain over human rights with China and a shift in domestic perception of external pressure and condemnation, it appears that the window of opportunity to influence Beijing's human rights decisions through strategic bargaining is gradually closing.

Persuasion

Unlike strategic bargaining, persuasion does not require material or social vulnerability to be successful. As is explained in Chapter 1 of this volume, persuasion operates with the logic of appropriateness. But has persuasion helped to push China from commitment to compliance? The most instructive case to look at is the EU–China human rights dialogue. Different from the American human rights diplomacy vis-à-vis China, the EU strategy is not based on incentives. With a regular dialogue being held at the technical level, human rights are largely kept outside of political consultations. Unlike the United States, the EU has not employed a carrot-and-stick diplomacy to negotiate concessions.[5] What has the EU achieved through this dialogue policy, namely: have the dialogue's goals been achieved? And what role did the dialogue play in bringing these changes about?

In 2001, under pressure from NGOs and the European Parliament, the Council of the European Union published eight benchmarks for the dialogue (Council of the European Union 2001). The benchmarks are rather wordy but they do include certain components that are directly measurable without margins of interpretation. Taking these points as a basis for the analysis of goal attainment, we can observe a number of positive developments, notably the ratification of the ICESCR in 2001; the visits of UN special procedures in 2003, 2004, 2005 and 2010; the return of the death penalty review to the Supreme People's Court in 2007; and the abolition of "custody and repatriation" in 2003.

The critical question remains whether dialogue, arguing and persuasion provide causal explanations for these developments. The first point, China's ratification of the ICESCR in 2001, is commonly explained not as a result of persuasion, but rather as a strategic move by Beijing to avoid censorship at the Commission on Human Rights and, maybe more importantly, as a tactical concession to counter human rights criticism raised in the context of China's bid for the 2008 Olympics (Baum 2009: 39; Lee 2007: 449; Peerenboom 2007: 194).

---

[5] In one case the EU did use issue-linking: in 2004 it introduced human rights concerns into a negotiation over its arms embargo against China. However, these concerns were only raised as an afterthought, notably after the United States had protested against the EU's willingness to lift the embargo. By citing human rights concerns, the EU found an explanation for its sudden change of mind on the embargo. The afterthought was not taken seriously in Beijing (Kinzelbach: 2010: chs 5 and 6).

Among the visits of UN Special Procedures to China, only the visit of the Special Rapporteur on Education can be unequivocally linked to the EU's dialogue. The invitation letter was handed over during the November 2002 session of the dialogue (United Nations Special Rapporteur on the Right to Education 2003: § 1). While it is ultimately impossible to ascertain to what extent persuasion may have influenced Beijing's decision, it would be wrong to conclude that no incentives were at play. Given that the United States had lost its seat in the UN Human Rights Commission, NGO lobbying for a resolution on China ahead of the Commission's 2003 session centered squarely on the EU. The EU thus needed a positive outcome from the dialogue in order to politically defend its decision not to sponsor a resolution. The invitation of the Special Rapporteur on Education was a comparatively cheap concession to make, not least because it also underscored Beijing's plea that UN human rights bodies ought to pay more attention to social, economic and cultural rights. Similarly, the visit to China by the Special Rapporteur on the Right to Food in 2010 gave Beijing an opportunity to demonstrate its cooperation with UN procedures while simultaneously reconfirming its long-held position that the most important human right was the right to subsistence.

The visit of the Special Rapporteur on Torture, on the other hand, was far less welcome in Beijing. He was first invited by China in 1999 but only for a "friendly visit." Beijing refused to accept the Special Rapporteur's standard terms of reference, taking issue with unannounced visits to places of detention and private meetings with detainees. The Special Rapporteur insisted on the conditions and was eventually allowed to visit in 2005. There is little to suggest that the standard terms of reference were applied because they were finally accepted in Beijing as *appropriate*. Rather than persuasion, the necessary factor appears to have been US pressure. This interpretation is also supported by the EU's own analysis drawn at the end of 2004: according to the EU's Heads of Mission, the difficulties with the visit of the Special Rapporteur on Torture had to do with a "lack of cooperation by other relevant Ministries involved" (Presidency-in-Office of the Council of the European Union, Netherlands 2004: § 3.3.5.). Without external pressure, the Chinese Ministry of Foreign Affairs (the counterpart in all human rights dialogues) was simply not powerful enough to overrule the security apparatus. The Ministry of Foreign Affairs only won the upper hand in inter-ministerial politics when the United States offered an incentive – according to confidential interviews, the visit was identified as a condition by the United States for its agreement to the resumption of the US–China human rights dialogue. The same conditionality also explains the visit by the Working Group on Arbitrary Detention in 2004.

Among the above-mentioned developments, the most significant moves toward human rights compliance are the abolition of "custody and repatriation" detention in 2003 and the return of the death penalty review to the Supreme People's Court in 2007. What role did discourse and persuasion and specifically the EU–China human rights dialogue play in these two developments? Regarding the death penalty review, EU Commissioner Ferrero-Waldner claimed that the EU–China human rights dialogue had had "a certain influence" (European Commission 2007b). China's extensive use of the death penalty has, indeed, been among the key concerns expressed by the EU in the dialogue. During a meeting in October 1999, the Chinese delegation first announced the plan to work toward full abolition. Hopes were raised in the EU that a breakthrough on this topic might be imminent. Later, this hope faded and the EU even dropped the death penalty from its priority concerns. Instead, it highlighted four other issues between 2005 and 2006: the release of remaining Tiananmen prisoners, ratification of the ICCPR, reform of the re-education through labor system (RTL),[6] and greater freedom of expression (Kinzelbach 2010: ch. 6). Strikingly, it was during this very period when a public discussion on the dangers of the death penalty developed in China.

The domestic mobilization on the death penalty in China was triggered by the case of Nie Shubin who was sentenced to death after he confessed (purportedly while being tortured) to raping and murdering Kang Juhua. Ten years after Nie had been executed, the verdict was recognized as wrongful: in January 2005, Wang Shujin confessed his guilt. The *Henan Business News* published information on the execution of innocent Nie Shubin, and other papers such as the *Southern Weekend* published additional reportage (Zhao 2005). A public outcry followed. A number of Chinese legal scholars quickly entered and helped to shape the public debate. More wrongful verdicts were uncovered, notably that of She Xianglin, who was declared innocent and released from jail in April 2005, after serving eleven years in prison for murdering his wife – who later turned out to be alive (Liu 2005).

While this was happening in China, the EU could have intensified its call for abolition, but it did not. As far as could be ascertained through confidential interviews and a review of internal documents, the death penalty was not a primary issue of concern during governmental talks with China at the time. It is, however, likely that the EU's comparatively prominent position on the abolition of the death penalty, as well as two technical cooperation projects funded by the EU, influenced the domestic scholarly debate. Here it must be stressed that the EU's advocacy on the abolition of the death penalty has been implemented on a global scale and in public – it has not been confined to diplomatic discussions behind closed doors. While the logic of appropriateness can explain the success of domestic mobilization around the death penalty review, it appears that the logic of consequences is more suitable for explaining the government's response because, ultimately, the decision on the death penalty review in China

---

[6] RTL is a form of administrative detention than can last up to four years without a decision by a court.

accommodated a domestic demand that was modest enough not to challenge fundamental state or Party interests.

Also the decision to abolish custody and repatriation detention followed a process of domestic mobilization which was sparked by the death of a young graphic designer called Sun Zhigang held in police custody in Guangzhou on March 20, 2003. The editors of the *Southern Metropolis Daily* published a daring article on the case (for a detailed account of the decisions in the paper and the following events leading to the editors' arrest see Pan 2008: 250–267). The story of Sun Zhigang immediately hit the Internet. A decisive role was again played by a number of legal scholars, who made unprecedented submissions to the Standing Committee of the National People's Congress (Pils 2006–2007). According to Keith Hand, "legal reformers could work within China's authoritarian system to accelerate legal reform without triggering the type of damaging backlash directed against other, more 'politicized' rights actions" (Hand 2006–2007: 117–118). Although the system of administrative detention, including "custody and repatriation," had repeatedly been discussed in the EU–China human rights dialogue, the external appeals and persuasion attempts did not achieve any result until the necessary factor – domestic demand – materialized.

The above examples, including not only the death penalty review and the abolition of custody and repatriation detention, but also China's ratification of the ICESCR and the visits of UN special procedures, suggest that the People's Republic of China has not progressed far enough along the phases of the spiral model for persuasion strategies to be successful – at least not in isolation. Persuasion and the logic of appropriateness only appear to facilitate China's move toward compliance with civil and political rights when coupled with incentives and the logic of consequences.

Conclusion

Similar to the governments examined in the original PoHR project, the Chinese authorities also engaged in discussions with their human rights critics. However, unlike the original set of countries, China used its increasingly strong position in the international system to undermine the institutional processes through which international human rights scrutiny is implemented, particularly at the United Nations. Furthermore, China employed a combination of threats and awards to prevent Western governments from raising human rights issues in high-level political summits; it launched a multi-faceted counter-discourse, and it has sustained domestic repression without prompting regime change. Although transnational network pressure has been maintained over time, the boomerang effect only kicked in occasionally.

The China case delineates limits of the power of human rights but also demonstrates that even under particularly unfavorable circumstances, advances toward compliance can be made in accordance with the spiral model's predictions. The move from commitment to compliance appears to play out very differently depending on the right in question, and that not only with regard to centralized or decentralized implementation. Authoritarian regimes whose legitimacy is based on economic growth will not only move more easily toward compliance with economic, social and cultural rights. Within the group of civil and political rights, they are most unlikely to comply with a subset of rights that limit the regime's discretion to exercise political control. As examples discussed in this chapter have shown, notably on the death penalty review as well as on the abolition of custody and repatriation detention, domestic actors can still seize and create exceptional openings to demand modest reforms. On such occasions, the logic of appropriateness plays a dominant role. It appears, however, that the logic of appropriateness primarily explains why mobilization is successful – reform decisions, on the other hand, continue to be shaped by the logic of consequences.

External incentives that target China's social vulnerability have proven to be effective in soliciting marginal advances toward compliance, including the release of select political prisoners, not however in facilitating any significant move toward greater protection of civil and political rights. In addition, China's social vulnerability to external criticism is declining because the regime has launched a powerful counter-discourse against such criticism and because international governmental actors have, for material reasons, become more and more wary of engaging in strategic bargaining over human rights with Beijing.

In the case of norm-violating emerging powers, there appears to be a window of opportunity during which incentives employed by external actors can be successful. These opportunities are determined by two factors which again point to an interaction between the logic of consequences and the logic of appropriateness: first, the target government must assess its social vulnerability as more significant for its international status than its material strength (logic of consequences). Second, external criticism must resonate with the public of the target country (logic of appropriateness). The steeper the rise of a country's material power, the easier it will be for the target government to label foreign critics as resentful and disingenuous.

The case of China confirms that the boomerang effect as described by the spiral model can manifest itself in an authoritarian regime with features of limited statehood that is, simultaneously, an emerging power. While China is unique in many aspects, a similar interaction of an unwillingness and an inability to comply, coupled with significant international power and a nationalist counter-discourse as competing forces to the power of human rights, also appears to be at work in other cases, for example in Russia and Iran.

In such situations, persuasion and capacity-building alone do not seem to suffice as drivers of human rights compliance. Rather, it appears opportune to offer incentives. Once the target country's material and social vulnerability is too small for incentives to work, international attention should shift away from the improbable prospect of soliciting reforms against the will of the norm-violating government, toward documenting and condemning violations as well as directly supporting domestic human rights groups. Such support may include financial aid or, where necessary, capacity-building. Most importantly, this support ought to include public and confidential diplomacy to protect human rights defenders at risk. Whenever the domestic activists manage to create a new window of opportunity for improvement, however modest, international actors should not only join their calls for the specific reform in question, but also use issue-linking in political negotiations to offer an additional impetus for compliance.

10

The "Arab Spring" and the spiral model: Tunisia and Morocco

VERA VAN HÜLLEN

The political uprisings during the "Arab Spring" of 2011 have significantly changed the political landscape in the Middle East and North Africa. Revolutions in Tunisia and Egypt, civil war in Libya, revolts in Syria and Yemen and protest movements in most other countries of the region have overthrown authoritarian rulers that had been in power for decades and put increasing pressure on the remaining authoritarian regimes. The Arab Spring has opened a window of opportunity for democratic change and thus increased the chances for a renewed commitment to and ultimate compliance with international human rights standards.

The Arab Spring challenges the "persistence of authoritarianism" that started to intrigue scholars when it became clear in the mid 1990s that the "third wave of democratization" had spared countries in the Middle East and North Africa. Human rights activists became increasingly frustrated as the human rights record in the region remained disastrous despite the formal commitment to international human rights norms. Often, human rights did not even gain prescriptive status as national constitutions and legislation did not conform to international standards, e.g. with regard to the prohibition of torture, the abolition of the death penalty, or gender equality. Where human rights were guaranteed by law, rule-conforming behavior often seemed the exception rather than the rule, defying the hope for a linear or "natural" development from commitment to compliance triggered by the mobilization of transnational human rights networks.

This chapter assesses the explanatory power of the spiral model developed in *The Power of Human Rights* (PoHR) in light of the recent events in the region by investigating the diverging developments in Tunisia and Morocco, ranging from revolution to reform. The Arab uprisings started in Tunisia in late 2010 and grew into a revolution. When the authoritarian regime broke down and long-time President Zine el-Abidine Ben Ali fled the country on January 14, 2011, political protest had already started to spread to other countries, instilling either the hope for or the fear of a domino effect in the hearts and minds of the masses and elites in the region and beyond. The Moroccan protest movement only gained momentum on February 20, 2011, but it never succeeded in mobilizing the masses to the same extent as in other countries. Nevertheless, Mohamed VI responded to the increasing domestic and international pressure with political concessions and Moroccans adopted a constitutional reform by referendum on July 1, 2011. How far are these diverging developments in line with expectations generated under the spiral model?

Investigating the human rights situation in Morocco and Tunisia and the interaction between the regimes, transnational human rights networks, and external actors since 2000, this chapter analyses the role of different mechanisms of influence and scope conditions for the human rights records of the two regimes between commitment and compliance. It argues that in particular the specific combinations of different degrees of political liberalization and statehood as well as material and social vulnerabilities can account for the divergent developments in Morocco and Tunisia before and during the Arab Spring. Whereas the spiral model has been at work in Morocco, where the authoritarian regime slowly moved from commitment to compliance, the spiral model could not gain momentum in Tunisia for twenty years despite the regime change in 1987. However, the Arab Spring marks the ultimate failure of the Tunisian model of closed authoritarianism. It provides the opportunity to improve the human rights situation in both Morocco and Tunisia if transnational human rights networks can maintain their pressure from below and from above. The article starts by reviewing the original findings on the spiral model in Morocco and Tunisia in the twentieth century before it traces developments in 2000–2010 and turns to the events of the Arab Spring in 2011.

The power of human rights in Morocco and Tunisia until 1999

At the end of the 1990s, the spiral model seemed to capture developments in Morocco much better than in Tunisia.[1] In both countries, regimes were formally committed to international human rights standards and engaged in tactical concessions in light of transnational mobilization of human rights networks, but only Morocco seemed on the path from commitment to compliance whereas the spiral model had lost momentum in Tunisia.

After gaining independence from France in 1956, both regimes reacted with repression to growing socio-economic and political challenges, including systematic violations of human rights through extrajudicial killings, disappearances, torture and arbitrary arrest. In both countries, human rights activism increased during the 1970s with the significant difference that the Tunisian government had already committed itself to international human rights standards

---

[1] This section primarily draws on Gränzer (1999) and chapter five in Risse et al. (2002: 139–177) and summarizes the original findings in PoHR on Morocco and Tunisia until 1998 and 1999 respectively.

while the Moroccan regime was still in denial: Morocco ratified the International Covenants on Civil and Political Rights and on Economic, Social and Cultural Rights (ICCPR and ICESC, 1966) only in 1979, ten years after Tunisia. Founded since the 1970s, Moroccan and Tunisian human rights organizations engaged in transnational human rights networks and put growing pressure on their regimes during the 1980s for their continued human rights abuses, adding to the crisis of the incumbent regimes in the face of socio-economic difficulties.[2]

When then Prime Minister Ben Ali deposed President Habib Bourguiba in 1987 in a "medical coup," domestic and international actors hoped that the regime change would be a breakthrough for human rights and democratization in Tunisia. The new regime's legitimacy was initially built on its commitment to human rights and democratization and it quickly established the prescriptive status of the protection of human rights. But in the early 1990s, Tunisia experienced an authoritarian backlash. The new constitution introduced multi-party elections, but Tunisia remained a de facto one-party system with the absolute predominance of the ruling Constitutional Democratic Rally (*Rassemblement Constitutionel Démocratique*, RCD), the successor of the post-independence Neo Destour Party. After the participation of the newly legalized Renaissance Party (*Hizb En-Nahda*) in the 1989 parliamentary elections, the regime quickly returned to its confrontational strategy vis-à-vis Islamist opposition movements and banned all political parties and civil society organizations with religious foundations (Allani 2009: 265). At the same time in Morocco, Hassan II initiated institutional and legal reforms that slowly advanced political rights and freedoms. He established an Advisory Council on Human Rights (*Conseil Consultatif des Droits de l'Homme*, CCDH) in 1990 and created a number of reform commissions upgrading the prescriptive status of human rights. This sense of political opening was strengthened when Morocco underwent its first change in government or *alternance* after the Socialist Union of Popular Force (*Union Socialiste des Forces Populaires*, USFP) won the 1997 parliamentary elections.

In contrast to other case studies in PoHR, the spiral model seemed to be at work in Morocco even without a regime change whereas it failed to maintain momentum in Tunisia despite regime change. After its first political opening in the early 1990s, Morocco was on the path from commitment to compliance, carried by the mobilization of transnational human rights networks resulting in tactical concessions by the regime. Observers noted a slow improvement in

---

[2] The most important organizations founded in Morocco during the 1970s and 1980s were the Moroccan League for the Defense of Human Rights (*Ligue Marocaine pour la Défense des Droits de l'Homme*, LMDDH), the Moroccan Association of Human Rights (*Association Marocaine des Droits de l'Homme*, AMDH), and the Moroccan Organisation of Human Rights (*Organisation Marocaine des Droits de l'Homme*, OMDH). In Tunisia, the human rights movement of the 1970s organized in the Tunisian League of Human Rights (*Ligue Tunisienne des Droits de l'Homme*, LTDH).

the human rights situation during the last years of the reign of Hassan II and the succession of Mohamed VI to the throne in 1999 gave rise to hopes for more fundamental and lasting reforms. While the mobilization of the domestic and transnational human rights movement in Tunisia played a role in bringing about the regime change of 1987, the new regime under President Ben Ali effectively interrupted the dynamic of the spiral model. The regime appropriated the human rights discourse and adopted institutional reforms, but the political opening of 1987 was quickly followed by a backlash of authoritarianism and repression. The regime successfully co-opted the human rights movement and suppressed independent human rights activists and political opponents, cutting them off from the international human rights community. This strategy was facilitated by the fact that the Tunisian human rights movement – and opposition, for that matter – was organized in only one organization, the LTDH, and not backed by a plurality of political parties and movements, as was the case in Morocco. The success or failure of continued transnational mobilization thus depended on differences in the polities and politics of Morocco and Tunisia since independence: the Moroccan monarchy accommodated a higher degree of political and social pluralism than the republican regime in Tunisia, which institutionalized political power in the ruling party and always tightly controlled the formation of alternative actors.

This reference to structural differences between the two regimes shaping the form and strength of domestic human rights movements already pointed to the relevance of scope conditions for the functioning of the spiral model. The following section more systematically investigates the explanatory power of the scope conditions identified in Chapter 1 of this volume for the further development of the human rights situation in Morocco and Tunisia since 2000 as well as the interaction between the two regimes, transnational human rights networks and other international actors.

The power of human rights in Morocco and Tunisia in 2000–2010

The diverging tendencies that became apparent in the late 1990s continued throughout the following decade. While both regimes remained formally committed to international human rights standards, adopted an official discourse on human rights protection and democratization, and implemented legal and institutional reforms superficially suggesting a prescriptive status of human rights, developments differed significantly between the two countries with regard to the actual human rights situation. Morocco seemed on a long and cumbersome journey toward compliance whereas the human rights situation in Tunisia further regressed compared to the early 1990s. In comparison to the first thirty years after independence, the human rights record of both Morocco and Tunisia has significantly improved with regard to violations of fundamental

· human rights by the authorities. For example, extrajudicial killings and disappearances have hardly occurred since 2000, but there are still regular reports of torture and arbitrary detention in both countries even though both regimes signed and ratified the Convention against Torture and Other Cruel, Inhuman or Degrading Treatment or Punishment (1984) in the late 1980s and early 1990s. These human rights abuses, committed in particular by the police forces, seem to be less systematic and widespread in Morocco than in Tunisia, where they are definitely part of the regime's repressive strategy. Thus, while Human Rights Watch (HRW) came to the conclusion that "[i]n 2010 human rights conditions in Morocco were mixed, and in some aspects, decidedly poor" (Human Rights Watch 2011: 568), it asserted that "[t]he human rights situation remained dire in Tunisia" (Human Rights Watch 2011: 591). This assessment echoes reports by HRW and other international human rights organizations and observers, such as Amnesty International (AI) and the International Federation for Human Rights (*Fédération Internationale des Ligues des Droits de l'Homme*, FIDH), but also by Freedom House and the US Department of State, throughout the 2000s.[3] In addition, Morocco has qualified as "partly free" with regard to political rights and civil liberties since the mid 1990s whereas Tunisia was consistently ranked as "not free," having among other things "one of the worst media environments in the world" (Freedom House 2011). Moroccan authorities still tightly controlled media and human rights activists through restrictive laws, upholding in particular the three big taboos of Moroccan public life, namely the monarch, Islam, and the Western Sahara (Howe 2000: 69; Kausch 2009a: 169). Within these limits set and enforced by the regime, the freedoms of expression and association were nevertheless much greater than in Tunisia, where authorities restricted any form of contestation. In both countries, regimes adopted restrictive anti-terrorism laws after the events of 9/11 and terrorist attacks in the region which further undermined the prescriptive status of human rights.

Morocco: cooperation and reform, but little change

In Morocco, Hassan II had already initiated changes in the regime's human rights practice during the last years of his reign, but the succession of Mohamed VI to the throne in 1999 was generally celebrated as the advent of a new era for democracy and human rights in the country (Campbell 2003). In a symbolic act, he directly dismissed Driss Basri, the long-time minister of the interior under Hassan II, in order to distance himself from the practice of state repression during the "leaden years" (Howe 2000: 67; also Vairel 2008: 230).

More importantly, the regime started to admit to human rights violations in the past and initiated a top-down, state-led process that sought closure

---

[3] On the situation in 2010, see, for example, Amnesty International (2011a), Freedom House (2011), US Department of State (2011).

through compensating victims rather than prosecuting perpetrators. This was as a response to the continued mobilization of the Truth and Justice Forum (*Forum Vérité et Justice*, FVJ), founded in 1999, and other human rights organizations. Clearly not satisfied with the work of the Independent Commission of Arbitration (*Instance Indépendante d'Arbitrage*, IAA) set up by Mohamed VI in 1999, they pushed the king to create the Equity and Reconciliation Commission (*Instance Equité et Réconciliation*, IER) in 2004 (Vairel 2008: 231). Modeled after the South African Truth and Reconciliation Commission, it was the first transitional justice mechanism in the Middle East and North Africa and is still unique in the region. The IER, composed of experts, reviewed complaints and held public hearings of victims in 2004–2005 before it issued a final report with recommendations for legal and institutional reforms that was presented by the king and approved by the parliament in 2006. The work of the IER was closely followed by international human rights organizations (see FIDH 2004; Human Rights Watch 2005a; International Center for Transitional Justice 2005). While it was highlighted as an important step, it was also criticized for its strictly limited mandate that protected torturers from identification and judicial consequences and that turned a blind eye to human rights violations in the context of the Western Sahara conflict (Amnesty International 2011a: 48; FIDH 2011a). By including human rights activists in this highly formalized process, the IER "allows the palace to depoliticize the political stakes by organizing a consensus under the king's supervision" (Vairel 2008: 235), establishing an official truth rather than justice. The CCDH was mandated with the follow-up, but the implementation of the IER's recommendations by the regime has been painstakingly slow. By the end of 2010, Morocco had not yet ratified the statute of the International Criminal Court or abolished the death penalty.

The regime has, however, successfully created a dynamic (or impression) of change as "the Moroccan state has explicitly acknowledged the need for reforms and started to gradually implement them in a number of areas including the economy, administration, the media, the religious field, and human rights" (Maghraoui 2009: 143, also Joffé 2009). Mohamed VI has continued his father's practice of royal reform commissions as a highly institutionalized and top-down approach to political reform. In particular the revision of the Personal Status Code (or *Moudawana*) in 2004 was highlighted as a major reform initiative to improve women's rights and establish gender equality (Willis 2009: 232), even though critics pointed again to the limited scope of the reform, leaving legal restrictions in place, and in particular its incomplete implementation in practice. The appointment of yet another reform commission was clearly a response to the sustained mobilization of the women's rights movement and the politicization of the issue after 2000 (Elliott 2009: 214).

Overall, the human rights situation in Morocco remained patchy: especially after 9/11, the regime increased repressive measures against alleged Islamists and political rights and civil liberties were severely limited in the Western

Sahara. Accordingly, domestic and international human rights organizations regularly cautioned against overly optimistic assessments of change in Morocco (e.g. Amnesty International 2011a: 48). Nevertheless, the international community clearly appreciated the reform efforts of the Moroccan regime that readily cooperated with state and non-state actors on human rights and political issues. The regime was open to dialogue with civil society: it has hosted a range of workshops and conferences with domestic and transnational human rights organizations over the years and has jointly implemented projects with AI. International actors such as the European Union (EU) have directly supported domestic reform initiatives through financial assistance, e.g. for the follow-up of the IER and the modernization of the judiciary, and sought to encourage and stabilize reforms through political dialogue (European Commission 2006). In addition, Morocco has been rewarded politically and financially by international actors, signing in 2008 a five-year Compact for almost US$700 million of additional aid with the US Millennium Challenge Corporation and receiving an "advanced status" in Euro-Mediterranean relations the same year.[4] Except for coercive measures, Morocco has thus been subject to various mechanisms of influence through cooperation with domestic and international actors. The continued mobilization of transnational human rights networks has been crucial for advancing reform projects whereas international actors have exerted little pressure and the impact of their capacity-building and persuasion efforts seems limited (van Hüllen and Stahn 2009).

Observers disagree on the causes of the slow pace of reforms and their difficult implementation between a lack of capacity or willingness and sometimes claim that the regime's tactical concessions have been successful in deflecting pressures from above and from below without engaging in fundamental reforms. The Moroccan regime has definitely walked a fine line between engagement with domestic and international critics and control, given the persisting limits on the freedom of expression in the media.

Tunisia: further regression behind the façade of liberal reforms

In Tunisia, the regime continued to dominate the human rights discourse, especially vis-à-vis international actors, while repressing all forms of political competition, critical media and human rights activism in the country. It has thus not only minimized domestic pressure from below but also impeded an effective mobilization of transnational human rights networks.

The regime had attempted to align Tunisian human rights organizations through co-optation and infiltration, but at the end of the 1990s, many human rights activists started to turn against the regime more openly, prompting renewed

---

[4] Millennium Challenge Corporation: Morocco Compact, www.mcc.gov/pages/countries/program/morocco-compact.

repression. The regime never legalized the National Council for Freedom in Tunisia (*Conseil National pour les Libertés en Tunisie*, CNLT) founded in 1998. When the LTDH adopted a more critical stance in 2000, it also became the target of increasingly repressive measures (Geisser and Gobe 2004: 249; Langohr 2004: 184). Remaining within the limits of the "rule of law," the Tunisian regime pressed charges against members of the LTDH on various grounds, froze EU funds, and initiated media campaigns that together effectively precluded its effective operation (Chouikha 2006: 35; Geisser and Gobe 2004: 250).

In fact, the regime adroitly used constitutional and legislative reforms to consolidate its power while maintaining a façade of political liberalization. Legislative and constitutional reforms formally increased freedoms but left repressive clauses in place that allowed to restrict the scope of action of political parties, media and independent civil society (Chouikha 2006). Especially since the events of 9/11, the framing of political repression in the context of the fight against terrorism and Islamism created a certain degree of both domestic and international legitimacy, even though international NGOs have repeatedly denounced systematic human rights violations by the regime. Both the new anti-terror law of 2003 and a reform of the penal code in 2010 served to impede the joint mobilization of domestic and transnational human rights activists, restricting exchanges with the international community in terms of information and external (financial) support for Tunisian organizations (Del Sarto and Schumacher 2011: 944; Kausch 2009b: 6).

The Tunisian case clearly shows that tactical concessions do not necessarily backfire against the regime through a "boomerang effect" (Risse and Sikkink 1999) – at least for twenty years, the Ben Ali regime was successful in suppressing the mobilization of domestic actors. Without an independent judiciary, the legal guarantee of fundamental rights does not in itself trigger a broad mobilization to demand the effective move from commitment to compliance. Drawing on an extensive police apparatus and the judiciary, authorities used their discretion to discriminate against opponents to the regime. Mere inaction – e.g. not responding to a request for legalization by civil society organizations or political parties – provided the basis to then prosecute their members for illegal activities without giving them the opportunity to file complaints against this arbitrary but not random practice. While the regime thus effectively limited the scope of action of truly independent civil society organizations, it actively promoted organizations loyal to the regime (Geisser and Gobe 2004: 347). The regime has systematically limited the access of international human rights activists and observers, including United Nations (UN) special rapporteurs, to the country and impeded their contacts with domestic activists. Thus, AI placed the Tunisian 2010 reform of the penal code in the context of the regime's negotiations with the EU on an "advanced status" (Amnesty International 2011a: 325), trying to protect Tunisia's international reputation by preventing cross-border exchanges. The Euro-Mediterranean Human Rights Network (EMHRN), for example, had organized meetings with Tunisian and international human rights organizations in 2009 and 2010. It sent open letters together with AI, HRW, FIDH and other human rights organizations to the EU in July 2010 which triggered, however, little response.

Despite the regular exposure of repressive practices and outright human rights violations such as torture by international human rights organizations, the international community did not respond with pressure. On the occasion of the World Summit on the Information Society (WSIS) in Tunis in 2005, the violation of fundamental rights, e.g. through Internet censorship, and the repression of journalists and human rights activists were so blatant that the international community had to react (Chouikha 2006: 35; Geisser and Gobe 2004: 348). Tunisia's standing as a reliable partner of Western democracies was, however, not affected and the regime did not suffer from any coercive measures or sanctions. More generally, Tunisia's bilateral economic and political relations with the West have not suffered from the regime's human rights record and its refusal to cooperate in democracy promotion efforts, isolating the regime from all external attempts at influence. The EU and in particular the European Parliament (EP) complained several times when the Tunisian government blocked EU funding for the LTDH under the European Initiative for Democracy and Human Rights (EIDHR) but without avail.[5] The Tunisian authorities criminalized external support for domestic actors and made direct cooperation with Tunisian civil society organizations impossible. Even in intergovernmental relations, Tunisian authorities delayed the implementation of a large-scale project for the modernization of the judiciary under the EU's regional cooperation program MEDA between 2003 and 2007 until the European Commission officially suspended its efforts to implement democracy assistance projects with the Tunisian government (European Commission 2007a: 13). In a similar vein, the Tunisian authorities have always been reluctant to engage in political dialogue with international actors on issues related to human rights and democratization (see van Hüllen 2012; van Hüllen and Stahn 2009). Pointing to existing legal guarantees, ongoing political reforms, and its achievements on women's and socio-economic rights, the regime fended off any criticism as unacceptable interferences in domestic affairs and denied systematic violations of human rights. While international actors did not reward Tunisia as they did with Morocco, they neither cut assistance nor imposed sanctions. The United States even increased its Foreign Military Financing in 2009 and 2010 from around US$8 million to US$12–15 million (Sharp 2010: 15). The EU apparently used the request for an advanced status similar to the Moroccan one to gain some leverage over the country with regard to political reforms in 2008–2010, but concessions by the regime were

---

[5] See e.g. EP resolutions on the human rights situation in Tunisia and in particular the LTDH of December 14, 2000, September 29, 2005 and June 15, 2006 (Bulletin of the EU 12–2000, 9–2005, 6–2006).

rhetoric at best, considering the reform of the penal code in as late as June 2010 that further criminalized international contacts.

Scope conditions for the diverging developments in Morocco and Tunisia

While in both countries, authorities have appropriated the human rights dis-course and maintained a rhetoric of (democratic) change, they have done so in different ways: the Moroccan regime has actively cooperated with domes-tic and international actors, including human rights organizations and democ-racy promoters, and made their criticisms and demands part of its own agenda for reform. The Tunisian regime, by contrast, consistently refused to engage in similar exchanges with domestic and international actors. It successfully estab-lished a counter-narrative, claiming effective compliance with international human rights standards, e.g. in reference to women's rights, and denouncing international concerns either as threats to national security or as interferences in domestic affairs. By the end of 2010, the human rights situation in Morocco was still far from good, challenging the regime's sincerity in pursuing com-pliance, but there had definitely been improvements, especially compared to the "leaden years" under Hassan II, and politics and society were marked by a dynamic of change. By comparison, the situation in Tunisia had further regressed without any indication that the regime might relent – the weakness of the domestic human rights movement effectively precluding the mobilization of transnational networks.

Complementing the argument of structural differences leading to a more or less successful mobilization of transnational human rights networks advanced in the 1990s (Gränzer 1999: 115–118; Risse *et al.* 2002: 145–149), the scope conditions identified in Chapter 1 of this volume can account for the diver-ging human rights dynamics in Morocco and Tunisia (see van Hüllen 2012). First of all, while both countries fall into the category of authoritarian regimes with limited statehood, they still differ in their respective degrees of political liberalization and statehood. A more fine-grained analysis going beyond the dichotomous conceptualization of these two scope conditions reveals that the combination of political liberalization and statehood was much more favor-able to the regime's engagement in tactical concessions in Morocco than in Tunisia. As mentioned above, society and politics in modern Morocco had always been more pluralist than in Tunisia, making the monarchy more adept in reconciling regime survival with limited participation and competition than the republican (de facto) one-party system. At the same time, Tunisia was by far the most consolidated state in the region, providing the regime with the resources for repression and making it a stable and reliable partner in international relations. This was certainly one of the reasons why the Tunisian regime was remarkably successful in establishing a counter-narrative on human rights that effectively protected the country against external pressure. In addition, the lower level of socio-economic development, the ongoing conflict in the Western Sahara, and its strive for modernity made Morocco much more vulnerable to international demands. Finally, the systematic and centralized nature of human rights violations in Tunisia, e.g. through legal prosecution and torture, points to their strategic use by the Ben Ali regime, whereas the role of Moroccan authorities for the unsatisfactory implementation of reforms remains more ambiguous.

While the distinction between democratic and authoritarian regimes is not applicable to the cases of Morocco and Tunisia, the two countries differ with regard to their degrees of political liberalization. The more pluralistic organization of political and social life and greater freedoms of expression and association in Morocco are captured by indicators such as the Freedom in the World index (Freedom House 2011) or the Worldwide Governance Indicator (WGI) for "Voice and Accountability" (Kaufmann et al. 2010).[6] These differences in pluralism go back to structural differences between traditional monarchies, where the power of the king is not subject to political competition, and republican regimes, where the power of the presidency is inextricably linked to party politics (Langohr 2004: 189).

Morocco's greater engagement in reforms and cooperation with domestic and international actors was part of its survival strategy of "political inclusion" that offers limited political participation and contestation in exchange for loyalty to the monarchy (Cavatorta 2009; Dillman 1998; Lust-Okar 2007; Najem 2003). Since independence, the regime has reconciled the continued supremacy of the king with a semblance of political competition through multi-party elections. The *alternance* of 1997/1998 illustrates well that a change of government does not affect the distribution of political power effectively held by the monarch. The king can graciously grant political reforms to its subjects, using tactical concessions to alleviate public discontent and generate legitimacy for the regime without challenging its own position (Desrues and Moyano 2001). By contrast, the Tunisian regime had opted for a survival strategy that primarily compensated "political exclusion" with "economic inclusion," facilitated by sustained economic growth rates after the successful implementation of structural reforms in the 1980s (Dillman 1998; Najem 2003). This strategy led to the "Tunisian paradox," combining socio-economic modernization with increasing repression (Entelis 2005; Kausch 2009b). Despite the move to a multi-party system in 1987, this "façade democracy" (Sadiki 2002a) could not accommodate political dissent as easily as the Moroccan monarchy. The holding of competitive

---

[6] There have been no significant changes in the respective degrees of political liberalization in Morocco and Tunisia since the mid 1990s. This suggests that the indices rather capture scope conditions for than the impact of the two regimes' diverging responses to the mobilization of transnational human rights networks.

elections would have directly challenged the power and legitimacy of the incumbent regime. For the highly personalized presidential regime, it became crucial to eliminate all political opposition through co-optation and repression (Sadiki 2002b).

The effect of the respective level of political liberalization on the two regimes' willingness to yield to the dynamic of tactical concessions and mobilization of transnational human rights networks under the spiral model is reinforced by their diverging degrees of limited statehood. Indicators such as the WGI for "Government Effectiveness" (Kaufmann *et al.* 2010) or the "stateness" dimension of the Bertelsmann Transformation Index (BTI) (Bertelsmann Stiftung 2009b) attest Tunisia a higher capacity for effective governance than Morocco. This provided the Tunisian regime with the sheer capacity to build an extensive police and security apparatus, but also to systematically use legislation and prosecution as more elaborate means of repression. While Tunisia used its capacities to maintain a strategy of repression, the lower capacities in Morocco might explain in part why the implementation of political reforms has often been deficient, creating a gap between legal prescriptions and effective human rights protection. In fact, the Tunisian ability to maintain political stability, together with appeals to national unity (Sadiki 2002b), have generated a certain degree of legitimacy of repressive measures against political opponents and in particular Islamists in the name of a "war against terrorism" (Allani 2009; Willis 2006), both among secular Tunisian elites and many international actors. By contrast, the Western Sahara conflict threatens the stability and legitimacy of the monarchy in Morocco.

These two aspects directly link the degree of statehood to the two regimes' vulnerability to international demands. The perception of Tunisia as a harbor of stability in the region and as a reliable partner in the fight against terrorism (and Islamism) has shielded the country from international pressure even though it does not possess any significant economic or military resources on a global scale (Durac and Cavatorta 2009). At the same time, the Western Sahara conflict and the monarchy's pledge for territorial unity makes the Moroccan regime much more dependent on international support in order to defy various UN resolutions calling for a referendum (Darbouche and Zoubir 2008; Gillespie 2010; Willis and Messari 2005). In addition, the level of socio-economic development is much lower in Morocco than in Tunisia and, as an Islamic monarchy, the regime conforms much less to expectations of modernity in the international community than the secular republic of Tunisia, generating itself as the defender of women's rights in the Arab region (Grami 2008). Taken together, these factors suggest a greater material and social vulnerability of Morocco, making the regime more amenable to external demands for cooperation and reform, allowing the spiral model to work. By contrast, Tunisia successfully established a counter-narrative to the international human rights discourse that further deflected pressure from above.

Finally, the argument about the (de)centralization of rule implementation links well to the question of willingness and capacity for (non-)compliance with domestic and international human rights standards, captured by the combination of political liberalization and statehood. In the case of Tunisia, the political leadership was clearly responsible for human rights violations, maintaining a firm control of the executive and the judiciary. While it might not have directly commanded acts of torture, the systematic nature of human rights abuses by the police forces and the lack of their prosecution suggest their endorsement from higher up. In Morocco, the situation is more ambiguous. Human rights violations and the deficient implementation of legal reforms might be a problem of capacity as they are removed from the central authorities. However, the regime is able to enforce its rules of the game when it systematically prosecutes journalists and human rights activists that break established taboos. Similarly, the disastrous human rights record in the Western Sahara and the targeted repression of Sahrawi activists suggest a strategic choice of not granting human rights to this part of the population.

The "Arab Spring" in Tunisia and Morocco in 2011

The wave of popular protest that spread across the countries of the Middle East and North Africa in early 2011 has dramatically changed the political landscape in the region – and created new conditions for the spiral model to work. The "Arab Spring" is the result of an unprecedented mobilization of the masses and was not (primarily) brought about by transnational human rights networks. The different histories of Morocco and Tunisia with the spiral model can account, however, for their diverging trajectories during these times of change. Furthermore, recent events might facilitate the move from commitment to compliance in either country in the future: through regime change in Tunisia and regime transformation in Morocco. Indeed, the Arab Spring marks the ultimate failure of the Tunisian approach to regime survival, combining economic inclusion with political exclusion, whereas the "reformist" Moroccan regime might weather this challenge maybe not unscathed, but still in power.

In late 2010, the self-immolation of Mohamed Bouazizi triggered a mass mobilization around economic grievances that quickly acquired a political dimension and spread from the provincial town of Sidi Bouzid to the capital.[7] Socio-economic inequalities and especially high unemployment rates mobilized in particular the youth and led to more fundamental challenges to the incumbent regime's legitimacy in the name of "human dignity." In order to address corruption and mismanagement among the old elites, protesters claimed their

---

[7] For a number of assessments of the immediate causes for and the course of events in Tunisia, see e.g. Ayadi *et al.* (2011), Cassarino (2011), Murphy (2011), Paciello (2011) and Schraeder and Redissi (2011).

right to political freedoms and participation. At first, the regime tried to violently suppress the uprising, but as the movement gained momentum in January 2011, the military leadership finally refused to crack down on protesters and turned against President Ben Ali. The flight of Ben Ali with his family to Saudi Arabia on January 14, 2011 marked the breakdown of the old authoritarian regime. A civilian interim government and presidency under the protection of the military has taken over power in order to manage Tunisia's lengthy transition to democracy. As the process of dismantling old elites, forming political parties, and establishing new institutions proved increasingly complex and controversial, the elections for a Constituent Assembly were postponed to October 23, 2011. The clear winner was the moderate Islamist Renaissance Party (*Hizb Al-Nahda*), banned under Ben Ali since 1989 and legalized as a political party in March 2011, winning ninety of the 217 seats in the Constituent Assembly.[8] The Tunisian revolution had an immediate impact on the human rights situation regarding political rights and civil liberties and the interim government renewed its commitment to international human rights norms through the ratification of several international human rights conventions in June 2011.[9] Organized civil society only played a minor role in the mobilization of the masses, as did domestic and international human rights organizations (Schraeder and Redissi 2011: 11–13). Among the major international human rights organizations, the FIDH was the first to pick up on the events in Tunisia with a press release on December 27, 2010, whereas AI and HRW only followed in January 2011.[10] Acting as watchdogs, they have critically covered the developments ever since through a number of press releases, public statements, and urgent calls for action. In several reports, they called for a systematic investigation of "state violence during anti-government protests" (Amnesty International 2011b) and pointed to ongoing violations of human rights under the interim government (FIDH 2011b). The international community reacted late and most actors did not take

---

[8] See e.g. Al Jazeera news articles on "Ennahda Wins Tunisia's Elections" and "Tunisian Coalition Government 'in 10 Days'" of October 28, 2011 on http://english.aljazeera.net (last accessed October 31, 2011).

[9] These include, among others, the Optional Protocol to the ICCPR (1966), Optional Protocol to the 1986 Convention against Torture (2002), and the International Convention for the Protection of All Persons from Enforced Disappearance (2006); see United Nations Treaty Collection, http://treaties.un.org/.

[10] FIDH: Émeutes dans la région de Sidi Bouzid après la tentative de suicide d'un jeune, press release December 27, 2010, www.fidh.org/Emeutes-dans-la-region-de-Sidi-Bouzid-apres-la; AI: Tunisians Must be Allowed to Protest Peacefully without Fear, press release January 6, 2011, www.amnesty.org/en/news-and-updates/tunisians-must-be-allowed-protest-peacefully-without-fear-2011-01-07; HRW: Tunisia: End Use of Excessive Force; Free Political Prisoners, press release on January 14, 2011, www.hrw.org/news/2011/01/14/tunisia-end-use-excessive-force-free-political-prisoners (last accessed October 31, 2011).

a clear stance on the political uprising until the old regime had broken down and protests started to spread across the region.

During the Arab Spring, Morocco saw a first major manifestation of political discontent on February 20, 2011, when youth movements organized demonstrations throughout the country, starting the "February 20 Movement for Change" which rallied human rights and other civil society organizations.[11] In Rabat, these demonstrations were peaceful and apparently tolerated by the authorities, but protesters and the police clashed in a number of other Moroccan cities and international human rights organizations have repeatedly criticized the use of police violence to contain protests in 2011.[12] As in the case of Tunisia and other countries, demands for greater social equality were combined with political claims for democracy and human rights, denouncing corruption among the ruling elites and demanding legal and constitutional reforms – but not the deposition of Mohamed VI nor the abolition of the monarchy. In light of increasing protest in Morocco and throughout the region, Mohamed VI started to make further (tactical) concessions for fear of a domino effect. In a throne speech on March 9, 2011, he repeated his commitment to human rights and democratization and announced the creation of a commission that would elaborate constitutional reforms (see Ottaway 2011). As before, the commission only comprised experts appointed by the king, but it consulted political parties, human rights and other civil society organizations as well as individuals. Many organizations and especially the 20 February Movement, however, refused to participate in this top-down initiative for reform and political protests continued. The commission finalized its work in June 2011 and the king officially presented the new draft constitution on June 17, 2011. Supported by most political parties, it was adopted by referendum on July 1, 2011 despite repeated criticism that the changes did not go far enough to effectively limit the power of the king and transform the authoritarian character of the monarchy. The jury is still out on the impact of the constitutional reform on political life and the human rights situation in Morocco.[13] Throughout the reform process, authorities have

---

[11] The reform process in Morocco has received much less attention among scholars than the revolution in Tunisia, but see e.g. Colombo (2011) and Ottaway (2011).

[12] See e.g. the following press releases and public statements: AI: Moroccan Authorities Must Uphold Freedom of Assembly, Index Number: MDE 29/001/2011, Date Published: February 24, 2011, www.amnesty.org/en/library/info/MDE29/001/2011/en; AI: Morocco: Investigate Torture Allegations, Index Number: MDE 29/008/2011, Date Published: June 17, 2011, www.amnesty.org/en/library/info/MDE29/008/2011/en; HRW: Morocco: Thousands Demonstrate Peacefully. Police Restraint Contrasts with Previous Week's Violent Repression, March 21, 2011, www.hrw.org/news/2011/03/21/morocco-thousands-demonstrate-peacefully; FIDH: Maroc: la lumière doit être faite sur les violences policières à l'encontre des manifestants, June 8, 2011, www.fidh.org/Maroc-la-lumiere-doit-etre-faite-sur-les (last accessed October 31, 2011).

[13] E.g. FIDH: Arab Spring at the Heart of World Coalition Debates, August 23, 2011, www.fidh.org/Arab-spring-at-the-heart-of-World (last accessed October 31, 2011).

continued to crack down on protesters and journalists. At the same time, media coverage has been more critical than ever, apparently pushing the limits of the official discourse, touching upon traditional taboos. Again, international human rights organizations have acted as watchdogs, highlighting both shortcomings and positive developments.[14]

The events in Morocco throughout the Arab Spring in 2011 are in line with previous developments and expectations generated by the spiral model. There has been a mutually reinforcing dynamic of political concessions and the mobilization of domestic and transnational human rights organizations, but the path from commitment to compliance is still long: human rights violations in particular by the police forces persist and are only unsatisfactorily addressed by the regime. Legal and institutional reforms initiated are not yet reflected in sustained levels of political liberalization. These observations challenge the credibility of the incumbent regime as a driver of fundamental change. Often, the effective implementation of reforms might be hampered by a lack of capacity rather than willingness, but the Moroccan case nevertheless illustrates the limits of transformation without regime change. The pace of reforms and their implementation are slowed down by the fact that the king would undermine his own position, together with and against the ruling elite. Concessions are intended as much to contain discontent and maintain political power as to genuinely accommodate popular demands, opting for continuity through change (Ottaway 2011). Through appropriating the discourse on human rights and democratization, the regime controls the national agenda for reform and becomes a legitimate partner for both domestic and international actors (Colombo 2011).

The case of Tunisia, by contrast, demonstrates the importance of scope conditions for the spiral model to work. The successful mobilization of transnational human rights networks at one point in time does not necessarily trigger a linear development from one phase of the model to the next. Over a period of more than twenty years, the authoritarian regime under Ben Ali was able to stifle the domestic human rights movement and cut its link to international human rights organizations. Legal reforms merely served the purpose of maintaining the image of a progressive and reformist regime in the international community while the authoritarian interpretation of the "rule of law" allowed an even more effective repression through prosecution. Reframing the human rights discourse in terms of national unity and security, the international community let

---

[14] See e.g. AI: Morocco Royal Pardon an Encouraging Step, Index Number: MDE 29/002/2011, Date Published: April 15, 2011, www.amnesty.org/en/library/info/ MDE29/002/2011/en; HRW: Morocco: Thousands March for Reform. Demonstrations End Peacefully as Police Stay Away, February 20, 2011, www.hrw.org/news/2011/02/20/ morocco-thousands-march-reform; FIDH: Discours du roi Mohammed VI: la FIDH appelle à la mise en œuvre effective des réformes annoncées, March 16, 2011, www.fidh. org/Discours-du-roi-Mohammed-VI-la-FIDH-appelle-a-la (last accessed October 31, 2011).

Tunisia get away with this strategy despite increasing criticism by international human rights NGOs. Even though the country does not possess any impressive power resources, most Western countries valued the regime as a reliable partner for stability and against terrorism and Islamism in the region, refraining from the use of coercive measures or sanctions. Ultimately, the regime's strategy backfired and with hindsight it is not at all surprising that Tunisia experienced a revolution whereas the protest movement in Morocco was more moderate. The complete refusal to allow any form of pluralism – expressed in public debates, political parties or civil society organizations – deprived the Tunisian people of any outlet for increasing discontent with the political and human rights situation. The current economic crisis added to this situation, but also the growing socio-economic inequalities usually ignored by international observers in light of the country's seeming success in modernization and development (Ayadi *et al.* 2011: 2–3; Paciello 2011; Schraeder and Redissi 2011: 7). Change in Tunisia needed to be radical, challenging the legitimacy and the survival of the regime as such.

Conclusions

This chapter has reviewed the original findings on the spiral model in Tunisia and Morocco by tracing further developments between commitment and compliance since 2000 and in particular in light of the "Arab Spring" and recent events in both countries. Until 2010, Morocco slowly moved from commitment to compliance. The regime responded to the continued mobilization of transnational networks and an increased engagement of international actors by appropriating the human rights discourse as a part of its reform agenda. While making tactical concessions, it thus effectively controlled the pace of reforms and their implementation. By contrast, the Tunisian regime cut the link between domestic and international human rights activists through increased repression, insulating itself against pressures from below and from above. Despite increasing international criticism, it maintained a discourse of progress and reform and fended off demands for reform voiced by international actors. These differences between Morocco and Tunisia can be accounted for by the specific combinations of political liberalization and statehood and Morocco's greater vulnerability to domestic and external demands.

While the Tunisian strategy of "political exclusion plus economic inclusion" was relatively successful over the past twenty years, growing economic grievances caused a popular uprising in 2010 that quickly acquired a political dimension, leading to the breakdown of the authoritarian regime with the flight of Ben Ali. The legitimacy of the transitional regime is built on demands for democratic participation and it has renewed its commitment to international human rights norms. Nevertheless, the outcome of transition is still open and if the new regime is not bound by continued mass mobilization and strengthened civil society organizations, Tunisia risks to repeat its experience with the short-lived political opening of 1987. In Morocco, popular protest has never directly challenged the legitimacy of the monarchy, but increasing pressure from below and fear of a domino effect have prompted Mohamed VI to make further tactical concessions in the form of a constitutional reform. Again, the jury is out on whether these reforms will speed up Morocco's progress toward political liberalization and the effective protection of human rights. Organized civil society has only played a marginal role in the course of the Arab Spring, but the mobilization of transnational human rights networks can help consolidate changes and avoid authoritarian backlashes on the way from commitment to compliance.

PART IV

From commitment to compliance:
companies, rebels, individuals

11

Encouraging greater compliance: local networks and the United Nations Global Compact

WAGAKI MWANGI, LOTHAR RIETH AND
HANS PETER SCHMITZ

Human rights norms are today a central aspect of the corporate social responsibility (CSR) agenda. After decades of exclusive attention to the behavior of states, human rights activists began during the late 1980s and 1990s to increase their pressures on corporate actors and demand commitment to and compliance with basic human rights in the business world.[1] Unlike states, corporations lack international legal personality and cannot express commitment by signing on to formal international human rights treaties. Apart from voluntary standards, codes of conduct, and other United Nations standard-setting activities directed at businesses (Mantilla 2009), the Global Compact (GC) represents to date the main UN-sanctioned soft law designed to commit corporations to international standards of human rights and environmental protection. The GC does not replace the main compliance mechanisms set out by the legal obligations assumed by states under international law, but its goal is to supplement those existing mechanisms with an additional, non-binding avenue of promoting universal human rights principles (Rasche 2009; Shelton 2000).

The GC has attracted the most diverse membership, making it the "world's leading corporate citizenship initiative" (Annan 2006). With its emphasis on corporate citizenship, not legal accountability, as well as low entry barriers and minimal reporting requirements, the Compact offers a compelling

Previous versions of this chapter were presented at the Global Politics Seminar, Syracuse University, April 17, 2009, the workshop "The Power of Human Rights," University of Wyoming, August 25–27, 2009, as well as the workshop "From Commitment to Compliance: The Persistent Power of Human Rights," Berlin, June 3–5, 2010. We would like to thank Michael Beckstrand, the editors and reviewers of this volume, and the workshop participants for their feedback and support.

[1] In 1991, Amnesty International dropped its policy of targeting solely the government with *de jure* control over a given territory, even if violations were not committed by government agents. Many critics at that time argued that the new policy of shaming private actors would divert attention away from the responsibility of governments.

test case for the significance of discourses, learning, and capacity-building as pathways to compliance. The GC pursues an explicit strategy of using low entry barriers as well as "norm diffusion and the dissemination of practical know-how and tools" (Ruggie 2007: 820) to quickly expand the reach of its norms into the corporate sector. It uses non-coercive measures for achieving its goals by creating incentives connected to a firm's reputation-building efforts. But commitment to norms is meaningless if it does not have an impact on the behavior and compliance of private actors. In this chapter, we focus on compliance and ask if membership in the GC has a positive impact on the behavior of corporations or is merely a public relations stunt designed to "blue-wash" their image by adding the UN logo to the corporate social responsibility (CSR) statements.

After ten years of existence, corporate membership in the GC remains limited to a relatively small number of corporations largely based in Western Europe. Size is a strong predictor of likelihood to join, indicating that being a part of this UN venture remains primarily important for globally operating firms as well as for smaller and mid-sized companies linked to those global players. Considering that the GC is only a decade old and many of its members joined even more recently, assessing its impact on corporate behavior is challenging. We find that membership in the GC alone is unlikely to move a company in significant ways toward progressive and continuous implementation of the core GC principles. We argue that the existence of active regional and local GC networks is a crucial ingredient for setting in motion specific mechanisms, such as peer learning and capacity-building, that can contribute effectively to improved performance of individual member companies (Gilbert 2010; Rieth *et al.* 2007).

The chapter is organized as follows. We first provide some background on the emergence of norms related to corporate citizenship as well as a brief overview of the GC and its operation. We then move to the issues of commitment and compliance, defining each within the corporate context where obligations remain voluntary at the global level and measuring outcomes of specific firm policies can be difficult. In the empirical sections, we first address variation in the commitment to the GC among corporations and discuss why membership is concentrated geographically in Europe and remains largely limited to the largest global companies. In the second part, we first show that membership in the GC is strongly correlated with additional and usually subsequent steps toward integrating the ten principles into the managerial and strategic culture of a company. We use evidence from the Global Reporting Initiative (GRI) on the twenty largest companies in the automotive and utilities sector to support our conclusions. In the final empirical section, we then elaborate on two specific mechanisms – peer learning and capacity-building – to elaborate in what ways local networks can contribute to improved corporate performance along the ten principles.

The corporate social responsibility (CSR) movement: from denial to commitment

Debates about the transnational human rights effects of corporations date back to the colonial era (Ratner 2001), but played a relatively minor role compared with the domestic context where businesses and their behavior was first regulated. Major economic crises, such as the Great Depression, led to significant regulatory efforts by governments, but also gave rise to ideas such as corporate social responsibility (CSR) among management scholars and neighboring academic fields. With the proliferation of stock markets and private investments after World War II, the general public became a recognized stakeholder for corporations (Kell and Ruggie 1999; Whitehouse 2003). While the idea of corporate citizenship slowly took hold, its geographic scope remained limited to the domestic context of business operations and its primary tool became philanthropy. As a result, the ethical behavior of corporations was largely divorced from their actual practices and framed as a matter of re-investing profits in (domestic) society.

During the 1960s and 1970s, transnational activists began to focus attention on the role of multinational corporations in sustaining systematic human rights abuses abroad. Early results of these efforts were the 1976 OECD Declaration and Decisions on International Investment and Multinational Enterprises, the 1977 Sullivan Principles on Apartheid, the 1977 US Foreign Corrupt Practices Act (FCPA), the International Labor Organization's 1977 Declaration of Principles Concerning Multinational Enterprises and Social Policy, and the United Nations Draft Code of Conduct for Transnational Corporations initiated in 1980 and concluded in 1992 (Asante 1989). While these initiatives may have had only limited effects on corporate behavior, they played a crucial role in establishing normative expectations for corporate accountability and citizenship.

With the end of the Cold War, corporations became a more direct target of transnational activist networks focusing on labor rights and environmental destruction (Jenkins 2005: 527; Kell and Ruggie 1999). At the same time, corporate actors developed increasingly elaborate industry- and firm-level codes of conduct (Cutler *et al.* 1999; Kolk and van Tulder 2005). The preferred frameworks consisted of adopting voluntary regimes such as the "Principles of Business" committing companies broadly to improving economic and social conditions (Broad and Cavanagh 1997: 21–24). But developing and accepting such voluntary standards represents only a very first step away from the outright denial of responsibility for certain conducts violating human rights. The key challenge is to determine if and how mechanisms designed to diffuse the GC principles can positively contribute to moving corporations beyond the mere rhetorical acceptance of such norms. This process can be understood as a gradual expansion of CSR efforts, starting with their inclusion in internal management processes, continuing with the integration into core business strategies, and ending with a proactive promotion of those principles across a sector and industry (Zadek 2004).

While enforcement remains limited at the global level, we can observe a norms cascade of increasingly well-defined expectations targeted at corporations and their behavior at home and abroad. Similar to states shaping international human rights treaties, corporate actors have also been involved in the creation of these norms (see Chapter 12, this volume). Most importantly, this normative framework shifted markedly by focusing more directly on the actual business practices and by overcoming territorial boundaries as traditional limits to corporate responsibility. Establishing such standards is a crucial step in engaging corporate actors within the logic of the "spiral model" using tools of socialization, learning and capacity-building (see Chapter 1, this volume).

The Global Compact: governance and membership

The Global Compact was formally launched on July 26, 2000 and represents the first effort by the United Nations to create a multi-sectoral network of corporations, professional associations and NGOs designed to advance a commitment to corporate social responsibility. Apart from the main target of corporations, other membership categories include NGOs,[2] unions, business associations, cities, academic institutions and UN agencies. The GC is not legally binding and asks its members to "embrace, support and enact, within their sphere of influence, a set of core values in the areas of human rights, labor standards, the environment, and anti-corruption" (United Nations Global Compact Office 2010a).[3] Corporations join the GC by submitting a letter of commitment signed by the chief executive.

Exclusive control of the GC is maintained by the UN and members do not participate in the governance of the institution. The primary tools used by the GC to advance its core mission are achieving "scale" to further its own legitimacy and creating platforms for learning through regional and local networks fostering collaboration among members (Bremer 2008; Ruggie 2002; Waddock 2005). In the context of this book and its four compliance processes, the GC emphasizes learning and capacity-building with some incentive-based strategies added as a result of governance reforms in 2003 and 2005.

Membership of the GC grew quickly from an initial forty-four organizations to 300 by its first anniversary, 1,457 by April 2004 (McKinsey & Company 2004: 10), 3,800 by January 2007, 6,200 members by April 2009, and 7,700 participants in 130 countries by June 2009. As of July 2011, the GC had more than 8,000

---

[2] A number of major transnational NGOs are members of the GC, including Amnesty International, Conservation International, Human Rights Watch, Oxfam, Transparency International and the World Wild Life Fund.

[3] The ten core principles of the GC are available at: www.unglobalcompact.org/.

total members and more than 6,000 business members in 135 nations (United Nations Global Compact Office 2010b). Membership growth has slowed in recent years as a result of active delisting of non-reporting companies by the UNGC office. While current GC membership is only a fraction of the 140 million businesses in Dun & Bradstreet's global corporate database, most research on the GC focuses on a smaller sample of the largest companies, such as the Russell Index of the 10,000 largest listed companies.

At the end of 2006, Bremer finds that total participation of Russell 10,000 companies in the GC was about 3% globally, reaching close to 9.5% in the developed world (Bremer 2008: 236). While 28% of all Western European Russell 10,000 companies are in the GC, membership in other regions remains between 1% and 5%. Thus, the GC is still far away from a "tipping point" globally (both in the developed and the developing world), although it has reached such a level in Western Europe. Despite deliberate efforts by the GC Secretariat, recruitment in the United States lags behind other regions. While corporations from the developed countries are predominately larger, transnational businesses, the majority of the members from the developing world are small- and medium-sized enterprises focused on the networking and learning opportunities associated with the GC (Cetindamar and Husoy 2007: 167).

Early critics of the GC charged that corporate members were simply reaping reputational benefits without being held accountable in any meaningful way (Sagafi-Nejad 2005; Thérien and Pouliot 2006). In response, the GC established a formal "Communication on Progress" (COP) mechanism in 2003, requiring all members to submit an annual report (Arevalo and Fallon 2008). Businesses are now asked to renew their commitment annually and submit a COP detailing their efforts to "adhere to the principles and to encourage other companies, such as suppliers, to comply" (Bremer 2008: 230).

Following a review of its governance structure in 2005, the GC also added an advisory board with twenty members from the four core constituencies (business, civil society, labor and the United Nations) and also established a Global Compact Leaders Summit, to be held triennially to discuss the overall direction of the GC. In a shift toward adding forms of reputational sanction, the GC also began to formally classify companies as "non-communicating" if they missed their deadline for submitting the annual report and as "inactive" following one year of non-communication. Companies may also be labeled "inactive" as a result of the GC's complaints mechanism. If a complaint is accepted by the GC office, the company is required to respond to it within three months of being informed. Names of delisted companies are published on the GC website and such companies may no longer use the GC name or logo (unless they re-join the GC). Beyond keeping track of the annual reporting requirement, the GC does not monitor actual compliance of its membership.

The role of networks in implementing GC principles

We primarily focus on how companies move from an initial commitment to the GC toward the progressive implementation of its principles across the four key areas (human and labor rights, environment, and corruption). Corporations are also subject to legal enforcement in the national context of their operations, but the emergence of the GC and other voluntary initiatives indicates that this hierarchical model of compliance is less effective in ensuring rule-consistent behavior. Moreover, in the context of limited statehood or authoritarian states (see Chapter 1, this volume; also Chapter 4), transnational corporate actors are increasingly seen as an alternative tool in advancing human rights under conditions of outright resistance (autocracy) or lack of political and administrative capacity (limited statehood). Hence, our focus here is on exploring the viability of those "softer" mechanisms targeting corporations developed by the GC.

In the case of the GC, the governance reforms of 2003 and 2005 added two mild forms of sanction (see above). Bremer finds that "97% of all industrialized country companies that joined in 2000, the GC's first year, remained fully compliant" (Bremer 2008: 240) by the end of 2006. This rate drops to 65% for the same set of companies joining in 2004. By late 2010, 1,377 businesses were listed as "non-communicating" and 1,717 had been delisted for failing to submit their progress reports (United Nations Global Compact Office 2010b). Regional membership development varies significantly, in particular following the GC's decision to delist inactive companies. While Europe dominates the GC with close to 4,000 members in 2009, membership from the Americas actually dropped after 2008 while the growth rates in Asia/Oceania and especially the Africa/Middle East regions remain modest (United Nations Global Compact Office 2010c: 19). The main positive incentives provided by membership in the GC are reputational and financial. Members of the GC can use its logo in advertising and especially smaller businesses mention the networking opportunities offered as part of the GC local networks as a positive. Since more than half of the GC membership is comprised of small- and medium-sized enterprises (SMEs) whose operations are almost entirely local, their continued engagement depends largely on the strength of local GC networks (Whelan 2010: 338).

Additionally, the GC networks facilitate the two other mechanisms mentioned in the introduction: discourse/peer learning and capacity-building. Persuasion can take two distinct forms, one being the more prominent "naming and shaming" activities of transnational NGOs targeted at states and other non-state actors, the other a more collaborative discourse aimed at solving a joint problem. Major prominent businesses, including Shell, Nestlé and Nike, have become subject to high-profile advocacy campaigns (see Chapter 12, this volume) which took by and large the trajectory outlined by the spiral model, beginning with initial vehement denial and leading to tactical concessions and usually some changes in corporate behavior. Although these campaigns permanently altered how the global public perceives corporate responsibility, they are not necessarily representative of the main mechanisms by which norms influence corporate actors. In this chapter, we focus primarily on less contentious mechanisms, especially capacity-building as a first step necessary in decentralized rule implementation.

Participation in local and regional networks not only brings companies together with potential business partners, but also facilitates discourse with civil society actors or UN agencies. The number of such local networks reached ninety-two in 2009 and each pledges to hold at least two meetings annually, one dedicated to organizational questions and one devoted to substantial questions of advancing the ten principles. As part of these regular meetings, business representatives learn about "best practices," complete exercises in analyzing Communication on Progress (COP) reports, and develop partnerships with academic and governmental institutions as well as civil society groups. While the level of activity varies widely across these networks, a few have pushed well beyond the general and weak GC requirements. For example, the GC local network in the United Kingdom requires that all companies must submit their COP for peer review (United Nations Global Compact Office 2010c: 47). In this sense, the local or regional networks serve as an intermediary step facilitating movement from commitment to compliance and increasing the demands on membership in terms of translating the ten principles into business practices. They also represent the main site where the most appropriate tools to advance human rights can be developed and applied to a diverse membership. While capacity-building may be the most appropriate mechanism for a small company just joining the GC, networks can also provide localized incentives or even sanctions in order to advance the GC agenda.

The definition and measurement of commitment for corporate actors is complex and joining the GC is certainly not an example of "prescriptive status" as defined in the Chapter 1 by Ropp and Risse. Membership in the GC puts a corporation somewhere between the stage of tactical concessions and prescriptive status, depending on the extent of translating the ten principles into standard operating procedures in daily business practices. There are no generalized standards on how corporations ought to incorporate the ten principles into their operations, but examples of such efforts may include regular training of employees, establishing compliance hotlines for employees and other stakeholders,[4] and appointing an Ombudsman. This "output" dimension combined with a measure of compliance with the modest annual reporting requirements

---

[4] The German chemical company BASF reported forty-eight calls to such a hotline for 2009. "Of these complaints, 12 calls were verified as actual violations of our standards of behavior. The resulting personnel measures ranged from refresher courses on our standards of behavior through verbal and written warnings or even dismissals" (BASF 2010).

of the GC allows for establishing the place of a specific company along the continuum from commitment to compliance.

Even more difficult to assess is "rule-consistent behavior" as an outcome measure. Business operations can have a wide variety of intended and unintended consequences across many human rights issues and each firm has different relations with suppliers, governments and local communities. In addition, data about human rights conditions is collected at the level of nation states, not firms. And even if some corporations, such as Nike, now report annually violations of its CSR standards across its suppliers, there are no standardized measures allowing for a comparison of rule-consistent behavior across corporations within or across sectors.

In the absence of clear indicators measuring independently the actual impact of corporate conduct, the contributions of firms to the promotion of human rights is best understood as a continuum beginning with an initial acceptance of such responsibility usually expressed in joining a voluntary initiative such as the GC (commitment). What follows are several steps of behavioral change (Zadek 2004), beginning with an integration of such norms into daily operations (managerial level), a next step of making human rights norms a core part of the company's self-understanding (strategic level), and finally an active promotion of these norms not only within the company, but the sector overall (industry or societal level).

Commitment: GC membership patterns

Our sample of firms here is the Forbes Global 500 list, which ranks the world's largest corporations.[5] Global Compact participation is assessed by comparing the Forbes list to the GC membership.

Figure 11.1 shows the ten nations with the highest number of corporate headquarters on the Forbes Global 500 list. Overall 197 firms (39.4%) were GC members and membership would be well above 50% if participation in the United States was more widespread. Of 162 US-based corporations, only 23 (14.2%) were GC members, compared to rates above 80% for major European economies, including Spain (100%, total: twelve companies), Germany (90%, total: 20), France (82.8%, total: 29), and the Netherlands (81.8%, total: 11). From a total of 32 Chinese companies, seven (21.9%) were GC members.

These results confirm and enhance the results of earlier studies explaining GC membership patterns based on firm size and supplier relations with the United Nations (Bernhagen and Mitchell 2010). Firm size is a key predictor of membership, while companies doing business with the United Nations are generally

---

[5] Five of the Global 500 firms are listed with headquarters in two countries. These firms were counted twice for each country.

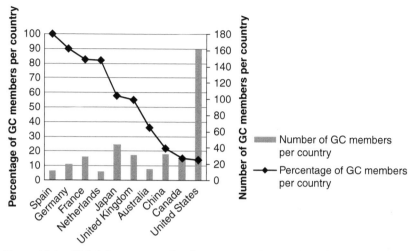

Figure 11.1   Global Compact membership among Forbes 500 firms

expected to be members of the GC. Among the Forbes Global 500 companies overall participation in the GC is significantly higher compared to the *Forbes 2000 Global* list, where US participation drops to 2% and European companies have membership rates in the 40% range (Bernhagen and Mitchell 2010: 1180). The initial membership drive for the GC was likely dominated by larger industry leaders with already well developed CSR policies.[6] Large firms not only have the resources to engage in these types of activities, but also have more interest in proactively engaging these issues, in particular in a transnational context where business success depends on dealing with a variety of governmental and non-governmental actors. A majority of US-based companies in the Forbes 500 list have largely domestic business activities and thus much lower incentives to join the GC. The minority of US companies in the GC are mostly global businesses, including Microsoft, Nike, Coca-Cola and Cisco Systems.

Lower participation of US companies shows that a generally negative attitude toward the United Nations in the home environment (Bennie *et al.* 2007: 748) will dampen the effects of size and global exposure (Bernhagen and Mitchell 2010). This claim is also confirmed by a 2004 McKinsey study explaining a lack of US participation with reference to fear of "potential

---

[6] This can also mean that CSR leaders quickly realize that the Global Compact offers few additional benefits to them. Runhaar and Lafferty (2009) find in a study of three telecommunication companies (Telenor, British Telecom, Deutsche Telekom) that they see the local networks established as part of the GC as its main benefit. Overall, they found that the GC "does not provide industry-specific input or resources (in terms of either knowledge or partners)" (492) which indicates that the learning approach taken by the GC is more appropriate for corporations with less experience in this area.

legal liabilities," outright rejection of the labor rights provisions, and "a relatively low assessment of the potential benefits of association with the UN"
(McKinsey & Company 2004: 11).

With the establishment of an explicit self-reporting requirement in 2005 and
its enforcement since 2008, the GC Secretariat now regularly suspends and ter-
minates membership of those corporations failing to submit their COP reports.
Only about one-third of all members regularly submit these required reports
and enforcing the requirement will likely lead to a significant slow-down in
membership development in the future. For example, almost all business members based in Romania and the Philippines as well as more than half of those
based in Egypt, Cameroon and Mexico were delisted in late 2009 (Rieth and
Glindemann 2010: 2).

The membership development of the first decade reveals that the GC is not
viewed as a costless proposition for corporations. If corporations saw the GC as
"cheap talk," we would expect to see much more impressive growth in membership over time as well as rampant non-compliance with the reporting requirements.[7] GC membership development overall thus challenges claims that
commitment to universal principles is just an "empty promise." Other studies
confirm that firms do not assume that human rights activists and the general
public are "easily satisfied or inattentive" (Bernhagen and Mitchell 2010: 1179).
Hence, joining the GC or other CSR initiatives is understood to be a meaningful
step that entails follow-up in terms of changing corporate behavior.

Explaining progressive implementation of GC principles

A few qualitative and quantitative studies on the effects of GC membership on
corporate behavior exist today (Bernhagen and Mitchell 2010; Clapp 2008), but
there remains a significant dearth in "studies about the impact of the Compact
on existing business practices" (Rasche 2009: 532). Scholars offering quantitative assessments of the effectiveness of voluntary CSR initiatives have argued
that "fruitful research in this area could examine qualitatively the impact that
comprehensive voluntary social initiatives have on CSP (corporate social performance)" (Tashman and Rivera 2010: 509). We argue here that local networks
organizing interactions between GC members (including businesses, unions,
academic institutions and civil society) are crucial in going beyond mere legal
requirements and strengthening the ability of an individual company to contribute positively to continuously and sustainably improving human rights
and environmental conditions. "Their role is to facilitate the progress of companies (both local firms and subsidiaries of foreign corporations) engaged in
the Compact with respect to implementation of the ten principles, while also

---

[7] Simmons (2009: 60) makes a similar argument with regard to state commitments to human
rights treaties.

creating opportunities for multi-stakeholder engagement and collective action" (United Nations Global Compact Office 2010d).

A key challenge for scholars is to define and measure such effects going beyond compliance with legal and reporting requirements. Measuring a firm's performance on human rights is a complex task because systematic data on human rights violations are organized around nation states, not firms and any changes in human rights are more likely to be driven by governmental policies. Scholars have taken some steps towards assessing the level of corporate compliance, for example by surveying firms and independently assessing their implementation efforts in training and monitoring their employees (Christmann and Taylor 2006). Others have taken explicit references to human rights in company policies as a proxy along with relying on external rankings of corporations (Bernhagen and Mitchell 2010). Our focus is on elaborating how specific mechanisms such as discourses, peer learning and capacity-building contained in the regular practices of local networks can contribute to improvements in corporate performance regarding rights protection.

A number of initiatives now regularly rank corporations in terms of their environmental and human rights performance, although all of these measures are composites and cannot be broken down to analyze specific human rights compliance. Such independent assessments include the Global Reporting Initiative (GRI), the Global 100 list of most sustainable companies (Global Responsible Investment Network 2010), the Global 1000 Sustainable Performance Leaders (Justmeans 2010), the Dow Jones Sustainable Indexes (DJSI), and Tomorrow's Value Rating (Two Tomorrows 2010). Commercial providers also increasingly offer investors assessments of corporate performance built on non-financial sustainability factors, such as the *Global Compact Plus* tool developed by the Riskmetrics Group (MSCI 2011). Asset4 offers a database to investors that combines levels of GC compliance for more than 2,400 global companies with any recent news stories related to human rights and labor standards (www.asset4.com).

While explaining membership in the GC has generated some interesting scholarly additions to the commitment literature, Simmons argues that compliance is primarily the result of citizen action, driven by "what they value (or come to value) as well as the probability of succeeding" (Simmons 2009: 154). Translated into the logic of corporate non-state actors, a movement toward compliance would be driven by stakeholders with vested interests in seeing the commitment translate into action. Cetindamar and Husoy find some preliminary evidence that membership in the GC increases the "involvement of stakeholders in their environmental problems," which is likely to shape business practices. They also find that the longer a business participates in the GC, "the greater the number of projects they develop" (Cetindamar and Husoy 2007: 173), potentially setting in motion processes of diffusion and learning. While the authors caution that their sample size is small, there is some evidence emerging that specific mechanisms (not the norms per se) developed as part of the GC facilitate a movement from commitment to compliance, especially if this compliance comes with other benefits, such as improved corporate image and better market performance.

But even if corporations become more proactive with regard to corporate social responsibility, moving from a managerial to a strategic inclusion of GC principles, biases in the geographic targeting as well as emphasis of selected principles can still limit the impact of CSR efforts. An analysis of more than 400 case studies presented by corporate GC members reveals that the vast majority of efforts are targeted at Western home markets and focus on environmental issues, rather than corruption, labor standards or human rights (Barkemeyer 2009). Those biases cannot be effectively addressed solely through increased interactions in local networks "at home," but would require especially multinationals based in Europe and North America to participate meaningfully in national networks where they maintain operations abroad, in particular in the developing world.

In the following, we present evidence about the role of local GC networks, in particular how they facilitate the specific mechanisms identified in Chapter 1 by Ropp and Risse, including discourses/peer learning and capacity-building. In each case, we also introduce the relevant scope conditions discussed in the introductory chapter and provide evidence for their role in enhancing or blocking the effects of those mechanisms. While incentives and sanctions associated with gaining or losing GC membership play some role early on, long-term improvements are driven by local and regional interactions. While corporations likely interact with the main GC office only once a year when submitting their annual COP, businesses have more frequent and meaningful interactions with other GC members at the regional and national levels.

With a multiplicity of voluntary CSR initiatives, the GC is only one among many options for corporate actors which further complicates measuring its discrete impact on the behavior of a particular firm. As one recent study of the effects of national networks argues, the Global Compact is primarily for those companies with little prior CSR experience interested in familiarizing themselves with issues of human rights and corruption (Rieth and Glindemann 2010: 4). But once a company has moved beyond this initial stage, other more specialized CSR-initiatives provide much more detailed guidance concerning the actual implementation of the basic principles. And the GC office explicitly encourages combining the ten principles with other standards, for example the Social Accountability 8000 Certification Standard (focused on workplace conditions), because they provide more concrete and operational definitions of the broad GC principles and also add independent, external audits.

GC membership and GRI: from commitment to transparency and stakeholder involvement

Before we elaborate on how membership in local networks contributes to movement toward progressive implementation, we first establish that membership

in the GC is positively correlated with a movement toward improved reporting practices, a key condition to understanding what progressive implementation will actually mean in a given context. If there is no relationship between
membership patterns and actual corporate behavior related to the ten principles, there is no need to explore the significance of mechanisms operating at
the national and local levels. In order to assess the relevance of GC membership
for corporate behavior, we correlate it with performance regarding the Global
Reporting Initiative (GRI) which is generally regarded as an indication of taking
steps beyond mere formal acceptance of the ten principles towards their progressive implementation in management and strategic planning (Zadek 2004).
In 2006, the GC and GRI entered a strategic alliance to offer a "'one-stop stop'
for guidance on the fundamental principles of CSR" where GRI provided "guidance on how to report on performance results, with an inbuilt materiality test,
enabling companies to select with their stakeholders the most relevant issues"
(Hohnen 2010: 300). In May 2010, the GC formally adopted the GRI reporting
guidelines as the framework recommended to its business membership.

In the utilities sector and among the top twenty utilities of the 2010 Forbes
list, we find that nine out of twenty companies moved from an initial rhetorical
commitment to the GC toward a more meaningful implementation of reporting
about progress in the context of the GRI. The sequence suggests an initial commitment to universal principles followed by a subsequent understanding that
GRI offered the appropriate venue to engage with stakeholders in a transparent
fashion. Conversely, six of the non-GC members in the list are either also absent
from the GRI or have filed only sporadically. Two utilities (EDP, Portugal and
EnBW, Germany) first began reporting under the GRI and later joined the GC.

In the automotive sector, we find confirmation of the above trend, but with
weaker results. Eight GC members also use GRI, six of those started out as GC
members and then moved toward more demanding reporting requirements. A
majority of the non-members has either not submitted reports to the GRI or
has done so only sporadically. The outliers are Fiat (Italy), Denso (Japan) and
Dongfeng (China), which have submitted at least two consecutive years under
the GRI procedure, but have yet to join the GC. Both sectors show some correlation between membership in the GC and GRI reporting patterns across major
industrial sectors.

Local networks: mechanisms facilitating progressive implementation

The final empirical section provides evidence about the mechanisms facilitating
progress toward the progressive implementation of GC principles. We argue that
local networks play a crucial role in sustaining the impact of important mechanisms such as peer learning and capacity-building. Companies are more likely
to take additional meaningful steps in aligning their business practices with GC
principles if vibrant local networks exist and offer specific services (Helmchen
2010), including encouraging dialogue across the civil society–business divide,

Table 11.1. *Twenty largest public companies/utilities (Forbes list 2010; GRI reports 1999–2010)*

Forbes rank	Name	Country	Joined GC in	First GRI report
24	GDF Suez	France	2000	2009
25	E.ON	Germany	2005	2006
27	EDF	France	2001	2004
42	ENEL	Italy	2004	2006
60	RWE	Germany	2004	2006
88	Iberdrola	Spain	2002	2004
175	Exelon	USA	n/a	2008 and 2009 only
186	National Grid	USA	n/a	2010
203	Gas Natural	Spain	2002	2008
206	Southern Co	USA	n/a	2009
207	Veolia	France	2002	2008
217	Centrica	Great Britain	2006	2006
233	FPL	USA	n/a	2009 only
235	Electrobas	Brazil	n/a	2009
250	Dominion Resources	USA	n/a	n/a
259	EDP	Portugal	2004	2001
266	Duke Energy	USA	n/a	2007
280	American Electric	USA	n/a	2007
281	EnBW	Germany	2010	2006
293	PG&E	USA	n/a	2007

providing ideas about concrete implementation tools, serving as an open forum to discuss challenges and doubts, establishing a peer review system for feedback on submitted COPs, and offering ways of adapting the broad GC principles to local conditions. Variation in the capacity of local networks in accomplishing these goals is an important factor in explaining the progress individual companies make in translating GC principles into their daily business practices.

To illustrate the important impact of local networks on the performance of corporations, we compare one of the oldest local networks launched in Germany in 2000 with the Australian local network launched in 2009 (United Nations Global Compact 2010c: 10). Using evidence from the operations of both networks as well as other examples, we show in what ways the local networks help

Table 11.2. *Twenty largest public companies/consumer durables-automotive (Forbes list 2010; GRI reports 1999–2010)*

Forbes rank	Name	Country	Joined GC in	First GRI report
58	Ford	USA	2001	2000
86	Honda	Japan	n/a	n/a
188	Hyundai	South Korea	2008	2003
197	BMW	Germany	2001	2005, 2007–09
310	Johnson Controls	USA	2004	2004
360	Toyota Motors	Japan	n/a	n/a
388	Daimler	Germany	2000	2004
424	Nissan	Japan	2004	2008
499	Fiat	Italy	n/a	2005
502	Suzuki	Japan	n/a	n/a
524	Porsche	Germany	n/a	n/a
530	Renault	France	2001	2006
537	Volvo	Sweden	2001	2000
553	Denso	Japan	n/a	2008
624	Bridgestone	Japan	n/a	2008 only
650	Dongfeng	China	n/a	2009
661	Peugeot	France	2003	2008
688	Continental	Germany	n/a	2008 only
706	Michelin	France	2010	2004 only
734	SAIC Motor	China	n/a	n/a

in overcoming challenges to improved performance regarding the GC principles. We are comparing local networks in the context of two highly developed nations to minimize the role of other possible factors, including overall resource availability or language barriers.

There are currently 170 GC member companies in Germany, compared to sixty-two in Australia. As Figure 11.1 illustrates, membership among Fortune 500 companies is significantly higher in Germany than in Australia. Among the 107 COPs listed under the advanced category for 2011, seven are from German-based companies, while none from Australia are highlighted. To move from a regular active membership to the advanced level, companies have to demonstrate continuous progress in implementation, establish meaningful transparency toward and communications with their stakeholders, and adopt advanced standard reporting guidelines such as the GRI.

Discourse and peer-learning

Membership in the GC increases dialogue among businesses as well as between businesses and civil society actors around non-financial issues. Some local GC networks regularly bring together not only business members of the GC, but also include academic institutions and NGOs. A regular discourse among these diverse set of actors may not exist otherwise and can help move individual firms toward greater compliance with the ten principles. Such open channels of communication are particularly useful for situations where companies "need tools they cannot develop on their own" (Ministry of Foreign Affairs of Denmark and UNDP Nordic Office 2010: 22).

The German local network supporting the GC has close to 170 business members, but also twenty-seven civil society member organizations regularly participating in meetings. The Australian network was incorporated in early 2011 and currently has twenty-six members, including only one civil society group (Plan International). NGOs critical to the principles of the GC, including Transparency International and Amnesty International, are members of the German network. Since the German network has been in operation for some time, it has already dealt with many basic questions, including its funding structure, and has modified its approach to peer learning in response to the different needs of its diverse membership. For example, the local network began to offer more focused meeting segments for smaller companies with limited capacity which "strengthen know-how and implementation on one particular topic, such as preventing climate change and fostering anti-corruption legislation" (Helmchen 2010: 366). This does not mean that other GC principles are neglected, instead, it shows how the local networks play a crucial role in recognizing the specific needs of the GC membership and develop more appropriate learning experiences.

Crucial to the relative success of the German network in facilitating dialogue between businesses and civil society[8] around the GC principles was the decision to put the Gesellschaft für Technische Zusammenarbeit (GTZ), a semi-autonomous development agency, in charge of coordinating the network. The GTZ was sufficiently independent from any of the main stakeholders in government, business and civil society, but had also a high level of credibility with all parties involved. In addition, the idea of a learning platform was fostered by meetings where Chatham House rules ensured frank discussion and exchange of ideas (Helmchen 2010: 357). When a few business leaders sought to take over the management of these meetings from the GTZ, other network

---

[8] Many individual partnerships between corporations and NGOs entail risks of cooptation for the not-for-profit organization (Baur and Schmitz, 2012). Such risks can be limited by establishing ongoing dialogue at the sectoral level within local networks which can identify conditions under which businesses and civil society can collaborate most effectively and fairly.

members warned that this would limit dialogue and likely lead to civil society groups no longer attending the discussions. "We are neither running a management consultancy nor merely offering businesses a platform for describing their activities" (Helmchen 2010: 367).

In the Australian case, the local GC network is currently based in an independent not-for-profit, the St. James Ethics Centre. Since the network is relatively new, its initial main goal is to reach a critical number of members among businesses, civil society groups, academic institutions and government agencies. But it has yet to evolve into a vehicle that contributes effectively to the progressive implementation of GC principles among Australian firms. Apart from attracting new members, the German case elaborates other crucial roles, including providing business-to-business dialogue on corporate responsibility and facilitating exchanges with civil society and other stakeholders interested in how corporations can contribute to improved rights enjoyment, anti-corruption and environmental protection. The global trend across all existing ninety-seven local networks is also sobering in this regard. Although civil society organizations represent the second largest member group following for-profits across all continents, their actual participation in network meetings has dropped since 2009 from an average of 60% to 26% (United Nations Global Compact 2011: 31). Only in Africa, NGO participation remained high, while elsewhere academic institutions now are second in participation rates following business and SMEs.

Capacity-building

This mechanism focuses attention on how a new GC member learns from others about implementing the principles. Many of these activities are sustained at the regional and local levels, not the main GC office in New York. One of the most widespread activities of the local networks is to disseminate information about how to implement the ten principles and put together a COP report. But local networks are not only a crucial player in helping businesses to report properly, but also in considering how progress along the ten principles can be accomplished and accelerated. The meetings facilitated by the German local network revealed that the individual representatives from members came from a variety of different places within their respective companies, including communications departments, compliance offices and environmental departments.

Capacity-building challenges revolved often around understanding not only the different roles participants play in their companies, but also addressing the often significant knowledge gap between them and the company colleagues actually responsible for the practices targeted for change. No one person in a given company has the expertise across all the major principles enumerated by the GC. If the regular representative sent to the local network meetings is from the communications department, he or she may not have the necessary credibility to effectively facilitate changes in the operations of the company on human

rights or environmental issues (Helmchen 2010: 359). These challenges in translating GC principles into company practice can only be revealed and addressed
through the operation of local networks, where people with similar challenges
faced within their companies can exchange ideas about how to approach such
problems more effectively.

Another key aspect of capacity-building facilitated by the local network is
the effect operations of many multinational corporations have in the developing
world. As industrialized nations, both Australia and Germany host significant
numbers of corporations that engage abroad in exploiting natural resources, use
suppliers and compete for access to markets. The local network in Germany not
only improves the capacity of individuals seeking to affect their own businesses
from the inside, but represents a unique forum where the private sector can
learn both from NGOs, but also the GTZ about development challenges and tap
into expertise previously largely separate from the business sector. In this sense,
local networks in developed nations and emerging markets play a particularly
important role in not only improving the local performance of companies, but
also creating global effects aimed at strengthening the importance of the ten
principles in nations where state capacity is limited and such voluntary commitments by business can temporarily improve conditions until more effective state
regulations accomplish the same goals.

The German Local Network facilitates such capacity-building by bringing
together and showcasing different stakeholder collaborations designed to aid
particularly mid-sized corporations engaged in global supply chain management. Puma, a producer of sports apparel, has worked for some time with
the Federal Ministry for Economic Cooperation and Development (BMZ)
and GRI to aid its suppliers in developing their own standards of corporate
conduct as well as establishing mechanisms for effective remedies accessible
to factory workers where those basic rights were violated (Global Compact
Network Germany 2011). Networks with a broad membership and a history
of establishing trust among them are more successful in developing beyond
simple tasks related to COP submissions toward aiding effectively in the progressive implementation of GC principles.

Conclusions

The Global Compact sets out a broad set of principles defining areas of corporate
responsibility to respect human rights, limit corruption and contribute to environmental protection. The GC does not constitute a compliance mechanism, but
a tool designed to nudge its members toward progressive implementation of universal principles into business practices. While the GC office has recently begun
to use some punitive measures to expel non-communicating business members,
the core mechanisms for progressive implementation are non-coercive and rely
on learning, discourse, peer reviews and capacity-building. We argued that for

the large majority of members of the GC these mechanisms do not operate at the global level, but are most visible in national GC networks with a vibrant and diverse membership. While a majority of the largest corporations have joined the GC and their implementation of principles may be increasingly situated at the global levels, the large majority of businesses rely on the local context and networks to learn about best practices, exchange ideas and engage with other stakeholders, including academic institutions, civil society and government agencies.

The most active local networks play a crucial role in overcoming specific impediments to progressive implementation. They create a meaningful national context for the abstract GC principles and aid individual GC members in preparing their annual COPs. They provide a forum for those individuals in charge of implementing GC principles to articulate challenges of getting the "buy-in" from others in the corporate hierarchy. They bring together businesses with civil society to facilitate an open exchange of ideas and differing perspectives. And such networks increase the capacity of all involved by sharing the resources and expertise often concentrated only in one of the relevant stakeholder groups. In the German case, the GTZ, with its long-standing presence in many developing nations, provided a key resource for other members benefiting from its extensive development expertise. Finally, local networks play a role in feeding back to the global GC office experiences that are relevant to decision-making about the governance and operations of the GC.

A key challenge to strengthening local networks is their sustained funding and their legitimacy across a cross-section of stakeholders, in particular outside of business membership. With a very broad set of four issue areas (human rights, environment, labor and anti-corruption), local networks face challenges related to sustaining appeal across a wide set of stakeholders with diverse interests, a changing membership, and possible competition from other initiatives. The collaboration with GRI and more widely shared expertise offers an opportunity for many local networks to shift attention away from only helping members with the COP submissions and expand further into activities designed to push the boundaries of what its members can contribute to global challenges such as biodiversity or climate change. Local networks are most likely to thrive if they can occupy a niche that fosters multi-stakeholder dialogue and can facilitate concrete steps for its for-profit membership to progressively align business practices with the GC ten principles.

12

Business and human rights: how corporate norm violators become norm entrepreneurs

NICOLE DEITELHOFF AND KLAUS DIETER WOLF

Governance beyond the state is characterized by remarkable individual and collective involvement of business corporations in norm production. In fact, "the blurring of boundaries and responsibilities for tackling social and economic issues" (Stoker 1998: 18) is one of the decisive features of governance in the post-national constellation. By engaging in norm-setting and norm implementation in the context of public–private or private–private governance arrangements, corporations are undergoing a role shift from norm violators to actors who commit themselves to human rights norms and even serve as agents of human rights promotion. This is particularly important in the light of the growing demands that these corporations face to take on new responsibilities when states lack capacity or willingness to provide public goods (see Chapter 4, this volume).

The turn of the international community to partner with the business sector in global governance can be framed as a second wave of human rights socialization targeting companies, but with an attempt to further the human rights situation in countries in which human rights still have a precarious status (Chandler 2003). With the accelerated speed of economic globalization in the 1990s in the wake of privatization and liberalization of markets, the business sector has greatly increased its influence in many regions while the governance capacities of governments stagnated or even decreased.

The turn toward business in securing human rights was fueled by a number of NGO and media campaigns and protests during the 1990s that named

The following findings are based on two research projects on the role of business in global governance and on business in conflict that were conducted by the authors between 2005 and 2009 at Darmstadt University of Technology and the Peace Research Institute Frankfurt. The results of these projects have been published in two volumes in Palgrave Macmillan's Global Issues Series. For a more comprehensive elaboration of the arguments presented here see Deitelhoff and Wolf (2010) and Flohr *et al.* (2010). We wish to thank our co-authors Moira Feil, Susanne Fischer, Anne Flohr, Andreas Haidvogl, Lothar Rieth, Sandra Schwindenhammer, Linda Wallbott and Melanie Zimmer for letting us draw on the results of our joint research in this chapter.

and shamed companies for misbehavior in their areas of operation. The most well-known among these are the campaign against Shell for its complicity in the arrest and execution of Ogoni leader Ken Saro Wiwa in 1995 in Nigeria (Rieth and Zimmer 2004; Zimmer 2010), against Nike for its practice of using sweatshops, against Coca-Cola for complicity in the mistreatment and disappearance of labor union workers in Latin America, or the "blood diamond" campaign, focusing on the business sector's role in conflicts in Angola, Sierra Leone and the Democratic Republic of Congo (Bone 2004; Smillie *et al.* 2000).

In this chapter we assess the status of the relationship between business and human rights. Following a brief account of the development of the human rights and business agenda, we turn to a critical application of the spiral model to the business sector. As we attempt to demonstrate, socialization in the business sector displays surprising extensions of this model regarding its phases and causal mechanisms. Under certain conditions, corporations can be observed transforming themselves from norm-consumers to norm-entrepreneurs as agents in a socialization process through which they attempt to commit other actors to a form of collective rule-conforming behavior. We then discuss the scope conditions under which corporations sometimes act (or do not act) as norm-entrepreneurs and conclude with an assessment of the similarities and differences between the socialization of governments and companies, and of some specific problems related to the socialization process in the business sector. The specific challenges facing companies moving toward compliance with human rights are related both to the nature of the compliance problem itself and to the nature of the local context. They are particularly daunting for companies operating in zones of conflict and areas of limited statehood.

Enlarging the human rights agenda: business and human rights

The turn to business to promote human rights raises several questions. What should the role of private business companies be in promoting rights that primarily address the relations between states and their citizens? Do private companies have any responsibility for such rights and if so what kind of responsibility is it?

The preamble of the UN Declaration of Human Rights of 1948 already stated that "every individual and every organ of society (is called upon) to promote respect for these rights and freedoms and by progressive measures, national and international, to secure their universal and effective recognition and observance."[1] Thus, in principle, business companies and the business sector in general have long fallen within the purview of the international human rights regime. Still, it took a long time before the business sector was willing to accept this responsibility, a responsibility which it perceived as falling within the "political

---

[1] www.un.org/en/documents/udhr/index.shtml (last accessed September 14, 2010).

sphere" of states and other public entities (Black 2006: 76). Moreover, most of the existing regulations that did focus explicitly on the responsibilities of companies regarding human rights were of a voluntary nature. Among them were the International Labor Organization (ILO) Tripartite Declaration on Principles Concerning Multinational Enterprises and Social Policy of 1972, which highlighted a set of principles in the fields of employment, training, labor unions, workplace safety and working conditions.[2] Additionally, the OECD Guidelines for Multinational Enterprises of 1976 stipulated that transnational companies should respect and promote the rights of their employees in their areas of operation and also to respect the rights of those affected by their activities consistent with the host government's international obligations and commitments.[3]

Previous attempts to address the human rights responsibilities of companies in a legally binding fashion had largely failed. For example, the UN Commission on Transnational Corporations that was to negotiate a code of conduct for TNCs in the 1970s failed due to political opposition which arose in many member states (Probst 2007: 26). Given the persisting climate mitigating against the successful promulgation of legally binding initiatives dealing with the human rights responsibilities of TNCs, the trend since the 1990s has been toward promoting a sense of *social* responsibility within companies and on voluntary initiatives to further human rights (Probst 2007: 34–35; Ruggie 2007: 244). This trend has resulted in turn in the development of numerous transnational governance arrangements, in which business actors are active as norm entrepreneurs and which can be distinguished according to differences in the configurations of relevant actors. They may (a) be initiated, sponsored (or even dominated) by the public sector. They may (b) consist of multi-stakeholder initiatives, where civic groups and business corporations meet on an equal footing. Or they can (c) be pure instances of private self-regulation among business actors with no direct public sector or civil society participation.

A major milestone in this regard was the establishment of the UN Global Compact by former UN Secretary General Kofi Annan. By 2011, it had grown to more than 8,000 participants, including over 6,000 businesses in 135 countries around the world (see Chapter 11, this volume). The Global Reporting Initiative (GRI) provides us with another example of a multi-stakeholder governance arrangement that includes corporations, accountancy agencies, human rights, environmental, labor and governmental organizations. Established in 1999, the initiative provides a worldwide framework for voluntary sustainability reporting of some public but mainly private organizations. This multi-stakeholder

---

[2] www.ilo.org/wcmsp5/groups/public/–ed_emp/–emp_ent/–multi/documents/publication/ wcms_094386.pdf (last accessed September 14, 2010).
[3] www.oecd.org/officialdocuments/displaydocumentpdf?cote=DAFFE/IME/ WPG(2000)15/FINAL&doclanguage=en (last accessed September 14, 2010).

process aims to develop a common framework for voluntary reporting on the economic, environmental and societal impacts of corporate activities.

Specifically focusing on human rights, the Voluntary Principles on Human Rights and Security comprises a sector-wide initiative, developed by companies in the extractive and petrochemical industries (e.g. Shell and BP), NGOs and the governments of UK and the United States. The guidelines of 2000 contain a set of criteria companies should apply to assess the human rights impact of their security arrangements with public or private security forces in their areas of operation.

As an initiative purely for the private sector, the Business Social Compliance Initiative (BSCI) was founded in March 2003 to improve and monitor compliance with workers' rights in the global supply chain. The system is based on a code of conduct (SA 8000), enshrining principles from the ILO's core conventions, and includes a comprehensive monitoring and qualification process that covers all products sourced from any country. The driving force behind the BSCI is the Brussels-based Foreign Trade Association (FTA). It is mainly intended as a sector solution for retail in Europe but is also open to any non-European company or business association. It established roundtables in the major import markets of its members to strengthen stakeholder involvement and improve social standards in supplier countries.

In addition to such collective initiatives, the debate on corporate social responsibility (CSR) has also increased corporate norm promotion at the level of individual companies. Company codes of conduct have spread into policy areas such as human rights, social standards, environmental protection and the fight against corruption. The spread of company and industry codes of conduct and public–private partnerships on human rights (Haufler 2004: 160; Ruggie 2006) signals that we might be on the edge of observing a norm cascade within the business community (Deitelhoff *et al.* 2010: 206; Ruggie 2006: 7, 2007: 254, 2009: 13). However, the mushrooming codes and standards not only refer to human rights norms narrowly defined (Black 2006: 70; Ruggie 2006, 2007) but rather to a broad range of normative principles covered by the UN Global Compact. This compact demonstrates that human rights are only one element of a much broader "CSR norm" that we observe to be cascading. Still, as the following sections highlight, companies are active in this regard only under certain conditions.

The spiral model of human rights change

Can the original spiral model as introduced in *The Power of Human Rights* (PoHR) (Risse *et al.* 1999) be applied to these developments in the business sector at all? The original spiral model assumes that there is a basically confrontational relationship between a transnational movement and a government, i.e. a norm-violating target. The main hypothesis is "that the diffusion of international norms in the human rights area crucially depends on the establishment and sustainability of networks among domestic and transnational actors who manage to link up with international regimes, to alert Western public opinion and Western governments" (Risse and Sikkink 1999: 5). These networks are supposed to put the norm-violating state on the international agenda, using strategies such as shaming and blaming, to empower the domestic opposition groups vis-à-vis the norm-violating government, and to create a transnational structure capable of exerting pressure from above and below on the norm-violating government. In sum, the model puts highest emphasis on the existence and strength of transnational NGO networks and the pressure they can exert on repressive governments as well as on the vulnerability of the target government to international pressure (Risse and Sikkink 1999: 24).

When applying the spiral model to human rights socialization in the business sector, several adjustments are necessary. First, companies differ from repressive governments. They usually do not oppress the domestic opposition or stakeholders in their respective zones of operations. Instead, they tend to ignore the human rights situation there or to take advantage of government repression. Indeed, government repression can "reward" them by lowering their costs of production through the availability of cheap labor, lack of regulatory control of workplace safety, the absence of labor unions, and the like.

Thus, companies are far more likely to be quietly complicit in human rights violations by government agencies and actors than to be human rights violators themselves. This "quiet complicity" in turn affects the type of denial applicable to companies: by frequently referencing a notion of appropriate corporate behavior that is closely associated with Milton Friedman in which "the social responsibility of business is to increase its profits" (Friedman 1970), companies do not question the validity of human rights norms as such. Rather, they reference their own more narrowly defined corporate responsibility and plead ignorance of both human rights violations and/or of human rights law.

Thus, commitment and compliance also need to be re-conceptualized for companies. We can talk of *commitment* to human rights when companies publicly declare their acceptance of human rights norms by either statements of compliance with international human rights law, by acceding to national, regional or global CSR-initiatives or by issuing company codes of conduct. With regard to *compliance*, we can think of a continuum (see also Chapter 5, this volume). Companies move toward compliance when they begin to institutionalize human rights within the company, i.e. when companies incorporate human rights norms into their management structures and risk management strategies or establish CSR units or departments. Further along the continuum, companies may begin to commit others as well by developing measures to ensure enforcement of their commitment along their supply chain or among their employees, and, finally, by proactively committing other companies and public actors alike through the development of new initiatives (norm-entrepreneurship), thus deepening and widening compliance on a collective level respectively.

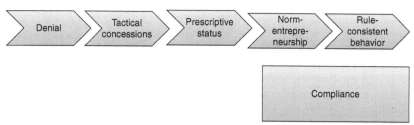

Figure 12.1 The spiral model of human rights socialization in the business sector

The second difference between corporations and repressive governments directly affects the strategies corporations employ on their way from commitment to compliance. In contrast to governments, corporations operate in a market environment: norm-violating and norm-abiding corporations are often competitors for the same market. Once committed and willing to comply themselves, pioneer companies thus have a strong interest in leveling the playing field: in order to comply they need to get others to comply as well so as not to be at a competitive disadvantage. Keeping these adjustments in mind and drawing on evidence from some of the better-known NGO campaigns, we have concluded that the socialization process within the business sector shows some astonishing similarities as well as differences as related to the classic spiral model.

In the following section, we draw on three cases: (1) Shell in Nigeria, (2) the coltan-campaign against companies manufacturing tantalum-containing end devices, and (3) the Nike sweatshop campaign in order to illustrate how and under what scope conditions companies move from denial to tactical concessions (i.e. commitment). Drawing on our cases, we show that the socialization process in its early phases is conditioned by similar scope factors as originally developed by PoHR: the strength of the transnational campaign and the vulnerability of the target. However, the move from commitment to compliance is also conditioned by the nature of the compliance problem and the local context in which actors have to comply (see Chapter 1, this volume).

Adjusting the spiral model for companies (see Rieth and Zimmer 2004) by starting with a "business as usual" phase, one can easily identify the classical pattern of socialization described by the original model. Once companies become the object of a transnational NGO campaign, they usually react by denying their responsibility for the human rights situation in host countries. As argued above, NGO campaigns targeting transnational companies usually focus on companies' complicity in the human rights violations of governments in their zones of operation.

From denial to tactical concession

The campaign of the early 1990s against Shell's activities in the Niger Delta highlights this pattern. NGOs accused Shell of implicitly supporting the Nigerian government's human rights violations vis-à-vis local communities in the Niger

Delta. The campaign got off the ground following the arrest and sham trial of eight leaders of the Ogoni Movement, a local tribe in the Niger Delta which had begun to demonstrate against Shell's operations on their territory (Zimmer 2010: 76). The Ogoni pressed for compensation for environmental degradation, they wanted a fair share of oil revenues and a change in the practices of oil drilling. When the Ogoni leaders around Ken Saro Wiwa were arrested (and executed in 1995) and transnational protests arose, Shell declared that it had not interfered with the government's decision and would not do so in the future as it was a private company with no legitimacy whatsoever to interfere with domestic political affairs. The company claimed that it was just doing business and could not influence the political situation in Nigeria.

Likewise, in the early 2000s the coltan campaign highlights a similar dynamic. The illegal trade and smuggling of the ore coltan served to finance the war in the Democratic Republic of Congo (DRC). NGOs targeted transnational companies using tantalum for their end-devices production for being complicit in human rights violations in the ongoing conflicts in the DRC by purchasing the ore without any regard to its origin. Once accused, companies denied any responsibility, emphasizing the fact that they could not verify the origin of the ore that they purchased. Instead, they shifted the blame onto their suppliers (Wallbott 2010: 92).

Another example of this pattern of corporate denial is Nike's reaction to the anti-sweatshop campaign it faced in the 1990s. By then, Nike had nearly completely outsourced its footwear, apparel and equipment production to hundreds of contract factories with more than 800,000 workers in forty-six countries (Connor 2010: 2), largely ignoring or even in fact exploiting the repression of human rights associated with their suppliers. "Nike, it appeared, was a nearly ideal target for activist attack – a perfect symbol of low-wage labor, and a symbol so prominent that attack was easy. And once the activists targeted the firm, they showed no sign of letting go" (Spar and La Mure 2003: 89).

When labor activists began to focus their campaign on Nike to pressure for global codes of conduct to counter the miserable conditions in the textile industry, the company at first reacted by denying its responsibility for their suppliers' practices: "We're about sports, not manufacturing" was a reaction of a company spokesman typical of that stage of confrontation (quoted in Spar and La Mure 2003: 90). In sum, during the denial stage companies usually do not question the validity of human rights as such but rather declare either that the problem that exists is a political one (and thus lies outside the sphere of competence or responsibility of the business sector), or that is one that has been created by other companies (Black 2006; Deitelhoff et al. 2010; Feil et al. 2008; Probst 2007).

In line with the original assumptions of the spiral model, the move to "tactical concessions" seems to be a function of (1) the strength and global resonance of the transnational campaign and (2) the social and material vulnerability of the targeted company. Vulnerability in the business sector depends on several factors, relating to company, product(ion) and home state characteristics: the risk of being targeted by consumer boycotts which may vary with the location in the supply chain, the visibility and prestige of a product, or the size of the company; the dependency on certain areas of operation, such as the location of natural resources or the amount of sunk costs through previous investments; and the risk of litigation or regulation by the home state (Deitelhoff and Wolf 2010; Wolf *et al.* 2007).

The impact of these two factors can be illustrated by our three cases. Although the coltan campaign generated public awareness and pressure, most of the targeted companies did not become active at all while some of them (almost all from the telecommunications sector) issued policy statements on coltan but dismissed any further need for action. This comparative lack of success of the coltan campaign results from two factors: the varying social vulnerability of the companies and, related to this, the missing or rather complicated link between the human rights violations, the product, and the respective companies involved (Hayes and Burge 2003; Wallbott 2010), thus weakening the transnational campaign. Not all companies and sectors are equally vulnerable to consumer boycotts. In this regard, companies that produce for end consumers are much more visible to them than are those companies that produce for other businesses in the supply chain. Furthermore, hardly any of the transnational companies targeted by the campaign worked "on the ground" in the DRC. Rather, they purchased coltan from various suppliers to whom they could shift the blame for any perceived violations (Wallbott 2010: 92).

Moreover, it proved to be extremely hard to clearly identify specific wrongdoers because coltan is used in a number of technical processes and products and by a widely diverse range of companies. This problem has long been discussed within debates among constructivists about successful framing strategies for NGOs concerned with human rights. Their success depends heavily on the possibility of translating complex problems into neat story lines that can dramatically highlight responsibility and guilt (Keck and Sikkink 1998: 20; Zald 1996: 266). Thus, the difficulty of the transnational campaign in exposing specific companies and the comparatively weak vulnerability of the companies involved can explain why companies only issued policy statements but did not take any further actions. Only telecommunication companies became active at all as they were the ones most visible to consumers and thus also the most vulnerable to a loss of reputation.[4]

---

[4] Companies even proactively change their business strategy to avoid the risk of consumer boycotts. In the disinvestment campaign against multinational oil companies in Burma, for instance, oil companies, such as Texaco and Amoco, chose to withdraw from Burma under severe attack by transnational NGOs. Unocal, however, decided to stay but eliminated most of its downstream activities (e.g. gas stations). Thus, this company attempted to become invisible to the regular consumer and to insulate itself against the risk of consumer boycotts (Spar and La Mure 2003: 86–89).

In contrast, when a transnational network is dealing with a company that is relying heavily on the image of its product and the network is able to connect with local opposition groups or mobilize consumers, the move to the next stage of "tactical concessions" is very likely. This is demonstrated by the campaign against the sweatshop practices of Nike's overseas suppliers or by Shell's reaction to the sustained criticism of its operations in Nigeria. Both of these companies are highly vulnerable to public pressure and to consumer boycotts. Nike produces a high-profile brand that relies heavily on its positive image for sales. The public floggings of the 1990s had turned the company into "a poster child for corporate villainy stemming from sweatshop practices in Southeast Asia factories" (Connor 2010: 1). Nike responded by putting into place a code of conduct for all of its suppliers. Shell is an equally recognizable brand and has gas stations worldwide that are easily targeted by boycotts. Thus, confronted with massive public campaigns, both companies began to adapt to the human rights discourse, by, on the one hand, highlighting their compliance with international human rights standards and, on the other hand, agreeing to activities addressing the specific problems at hand. Nike, for example, agreed to labor codes to counter the miserable working conditions of some of its suppliers and to a one-shot external audit on their performance (Zadek 2004: 128). Shell began to initiate a dialogue program on "Society's Changing Expectations" at the global level and increased its community development programs in the Niger Delta (Rieth and Zimmer 2004: 24). Public commitments in the form of unilateral collective codes of conduct may thus be observed as regular instances of tactical concessions.

From commitment to compliance

While the coltan campaign hardly reached the status of tactical concession given the lack of vulnerability on behalf of the involved companies and the difficulties the NGO campaign faced, the campaigns against Nike and Shell show a different dynamic. Tactical concessions often do not have their intended effect of pacifying the transnational public or consumers. Instead, they may serve as new anchors for the transnational networks to intensify their pressure. In the case of Shell, such concessions even resulted in a number of lawsuits and a call by the UN special rapporteur for Nigeria to investigate the activities of Shell in the Niger Delta.

The more the transnational networks can sustain the pressure on companies and win new coalition partners such as international organizations, the more likely companies move toward an institutionalized human rights profile. Responding to transnational public pressure, Nike, for example, established an extensive code of conduct, pointed to many examples of improvement in its behavior, and established a corporate responsibility department in the late 1990s. Thus, the corporation began to institutionalize its commitment to human rights within the company's structure (Zadek 2004: 129). Similarly, Shell included adherence to human rights in its general business principles in 1997 and established a social accountability committee soon afterwards (Rieth and Zimmer 2004: 25). Nevertheless, both companies remained under public scrutiny and NGOs were eager to reveal any misbehavior that would support the suspicion that the companies were only engaging in window dressing but did not significantly change their practices.

As a result, both companies began to further intensify and institutionalize their commitments. Shell regularly issued sustainability reports and became a member of various international and regional initiatives, such as the UN Global Compact, the Voluntary Principles on Security and Human Rights, or the Nigerian participation in the Extractive Industries Transparency Initiative (Rieth and Zimmer 2004: 26; Zimmer 2010: 63). Nike even started to change its production and inventory management procedures to be better able to comply with its code of conduct and became a member of the Global Compact and other initiatives (Zadek 2004: 130–132). According to Rieth and Zimmer (2004: 28–30), Shell's gradual acceptance of the CSR norm and continuous extension of its CSR policy at local, national and global levels, as well as its change in line of argument, are the result of a process of self-entrapment. Subjected to persistent NGO pressure, shamed by the violation of human rights in Nigeria and accused of environmental degradation, Shell started to reflect on its corporate strategy. The company seemed to realize that its bad human rights record was a result of focusing only on the financial bottom line, and increasingly signaled that it was giving the principle of sustainability equal consideration (Shell 2009).

These illustrative cases of transnational campaigns against companies highlight the fact that the spiral model of human rights change can fruitfully be applied to the socialization process of corporations. The strength of a transnational campaign and the social and material vulnerability of the company as scope conditions help account for the varying success of companies' socialization on their way from commitment to compliance. However, taking a closer look at the business sector, a curious and unexpected side effect can be observed: the socialization process may even transform corporate norm-takers into norm-makers. On their way from commitment to compliance individual companies' willingness to move toward rule-consistent behavior may also depend on the need to get competitors to comply as well. In order to achieve a level playing field, companies then might become norm-entrepreneurs. This development points to the nature of the compliance problem as a powerful scope condition.

A new element in the spiral: corporations as norm-entrepreneurs

To conceive of business corporations as norm-entrepreneurs may seem somewhat surprising. When initially addressing the formation and diffusion of norms, constructivist writing (Keck and Sikkink 1998; Risse *et al.*

1999) had a certain range of actors in mind. Activist networks (Keck and Sikkink 1998; Price 1998), epistemic communities (Haas 1992), international organizations (Finnemore 1993; Schimmelfennig *et al.* 2003) and governments (Deitelhoff 2006) were all considered agents with the potential for norm-entrepreneurship, that is, actors with strong notions about appropriate behavior (Elgström 2000: 459) who "attempt to convince a critical mass" (Finnemore and Sikkink 1998: 895).

With the debate about corporate social responsibility (CSR), the awareness of corporate norm related behavior increased. Company codes of conduct and collective self-regulatory initiatives in policy areas such as human rights, social standards, environmental protection and the fight against corruption seemed to reflect activities similar to those of classical norm-entrepreneurs. If actors qualify as norm-entrepreneurs in the early stages of a norm life cycle (Finnemore and Sikkink 1998) by redefining "an activity as a problem" (Nadelmann 1990: 482), this has definitely also been the case with corporate behavior in the evolution of CSR norms. Corporations were engaged as "meaning managers" by creating new "cognitive frames" and establishing "new ways of talking about and understanding issues" (Finnemore and Sikkink 1998: 897).

Corporate norm-setting and norm development

The strategies of corporate norm-entrepreneurship differ from those of other norm-entrepreneurs: NGOs, in seeking to change the practices of states, work mainly through discourse, shaming and lobbying strategies. Corporations often start by changing their own behavior, thus offering best practice for imitation by other companies which may lead into collective self-commitments. In the latter case, corporations voice the proposal for the norm in public or build alliances with other companies, civil society, international organizations and even governments to initiate a process of norm institutionalization. Similarly, by adopting codes of conduct and applying them to their supply chain management, corporations support the diffusion of the respective norms in the business sector (Black 2006: 69).

Corporations thus get involved in an early stage of the norm cycle and engage in reframing a formerly legitimate activity as a problem. Typically, norm-setting by corporations does not entail the invention of an entirely new norm but rather the new commitment by companies to a norm as a standard for appropriate *corporate* behavior. Even after a norm has reached a certain level of acceptance and institutionalization a corporation can still be a norm-entrepreneur through norm-development activities, for example, by further specifying a broader norm's exact content and implied requirements. In contrast to their traditional role as norm-consumers, corporate norm-entrepreneurs are not only accepting and implementing norms but also set and develop norms for the business sector. In addition to norm setting, corporations can therefore also engage in further developing the scope of norms, their content and the procedures which serve as enforcement mechanisms. These elements can be demonstrated by Nike's development since the 1990s, which also illustrates the conditions under which a corporation can turn into a norm-entrepreneur.

From norm acceptance to norm-entrepreneurship: the Nike case

Nike started with unilateral measures, such as committing factories within the supply chain to observance of human rights norms, pointing to single examples of improvement, or, from 2001 on, issuing responsibility reports. However, there were more than enough incidents of violations left to make the company an easy target. CEO Parker reflected on the need for an additional step towards norm-entrepreneurship quite openly: "Another hard lesson came after years of pushing our suppliers with monitoring and policing tools. We thought that we could be a unilateral force for systemic change. Instead, we learned that meaningful reform was not going to come from external pressure alone. Awareness and monitoring of any mandated Code of Conduct had to be embraced and enforced at the local level" (Nike 2010: 4).

Another difficulty facing corporations that genuinely wished to observe human rights norms was that norm-violating contractors often produced for other companies as well. As a result, Nike became a strong advocate for industry-level systemic change:

> Consider our efforts to improve working conditions across our supply chain. We have made incremental improvements but real, long-term solutions lie in changing systems. Systemic change requires fundamental shifts in working conditions across the entire apparel and footwear industry. The work of a single brand or manufacturer is not enough. Yet, as an industry leader, we can begin to change the behaviors and expectations of those who work in the industry through influencing policy and encouraging collaboration between civil society, industry and government.
>
> (Nike 2010: 25)

In order to achieve system-wide improvements Nike began to collaborate with its competitors to level the playing field by joint factory audits and standardization efforts (Connor 2010: 2).

Nike's proactive role as a corporate norm-entrepreneur can be observed in a number of initiatives. In 1998, the company played an active role in forming the Fair Labor Association (FLA), an entity designed to audit, monitor and enforce working conditions in member factories around the world (Spar and La Mure 2003: 91). In 2008 Nike became chair of the World Economic Forum's Consumer Industries Working Group on Sustainable Consumption, with the declared intention "to galvanize industry collaboration." Nike is also part of the International Labor Organization's Better Work program in order to develop a coordinated approach by multiple companies to improve conditions in their shared supply chain. "Working with member companies, we hope to achieve improvements on a greater scale than our individual initiatives" (Nike 2010: 25).

In sum, Nike went quite some way along the road to rule-consistent behavior. Human rights norms gained prescriptive status within the company. When specific cases of labour rights violations in the supply chain were brought up, Nike took steps to address these problems, although there is still some way to go. As Oxfam (2010) suggests, "many, if not most, of their other factories continue to have oppressive work practices." What is more important in support of our argument here is that the case of Nike illustrates how proactive norm-entrepreneurship was employed for leveling the playing field for system-wide improvements in the whole industry on the way to rule-consistent behavior. Corporate norm entrepreneurship thus has to do with market conditions and concerns. To reduce competitive losses, compliance with human rights is more likely the more competitors comply as well. This amounts to strong incentives for the more vulnerable companies to engage in norm-entrepreneurship.

The specific challenges of the compliance context for business

As Nike's development has shown, corporate norm-entrepreneurship may be needed to level uneven playing fields that may be a major obstacle on the way from commitment to compliance. Besides this particular challenge, business companies face more general difficulties to move from commitment to compliance that relate to (1) the nature of the compliance problem and (2) the political environment in which they operate, in particular zones of conflict or limited statehood. Both factors work as powerful scope conditions on companies' move from commitment to compliance with human rights.

The nature of the compliance problem companies face poses a severe challenge to achieve sustained compliance. Usually, companies need not only comply with human rights norms themselves but also have to commit other actors as well. This is because companies have to enforce their commitments along their supply chain. Even the strongest code of conduct a company may adopt necessarily fails if that company's suppliers do not adhere to the agreed upon standards. Enforcing commitments in the supply chain, however, can be difficult if the market of suppliers is small (suppliers cannot easily be replaced) or if the supply chain lacks transparency so that companies find it hard to monitor compliance. Second, as the discussion on norm-entrepreneurship highlights, companies also need to commit their competitors within a given market. Initially, companies that commit themselves to compliance with human rights face higher costs than competitors who refrain from doing so. In highly competitive market segments there is always an incentive for companies not to comply. The more companies in such cases have a chance to insulate themselves against public pressure the less likely they will comply and vice versa as our discussion of norm-entrepreneurship above implies.

Finally, companies often struggle to commit public actors (e.g. governments and their agents) to comply with human rights. This is especially the case in zones of conflict and of limited statehood more generally (see Chapter 4, this volume). Zones of conflict are usually those places where human rights are violated most severely and where governments regularly fail to protect them effectively, either out of unwillingness or because they lack the capabilities to do so.

Findings from our research on corporate governance contributions to peace and security in zones of conflict (see Deitelhoff and Wolf 2010) indicate that, although companies avoid contributing to peace and security directly, they contribute quite frequently to peace and security indirectly by taking up issues closely related to conflict drivers and causes, especially with regard to socio-economic issues (segregation, poverty) and political issues (rule of law, human rights (Deitelhoff *et al.* 2010: 205)).

These kinds of contributions are triggered by the same set of factors we discussed above, pertaining to company characteristics, product(ion) characteristics, and the social and political environment in home states, all adding to the vulnerability of companies toward adverse campaining. However, two additional factors seem to affect the human rights activities of business in zones of conflict, both of them highlighting the importance of (host) state strength as another scope condition in the process from commitment to compliance that is relevant for states and for business actors alike: the risk of large-scale violence and the existence of reliable partners in the public sector. Conflictual settings reflect extremely difficult operating contexts for companies. Our research highlights that large-scale violence in a company's environment works as a show-stopper to corporate governance contributions of any kind (Feil 2010; Wolf *et al.* 2007). If companies do not outright withdraw from the scene, they are mainly concerned with the protection of their staff and facilities, leaving no room for any further voluntary governance contributions to live up to their commitments. Such governance contributions are more likely in post-conflict phases in which the scale and intensity of violence have significantly decreased. Still, it makes a difference whether companies' facilities and staff are located close to violent conflict and whether violent encounters are regularly recurring (Feil 2010: 47). If both apply companies seem to be more likely to contribute to governance.

Large-scale violence is an extreme but very common feature of the host state environment in which companies operate. Of course, the politico-legal environment of the host state varies, but quite often companies are confronted with varying degrees of state failure and the under-provision of collective goods (see Chapter 4, this volume). In this respect, it is important to distinguish between formal regulation and implementation of existing laws. While legal frameworks often exist, states either lack the willingness or the capacity to implement them or to provide certain public goods. Our findings suggest that in a state that is willing to improve its performance but has weak capacities to do so, companies might also be more willing to contribute to governance and might do so to support governments. Companies value a stable environment to do business after all (Wolf et al. 2007: 301). In states with strong capacities but rather weak willingness companies neither need to be afraid of further regulation or proper implementation (Ballentine 2007: 130) nor might their engagement be welcome when it comes to furthering good governance (especially in authoritarian or repressive states). This was also the case in Nigeria where consecutive governments did not display any incentives for companies to engage in any form of human rights protection or even explicitly discouraged them. Only since Nigeria has slowly started a transition process to democracy, the political climate has begun to change. In the course, the oversight of the oil industry and regulatory reforms have increased and meanwhile the oil companies have begun to start to partner with the Nigerian government to support its effort to establish a public governance framework (see Zimmer 2010: 75).

In sum, as far as (host) state strength as a scope condition is concerned, the most favourable setting of the local context seems to be a mixture of a strong political willingness and low capacities. The risk of large-scale violence in their operating environment leaves companies hardly any room to maneuver, and host state governments that are primarily responsible in such areas for human rights protection are often either unable or unwilling to support companies' attempts to further human rights. To be sure, companies might cooperate with all kinds of local strong men and shaky authorities to keep their business running but they only engage in corporate governance contributions to further human rights once a reliable state authority emerges which displays at least sufficient political will to establish and implement a public governance framework (Feil 2010: 52–53). Socialization of companies into human rights activities in zones of conflict thus follows similar patterns as the socialization process for companies in zones of peace. However, even companies who might be willing to engage in human rights activities in conflict, i.e. who have been successfully socialized, face often insurmountable additional challenges in living up to their commitments in these operating contexts.

Conclusions: what can we learn for the "power of human rights"?

The spiral model of human rights change can be fruitfully applied to the development of human rights awareness and activities in the business sector. Companies go through a similar process of denial, tactical concessions, norm acceptance and institutionalization. Apart from the general similarity of the socialization in consecutive stages, companies also show a similar logic of institutionalization. Institutionalization in the business sector points to two different levels. One is the accession to existing human rights initiatives on the regional, global or sectoral level, the other is the adoption of company codes of conduct and the formation of specific CSR departments and management structures within the company making human rights become incorporated in the standard procedures.

Despite these similarities, the spiral model has to be adjusted to account for the behavior of corporate actors. Socialization in the business sector displays surprising extensions of this model regarding its phases and causal mechanisms. Companies are not like repressive governments. They are usually not the principal human rights violators and have for a long time declined responsibility for the human rights situation in their operating contexts. With regard to the business sector, "denial" does not involve corporate questioning of the validity of human rights norms but rather denial of the responsibility of corporations to promote them. It therefore comes as a surprise to observe that a number of companies move further along the path toward commitment and compliance than do some notoriously norm-violating states by becoming norm-entrepreneurs that proactively engage in norm-setting and development (Black 2006: 81–82). While the original spiral model focused on processes of change related to repressive governments and presumably ended with the rule-consistent behavior of its target states (who, at best, turned into reliable norm-takers), we find that rule-consistent behavior in the business sector is preceded by an even more far-reaching role shift. As shown above, this unanticipated development may be influenced by the strategic projection of companies to remain ahead of stakeholder and public expectations or to reduce competitive losses that could result from the compliance with human rights standards of some but not all competitors in a given market segment (Zadek 2004: 127).

However, our finding that corporate socialization into norm-entrepreneurship is usually triggered by rationalist calculations regarding the re-definition of fundamental business interests does not rule out the existence of underlying notions of appropriate business behavior which may in turn support or challenge what is perceived as the "business case" in any given context. In fact, one can very well argue that competitive utility maximization has been the basic standard of appropriateness for the business sector (see Müller 2004) most of the time in most of the important home states. Markets are not "natural" spaces in any meaningful sense but social constructs whose rules are predetermined by political decisions of governments, individually or collectively. Thus, Friedman's claim that the social responsibility of business is to make profits holds true for a specific understanding of business–governance relations within the state in which the state is responsible for providing public goods while the business sector supports this provision by generating wealth and economic development within society.

This notion of appropriate corporate behavior and the narrow market rationality that goes along with it only causes problems once socially constructed boundaries fall apart. For example, such is the case within globalized markets as a whole, and within areas of limited statehood in particular, where the provision of public goods based on the former attribution of responsibilities has failed. Against such a background of market failure, the absence of globalized political mechanisms capable of re-establishing the social boundaries of the market and

transnational public pressure reflecting the need for new standards of appropriateness, induces companies to develop more complex notions of market rationality. The emerging CSR structure thus works as the functional equivalent of
socially bound markets, inducing companies to include human rights concerns
in their interest calculations (Deitelhoff *et al.* 2010: 206).

As the impressive existing list of CSR initiatives and codes of conduct suggests, the relevance of human rights principles is no longer regularly challenged within the business sector. However, at least three problems remain.
One is the question of what exactly the CSR norm is – that is, which specific
human rights norms should be considered as part of the CSR norm? Corporate
norm-entrepreneurs continuously struggle with interpreting and applying CSR
standards precisely because they feel uncertain about what standards demand
and which standards to apply.

Another critical issue is the voluntary nature of CSR. The turn to self-
regulation of the business sector has certainly fueled the diffusion of human
rights. However, it also makes it much more difficult to monitor and hold companies accountable (Ruggie 2007; see also Chapter 11, this volume). Even those
companies that are highly visible to consumers, vulnerable to public pressure
and potential targets often refuse to accept external monitoring procedures, not
to mention the majority of companies that can hide completely from the public
(Black 2006: 79).

Finally, and as a consequence of the above, companies' activities in human
rights promotion can only be a complement to, but can never permanently
replace, public regulation. In fact, as we argued above, the socialization that
results in turning companies into human rights advocates might be understood
as a second wave of human rights socialization pressuring governments into
observance by targeting companies. However, the mushrooming of CSR initiatives at the regional and international level and of company codes of conduct
should not blind us to its limits. As our brief illustration of the behavior of businesses in zones of conflict has highlighted, companies face the biggest challenges
in living up to their human rights commitments in zones of violent conflict and
limited statehood. The prospects of them contributing are good when they face
public authorities that display a political willingness to further human rights
standards but lack the capacity to do so. This observation supports the general
finding from the management approach to compliance. In other words, corporate prospects for affecting human rights change will be negligible in instances
where actors are confronted with state or local authorities who show no political will of their own (Deitelhoff *et al.* 2010: 213–215). These latter zones are of
course exactly the hot spots where human rights protection is most precarious.

13

Taming of the warlords: commitment and compliance by armed opposition groups in civil wars

HYERAN JO AND KATHERINE BRYANT

Respect for human rights is difficult to attain even during times of peace. But when conflict occurs, human rights protection and humanitarian assistance becomes an almost insurmountable task.[1] How do we induce compliance from non-state actors such as armed opposition groups? Based on several decades of research on compliance, we seem to know a lot about how states behave, but we know much less about how non-state actors comply with international rules (Simmons 2010). This is an important gap to fill, as non-state actors have become active participants in world politics.

The non-state actors we examine are rebel groups[2] in civil wars. They provide a hard test for commitment and compliance with international rules. The baseline expectation of rebel groups committing to and complying with international standards is low because they are, by definition, political entities fighting against existing authority. The political context they are situated in, namely internal conflict, is a difficult landscape for international law to operate in for two main reasons. First, civil wars tend to be bloody venues where we would least expect compliance to occur, as warring parties tend to privilege their military goals over compliance with human rights and humanitarian rules. Second, norms for non-state actors in civil conflicts are not well established.[3] While the Geneva Conventions provide a common and shared understanding of the laws

We acknowledge financial support from the Scowcroft Institute at Bush School, Texas A&M University.

[1] In this chapter, following Clapham (2006), we assume that both international human rights and international humanitarian law are applicable in the case of internal armed conflicts.
[2] We are agnostic about connotations among the terms "insurgents," "rebel groups" and "armed opposition groups."
[3] The obligations of insurgent groups are codified in Common Article 3 of the Geneva Conventions and the Additional Protocol II. For the legal obligations of non-state actors, see Zegveld (2002), Clapham (2006), Sivakumaran (2006) and Steiner *et al.* (2008). In particular, Clapham (2006) develops an argument that human rights law is applicable to armed opposition groups in protracted internal conflicts.

of war for states, they are less clear when applied to non-state actors.[4] As public international law is the realm of state parties, non-state actors do not have formally established ways to express their intention of being bound by international law. The puzzle for compliance researchers is then how – under what conditions and by what pathways – commitment and compliance arise among armed opposition groups.

The main contribution of this chapter is to advance arguments about commitment and compliance in the context of non-state actors. Along with other chapters in this volume (Chapters 11, 12 and 14), we examine a type of non-state actors that are increasingly active in world politics. We find, consistent with the insights from Jinks and Goodman (Chapter 6), that material incentives work together with non-material motivations in inducing actors to move from commitment to compliance. More concretely, we demonstrate that incentives to attract more material support for their cause as well as non-material incentives to gain legitimacy are central in understanding commitment and compliance behaviors of non-state armed groups.

We argue that organizational characteristics that allow the rebel group to enforce centralized compliance decisions and the motivation for them to establish legitimacy (i.e. social vulnerability) are key scope conditions for commitment and compliance. We provide both quantitative and qualitative evidence on the importance of centralization and vulnerability in explaining how these groups move from commitment to compliance. Our empirical evidence comes from a dataset of humanitarian access granted to the International Committee of the Red Cross (ICRC) in conflict zones between 1991 and 2006. To further elucidate the role of centralization and vulnerability, we also provide a case study of three rebel groups in Sudan. We conclude this chapter with a discussion of the implications of our analysis for future studies of compliance behavior among non-state actors.

Defining commitment and compliance in the case of armed opposition groups in civil wars

We define "commitment" as actors accepting international human rights norms to be valid and binding. For state actors, commitment usually means the act of signing and ratifying treaties. Non-state actors such as rebel groups do not have these traditional legal means available and must instead resort to alternatives. Some insurgent groups developed their codes of conduct to abide by international humanitarian law (La Rosa and Wuerzner 2008: 333). Other groups even expressed their desire to adhere to the Geneva Conventions and

---

[4] One of the two Additional Protocols signed in 1977 – Protocol Additional to the Geneva Conventions of 12 August 1949, and relating to the Protection of Victims of Non-International Armed Conflicts – addresses non-international armed conflicts.

Additional Protocol I (Veuthey 1983: 122–123).[5] Several dozen national liberation movement groups participated as observers in the negotiation of the 1977 Additional Protocols to the Geneva Conventions, and three of these ultimately signed the Final Act of the Diplomatic Conference (Henckaerts 2002: 128).[6] Additional instances of commitment behavior include the signing of international agreements. Examples of such agreements include Operation Lifeline Sudan (OLS), an agreement between UNICEF and the Sudan People's Liberation Army/Movement (SPLA/M),[7] and the work of Geneva Call on the Deeds of Commitment for Adherence to a Total Ban on Anti-Personnel Mines and for Cooperation in Mine Action. Although these agreements have weak enforcement systems, a rebel group signing them is analogous to the behavior of a state when it signs international treaties.

We define "compliance" as sustained behavior and domestic practices that conform to international norms. Compliance by rebel groups includes behaviors consistent with international human rights and humanitarian law, particularly their legal obligations as written in Common Article 3 and Additional Protocol II. Prohibitions include such acts as no civilian killing, no use of landmines, no recruitment of child soldiers, and humane treatment of detainees.

Along the commitment–compliance continuum, there are several behaviors that fall in-between. One such example, for which we provide a quantitative analysis, is rebel groups granting the ICRC access to their detention centers. When a rebel group grants access to the ICRC, it allows the organization to monitor its treatment of security and civilian detainees (Aeschlimann 2005).[8] We propose that granting humanitarian access constitutes more than commitment behavior but does not quite amount to compliance behavior. Granting access goes beyond commitment because it is more substantial than simply making a promise and represents behavior consistent with recommendations in the Geneva Conventions.[9] Granting access does not amount to full compliance behavior,

---

[5] The list of insurgent groups that addressed their declaration to the ICRC include the African National Congress (ANC) of South Africa 1980, the South West Africa People's Organization (SWAPO) 1981, the Eritrean People's Liberation Front (EPLF) 1977, the National Union for the Total Independence of Angola (UNITA) 1980, the Afghan National Liberation Front (ANLF) 1981, the Islamic Society of Afghanistan (ISA) 1982, the Palestine Liberation Organization (PLO) 1982 and the Moro National Liberation Front (MNLF) of the Philippines 1981.

[6] The three groups are the Palestine Liberation Organization (PLO), the Pan-Africanist Congress (PAC), and the South West Africa People's Organization (SWAPO) (Henckaerts 2002: 128).

[7] For lists of rebel organizations signing agreements with international actors, see Clapham (2006), Ewumbue-Monono (2006) and Steiner et al. (2008).

[8] For the categories of civilian detainees and corresponding obligations of conflict parties, see Goodman (2009).

[9] Granting access to the ICRC is not a legal obligation, but warring parties are encouraged to recognize the role of the ICRC according to Common Article 3 of the Geneva Convention (Clapham 2006).

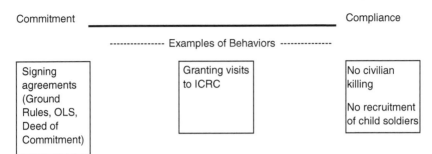

Figure 13.1   Commitment and compliance continuum in the case of armed opposition groups

however, because its legal foundation is less solid than other obligatory behaviors, such as not killing civilians or recruiting child soldiers.[10] For the purpose of our research, this transitional period of granting access will give us an understanding of what happens between commitment and compliance.

We summarize corresponding behaviors on the commitment–compliance continuum in Figure 13.1.

Scope conditions and mechanisms: commitment and compliance by armed opposition groups

We begin with the simple observation that rebel groups are not created equal. Some are political actors, much like states vying for legitimacy, whereas others are disorganized and lacking in political motivation. Groups with long-term political goals established by political wings may have a disciplined military, while others may take on lawless characteristics and potentially break into factions.

With this initial observation, we think that centralization and social/ material vulnerability are the most relevant in explaining rebel groups' compliance behavior among the five scope conditions introduced in Chapter 1. Centralization sets the boundaries of what rebel groups are able to do in terms of their decision-making procedures and their ability to enforce compliance. Vulnerability determines what the actors aim to do and how vulnerable they are to compliance demands. Some groups may be concerned about promises of material aid or their prospects of becoming legitimate political entities, while others may not.

Centralization facilitates compliance in two ways. First, centralization gives rebel leadership negotiating and decision-making authority. Groups

[10] The distinction between military personnel and civilians is a cornerstone of international humanitarian law, and is in fact considered to be a customary international law. The prohibition of recruiting children into the military is codified in the Convention on the Rights of the Child (CRC).

with central command and control structures are better able to negotiate with external actors such as humanitarian agencies. A centralized organizational structure also provides humanitarian actors the opportunity to pinpoint who they need to negotiate with and ensures that this person or group has ultimate decision-making authority. Second, centralization enhances the possibility of enforcement through internal discipline. Armed groups with strong command and control structures are able to control the behavior of lower rank soldiers through internal monitoring and enforcement mechanisms. This emphasis on organizational structure is consistent with findings in recent civil war literature (Weinstein 2007).

Organizational structure alone does not motivate rebel groups to abide by international norms. Vulnerability concerns are at the heart of some rebel groups' intrinsic motivations and shape their compliance behavior. Similar to states, rebel groups have political constituents. Sometimes these can be state or non-state external supporters[11] such as diasporas, while at other times they are local civilians. In serving their constituents, some rebel groups want to develop their reputation both internationally and domestically, making them socially and materially vulnerable actors. Having a positive record on human rights makes them more likely to receive humanitarian aid.[12] Rebel groups that want to develop a good relationship with civilians also usually want humanitarian aid to distribute amongst their core supporters.

All four social mechanisms (coercion, rewards, persuasion and capacity-building) are at work in the context of rebel group compliance. The first mechanism of coercion and legal enforcement relates to the international community's effort to develop international criminal law, landmarked by the Rome Statute and the establishment of the International Criminal Court. In making rebel groups responsible for war crimes, it is hoped that they will be deterred from committing crimes prohibited by the Statute. The second mechanism of sanctions and rewards relates to the power of humanitarian organizations in providing aid. International humanitarian communities can stop aid flow in the wake of human rights or humanitarian violations, or conversely can use aid as a reward for good behavior.[13] The third mechanism of persuasion and discourse is at the center of rebel group negotiations with humanitarian agencies prior to aid provision. Humanitarian organizations actively engage with rebel groups by negotiating the conditions and terms of their assistance and protection. The fourth mechanism of capacity-building is also related to the role of humanitarian actors, as they can educate rebel groups about humanitarian principles

---

[11] See Byman *et al.* (2001).

[12] The Sri Lankan LTTE's loss of $350 million after being designated as a terrorist group is a prime example of material vulnerability (Sivakumaran 2006).

[13] An example of this is US aid given to the SPLA/M because of its commitment to human rights.

Table 13.1. *Humanitarian access granted to the ICRC by armed opposition groups in internal conflicts 1991–2006*

	Frequency	Percent
Full visit	71	11.51
Partial visit	29	4.70
No visit	33	5.35
Missing	484	78.44
Total	617	100

or assist them in building human rights organizations.[14] By empowering local civil society, international actors promote compliance with human rights and humanitarian rules.

Warlords and samaritans in conflict zones: quantitative evidence of centralization and vulnerability

As part of the behavior that occurs between commitment and compliance, we examine access granted to the ICRC by rebel groups in internal armed conflicts between 1991 and 2006. The unit of analysis is conflict-year.[15] The list of conflicts is obtained from the Uppsala Conflict Data Program (UCDP) Armed Conflict Dataset and visitation records were coded from annual reports of the ICRC. Table 13.1 shows the breakdown of rebel group access.[16] Full visits refer to unrestricted access given to the ICRC, partial visits refer to somewhat impeded access, usually restriction to security detainees, and no access refers to when access is denied or humanitarian negotiation has failed.

Two observations immediately follow. First, armed opposition groups *do* grant humanitarian access 15 percent of the time when combining full and partial visits. This goes against conventional wisdom that armed opposition groups are lawless entities. The second observation involves missing values in the data. Missing data constitutes 78 percent of the dataset, reflecting the

---

[14] For example, the SPLA/M allowed ICRC officials to conduct workshops on IHL principles.

[15] The ICRC rarely distinguishes individual rebel groups and organizes visit information by conflict-year. Following the organization of the dependent variable, our unit of analysis is conflict-year rather than rebel group-year.

[16] Armed opposition groups that granted full access for at least one year include UCK (Macedonia), CPN (Nepal), PKK (Turkey), RCD (Congo), MILF (Philippines), SPLM/A (Sudan), UNITA (Angola), UCS-faction (Somalia), NPFL (Liberia), LTTE (Sri Lanka), GAM (Indonesia), FRUD (Djibouti), Abkhazia (Georgia), Chechnya (Russia) and MJP (Côte d'Ivoire).

realities of humanitarian operations. Several possible explanations for the missing cases include (1) instances when national governments denied access upfront to their territory, being heavy-handed about humanitarian assistance and operating as gatekeepers (as in India and Turkey), and (2) instances where humanitarian negotiations with rebel group leadership failed because of splitting factions, inaccessibility of terrain, or a conflict flare-up. Since we code all conflicts included in the UCDP database, there are simply many conflicts and rebel groups that the ICRC never discusses in its reports. As there is no mention of these conflicts or groups by the ICRC, we can with some confidence assume that they count as "no visits."[17]

In our empirical analysis, centralization is measured by rebel groups' organizational characteristics, including strong command and control structure, and territorial control. Rebel groups with strong command and control are more likely to negotiate with humanitarian agencies compared to splitting factions with weak leadership. Groups that control specific areas of territory are also more likely to have a firm handle on the decision to grant access to the ICRC. Vulnerability measures include levels of civilian support, military strength of the rebel group, and whether the group has a political wing. Rebel groups with high civilian support are more likely to be concerned about their political reputation vis-à-vis their core constituents. Militarily strong rebel groups are generally those with political aims to take down the government and would be concerned about their future political survival. The presence of a legally permitted political wing in the country is another indication that rebel groups are vulnerable to social and international pressures. Data sources and variable descriptions are shown in Table 13.2.[18]

Given the nature of the dependent variable, we use ordered probit analysis. The statistical analysis of humanitarian access reported in Table 13.3 shows the effects of centralization and vulnerability.

We report four models to explain humanitarian access in Table 13.3. Model 1 presents the effects of the strength of central command and having a legal political wing. In Models 1 and 3, we control for the regime type of the opposing government because the legality of political wings often depends on whether the government allows such political opportunity. Model 2 shows the effects of the military strength of rebel groups, high civilian support for the rebel group, and territorial control. Model 3 includes all the correlates of centralization and vulnerability except for high civilian support, which heavily reduces the number of observations due to data being available only after 2000. Model 4 examines the effect of international criminal law on rebel group behavior. We conjecture

---

[17] Jo and Thomson (2011) statistically test whether this assumption is innocent or not. The core results are left unchanged after accounting for the factors that generate the missing data.

[18] For more detailed data descriptions, see Jo and Thomson (2011).

Table 13.2. *Variables and data sources*

Variable	Description	Data source
Strength of central command	3 = high degree of central command control, 2 = moderate control, 1 = low control, 0 = the control of the central command is unclear	Cunningham *et al.* (2009)
Territorial control	0 = no control over territory, 1 = rebels control territory	Cunningham *et al.* (2009)
Legal political wing	4 = Yes, 3 = unclear, 2 = does not apply, 1 = No	Cunningham *et al.* (2009)
Rebel group strength	1 = much weaker than government, 2 = weaker than government, 3 = power parity, 4 = stronger than government, 5 = much stronger than government	Cunningham *et al.* (2009)
Civilian support for rebel groups	1 = the peak number of active civilian supporters of the insurgents exceeds 100,000, zero otherwise	Valentino *et al.* (2004)
Political regime type	Index of Political Regime (ranges from –10 to 10, with –10 being most autocratic and 10 being most democratic)	Polity IV Project (Marshall and Jaggers 2002)
Signatory of the Rome Statute	0 = not a signatory, 1 = signatory to the Rome Statute	International Criminal Court[a]

Note: [a] Data coded from www.iccnow.org/documents/
Signatures-Non_Signatures_and_Ratifications_of_the_RS_in_the_
World_November_2009.pdf.

that considerations regarding the future consequences of ICRC visits may be another factor affecting rebel groups' decisions to grant humanitarian access. The model tests this conjecture by adding a dummy variable to indicate whether the country has signed the Rome Statute. Because the Rome Statute was opened for signature in 2000 but our temporal scope is 1991–2006, the addition of this variable significantly drops the number of observations and restricts our ability to make inferences. In all four specifications, we include a lagged dependent variable to account for temporal dependence.

The positive coefficients of rebel group characteristics in Models 1–4 indicate that rebel groups with a legal political wing, a strong military, high civilian support, and territorial control are more likely to grant access to the ICRC.

Table 13.3. *Statistical models of humanitarian access granted by armed opposition groups*

	Model 1	Model 2	Model 3 Baseline	Model 4 ICC effect
Strength of central command	0.499*** (114)		0.299** (0.121)	0.571*** (0.215)
Territorial control		1.431*** (0.266)	0.888*** (0.184)	1.321*** (0.443)
Legal political wing	0.161** (0.077)		0.324*** (0.094)	0.598*** (0.231)
Rebel group strength		0.944*** (0.226)	0.638*** (0.109)	1.303*** (0.332)
High civilian support		1.110*** (0.307)		
Political regime type of opposing government	−0.041*** (0.012)		−0.033** (0.015)	−0.060** (0.029)
Signatory of the Rome Statute				−0.841*** (0.306)
Lagged dependent variable	1.342*** (0.179)	0.483* (0.295)	0.873*** (0.189)	0.586* (0.336)
Cut1	2.660(0.346)	5.543(0.780)	4.279(0.524)	6.672(1.192)
Cut2	2.969(0.366)	6.060(0.811)	4.653(0.550)	6.937(1.223)
Total number of observations	499	140	494	210

Robust standard errors are given in parentheses. * $p<0.10$, **$p<0.05$, ***$p<0.01$.

Model 4 shows that armed opposition groups are not immune to recent developments in international criminal law. When a state ratifies the Rome Statute, it may change the incentives of insurgent groups in committing human rights violations. Fear of being captured and tried at the ICC may deter rebels from committing heinous violations, such as civilian killings. However, the above analysis shows that in terms of granting visits, rebel groups are more likely to restrict access. This result needs more investigation, but our tentative interpretation is that this negative effect is due to the fear of their violations being found out. Although the ICRC has announced that they are not obligated to share information with the ICC prosecution (Mackintosh 2004), rebel groups seem to be aware that humanitarian visits can provide compliance information to humanitarian agencies.

Table 13.4. *Humanitarian access and civilian killing: linkage*

		Civilian killing	
		Civilian killing fewer than 25	Civilian killing more than 25
Granting of visit to ICRC	No visit	17	41
	Partial visit	6	14
	Full visit	16	8

Source: Eck and Hultman (2007); Jo and Thomson (2011).

The road from commitment to compliance is not automatic. Table 13.4 shows how humanitarian visits are related to another substantive compliance behavior – civilian killing, for which Eck and Hultman (2007) provide systematic data.

We classify an instance as civilian killing if more than twenty-five civilians are killed by rebel groups in that conflict-year.[19] Groups that grant full visits and kill fewer than twenty-five civilians (sixteen instances) consistently follow humanitarian norms. Groups that grant no visits and kill more than twenty-five civilians (forty-one instances) are the non-compliant group. The groups that grant no visits and kill fewer than twenty-five civilians (seventeen instances) are compliant with humanitarian rules but did not engage humanitarian actors. Most of these instances involve militarily weak groups, which may be too weak to attack civilians or which humanitarian actors failed to engage due to the group's unimportance. The groups that grant full visits but nonetheless kill civilians (eight instances) failed to reach a stage of rule-consistent behavior. Alternatively, these groups may have had ulterior motives to receive humanitarian aid that is associated with visits to detention centers. Centralized organization can therefore play a dual role across different issues of commitment and compliance: it can make access easy by facilitating humanitarian negotiation, but can also be amenable to civilian killing.

Due to the lack of reliable data on various dimensions of human rights and humanitarian compliance of non-state actors,[20] in this chapter we do not examine

---

[19] Eck and Hultman's one-sided violence data use a threshold of twenty-five deaths.

[20] Except civilian killing data, we are unable to find systematic data for other compliance behaviors of armed opposition groups. Data for state behavior are more readily available than those for non-state actors. For example, the data for the use of child soldiers exist (Achvarina and Reich 2006; Simmons 2009), but their studies are for analysis on the behavior of state actors, not of non-state actors. The most used dataset about human rights violations, Cingranelli-Richards (CIRI) Human Rights Dataset, also records human rights violations of states, not of non-state actors.

the connection between access and compliance behaviors in a systematic fashion. Hopefully the case study presented in the next section will give readers a sense of how centralization and vulnerability move actors from commitment to compliance.

Commitment and compliance by the Sudanese rebel groups: qualitative evidence of centralization and vulnerability

Introduction and case selection

Over the last several decades Sudan has been devastated by two civil wars involving three very different rebel groups. These differences provide a unique opportunity to further analyze the causal mechanisms of rebel compliance with human rights norms.[21] Through this case study, we hope to add to the robustness of our empirical findings and present a comprehensive view of how commitment and compliance occur in the case of rebel groups.

We have three motivations in choosing Sudan as a case study. First, Sudanese rebel groups display a substantial amount of variation. The rebellion in Southern Sudan began in the early 1980s and has recently resulted in independence for the region, whereas the Darfur conflict did not begin until early 2003 and the fighting continues to this day. Additionally, the two main Darfur rebel groups are differentiated by ethnicity, religion, political goals, organization and military capacity. Our second motivation is one of error minimization. By focusing on rebel groups that exist within the same country, we are able to control for cross-case variation and reduce the risk of creating biased inferences (King *et al.* 1994). Finally, a key benefit of case study analyses is that they allow for process-tracing (Gerring 2004; King *et al.* 1994). By comparing rebel groups, we can observe why they chose different levels of engagement with the international community and how this contributed to subsequent compliance. Below, we show that the strong centralization and vulnerability of the Sudan People's Liberation Army/Movement's (SPLA/M) in Southern Sudan has allowed it to successfully progress toward compliance. On the other hand, the chaos that characterizes the Darfur rebel groups (the Sudan Liberation Army/Movement (SLA/M) and the Justice and Equality Movement (JEM)) make it unlikely they will advance along the commitment–compliance continuum without first undergoing substantial internal change.

In the following sections, we discuss how centralization and vulnerability drove each rebel group to reach different levels of compliance. Next, we examine each group's performance on four crucial issues of human rights, providing

---

[21] Case studies have been acknowledged as being particularly useful in clarifying causal mechanisms (Gerring 2004; King *et al.* 1994). In a recent demonstration of this, Sambanis (2004) uses case studies to elucidate the causal mechanisms at work in civil wars.

further evidence of their compliance behavior. Finally, we offer our conclusion as to each group's prospect of reaching rule-consistent behavior.

Leadership, unity and the transition to prescriptive status: the case of Southern Sudan

The SPLA/M was established in 1983 to address the Sudanese government's marginalization of its southern regions and blatant (oftentimes violent) discrimination against non-Arabs. Instead of promoting an elite ethnic group like the Sudanese government, the SPLA/M wanted to establish a state that would protect the rights of all citizens. In a 1985 statement, the SPLA/M's leader John Garang avowed, "We are committed to the establishment of a new and democratic Sudan in which equality, freedom, economic and social justice and respect for human rights are not mere slogans but concrete realities" (Deng 2010: 40). These priorities were echoed throughout the conflict by the SPLA/M and were enshrined in the 2005 Comprehensive Peace Agreement (CPA)[22] negotiated between the SPLA/M and the Sudanese government. Then, in January 2011 Southern Sudan voted to split with the north, and the new nation declared its independence in July. With the SPLA/M largely controlling the government, its ultimate adherence to these principles remains to be seen.

From its beginning, the SPLA/M's strong political foundation, coupled with the potential for rewards from the international community, gave the group a strong incentive to comply with international law. The SPLA/M's political vision made it essential for them to appear as rule-abiding and legitimate members of the international community. Since it had secessionist aims, the SPLA/M needed to demonstrate it was worthy of international recognition. If the group was seen as violating these standards, it risked losing much-needed international support. To demonstrate its resolve, the SPLA/M even allowed the ICRC to conduct instruction sessions on humanitarian law[23] for its armed forces and officially incorporated IHL principles into its training in 2003 (ICRC Annual Report 2003). Such actions indicate the group has moved beyond merely making commitments and is actively taking steps towards compliance.

A high degree of centralization in the SPLA/M also enhanced its ability to successfully engage with international humanitarian organizations (IHOs). The SPLA/M's chairman and commander-in-chief John Garang maintained strong control over the organization from 1983 until his death in 2005. Despite internal discord in the early 1990s and occasional rumors of discontent, Garang

---

[22] Comprehensive Peace Agreement Between the Government of the Republic of the Sudan and the Sudan People's Liberation Army/Movement, 2005.

[23] IHL training sessions were discussed in ICRC Annual Reports for the years 1996 and 1998–2008.

remained the SPLA/M's undisputed leader (Young 2008). While Garang's pre-ponderance of power within the SPLA/M was sometimes criticized by others within the rebel movement, it enhanced coordination with humanitarian agen-cies. McHugh and Bessler (2006a) highlight the importance of central lead-ership for rebel group compliance, stating that, "When a chain of command (however limited) is functioning, it increases the likelihood that lower-ranking members of the group will respect the undertakings and agreed outcomes nego-tiated by and with their leaders" (5). The ability of humanitarian organizations to pinpoint Garang as the person they needed to talk to in order to deliver aid and discuss humanitarian violations eliminated the uncertainty IHOs often face when dealing with rebel groups.

The internal conflict experienced by the SPLA/M in the early 1990s demon-strates the consequences of leadership disruption for compliance. As the group split into three factions, the environment became much more complex for IHOs (ICRC Annual Report 1994). Rather than having to cooperate with only one rebel group, they suddenly had to coordinate operations with three groups that were busy fighting each other and the government. The violence that ensued from 1994 to 1995 made it particularly difficult for IHOs to pressure the rebels to conform to humanitarian norms. As a result, the ICRC was denied access to detainees in 1995 (ICRC Annual Report 1996; Jo and Thomson 2011). In 1996, however, the factions each made at least a partial inroad toward peace. The Southern Sudan Independence Army (SSIA/M) and the SPLA/M-Bahr-el-Ghazal faction signed a political charter with the Sudanese government that essentially eliminated them as rebel groups. At the same time, the SPLA/M-Garang signed a provi-sional agreement with the government and declared a ceasefire. The restoration of clear leadership within the SPLA/M allowed the group to re-signal its inten-tion to comply with international humanitarian norms, and ICRC visitations to the SPLA/M's detainees were again permitted (ICRC Annual Report 1996; Jo and Thomson 2011).

Despite facing some difficulties during periods of internal turmoil, the SPLA/M has been able to effectively transition from a rebel group to an estab-lished political entity committed to protecting human rights. Without such a strong commitment to human rights and a concern for its political repu-tation, we believe it is quite unlikely that the SPLA/M would have been as accommodating to IHOs. The SPLA/M's sudden lack of centralization in 1995 led to obvious cooperation problems with IHOs. Only when Garang re-estab-lished control could the group proceed along the commitment–compliance continuum. In sum, the qualitative evidence demonstrates how centralization and vulnerability concerns – key scope conditions as borne out by the group's leadership and political motivation – interact with mechanisms of rewards and capacity-building in the form of external political support and humani-tarian engagement in the process of fostering compliance behavior among non-state armed groups.

"Hotel Guerrillas," fractured factions and stagnation: the rebel groups of Darfur

While the Darfur rebel groups that emerged in 2003 may resemble the SPLA/M in terms of their political motivations, the SPLA/M possessed a level of sophistication and unity that the Darfur rebel groups severely lack. Dominated by leadership struggles and a lack of internal cohesion, the Darfur groups are far from realizing their political goals. As a result, these groups are stuck in a pre-commitment phase, and incorporating them into the international community as legitimate, rule-abiding actors remains a slim possibility.

The Darfur rebel groups have never shown as much commitment to their political foundations as the SPLA/M. It could even be argued that the political foundation of the SLA/M was simply borrowed from the SPLA/M, as its political manifesto shows a strong resemblance to the SPLA/M's (Flint and de Waal 2005) and was published only two months after the two groups met. By not carefully establishing these guidelines independently, it became much easier for the SLA/M to abandon them later.

Leaders of the other main Darfur rebel group, JEM, had a much clearer understanding of their political goals. While JEM does not support the separation of church and state as the SPLA/M and the SLA/M does, religious and political freedoms are still considered important aspects of the movement. Although initially smaller than the SLA/M, JEM's clearly established political aspiration has made it easier for them to adhere to those ideals.

In addition to lacking a firm commitment to their political orientation, the SLA/M also lacks strong and consistent leadership. Key positions within the SLA/M were initially divided among the three ethnic groups: Abdel Wahid of the Fur was chosen as chairman, Abdalla Abaker of the Zaghawa was chosen as chief-of-staff, and the Masalit position was left open. This marriage of convenience did not last long. Only two years after the SLA/M was formed, dissatisfaction with Wahid led a small group of Zaghawa to vote to make Minni Minawi, former secretary of Abaker before his death in 2004, chairman of the movement. Wahid and his supporters rejected Minawi's claim of leadership and the SLA/M permanently split into two factions (Flint 2007). In international affairs, each faction demands to be recognized as the head of the organization. This internal discord has made it increasingly difficult for IHOs to engage with either group.

Compounding the SLA/M's leadership difficulties are issues of decreased capacity and centralization. Hoping to gain international support for their cause, Minawi and Wahid spend much of their time abroad lobbying for assistance. Soldiers on the ground soon dubbed their leaders "hotel guerrillas," as Wahid and Minawi rarely visited the field or interacted with the soldiers. The disjuncture between the SLA/M's leaders and ground operations has created uncertainties in negotiations. Leaders could very rarely ensure that their orders were being carried out and had little knowledge of daily operations by their units.

Due to its smaller foundation and the political experiences of its members, leadership in JEM has been substantially stronger than in the SLA/M. In 2001 JEM members elected Khalil Ibrahim to be the spokesperson for the organization (Flint and de Waal 2005). Their united political vision has made JEM's leadership much less volatile, and Ibrahim remains the leading figure to this day.

The lack of centralization in the SLA/M and a meager commitment to its political goals has resulted in a severe lack of organization and discipline within the group. "Almost from the outset, the SLA was marked by division at the top and constantly shifting allegiances lower down. Organizational structures were never put in place and military command and control disintegrated" (Flint 2007: 141). The result was a surge of violence against civilians, especially by Minawi's faction. In 2006, Amnesty International condemned the SLA/M-Minawi for killing, injuring and raping more than 200 civilians in the Korma region over a period of five days.[24] The violence by Minawi's faction is even more surprising considering he was the only rebel leader to sign the 2006 Darfur Peace Agreement. The agreement did not create a lasting impact though, and only months later Minawi's faction renewed its violence and was once again condemned by Amnesty International.[25]

Changes among the centralization and vulnerability of the Darfur rebel groups over the last decade have resulted in substantial real world changes as well. Whereas the SLA/M possessed greater military capacity than JEM when both groups were established, today the opposite is true. According to the Sudan Human Security Baseline Assessment (HSBA), "JEM remains the strongest rebel force on the battlefield" (2011a: 3). The SLA/M has also diminished in terms of its domestic and international reputations, as the HSBA characterizes the group as "isolated" and having fallen out of favor with the United States (2011b: 2). Such changes have important implications for future compliance by these Darfur rebel groups.

Sudan's rebel groups and compliance with human rights and humanitarian rules: the importance of rebel characteristics

To further analyze compliance among Sudan's rebel groups, we compare their behavior on four human rights issues highly salient to conflict zones: (1) the treatment of civilians, (2) the treatment of detainees, (3) the use of landmines, and (4) the use of child soldiers. These four issues are cornerstones of international humanitarian law and together provide a good indication of where each rebel group falls on the commitment–compliance continuum. A summary of our findings is presented in Table 13.6.

The first issue area we analyze is rebel treatment of civilians. Civilians have been continually harmed by all of Sudan's rebel groups, although violations by

---

[24] Amnesty International (2006).　[25] Amnesty International (2007).

Table 13.5. *Sudanese rebel group characteristics*

		Rebel group characteristics	
		Political aspirations	Leadership and discipline
Southern Sudan	SPLA/M	Strong and consistent	Very strong and centralized
Darfur	JEM	Strong but not as radical as those of the SPLA/M or the SLA/M	Strong leadership and organization
	SLA/M-Minawi and SLA/M-Wahid	Moderate at best. Their ideology was never central to their movement	Very weak

Source: Flint and de Waal (2005); Flint (2007); Young (2008); Deng (2010).

the SPLA/M are occurring less frequently. The SPLA/M laid the foundation for its commitment to human rights in its manifesto and reaffirmed this commitment in 1995 when, in an agreement between the SPLA/M and Operation Lifeline Sudan (OLS) on humanitarian aid distribution, it expressed support for the 1949 Geneva Conventions, the 1977 Geneva Protocols and the 1989 Convention on the Rights of the Child (McHugh and Bessler 2006b). This commitment was reiterated in its 1998 Fifteen-Point Programme stating that, "The Movement stands in support and respect of international Conventions on human rights and similar international protocols on human rights" (SPLM Political Secretariat 1998). The SPLA/M even established the Sudan Relief and Rehabilitation Association (SRRA) and Operation Save Innocent Lives (OSIL) as humanitarian wings of its movement (Ewumbue-Monono 2006: 919). Despite these verbal commitments, however, violations by the SPLA/M still occur, and in 2009 it was accused of not properly protecting the rights of the Southern Sudanese people by Human Rights Watch (2009b). Recent controversy within the SPLA/M and continued fighting with Sudanese government forces, however, have led to increased violations (Human Rights Watch 2011; US Department of State 2010). As the group turns to the task of governing, it must be especially watchful of these occurrences escalating. Examining the Darfur groups, it is clear that the SLA/M-Minawi has an especially egregious record in this area, and has consistently been condemned for indiscriminate injuring, killing and raping of civilians. While the SPLA/M's tendency to commit these violations does appear to be decreasing over time despite their recent infringements, neither the SLA/M nor JEM show any signs of improvement.

A similar picture emerges when we turn to our second issue, the treatment of detainees. As discussed in our quantitative section, detainees are entitled to visitation from the ICRC.[26] Due to decreases in rebel capabilities, access to the ICRC often fluctuated with conflict levels. During more violent years access would be denied, whereas complete access was granted during more peaceful years. The SPLA/M has the most compliant record on this issue. Although sometimes criticized for violating the rights of detainees, the SPLA/M was generally engaged with humanitarian agencies, especially as the conflict drew to an end (ICRC Annual Reports; Jo and Thomson 2011). Once again, however, the Darfur rebel groups have a more negative track record, as their general pattern of behavior is to deny access to the ICRC (ICRC Annual Reports; Jo and Thomson 2011). This demonstrates how the SPLA/M has been able to progress along the commitment–compliance continuum while the Darfur groups remain stagnant.

The third area we analyze is landmine use. The international community has been very active on this issue area, as demonstrated in the Deed of Commitment for Adherence to a Total Ban on Anti-Personnel Landmines and for Cooperation in Mine Action under the Geneva Call. As of September 2011, the Deed has been signed by forty-one rebel movements.[27] Interestingly, on this issue it is the Darfur rebel groups who outshine the SPLA/M. In fact, there have been no reports of landmine use by the SLA/M or JEM, whereas the SPLA/M has been repeatedly criticized for employing them (Watchlist on Children in Armed Conflict 2007). While at first glance this may indicate compliance by the Darfur groups, we remain cautious about such conclusions. The fact that the Darfur rebels do not use landmines does not imply they avoid them for humanitarian purposes. It is quite possible that landmines simply do not give them a military advantage. Therefore while we are encouraged that the SLA/M and JEM have refrained from using landmines, we do not take this to be a reflection of their concerns for human rights. The SPLA/M on the other hand used landmines quite extensively throughout the 1980s until the mid to late 1990s, particularly in the Nuba Mountains and Eastern Equatorian regions. Under increasing pressure from the international community, the group passed a resolution banning landmines in 1996 (Ewumbue-Monono 2006). While the SPLA/M was again criticized for their use in 2003, it appears to have made strong improvements in this area.

---

[26] The reader may wonder why we do not simply present a table of visitation data for Sudan. The main reason has to do with the organization of the dataset. While the data is organized by country-year, Sudan has three rebel groups that sometimes operate during the same years. Therefore we cannot differentiate between different groups in the dataset. To address this problem, we went back and examined the ICRC Annual Reports again to see who the data refers to.

[27] "Signatories to the *Deed of Commitment* banning anti-personnel landmines." Geneva Call. Accessed on September 3, 2011 at www.genevacall.org/resources/list-of-signatories/list-of-signatories.htm.

Perhaps one of the most reviled violations of international humanitarian law today is the use of child soldiers. The SPLA/M and the SLA/M have both been strong violators of this norm. Although the SPLA/M agreed to stop recruiting child soldiers when it consented to the Ground Rules, reports continue to document offenses. With the help of UNICEF, the group was able to successfully demobilize 3,200 child soldiers in 2001 and another 2,500–5,000 in 2004, but it is estimated that thousands more remain (Child Soldiers Global Report 2008). Once again, however, it appears that the SPLA/M is attempting to comply, and has pledged to demobilize all child soldiers by the end of 2010 (Uma 2010). The same optimism does not appear in the case of the SLA-Minawi, which has been cited as forcibly recruiting children as young as twelve and is estimated to have thousands of child soldiers in its ranks. An agreement was attempted by UNICEF to help demobilize the group's child soldiers, but efforts on behalf of the SLA/M were not genuine and the talks collapsed. JEM's use of child soldiers on the other hand remains unclear. While there have been several reports of it recruiting and training child soldiers, the group vehemently denies such accusations. In an effort to challenge this, it agreed to allow the UN access to its camps in July 2010 (BBC News 2010). Should these inspections verify their statements, JEM would be well on its way toward compliance in this area.

As evidenced above, when analyzing rebel group compliance it is essential to account for their differences and how these differences impact the group's successful integration into human rights regimes. The SPLA/M's strong commitment to human rights since its beginning, consistently strong leadership, and clear political aims made it much more likely to engage effectively with IHOs, and therefore more likely to reach the latter stages of the spiral model. Characteristics such as centralization and vulnerability concerns made it easier for the international community to use persuasion and discourse, as well as the tools of capacity-building (through education and training of IHL) and rewards (in the form of aid), to induce compliance from the group. Critics may argue that the SPLA/M was simply making "hypocritical commitments" in order to achieve its goals (Cardenas 2007) and is not truly committed to human rights protection. However, the SPLA/M's continuing compliant behavior on a variety of issues leads us to conclude that it has indeed reached prescriptive status and is on its way to achieving rule-consistent behavior.

The Darfur groups present quite a different story. Lacking those qualities that allowed the SPLA/M to proceed towards compliance, the SLA/M and JEM appear to be stuck hovering around the "tactical concessions" stage. Although Wahid and Minawi may verbally agree to humanitarian norms, they are unable to enforce real change in their organizations, and have been repeatedly condemned for blatant violations of humanitarian principles. Until these groups undergo substantial internal change, it is unlikely they will progress toward compliant behavior.

Table 13.6. *Compliance indicators of Sudan's rebel groups*

	Southern Sudan	Darfur	
	SPLA/M	SLA/M	JEM
Treatment of civilians	Initially poor but improving	Very poor, especially Minawi's faction	Poor
Treatment of detainees	Varied but usually good	Generally poor	Generally poor
Use of landmines	Markedly improved	Not used[a]	Not used
Use of child soldiers	Moderately improved. Pledged to demobilize all child soldiers by the end of 2010	Very poor	Unclear. They maintain they do not use child soldiers

Note: [a]Although no systematic evidence of landmine use by either of the Darfur groups, we are hesitant to conclude that this represents compliance with international norms, as the groups have never signaled their views on the issue.
Sources: Amnesty International (2004, 2006, 2007); Child Soldiers Global Report (2001, 2004, 2008); Eck and Hultman (2007); Ewumbue-Monono (2006); Felton (2008); Hamberg (2010); Heavens (2008); Human Rights Watch (2009b, 2010); ICRC Annual Reports, various years; International Campaign to Ban Landmines (2003); IRIN (2004); Jo and Thomson (2011); Levine (1997); McHugh and Bessler (2006b); Uma (2010); UNDP Sudan; Watchlist on Children and Armed Conflict (2007).

Conclusion

We find that centralization and vulnerability are two key scope conditions for commitment and compliance by armed opposition groups in contemporary civil conflicts. We also find that persuasion and rewards are salient mechanisms for compliance, particularly for rebel groups that prize external recognition and support for their political cause. Rebel groups with state-like characteristics, such as organizational capacity and centralization, and vulnerability to reputational concerns are easier for humanitarian actors to engage. Our results are both inspiring and unsettling. They imply that many of these groups are possible to engage but, unfortunately, the groups that are the most unruly may not be easily engaged. Future research should address how humanitarian organizations should engage unruly rebel groups, which would be both highly useful for the policy community and informative to scholars of compliance and human rights.

Our research also shows the importance of political interactions among non-state actors. The relationship between non-state actors, rebel groups and international humanitarian organizations is important in catalyzing compliance behavior, as the Sudan case demonstrates. The empowerment of civil society was one of the SPLA/M's strategies in order to reach prescriptive status. Civil society and international pressure – key mechanisms put forward by the original spiral model – are important and relevant for rebel group compliance. Our research focuses on the interim step between commitment and compliance, namely the ICRC's access to detention centers, but future studies on commitment and compliance should examine other dimensions of non-compliance behaviors, including civilian killing and the recruitment of child soldiers. Whether the key scope conditions and mechanisms suggested by our analysis are applicable to other compliance settings will guide our understanding of compliance behaviors of non-state actors in world politics.

14

Changing hearts and minds: sexual politics and human rights

ALISON BRYSK

How does the "power of human rights" affect private wrongs – violations generated by non-state actors? Private actors with delegated authority, such as families, employers and religious communities, are increasingly recognized as potential human rights violators and subject to international campaigns – but not yet to consistent governance. Many modern states allow designated categories of private actors to exercise physical and even legal control over dependent members such as women, children and employees, and the exercise of such control may often violate international human rights standards of life, liberty and bodily integrity – even in states that normally guarantee protection from state abuse of such rights to their citizens in the public sphere. As a constructivist perspective suggests, transnational campaigns against private wrongs such as violence against women rely on a combination of logics of persuasion and institutionalization, with limited availability of coercion and incentives. This chapter will analyze a strikingly similar pattern of norm change through socialization in states and international organizations in the "hard case" of sexual politics, where male elites and social institutions face no incentives or coercion to change gendered patterns of subjugation. Yet immigration-weary states provide gender-based asylum and gender-neutral professional organizations lobby international organizations to delegitimize female genital mutilation (FGM). This is a story of the move from commitment to compliance; as norms change "from above and below," the state struggles to find purchase and leverage in authority structures, including both the state and other sectors of civil society.

In each case, communicative action and civil society movements have shifted hearts and minds to contest private wrongs and extend international standards to demand state accountability for the protection of *all* citizens. While such persuasion and social pressure *can* elicit *commitment*, as the amplified spiral model would predict, progress from such prescriptive commitment to *compliance* relies heavily on the degree of centralization and control of the decision-maker, complicating redress for private wrongs more than state-sponsored abuse. Thus,

Many thanks to Madeline Baer for research assistance on the cases.

this chapter will explore two further key issues for compliance: how much the state controls both abuse and redress, and how much the compliance decision is focused on a centralized source or small number of decision-makers. In this regard, the cases show clear differences; although many states have shifted commitments to eschew violence against women that emanates from private actors, in gender-based asylum states control redress and compliance is centralized in state immigration policy. By contrast, for the private wrong of FGM, compliance is decentralized and weakly subject to state control. However, it is striking that in the scattered but growing cases where decentralized compliance has improved on FGM, it is through explicit changes in norms – not shifts in authority relations, centralization or state capacity.

The persuasive power of human rights norms permeates the "spiral model," and articulates with a growing genre of global governance research on norm change. In the absence of authoritative coercion, states and transnational private actors may choose to change their behavior to accord with legitimate standards accepted by both local civil society and "world public opinion" – even where this contradicts their short-term material interest in profit or control. When it occurs, such change accords with a constructivist logic of appropriateness, in which power-holders internalize roles and seek status alongside material benefits, and results from a transnational dialectic of communicative action. Norm change, in the spiral model and elsewhere, is based on a combination of symbolic and information politics: hearts and minds. New rights norms engage and persuade when they are: (1) articulated by credible and charismatic speakers, (2) framed to resonate with universal or previously established values, (3) progressively explain and manage outstanding social problems, and (4) are delivered through accessible and salient media. Transnational ties are constructed through the communicative processes of identification with the Other, clear causal narratives of injustice and redress, and "branding" of locations and victims (Brysk 1995, 2007).

Human rights violations linked to sexual politics – assassination, assault, torture, discrimination, imprisonment and enslavement of a significant proportion of half of the world's population – pre-date the modern state system, and continue alongside the globalization and the modernization of many other forms of labor and social interaction. Sometimes coercion over gender roles is *state-sponsored*: in theocratic regimes, legal denial of reproductive health rights and discriminatory family codes (Cook 1994). But often the "private wrongs" of sexual politics are enacted by non-state individuals and social institutions such as family members, traffickers and clergy: to control and commodify the biological and social functions of reproduction and associated sexuality. The political nature of "the world's oldest oppression" is further elucidated as the private authority of violators depends upon either state *delegation* of coercive power or state *negligence* of women and girls – as second-class citizens with an unequal claim on membership, protection and political participation (Brysk 2005). As a gender-based refugee put it: "The discrimination and repression I lived with in Saudi Arabia had political and not cultural roots. When governments impose a certain set of beliefs on individuals, through propaganda, violence or torture, we are dealing not with culture but rather with political expediency" (Alfredson 2009: 143). Violence against women is a consequence of gender inequity and unequal state protection, and often serves to perpetuate discriminatory control of women's reproductive rights by states, social institutions and individual family members.

Following the spiral model, campaigns for reproductive rights and gender equity have achieved widespread recognition and some tactical concessions, but often stall between commitment and compliance. This is due in part to the multi-level targets of norm change, which appear to respond unevenly to pressure "from above and below." It also reflects limitations in state responsiveness to weakly legalized norms that affect a diffuse, marginalized and sometimes non-citizen population. The other chapters in this volume that deal with rights violations by non-state actors such as warlords and corporations reflect similar patterns of persuasive norm change engendering prescriptive commitment, followed by a critical governance gap in compliance due to limited state capacity and decentralized control over rights violators even by willing states and international organizations (see Chapters 11, 12 and 13, this volume). The importance of the governance gap can be seen in the relative success of gender-based asylum, where high-capacity states like Canada exercise control over migration, compared to slow and uneven change in FGM in states which typically exercise little governance of their own private sectors and rural areas.

Both the original spiral model and the international human rights regime assume that abusive states are capable but unwilling, so that transnational pressure and socialization can transform the incentives and logics of the source of abuse. In this scenario, strengthening international norms and resources along with empowering victims (in this case, women) within their states will improve attention to and enforcement of rights. But if states are negligent, complicit or truly powerless vis-à-vis local elites, grassroots social authorities, transnational economic actors and informal cross-border networks, the international human rights regime lacks traction. Formal international authority such as multinational corporations or international peacekeepers can be socialized on issues of gender equity and reproductive rights, but informal local or transnational actors like village tribal councils or human traffickers have alternative bases of legitimacy and control and are relatively impervious to communicative action. Both states and formal private authority depend on legitimacy as well as force and rewards, and generate formal commitments such as treaties, laws, codes and charters as part of their exercise of authority. Informal local or transnational actors draw on norms in a different sense, so persuasion may generate shifts in social understandings that shift incentives but do not operate through legal codes. For these actors, a shift in commitment may involve adherence to a new or different external formal standard (like a different interpretation of sharia law), a public pledge or understanding, or simply an agreement to permit public monitoring or dialogue concerning a private practice.

Thus, while both gender-based asylum and campaigns against FGM garner international commitment, they result in disparate levels of compliance with the new norms. Compliance is not equivalent to legal enforcement, although enforcement may be important for some kinds of abuses. In theory, compliance with a human rights standard may mean refraining from committing the abuse, regulating an abuse committed by others, providing succor or redress to victims, removing or reforming the source of a chronic or structural abuse, creating new institutions to perform any of the above functions, as well as monitoring and educating private actors in their performance of delegated social control. These various dimensions of compliance are relevant to different degrees for private wrongs than a state-sponsored abuse such as war crimes, and operate in different ways for different types of private wrongs – and international instruments require various levels of compliance to constitute provision and protection of rights. In asylum cases, the agent of redress is a centralized, capable state distinct from the abuses. Compliance is easy to assess by refugee admissions standards, processes, figures and rates. For FGM, both abuses and responses are decentralized in private actors, with both target states and international organizations playing an intermediary role in standard-setting, resource provision and some symbolic enforcement that signals but does not truly control the norm violators. Moreover, FGM compliance is more difficult to gauge because the decentralized outcome of a private wrong is an ensemble of shifting prevalence rates, changes in the severity of the practice, positive unreported prevention and negative unreported concealment. Despite these difficulties in assessment, it is fairly clear that in the past decade, gender-based asylum policies have diffused and acceptances have multiplied, while by contrast FGM continues to be practiced extensively and harmfully. However, there are some shifts in local practice of FGM associated with some kinds of interventions hidden within overall prevalence rates – such as small but significant inter-generational declines – that suggest that even the more modest forms of monitoring and service provision compliance may eventually spill over to more conventional behavioral compliance, and should not be discounted.

Norm change and sexual politics

Contesting sexual politics across borders therefore depends more heavily on a more complex form of transnational socialization than mobilizing the normative consensus for civil liberties of political dissidents, or even labor rights. It demands an extension of anti-discrimination norms to gender equity, alongside a simultaneous validation of women's unique vulnerability to abuse in reproductive roles; an uneasy blend of protection and empowerment. The dialectical and internalized construction of gender roles demands significant re-socialization of men, male-dominated institutions and patriarchal logics. Along with spiral model argumentation in which the victims of repression reach out for international support based on legal and rational grounds, we should expect to see significant framing efforts by experts, advocates and cultural figures. Key elements of the coalition will participate on the basis of their own identities and ideologies, beyond the generic consensus of the international human rights regime. Since violations are a varying blend of state-sponsored, state-delegated and wholly private wrongs, the sequence of appeals may not follow a "boomerang" model from local to global to state, nor even a world polity model of diffusion from global to state (Boli and Thomas 1999; Keck and Sikkink 1998). Rather, we will often see multi-level frame contests and dialectical reconstructions, as in the global-local-global shift from empowerment to health rights on FGM (Baer and Brysk 2009). Finally, as "the personal is political," symbolic politics including cause célèbres, media representations and charismatic appeals to transcendent tropes such as motherhood will play a larger role in legitimating and building Other-identification with reproductive rights than more established and visible public sphere violations.

The commitment: violence against women

Violence against women is a patterned violation of women's life, liberty and physical integrity on the basis of gender; either enabled by or in order to maintain women's physical, sexual, economic, political and legal subordination. Women's right to freedom from violent coercion by states and corresponding right to protection by their states from coercion by private parties flow from widespread core commitments such as the ICCPR, the International Covenant on Civil and Political Rights, as well as the International Convention on Economic and Social Rights (ICESR), and the Geneva Convention on the Rights of Civilians in Wartime. Fundamental norms of gender equity are covered in CEDAW, the Convention on the Elimination of All Forms of Discrimination Against Women. Self-determination around gender-based reproductive roles includes freedom of movement for unmarried or unaccompanied women, free consent to marriage, legal equality within marriage, equal rights to childrearing and custody, protection from domestic violence and marital rape, and protection from forced prostitution; some of these are covered in CEDAW, the Convention on the Rights of the Child, and optional protocols on Trafficking and Consent to Marriage. Since gender inequity is usually strongest in populations suffering other forms of abuse and vulnerability on the basis of race, class, culture or displacement; some kinds of coercive practices fall under various anti-discrimination norms, including but not limited to CERD, the Convention on the Elimination of Racial Discrimination, and the Refugee Convention. A full list of all applicable international instruments can be found at the website of the United Nations Special

Rapporteur on Violence Against Women, www2.ohchr.org/english/issues/ women/rapporteur/instruments.htm.

Rights protection from all forms of sexual violence including genital mutilation also requires reference to non-binding "soft law." The full panoply of gender-based violence is condemned in a non-binding Declaration on the Elimination of Violence Against Women. The linkage between gender-based violence and reproductive rights is acknowledged in the declaration of the 1995 World Conference on Women in Beijing: "The human rights of women include their right to have control over and decide freely and responsibly on matters related to their sexuality, including sexual and reproductive health, free of coercion, discrimination and violence" (United Nations 1996: para. 96). The United Nations General Assembly has passed a series of resolutions on female genital mutilation, in 1997, 1998 and 2001, calling on member states for legislation, policy, enforcement and education against "traditional practices that harm the health of women and girls" and citing female genital cutting.

Although there is no international *enforcement*, there are archipelagos of *implementation*. The UN Division for the Advancement of Women provides model legislation for violence against women, while numerous UN, regional and bilateral programs foster enforcement, assistance and educational programs against trafficking. Many transitional justice bodies, starting with the International Criminal Court, now include prosecution for sexual violence committed during war, genocide or massive civil conflict (but not chronic or routine sexual violence, even if state-sponsored or systematic). The foreign aid programs of human rights promoter states include programs to foster gender equity in education and reproductive health care, and legal assistance programs often address legal discrimination in gender roles, including marriage. Within global civil society, flagship human rights organizations such as Amnesty International and Human Rights Watch specifically campaign for women's protection from gender-based violence. Human Rights Watch's condemnation of impunity for rape in Mexico links state responsibility and private wrongs with the label, "The Second Assault" (Human Rights Watch 2006).

The following "hard cases" of women's rights socialization across borders show a similar process of communicative action mobilizing principled support. In these cases, the change agent derives no personal or group benefit from advocacy, and in gender-based asylum the state sacrifices its default interest in limiting refugee claims. The substantive rights at issue are predominantly private wrongs such as FGM and domestic violence, but there is some systematic critique of state negligence and/or legal regimes. There is evidence that normative appeal to actor identities mobilized advocacy. And in each instance, the victims participated in some fashion in reshaping the social agenda, but could not secure policy change without a coalition of like-minded but differently situated individuals and organizations.[1]

The personal is political: "global good samaritan" and gender-based asylum

The first case of state-level principled support for women's rights is the introduction of gender-based asylum, starting with Canada in 1993 and subsequently diffusing to a dozen other countries. Following a communicative action campaign by asylum seekers and advocacy groups, Canada drafted new refugee admission standards and processes to encompass gender-based persecution, defined to include state-negligent and severe domestic violence, FGM, and state prosecution for women's resistance to state-mandated discriminatory restrictions on dress and social behavior. These new refugee policies resulted in a measurable increase in refugee admissions on the basis of gender. The initial guidelines were strengthened via a 1996 update that also enhanced policy procedures to be more attentive to gender-based persecution (Alfredson 2009). In this case, compliance should mean equitable assessment of gender-based asylum claims at comparable rates to other forms of asylum.

The content of the Canadian model reflects progressive socialization on the nature and causes of sex discrimination, encompassing four gendered categories of persecution: gendered forms of harm (such as sexual violence) for persecution on some other basis, persecution on the basis of kinship, state collusion or negligence in protecting female citizens from severe discrimination or violence by private actors, and persecution for "transgressing, certain gender-discriminating religious or customary laws and practices" (Alfredson 2009: 5–6). Such recognition of a new and complicated basis for refugee admissions clearly contradicted the default state interest in controlling migration and the bureaucratic politics of immigration officials, who stated their resistance the previous year on precisely these grounds, reversing course after a concerted campaign that appealed to core Canadian values. Another measure of the success of socialization on this issue was its rapid diffusion to a set of diverse but "like-minded" humanitarian states, such as Ireland, South Africa, Australia and Sweden, at a time when most were grappling to restrict migration on other grounds. The culmination of this modeling was the 2002 adoption of UN High Commission on Refugees Guidelines on International Protection: Gender-Related Persecution (HCR/GIP/02/01), which explicitly cited the influence of pilot standards in Canada, the United States and Australia, and corresponding EU Recommendations calling for attention to gender-based

---

[1] Two additional studies by the author show virtually identical dynamics in the related areas of mobilization against human trafficking, and campaigns for gender equity by male public intellectuals (Brysk, in press).

persecution as a basis for asylum. In 2004, the EU issued a Qualification Directive and an Asylum Procedures Directive that specifically ask states to take into account gender and sexual violence in assessing individual applications and creating asylum procedures.

The core of the communicative action campaign was a set of media statements and interviews by half a dozen representative asylum seekers who told their stories, as well as group statements by women refugees from eighteen different countries, capturing the public imagination. One level of impact was simply to put a human face on the suffering of these women; several of them were mothers who spoke of their fears for their children. Another overall effect was to educate the Canadian public about the scope of gender persecution in their home countries, and the unavailing nature of their governments – and initially of Canadian immigration officials. They were supported by highly legitimate refugee, women's and religious organizations in a country with a relatively influential and internationalist civil society (Brysk 2009c). Favorable media coverage successfully linked the women's struggle for recognition to human rights frames well-established in Canada; one story was titled "Is Sexual Equality a Universal Value?" while an editorial in the *Montreal Gazette* contended "Indivisible: Until Women's Rights Are Human Rights, We Have Far to Go" (Alfredson 2009: 197–199).

The dialectical process that socialized the Canadian state is worthy of note. In response to several prior legal appeals in the early 1990s, the Canadian government initially contended that its policies were legitimated by the 1951 Refugee Convention, which Canada claimed was "gender neutral." Nevertheless, the defensive response characteristic of the middle stages of the spiral model, acknowledging the legitimacy of the norm even while denying it is being violated, is evident when the Immigration Minister's office replied to NGO queries: "the position of the government with respect to the persecution of women is irrelevant to the refugee status determination process. Nonetheless, let me assure you that the Minister does not condone discrimination against, or persecution of, women" (Alfredson 2009: 191–192). When the Canadian flagship human rights organization ICHRDD joined the campaign, they appealed to another aspect of transnational socialization typical of the boomerang model as well as specific to Canada's foreign policy niche as a norm promoter: "If [Nada] is forced to return to her country, Canada will be sending out a signal that it will not act to oppose the systematic violation of women's human rights ... This would be most unfortunate, *given the important initiatives that Canada has taken on behalf of gender equality and human rights in the Francophonie, the Commonwealth, and the Organization of American States*" (Alfredson 2009: 195, my emphasis). The domestic "mobilization of shame" deepened when the president of the ICHRDD, former MP Ed Broadbent, wrote an editorial for the country's two leading newspapers (the *Globe and Mail* and *La Presse*) that a colleague explained "embarrassed the hell out of the government." This time, the government adopted a culturally relative refusal to "impose its values on the rest of the world" – unwittingly radicalizing the public debate. The minister ended up retracting this statement, promising new policy guidelines acknowledging Broadbent's influence, and announcing consideration of representations to the United Nations (Alfredson 2009: 202–204).

For this campaign against a collection of gender-based private wrongs, compliance was relatively robust. In Canada itself, the reforms brought acceptance rates for gender-based claims up to a par with refugee admittance for other forms of persecution (roughly 58 percent). According to Alfredson's study, between 1993 and 2002 Canada accepted 1,345 gender asylum claims, and such claims have continued to constitute 1–2 percent of Canada's annual refugee claims – affecting thousands more women (Alfredson 2009: 78). Gender-based asylum standards have now been adopted systematically by the UK, Sweden, the United States and Australia, while dozens of other countries recognize some form of sexual violence as a factor in the determination of refugee status. The growing practice of gender-based asylum has affected small but significant numbers of critically endangered women refugees in half a dozen countries, including some keystone pilot cases such as a US and similar UK grant of asylum for African women threatened with FGM. The potential further impact on jurisprudence is striking, even in the relatively legally isolationist United States; a US federal appeals court recently ruled that Guatemalan women face such massive insecurity from thousands of unsolved murders of young single women that they may qualify for asylum on the basis of persecution by gender (www.google.com/hostednews/ap/article/ALeqM5jDsyN-sz_uLkkzpF8SwX2qIQE3QAD9GTQQN00).

Following a communicative action model, why did Canada come to protect, and later globally promote, the rights of powerless non-citizens suffering from private wrongs? First, the "innocent victims" became charismatic speakers who communicated directly with a receptive public. Their claims were reinforced by a coalition of highly legitimate insider advocates. The message that "private" violence against women was a public problem resonated strongly with domestic values, as a 1991 federal report on violence against women in Canada had stated: "These assaults on the person, dignity and rights of women as equal citizens undermine the values Canadians revere and upon which they are trying to build a tolerant, just and strong nation" (Alfredson 2009: 258). Providing refuge to abused women reinforced Canada's self-image as a humanitarian internationalist, at a time of growing migration tensions, inaction in Bosnia and debacle in Somalia (Brysk 2009c). In this case, commitment did translate into limited but meaningful compliance. In order to broaden the impact and achieve the spiral model's final stage of rule-based behavior, the normative and political challenge is to move from refugee protection to empowerment, and from succor to prevention for private wrongs.

Health rights and norm change: humanitarian professionals in the FGM coalition

At a different level of analysis, transnational communicative action has moved contested norms regarding FGM toward a consolidated commitment by most states and international organizations, though still falling short of compliance. The patriarchal practice of crippling women's sexual pleasure by removal of the clitoris evokes some of the strongest symbolic sexual politics, precisely because it is a practice of pure hegemony inscribed upon the body, vaguely rationalized as functional for social control. African states and local elites initially resisted colonial and later modernizing attempts to legislate against FGM, citing cultural relativism, a spurious religious basis in Islam, and national self-determination over "their" female citizenry. By the 1990s, however, there was broad consensus within the international rights community that FGM violated a number of core human rights: the right of women to be free from discrimination on the basis of gender, the right to life and physical integrity including freedom from violence, the rights of the child, and the right to health (Rahman and Toubia 2000; Skaine 2005). However, at one stage the spiral model was derailed when feminist groups, international organizations and human rights NGOs encountered unexpected resistance to perceived imposition of inappropriate norms from the very people they aimed to assist – African women, including many who opposed the practice. Since about 2000, these tensions have been reduced through the rise of a new and less controversial combined "health *rights*" framing for the issue, which appeals internationally but does not alienate locally. A critical component in the second phase reframing of the FGM coalition spiral model was the entry of highly legitimate and "neutral," non-feminist professionals as interlocutors between the rights community and national sensibilities: doctors and humanitarians. As a result, dozens of African countries have outlawed the practice, but perhaps just as important for implementation, have begun to encourage holistic attention to women's health rights and transnational support for some humanitarian programs of local women's empowerment.

In contrast to the classic spiral model, the goal of the FGM campaign was multi-level change in state policy and local behavior by private actors. The participants in the coalition also shifted and broadened: from global missionaries to local women to global feminists to international organizations to health and development NGOs plus some local and regional women's groups. In more typical fashion, the campaign brought slow and uneven change first in standards, then policies, and finally some implementation via transnational programs.

The charismatic authority and problem-solving modernity of medical professionals has played a critical role in delegitimizing FGM, with a joint effort above and below the state from health IGOs and NGOs. To assess this change, it is useful to recall that when the Economic and Social Council of the United Nations asked the WHO to study FGM in 1958, WHO leadership refused because FGM was seen as a cultural matter, not as an international medical issue (Boyle 2002: 41). But by the late 1970s and early 1980s, UN sub-committees began to study FGM and began providing outlets for national governments and NGOs to discuss the health issues related to FGM (Boyle 2002: 48). One such forum was the WHO-sponsored Seminar on Harmful Traditional Practices Affecting the Health of Women and Children in Sudan in 1979. After another generation of feminist consciousness-raising, in 1998 the WHO, UNICEF and the United Nations Population Fund issued a strong and influential joint statement against FGM, calling FGM a violation of the rights of women and girls to the highest attainable standard of health (*Female Genital Mutilation* 1997). This represents a breakthrough from the communicable disease model of public health to a rights-based perspective, and in a 2008 update of the joint statement, the WHO goes on to assert universal reproductive rights. The 2008 norm-setting standard calls FGM a practice with "no known health benefits" that reflects "deep-rooted inequality between the sexes" and is an "extreme form of discrimination against women."

The WHO now uses its legitimacy as a public health organization and source of knowledge to promote attention to issues of sexual and reproductive health. A study sponsored by the WHO was published in *The Lancet* in 2006 on the links between FGM and maternal and infant mortality and health consequences (World Health Organization 2006). The WHO provides training manuals for nurses, midwives and other health professionals on how to prevent FGM and how to provide health care to girls and women with FGM related complications. The manuals also provide strategies for involving families, communities and political leaders in preventing FGM (World Health Organization 2001a, 2001b, 2001c). Finally, the WHO has reviewed anti-FGM programs by other agencies to assess the effectiveness of public health interventions in this area (World Health Organization 1999).

At the level of global civil society, the World Medical Association, an independent confederation of about eighty national medical associations, condemns the participation of physicians in any form of female genital circumcision and encourages national medical associations to oppose the practice (World Medical Association 2003). Formed in the wake of the Nuremberg trials to oppose unethical medical experimentation, the organization has played a broader role in opposing physicians' participation in torture, as well as drafting guidelines on emerging ethical issues such as new genetic technologies. The WMA offers specific "best practice" guidelines for physicians in environments where women and girls are at risk of cutting, stating that "Regardless of the extent of the circumcision, FGM affects the health of women and girls. Research evidence shows the grave permanent damage to health." In terms of concrete policy work, in the late 1990s the WMA publicly encouraged the Egyptian Minister of Health to continue working to ban female circumcision in Egypt (World Medical Association 1997). The WMA has also extended its opposition to the transnational medicalization of the procedure in immigrant communities, especially in Western Europe. In a press release from 2003, Dr. James Appleyard, incoming president of the WMA, specifically mentioned FGM as a rights issue: "One form of a gross breach of the rights of young girls is female genital mutilation. Even in the UK where the practice is outlawed it is widely alleged that FGM continues to be practiced in private hospitals" (World Medical Association 2003).

Similarly, humanitarian service providers have reframed medical, development and missionary identities to adopt and transmit a rights-based perspective on FGM. Doctors Without Borders strongly opposes FGM as a human rights violation and a threat to health, and identifies medical staff involvement in the practice as a breach of ethical and professional standards. In addition, Doctors Without Borders attempts to ensure that the practice is not performed in facilities where the agency works and that instruments provided by Doctors Without Borders are not used for the procedure (Médecins Sans Frontières 1999). At the local level, CARE found that Somalis living in Kenyan refugee camps who had been exposed to the human rights dialogue used by international aid workers were open to rights-based discussions of FGM and health consequences, which led many people in the camps to abandon the practice. Catholic Relief Services, sponsored by the US Catholic Bishops to do justice-oriented development solidarity work, opposes FGM as a threat to human dignity and maternal health – although departing from a feminist view of reproductive rights. Nevertheless, CRS has used its transnational network and local legitimacy to partner with local dioceses to sponsor alternative rites of passage for young girls to discourage FGM and promote reproductive health. (DeVoe n.d.; Majtenyi 2009).

Compliance has been much less effective and difficult to trace than gender-based asylum, but there do seem to be some changes in practice linked to the international campaign and commitment. While at least fourteen African countries have outlawed the practice, estimated prevalence remains stubbornly high at over 90 percent in half a dozen core countries such as Somalia and Egypt – and while Egypt bans the practice, Somalia does not. However, high prevalence countries are highly concentrated in the Sahelian region and especially the Horn of Africa; even in Western Africa and certainly in the South, FGM is generally restricted to certain ethnic groups in isolated rural areas. The World Health Organization estimates that several million girls are still affected each year, with over 100 million women living with the consequences, and the spread to immigrant communities has affected thousands more in the heart of Europe. Many immigration receiving countries have also banned FGM, including Canada, Sweden, the UK and the United States, and many European countries such as France and Spain lack specific legislation but have prosecuted the practice in immigrant communities under child protection and assault laws.

A comprehensive 2010 report by the Population Reference Bureau shows persistent high prevalence rates in a core group of about a dozen African and

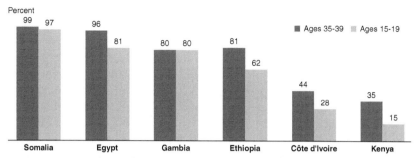

Figure 14.1   Prevalence of FGM/C among younger and older women
Source: Feldman-Jacobs and Clifton (2010).

Mideastern countries, but there are some encouraging trends. One indicator of emerging behavioral change is a significant inter-generational reduction in younger women affected even within some high-prevalence countries, and the possible emergence of a "tipping point" reduction in Kenya and some Western African states where lower rates have now almost halved, such as Benin, Liberia and Togo. Similarly, FGM has become much less common in urban areas in countries like Kenya, Liberia and Mauritania, suggesting increasing decline with the general modernizing trends of urbanization, education and media exposure. Although data is quite incomplete and uneven on forms and harms of FGM within these countries, there is also some evidence that the most harmful form of infibulation is increasingly concentrated as a widespread practice in a few core countries such as Somalia, while a few other countries such as Eritrea have shifted significant numbers of practitioners to a symbolic nick which does not involve the removal of flesh or impairment of future function.

Moreover, despite the overall gap between positive commitment in national laws and continuing negative grassroots behavior, there are field reports and studies of specific international programs that do seem to have reduced the practice and harms at the local level. The programs that do seem to effect greater compliance with the new norm are generally characterized by a holistic empowerment and dialogue approach that fits the health rights and development frame adopted by the transnational professionals profiled above. For example, the "Navrongo Experiment" appears to have reduced the risk of FGM by 93 percent in one area of Ghana, where FGM is traditional in some regions but illegal and enforced by a government that readily accepts international assistance, and overall prevalence may be reaching a "tipping point" of decline.[2] Similarly, the

---

[2] This section is based on a comprehensive review of dozens of UN, WHO and academic field studies by the NGO Stop Violence Against Women. See www.stopvaw.org/female_genital_mutilation.html for extensive discussions of geographic and statistical prevalence, charts of laws and policies by states and international organizations, reviews of NGO programs and model legislation.

Tostan grassroots education and civil society-building program originated in Senegal has reported positive reception in numerous areas of West Africa, suggesting that compliance with a private wrong cannot rest on law alone and must directly address civil society.

A broader and more recent study affirms and deepens this account of the power of persuasion to foster more decentralized compliance from non-state actors via transformation of social norms and transnational civil society. A UNICEF study from 2006–2009 based in Egypt, Ethiopia, Kenya, Senegal and Sudan applies social scientific understandings of norm theory, organized diffusion and tipping points to promote shifts in communities' expectations around gender roles and marriageability of girls to reduce the practice of FGM (Innocenti/UNICEF 2010). The Innocenti research program is guided by UCSD sociologist Gerry Mackie, who studied the interactive abandonment of footbinding in China and applied this historical experience and game theory to the complex process of changing internalized social conventions through education, dialogue and social networks. The five-country study concludes that:

> Participatory deliberation drawing on human rights principles appears to play a crucial role in bringing about this collective change … Public commitment serves as a mechanism to coordinate families within intramarrying communities on abandonment … The public commitment not only helps shift the convention, maintaining the marriageability interest and advancing the health interest, but just as importantly, it also shifts the social norm, so that families who do not cut are socially respected and those who continue to perform the practice are socially sanctioned.
>
> (Innocenti/UNICEF 2010: 9)

More specifically, the study provides evidence of significant progress in localized behavior and broad attitudes over the relatively brief period of a decade in four of the five countries studied, with effects following the logic outlined: "The first declaration publicly announcing the abandonment of FGM/C in Senegal took place in July 1997. More than 12 years later, in December 2009, 4,121 villages that had directly or indirectly been part of the Community Empowerment Programme had publicly declared the abandonment of the practice" (p. 15). In Egypt, where prevalence remains quite high but increasingly medicalized: "FGM/C prevalence rates are high, over the past decade there have been some significant signs of change in attitudes about the practice, particularly among the youngest generations. The percentage of ever-married women who think FGM/C should be continued has dropped from 82 per cent in 1995 to 63 per cent in 2008. The practice has also become less common among the youngest age groups" (p. 17).

Following the model above, "The decisive stance for the abandonment of FGM/C taken by representatives of three groups in particular – medical professionals, religious organizations and young people – has given greater legitimacy and credibility to the FGM/C abandonment movement ... By the beginning of 2009, 50 villages had publicly declared their intention to end FGM/C, with most villagers signing a public pledge" (p. 22). In Ethiopia: "Especially significant is the fact that younger mothers (15 per cent) are nearly five times less likely to have a daughter cut than older mothers (67 per cent), indicating that the practice is becoming less common among the youngest age group. Attitudes towards the practice have changed significantly during this period, with reported support for FGM/C halving, from 60 per cent in 2000 to 31 per cent in 2005" (p. 24). In that country, echoing the Chinese Natural Foot Movement that ended foot-binding: "In 2000, [transnational development NGO] KMG organized the first of a series of public weddings of couples who chose to break with the tradition. As many as 2,000 people attended the first wedding, including 317 girls who had not undergone the practice serving as bridesmaids. During the ceremony, the bride and bridesmaids wore signs that read, 'I will not be circumcised. Learn from me!' The groom wore his own placard saying, 'I am happy to marry an uncircumcised woman'" (p. 30).

As with gender-based asylum, global advocates who were not women or even feminists took up the cause of women's rights based on their own identities and norms: as doctors, clergy and aid workers. Amidst the spectrum of such abuses occurring in very poor and patriarchal countries, FGM stood out for its senselessness and threat to innocent mothers and children. The harms of FGM also helped to explain or contribute to a range of health and development problems, from fistulas to AIDS. The practice is a dramatic visual representation of sexual violence against women. Physicians have an additional ethos and social role as defenders of the body, which is violated by FGM. But as with gender-based asylum, communicative action mobilizes more protection than empowerment, and even more of a gap between norm change and enforcement.

Communicative action and the new human rights agenda

This chapter has tried to expand the spiral model's account of norm change, as a communicative action strategy to contest multi-level "private wrongs." Communicative action based on identities was a critical component of mobilization around gender-based violence and the consequent commitment. A liberal state pushed by a humane civil society, organizations of health professionals and male intellectuals were persuaded to become advocates and reformers by a narrative of gendered suffering that challenged their own vision of themselves. The narratives of domestic violence and FGM centered on highly affecting innocents who were personalized characters brought to public view. Advocates consciously combined rational argumentation and principle with symbolic and emotional appeals; persuading hearts *and* minds. Although the reforms secured are tentative and incomplete, they have gone beyond the starting stage of spiral level repression to secure state-level and global acknowledgment: recognizing the political character of gender-based persecution and self-determination for reproductive decision-making. However, these cases show that the pathway to compliance depends upon the complex architecture of power relations between state and civil society, and that sometimes it is easier to secure policy change across borders than within them.

Since the cases presented here are representative of the general dynamics of gender rights struggles, we should consider the larger implications of the spiral model for the redress of private wrongs. While the transnational project of the construction of a feminist human rights regime is in its very early stages, it is difficult to determine how far a model designed to explain transnational pressure on states for the public rights of (male-modeled) citizens can go in explaining the multi-level struggle for the private rights of a massive and diverse social condition. Yet this chapter suggests that the dialectical establishment and diffusion of norm change does follow some familiar patterns outlined by the spiral model. The importance of legalization, transnational coalitions, and the decisive shift from denial to lip service seem similar for women's rights and the first-generation democratization cases considered in the original spiral model. Gender rights campaigns do seem to put more weight on certain aspects of the spiral model than historic democratization struggles for civil and political rights: frame innovation, humanitarian appeals, and global pressures on international policy-makers to substitute for weak states. This means that the next wave of human rights research should consider how to govern abusers whose hearts and minds cannot be changed, by empowering victims, bystanders, and governments who can.

15

Conclusions

THOMAS RISSE AND KATHRYN SIKKINK

The big puzzle for this volume has been how to identify and explain human rights change in the world. Human rights violations continue to be one of the most serious threats to human security, and yet we do not understand fully how to reduce human rights violations. The intellectual and theoretical challenge is first to identify *if* positive human rights change is happening in the world, that is, are actors moving to greater compliance with international human rights law, and if so, *why and how* are they doing so. In this conclusion, we return to the main research question of the book: under what conditions and by what mechanisms will actors – states, transnational corporations and other non-state actors – make the move from commitment to compliance with human rights norms? In particular, we will revisit the mechanisms and models of social action and recap the ways in which a more robust consideration of a set of scope conditions for the movement from commitment to compliance contribute to theorizing.

These issues are all the more important because in the last decade the world has witnessed both some of the most important political and institutional developments designed to enhance human rights *and* it has witnessed some serious setbacks to human rights, in particular 9/11 and later large-scale terrorist attacks and the emergence of a global war on terror framed as an issue where human rights protections had to be set aside. The terrorist attacks on the World Trade Center on September 11, 2011, or the Madrid train bombings in March 2004 can be seen as crimes against humanity, because they were "widespread or systematic attacks" directed against a civilian population, in the language of the Rome Statute. At the same time, the response to 9/11 has led to violations of human rights, including the resurgence of torture, the use of disappearances ("black sites"), kidnapping and refoulement ("extraordinary rendition") and summary execution ("targeted killings") by the greatest global power.

With its chapters on the United States and China, this volume explicitly addresses the issue of human rights compliance in powerful states. But the volume has not discussed some of the other broader changes in the world with great implications for human rights such as the role of the responsibility to protect doctrine in the United Nations or the rise of individual criminal accountability for human rights violations. Yet, it is still important to put our study and

our conclusions into the larger global context and address some issues that
have not been fully taken up elsewhere in the volume, but nevertheless form
the backdrop against which analyses take place. In the section below on coercion and enforcement we will discuss briefly the importance of the practice and
doctrine of Responsibility to Protect (R2P) and the rise of individual criminal
accountability for the issue of compliance with human rights law. We conclude,
however, that military intervention under the R2P doctrine and international
criminal tribunals will be the exception and most of the routine work of human
rights promotion in the world will continue to be conducted through the less
dramatic mechanisms described and analyzed in this volume.

But we need to state at the outset that it is not clear that a general theory of
human rights change is possible, especially as we introduce non-state actors,
including corporations, insurgent groups and even individual families into the
equation. The reasons that lead an African family to permit or even encourage
the use of female genital cutting on their daughter (Chapter 14) are simply quite
different from those that lead the Chinese state to continue to imprison its political opponents (Chapter 9) or a state with areas of limited statehood to be unable
to control or punish criminality in those regions (Chapter 4). This volume does
not aspire to provide a general theory of human rights change applicable to all
actors, but rather to clarify the main social mechanisms through which human
rights change occurs and the scope conditions that affect such change, and signal under what conditions we would expect spirals of external and internal pressures to be more or less effective. In this volume, we highlight four different
mechanisms and modes of social action to induce compliance: (1) coercion;
(2) incentives – sanctions and rewards; (3) persuasion and discourse; and (4)
capacity-building. We stress these multiple mechanisms not just because the spiral model is "additive" and believes that more pressure is better. Rather multiple
mechanisms are necessary because human rights compliance involves multiple
actors, and those actors have different kinds of motivations (see Chapter 6). This
book examines both the motivations *and* the capacity of actors, whether target actors are "willing" (motivation) and whether they are "able" (capacity) to
improve human rights. We suggest that different policy responses may be necessary for actors who are willing but unable to bring about compliance than for
actors who are unwilling to do so.

The idea is not to produce a single (very complex) general theory of human
rights change, but rather to remind readers that dealing with different types of
human rights issues and different types of target actors will require diverse theoretical and policy approaches. Nevertheless, there continue to be some general
propositions that hold across the many diverse cases presented here, as discussed
in the introduction and some of the chapters. For example, all of the chapters in
this volume, as well as the much larger literature surveyed by Chapters 2 and
3 continue to stress the importance of principled action by non-governmental
organizations. As Simmons remarks, almost every study of the pathway from

commitment to compliance "has emphasized the ways in which purposive actors have used international human rights norms to persuade, cajole, pressure and shame governments to live up to the commitments they have made to respect the rights of their own people" (p. 57). In their overview of the qualitative and quantitative literatures, both Jetschke and Liese and Simmons (Chapters 2 and 3) agree that literatures consistently see domestic mobilization as a key variable for explaining progress toward compliance.

In the following, we start by discussing how to measure compliance, the "dependent variable" of this volume. We then survey the findings of this volume with regard to the mechanisms and modes of social action identified in Chapter 1 followed by an analysis of the scope conditions for human rights change in light of the empirical chapters. We conclude with some policy implications of this volume.

Understanding and measuring compliance

This volume has identified the problem of moving from commitment to compliance with human rights norms to be the central concern. As such, the definition and operationalization of compliance is crucial. For this reason, the volume has devoted an entire chapter (Chapter 5) to these issues. Scholars have studied a compliance gap between the increasing level of human rights commitments and the apparent lack of corresponding behavioral change (see e.g. Hafner-Burton and Ron 2009). But as Dai reminds us, the compliance gap is not only an objective measure of behavioral change, but a "subjective benchmark" by which behavior ought to be evaluated. This benchmark has been increasing over the years, in large part due to the advocacy efforts of the human rights organizations. There are now more human rights treaties than ever before, and more inclusive understandings of the rights spelled out by older human rights treaties. So, for example, much of what we consider as problems of human rights compliance in this volume, such as compliance by transnational corporations, insurgent groups, private actors enacting gender violence, and the state's inability to combat human rights violations by non-state actors in areas of limited statehood, would simply not have been considered human rights violations two decades ago. In other words, the human rights bar has been moving ever higher, and so states (and now increasingly) non-state actors, have to jump higher to clear the bar.

Moreover, there is also much more information available about human rights violations in the world, including new understandings of what constitutes a human rights violation. Recent human rights reports from non-governmental organizations and governmental sources typically contain much more and better information than earlier ones, and they document a wider range of human rights violations. As a consequence, social scientists have more data on human rights. The increase in the quality and quantity of information about human rights violations in the world and greater attention to the full range of human rights is good news for scholars and practitioners in this area, but it carries some potential problems for measuring changing levels of compliance with human rights. It is important to be aware how these two factors – the dramatic increase in human rights commitments and the information environment within which human rights violations take place – can affect our ability to reach consensus about whether human rights compliance is occurring and the causal factors related to human rights change over time (see Chapter 5, this volume; Clark and Sikkink forthcoming). This volume is committed to working with this constantly evolving notion of compliance, but it is important to be clear about the scholarly difficulty of measurement of compliance in a context of increasing commitments and information.

Social science theory often applies to a non-trivial but limited set of cases meeting certain scope conditions. The "classic" model of repression in *The Power of Human Rights* (PoHR, Risse *et al.* 1999) involved the violation of physical integrity rights in authoritarian states with low legitimacy but relatively high capacity. In these situations, a sustained spiral of increased information, pressure and sanctions from linked internal and external actors increased the social and the material costs of continuing such repression. Even under these classic situations, the spiral did not necessarily lead to change. Not all governments were equally vulnerable to pressures and consistent internal and external pressures were difficult to organize and sustain. Even so, the spiral model appeared to be useful in explaining change in multiple places (see Chapter 2). Sustained change, however, depended on whether these authoritarian states also made a transition to democracy. Even more interesting is that a number of chapters in this volume show that a somewhat modified spiral model can be fruitfully applied to understanding human rights change of non-state actors such as transnational corporations (Chapters 11 and 12 by Deitelhoff/Wolf and Mwangi/Rieth/Schmitz) and insurgent groups (Chapter 13).

Mechanisms and modes of social action

The role of enforcement

What difference does greater enforcement of human rights law make for the move from commitment to compliance? Historically many scholars and policy-makers have argued that human rights treaties did not have an impact because they were not enforced. By the early twenty-first century, a small number of human rights have become the object of enforcement regimes, including those that permit military intervention or international criminal accountability, at either the domestic or international level. Both the literature on compliance with institutions in international relations and the deterrence literature in sociology suggest that stronger enforcement should lead individuals to reduce human rights violations (Downs *et al.* 1996; Nagin 1998).

By enforcement, scholars have tended to mean two of the social mechanisms we discuss: (1) coercion; and (2) sanctions. The most extreme form of enforcement is the use of military intervention to stop human rights violations. Although none of the chapters in this volume or the previous one involved military intervention, such an option is now a possibility and thus forms the backdrop for any discussion of the move to greater compliance with human rights. In 2011, the first formal, explicit and multilateral exercises of military intervention using the Responsibility to Protect doctrine took place in Libya and the Ivory Coast. The "Responsibility to Protect" (R2P) was born in the perceived failure and impotence of the world's response to genocide, especially in Rwanda, but also in the Balkans (for detailed discussions see Bellamy 2009; Orford 2011). R2P was the brain-child of a group of like-minded states, including not only Western states, but also countries from the Global South that had experienced large-scale human rights violations, such as Argentina, Chile, Guatemala, Rwanda, and South Africa.[1] R2P consists of three propositions, or pillars: (1) first, that the state has primarily responsibility to protect its population against genocide, war crimes, crimes against humanity and ethnic cleansing; (2) second, that the international community has a responsibility to assist and encourage states in fulfilling this obligation, using appropriate and peaceful diplomatic and humanitarian tools; and (3) finally, should the state "manifestly fail" in its responsibility to protect, and should the international community's peaceful efforts be inadequate, the international community could take stronger measures, including the collective use of force through the UN Security Council (United Nations, General Assembly, 2005).

Responsibility to Protect reflected the justified frustration of many state officials who sat by and watched genocide occur and did nothing, hamstrung by UN rules and doctrine, as well as the caution of foreign ministries (Axworthy 2011). But R2P is about more than military intervention. It provides a firmer legal and doctrinal justification for international actions to promote human rights, which basically argues that states forfeit their right to be free from intervention if they manifestly fail in their responsibility to protect their populations from the most severe forms of human rights violations.

The first efforts in the UN to articulate the doctrine came during the term of Secretary General Kofi Annan in 2001. Yet in particular after the US sponsored invasions of Afghanistan and Iraq, the emerging doctrine collided with the fears of many small states that the doctrine could and would be used to justify military intervention to pursue a wide range of their foreign policy goals,

[1] For an archive of all the key documents relating to the emergence of the R2P doctrine, see the website of the International Coalition of Responsibility to Protect at www.responsibility-toprotect.org/

and not mainly to protect against core crimes like genocide and crimes against humanity. Critics correctly pointed out that R2P is characterized, as are all UN Security Council actions, by the deep power asymmetries of the international system, and thus such intervention would never be used against powerful states or their allies. The proponents of R2P persisted, arguing that a clear capacity for a multilateral response to gross violations of human rights would make unjustified unilateral intervention less, not more, likely. It was not until the 2005 World Summit that R2P was endorsed by a wide range of states, and not until 2011 that it was first invoked by the Security Council to justify military intervention.

In the context of the Arab Spring (see Chapter 10) and with the support of the Arab League and the African Union, the first real test of the third pillar of R2P came in Libya. It is still too early to evaluate the ultimate success or failure of that mission. But what we wish to stress in this volume is that while multilateral military intervention under the R2P doctrine will continue to be *one* high-profile tool in the toolkit of human rights promotion, it will be an exceptional and seldom used tool, only for a small subset of severe cases where an unusual foreign policy consensus exists among the members of the Security Council. It is not and should not be seen as a panacea for human rights violations in the world, nor, as its detractors have argued, as the most serious threat to human rights. Rather, the great bulk of human rights violations in the world, both those in fragile and in powerful states, will need to continue to be addressed through the far more routine policies and practices that we describe and analyze in this volume.

In this sense, it is the first two pillars of the R2P doctrine that provide a firmer basis for the human rights pressures and activities we discuss in this volume. It is also interesting to note that some of the states that were the objects of international human rights pressures in the PoHR volume became protagonists in the evolution of the R2P doctrine, in particular, Chile, South Africa and Guatemala. Although many states still fear that R2P will lead to excessive intervention, it has been endorsed most importantly by the African Union in the Ezulwini consensus, which also insisted on the need to empower regional organizations to take action in some cases.[2] The R2P doctrine also envisions other peaceful and diplomatic actions and "capacity-building" as steps the international community should routinely be taking to assist states in their responsibility to protect their citizens. So, for example, the General Assembly resolution on the 2005 World Summit Document, which is generally credited as the first multilateral

---

[2] The document known as the "Ezulwini Consensus" was produced in March 2005 by the African Union at its 7th Extra Ordinary Summit of the Heads of States and Government of the African Union. In it, African governments endorsed the Responsibility to Protect doctrine, and authority of the Security Council to authorize the use of force in situations of genocide, crimes against humanity, war crimes and ethnic cleansing, and also insisted that regional organizations in areas of proximity to conflicts should be empowered to take action (African Union 2005).

endorsement of the R2P concept, says the international community also intends "to commit ourselves, as necessary and appropriate, to helping States build capacity to protect their populations from genocide, war crimes, ethnic cleansing and crimes against humanity and to assisting those which are under stress before crises and conflicts break out" (United Nations, General Assembly, 2005). In this sense, R2P is an important backdrop for the chapters in this book, providing a doctrinal justification for the wide range of tools the human rights community uses to promote human rights, as well as the distant possibility of coercive enforcement in a small subset of extreme cases.

A second important human rights trend that forms a backdrop for this book is the rise of individual criminal accountability for human rights violations. This increase in criminal accountability, not only through international tribunals like the International Criminal Court (ICC, see Deitelhoff 2009) and the International Criminal Tribunal for the former Yugoslavia (ICTY), but also through an increase in foreign and domestic criminal prosecutions for human rights violations, is an important new type of enforcement for human rights norms that was not apparent at the time PoHR was published. Up to this point we have not considered the possible effect of such new enforcement for human rights compliance (but see Chapter 6).

Like R2P, the ICC, international tribunals and other foreign prosecutions are a back-up system for extreme cases. Most of the work in holding individual state officials criminally accountable for past human rights violations is being done in the domestic courts of primarily transitional countries where the human rights violations occurred, using a combination of domestic criminal law and international human rights law (Sikkink 2011). These trials are happening mainly in the transitional countries that were the topic of PoHR, but were for the most part excluded from this volume as we moved to focus on different topics. Nevertheless, this rise of individual criminal accountability provides more coherent and rule-based enforcement of human rights law. For example, all twelve of the transitional countries considered in PoHR have used domestic human rights prosecutions to hold former state officials accountable for past or current human rights violations.[3] Such domestic prosecutions are also being used in more recent transitional cases, as, for example, in the trial of former president Mubarak of Egypt for the deaths of protesters during the transition there.

Human rights prosecutions fit the definition of enforcement, since they have the capacity to impose real costs on perpetrators, not only through possible convictions and prison terms, but also through lawyers' fees, lost income through

---

[3] Chile, Poland, Czechoslovakia/Czech Republic, Guatemala, South Africa, Kenya and Indonesia have held both transitional trials for human rights violations during the previous authoritarian regimes, and trials for ongoing violations of rights during the newly established democratic regimes. Uganda, Morocco, East Timor, Tunisia and the Phillippines have held only have non-transitional trials. Transitional Justice Database, University of Minnesota and Oxford University. See www.transitionaljusticedata.com.

preventive detention, and the large political and reputational costs of criminal indictments. But prosecutions are different than most enforcement mechanisms in a number of respects. First, prosecutions operate mainly through consent when states commit to treaties like the Convention against Torture, and the Statute of the ICC that contain the possibility of enforcement. With the exception of the handful of legal enforcement actions set into motion by the UN Security Council, we can say that states "invited" the process of individual criminal accountability through treaty commitments and self-referrals to the ICC, even if they were often later unpleasantly surprised, as in the case of Pinochet, with the results of their actions.

Second, individual criminal accountability trials sanction individual state leaders (and sometimes individual insurgents) rather than the state as a whole. As Börzel and Risse point out in Chapter 4, enforcement approaches that focus on state sanctions assume a functioning state that is in principle capable of enforcing central decisions and the law. They argue that such enforcement will be less effective in areas of limited statehood. However, human rights prosecutions for individual criminal accountability target individuals not unitary states. As such, they may be effective even in situations of limited statehood where individuals (be they warlords or insurgents) nevertheless carry out human rights violations. To the degree that these areas are characterized by powerful individuals who control territory and may be responsible for violating rights, enforcement targeting such individuals could be effective. Cases before the International Criminal Court in three countries: Uganda, the Democratic Republic of the Congo and the Central African Republic, involve heads of insurgent groups in areas of limited statehood. Because none of these cases is yet completed, it is still too early to tell whether such a strategy leads to more compliance. Such individual enforcement could supplement institution- and capacity-building as compliance options in areas of limited statehood.

Even the US case considered in this volume (Chapter 8) shows that policy-makers were in fact intensely aware of the possibility of domestic prosecution under US statutes implementing international human rights law; many of their actions, including the infamous torture memos, were influenced by this awareness. But the US case shows the limitations of a pure enforcement model relying on the fear of punishment rather than a deeper internalization of norms. Motivation only by the fear of legal punishment can lead to the kind of perverse legal casuistry that the Bush administration employed in this case. This is one of the points stressed by Goodman and Jinks (Chapter 6) about the importance of intrinsic state motivation in order to ensure compliance.

Some scholars, however, have argued that human rights trials will not deter future violations and that, in some circumstances, they will actually lead to an increase in repression or to humanitarian atrocities (Goldsmith and Krasner 2003; Snyder and Vinjamuri 2004). For example, they contend that the threat of prosecution could cause powerful dictators or insurgents to entrench themselves in power rather than negotiate a transition from authoritarian regimes and/ or civil war. Goodman and Jinks likewise argue in this volume (Chapter 6) that material sanctions could "crowd out" other motivations and actually be counter-productive for human rights compliance.

But analysis based on new datasets (Kim and Sikkink 2010; Olsen *et al.* 2010) confirm that enforcement in the form of human rights prosecutions can have a positive effect on compliance with human rights norms. Such research shows, for example, that transitional countries in which human rights prosecutions have taken place are less repressive than countries without prosecutions, holding other factors constant. Contrary to the arguments made by the trial skeptics, transitional human rights prosecutions have not tended to exacerbate human rights violations. The findings of the literature on such prosecutions suggest that enforcement may be one important tool in the move from commitment to compliance with international human rights law.

Human rights prosecutions, however, are not only instances of punishment or enforcement, but also high-profile symbolic events that communicate and dramatize norms and socialize actors to accept those norms. It is thus difficult to separate out the enforcement or punishment effects of trials from their communicative or social dimension. This is more generally the case with the social mechanisms discussed by the spiral model. The spiral model looks at an eclectic blend of actions and pressures involving all the different forms of social mechanisms aimed at diminishing human rights violations. Because these mechanisms are used simultaneously, it is difficult to tease out the effects of different mechanisms. Yet a number of the chapters in this volume help to isolate the impact of various social mechanisms, and thus evaluate what is doing the work in bringing about human rights change.

Persuasion and discourse

Brysk's chapter on gender violence (Chapter 14) provides evidence for the power of persuasion and institutionalization, especially in the case of the decision to include gender violence as a criterion for Canadian asylum policy. Brysk argues that "male elites and social institutions face no incentives or coercion to change gendered patterns of subjugation" (p. 259) and yet communicative action has shifted policy and even compliance. More than any other chapter, however, the issue of gender violence illustrates how centralization of the compliance decision has important implications for compliance. Compliance is more likely in cases, such as that of Canadian asylum policy, where the compliance decision is centralized and the state directly controls compliance. Where compliance decisions are radically decentralized, and not under state control, such as family decisions about female genital mutilation (FGM), compliance will be more difficult. The case of FGM appears to be the clearest case discussed in this volume where processes that build intrinsic commitment through empowerment and dialogue have been most effective in promoting compliance in the absence of any enforcement. But we should also note that the continuing very high levels of FGM suggest that compliance has been modest at best.

Persuasion and learning also seem to matter with regard to bringing non-state actors such as companies from commitment to compliance (see Chapters 11 and 12). With regard to the Global Compact (GC), in Chapter 11 Mwangi *et al.* show that companies that actively participate in regional or local GC networks are particularly likely to move toward better compliance with human rights, because they are exposed to learning experiences. However, persuasion seems to rarely work in isolation here. In most cases, companies only moved toward better compliance with human rights norms after extended campaigns by trans-national advocacy networks as suggested by our spiral model. As the case of Shell in Nigeria demonstrates (see Chapter 12), these campaigns often resulted in consumer boycotts against transnational corporations that were exposed to these mobilizations because of their brand names and/or because they produced for high end markets (see also Börzel *et al.* 2011; Flohr *et al.* 2010; Thauer 2009). In other words, such companies seem to be particularly vulnerable to strategic framing coupled with the threat of material sanctions. We come back to this point below.

But public discourse also moves states from commitment to compliance as we already argued in PoHR. Clark's Chapter 7 in this volume provides one of the first quantitative tests of the discursive mechanisms suggested in the original spiral model. She shows that exposure to public naming and shaming by the UN Human Rights Commission resulted in significantly better compliance by states that had ratified the Anti-Torture Convention (CAT) as compared to those which either had not committed to the CAT or had not been exposed to public criticism. As in the case of companies, this mechanism seems to be related to the extent to which states are socially vulnerable to external criticism (see below).

In this context, it is rather irrelevant whether governments (or company leaders for that matter) are beginning to comply because they are deep down persuaded of their wrongdoing or because they believe that they have no choice other than to comply for some different and – maybe – instrumental reasons. It seems to be helpful to distinguish between what Jeffrey Checkel has called Type 1 as compared to Type 2 socialization (Checkel 2005). Type 1 socialization involves role-playing: actors know what is socially expected from them and behave accordingly, irrespective of whether they believe in the normative validity of the rule or not. In contrast, type 2 socialization requires normative persuasion: actors are convinced that complying with a particular norm – human rights in our case – is the "right thing to do." Both types of socialization constitute variants of the logic of appropriateness (March and Olsen 1998), but type 1 socialization does not require deep attitudinal change. The original PoHR did not distinguish between these two variants and implicitly assumed that sustained compliance with human rights norms requires deep socialization and internalization. While it is certainly the case that compliance should be the more likely the more actors are actually convinced of the normative validity of human rights, we now suggest that type 1 socialization is sufficient for compliance. As long as (a) human rights are institutionalized in international and domestic law, and, (b) public naming and shaming are likely to occur in cases of rights violations, it is sufficient that actors – whether states, companies, rebel groups or private citizens – know what is socially expected from them in order to induce compliance.

But the original PoHR also assumed that persuasion and discourse are uni-directional toward greater compliance with human rights (see Chapter 1, this volume). This assumption has been proven wrong, unfortunately (see Chapter 8 on the United States and Chapter 9 on China; see also Chapter 2). In the case of the United States, the terrorist attacks of 9/11 provided the Bush administration with a powerful counter-discourse vis-à-vis the prohibition against torture. While terrorism as such has always served autocratic regimes as a justification to violate basic human rights (see e.g. Jetschke 1999, 2010), it is a new development that stable democracies resort to similar arguments to justify violating human rights – and get away with it, at least for a number of years.

Another counter-discourse has been advanced by the People's Republic of China for some time (see Chapter 9). This discourse – similar to the "Asian values" debate of the 1980s and 1990s (Donnelly 2003: part 2; Kausikan 1994) – challenges the universality and generalizability of human rights and criticizes the individualist approach to human rights as Western or Euro-centric. While parts of this discourse undoubtedly serve to camouflage human rights violations by Chinese party autocrats, it cannot be denied that some arguments resonate with non-Western philosophical traditions such as Confucianism and with the opposition against Western neo-colonialism as well as with postcolonial studies. While we cannot do justice to this debate here, suffice it to say that we will probably see more of these type of debates, the more we move out of a Western-dominated international system into a "G20" world.

Capacity-building

PoHR regarded human rights violations primarily as resulting from the unwillingness of actors to comply. But, as Börzel and Risse argue in this volume (Chapter 4), "involuntary non-compliance" needs to be addressed, too. If non-compliance results from limited statehood, i.e. weakness of state institutions to enforce the law, neither enforcement nor sanctions, positive incentives or persuasion will result in human rights improvements.

Capacity-building is not only relevant with regard to states and national governments as rule addressees, but also concerning non-state actors. Companies

Table 15.1. *Target ability to comply*

		State capacity	
		High	Low
Centralization of compliance decision	High	High probability	Mid-level probability
	Low	Mid-level probability	Low probability

might have committed to human rights, but they often lack the managerial capacities to institutionalize the rules in their internal structures and down the supply chain, as Mwangi *et al.* point out in Chapter 11. They suggest that local and regional networks of the Global Compact provide a mechanism for capacity-building inducing companies to greater compliance with human rights. The same holds true for rebel groups requiring adequate training with regard to the Geneva Conventions (Chapter 13). Last but not least, combating FGM seems to be primarily a question of education and changing sexual behavior, as Brysk points out in Chapter 14. Here, persuasion and capacity-building go hand-in-hand.

Scope conditions

The main theoretical contribution of this volume as compared to PoHR is that we identified scope conditions under which compliance with human rights becomes more or less likely. In the introduction, we provided an overview of the four main scope conditions: regime type, degrees of statehood, centralization of rule implementation, and material and social vulnerability. In the following section, we discuss how these scope conditions interact, and we discuss these scope conditions in light of the empirical findings from the various chapters. Moreover, depending on which scope condition is at play primarily, different social mechanisms are necessary to move actors from commitment to compliance.

A schematic way to conceive of the scope conditions and the ways in which they interact is to build off the two dimensions of target characteristics: rule target *ability* to bring about change, and rule target *willingness* to bring about change. We can conceive of two of our scope conditions (state capacity and issue centralization) as being fundamentally about the *ability* of the rule target to bring about change (see Table 15.1). States with large areas of limited statehood lack the capacity, or ability, to bring about compliance, even if they would wish to do so. But the degree of centralization of the compliance decision also influences the ability of states (or corporations) to comply with norms. If the norm in question involves a centralized compliance decision, a state is more able to

Table 15.2. *Target willingness to comply*

		Regime type	
		Democratic	Authoritarian
Material and/ or social vulnerability	High	High probability	Mid-level probability
	Low	Mid-level probability	Low probability

comply, while if it involves a very decentralized compliance decision, like FGM, a state is less able to comply.

Second, actor *willingness* to comply is related to the remaining two scope conditions, regime type and target vulnerability (see Table 15.2). Democratic states tend to be more willing to comply with human rights norms, but target vulnerability also makes targets more or less willing to comply. States that have social vulnerability are more willing to comply because they have identities that make them more sensitive to pressure; states that have material vulnerability are more willing to comply to gain material benefits or stop sanctions. We can use these two main characteristics to create a representation summarizing some of the ways in which the scope conditions might interact to provide a greater or lesser likelihood for compliance.

This way of organizing the scope conditions discussed in this book helps us think about the possibility of human rights change on a particular issue with a particular target. So, for example, if we wanted to think about the possibility of ending FGM in an authoritarian state with low capacity, and low vulnerability, we should be very pessimistic about change, because it would fall in the worst possibility of change category on both ability and willingness for change. But if we wondered about changing the use of the death penalty in a democratic state with low capacity but higher vulnerability, we might be somewhat more optimistic. We discuss each of the scope conditions below, grouped into the two broad categories of willingness and ability to comply.

Scope conditions primarily influencing target willingness to comply

Regime type

The single most important factor for sustained state willingness to comply with human rights norms is regime type. In general, the literature has confirmed the importance of regime type as a crucial condition explaining the likelihood of movement from commitment to compliance. In order for such human rights change to be sustained, quantitative studies suggest that only quite high levels of democracy have a positive and sustained impact on human rights. One key explanation for why countries sometimes get stalled in the path from human rights commitment to compliance is that the quality of their democracy and rule of law systems is not yet sufficient to sustain more compliance.

In her survey of the quantitative human rights literature, Simmons states that this literature has largely confirmed the argument in PoHR that liberalization and democratization are essential for sustained human rights improvements, so much so that political liberalization should now be considered a necessary (but not sufficient) condition for sustained human rights compliance (Apodaca 2001; Landman 2005a; Neumayer 2005; Poe *et al.* 1999). This finding is robust so that we might want to modify the scope condition discussed in Chapter 1 of this volume. It is not just that the more democratic the state, the more likely it is to comply. Rather, liberalization might need to be seen as a necessary condition for human rights compliance. Exactly because domestic mobilization is so essential for human rights change, such change can only occur in countries that are sufficiently liberalized to permit domestic mobilization. In Chapter 10 on Tunisia and Morocco in this volume, Van Hüllen reminds us that the influence of regime variables on human rights compliance is complex. Initially in the 1990s the spiral model seemed to be at work in Morocco without regime change while it failed to maintain momentum in Tunisia despite initial regime change. But Van Hüllen concludes that the Moroccan government seemed more willing to bring about positive human rights change than did the regime of President Ben Ali in Tunisia, and that ultimately the Moroccan monarchy accommodated a higher degree of political and social pluralism than the republican regime in Tunisia. But with the Arab Spring, actual regime change occurred in Tunisia, while the Moroccan case illustrates the limits of this transformation without regime change.

In sum, a more nuanced picture emerges from these considerations. The mechanisms discussed above and in the original spiral model of PoHR seem to be particularly relevant in liberalizing countries to move from commitment to compliance. Neither stable autocratic regimes nor stable democracies are likely to be affected much by transnational as well as domestic mobilization. As to stable democracies, they are both less likely to violate rights, *and* more resilient to resisting external human rights pressures. Because democracies have greater legitimacy, they may be less socially vulnerable to outside pressures, as the cases of the United States under George W. Bush or of Israel suggest (see Chapter 8; Liese 2006). While we can depend on rule of law institutions in some democracies to protect rights, electoral mechanisms are only useful for protecting the rights of certain constituencies. It is possible that democracies are more prone to "crowding-out effects" – that is, more prone to feel immune from external pressures.

Material and social vulnerability

The willingness of a state to comply with human rights norms is not solely a function of regime type but of the interaction between regime type and social and material vulnerability. In the case of transnational corporations and insurgent groups, willingness to comply is primarily the result of social and material vulnerability. In this way, we try to explicitly include the material and ideational power relationship between sets of actors as a significant factor explaining the (lack of) movement from commitment to compliance.

If, for example, the international community sanctions Russia or China for human rights abuses, this is likely to be less effective than sanctions against materially more vulnerable targets. However, as the examples of North Korea or Zimbabwe demonstrate, even materially extremely vulnerable states are able to fight off material pressures by the international community for a long time, as long as the regime is capable of suppressing any substantial internal opposition and/or as long as the regime does not care at all about its international reputation. North Korea and Zimbabwe are, therefore, examples of regimes that have been able to compensate for their material vulnerability with a lack of social vulnerability.

These cases suggest that it is more interesting to look at the interaction effects between material and social vulnerability than to investigate these two factors in isolation. Moreover, we should not overlook that power is relational (Baldwin 2002), i.e. it depends on the material and ideational resources available to both rule targets and those campaigning against them. For example, we see evidence in Chapter 7 of the independent effect of UN Human Rights Commission resolutions, when combined with commitment (treaty ratification). Although the UN actions are not enforcement, in the sense of imposing material costs, they are a type of sanction involving important reputational costs. The Chinese government has worked very hard (and very successfully) to avoid Commission resolutions condemning China, which suggests that governments see these resolutions as costly and damaging. Chapter 7 suggests that commitment (treaty ratification) combined with reputational sanctions, short of enforcement, can lead to improvements in compliance. The more target countries want to become (or remain) members of the international community "in good standing," the more they are socially vulnerable to these reputational sanctions.

Chapter 9 on China also permits us to look at the independent effects of target vulnerabilities. China constitutes a materially powerful state which – at the same time – cares a lot about its international reputation, i.e. is socially vulnerable. It then uses its material power to compensate for its social vulnerability. Because the Chinese government has been successful in limiting the use of any form of enforcement, either coercion or sanctions, even including the reputational sanctions of the UN Human Rights Commission/Council, we can see the Chinese case as a test of the effectiveness of human rights pressures in the absence of enforcement or sanction. China has committed to many human rights treaties, but has not ratified the crucial treaty on the type of violations now most common in China (the International Convention on Civil and Political Rights). The case of China suggests that persuasion alone (such as the

EU–China dialogue process) does not contribute to ongoing improvements in compliance, if not coupled with incentives, sanctions or some kinds of logics of consequences. Similar to other cases that have resisted external human rights pressures, China has successfully used a counter-discourse of sovereignty and freedom from foreign intervention that has resonated with domestic audiences. This counter-discourse has been an effort to reduce the social vulnerability of the Chinese leadership.

But China is unique in a couple of ways that may make it difficult to generalize from this case. First, it has used its considerable material power to block and even punish external human rights pressures. Second, China has been able to eliminate and control exactly the kinds of domestic mobilization that the spiral model has always seen as essential to sustained human rights change. As Beth Simmons has shown in her work, commitment is more likely to lead to compliance if it is coupled with domestic mobilization (Simmons 2009). By blocking both external enforcement/pressures *and* efforts at domestic mobilization, the Chinese government has effectively been able to short-circuit the spiral model.

The US case also illustrates the role that power can play in limiting/stopping efforts at sanctions, enforcement or even incentives (see Chapter 8). Although other countries have criticized US torture policy under the George W. Bush administration, they stopped short of bringing any significant enforcement to bear on the United States to change its policy. Where powerful countries like China or the United States are the rule targets, it is likely that the countries and actors trying to apply pressure are more materially vulnerable than the target itself. Both China and the United States have shown themselves willing to use counter-sanctions and incentives to block human rights pressures, or to gain accomplices in the process of human rights violations, as the United States did when it sought the support of Eastern European countries in setting up "black sites" or secret prisons where CIA prisoners were held and interrogated. As a result, it is not a surprise that so few countries brought consistent pressure to bear on the United States for its interrogation, detention and extraordinary rendition programs.

Likewise, in the United States, the Bush administration's "deployment" of a powerful security counter-discourse succeeded temporarily in blocking internal pressures for change. The United States eventually changed its practices regarding torture, but primarily because the domestic institutions of a liberal democratic state forced the government back into compliance with human rights. The transnational outcry against Abu Ghraib or Guantanamo Bay was not particularly effective in this case. In other words, the United States represents an interesting case of both material power and lack of social vulnerability. The paradox of the interaction of regime type and vulnerability is that while democracies in general are often more willing to comply with human rights norms, at the same time, consolidated democracies may be less socially vulnerable to human rights pressures, especially in the context of powerful counter-discourses with broad-based public support.

The ability to use counter-discourses effectively to deflect criticism is not limited to key actors within powerful states. The Ben Ali regime in Tunisia was an example of a regime unwilling to bring about human rights change and at the same time very capable of co-opting the internal opposition and deflecting international criticism. It did this by using a counter-discourse which stressed that it was a stable, secular and reliable ally in the Middle East with a good record on socio-economic rights and gender equality, while providing "a secular bulwark against Islamic fundamentalism" (Chapter 10, this volume). The deployment of such a counter-discourse limited Tunisia's social vulnerability. The Mubarak regime in Egypt also used a counter-discourse of the loyal reliable moderate ally in the Middle East to effectively block both social and material vulnerability. As a result, it was not subject to external material pressures for human rights change and only changed as a result of bottom-up pressure for transition.

Conditions affecting the ability of targets to comply with human rights norms

Degrees of statehood

The first and most important condition influencing the ability of states to comply with human rights norms is the degree of statehood. Börzel and Risse argue that in areas of limited statehood, lack of capacity rather than lack of willingness may be at the root of the inability to move to compliance, but they stop short of saying that consolidated statehood is necessarily a precondition for compliance with human rights. Rather, they suggest that we should look for functional equivalents for the hierarchical law enforcement or for the "shadow of hierarchy" provided by consolidated statehood (see also Börzel and Risse 2010). In particular, since mostly non-state actors – rebel groups, companies and others (see Chapters 12 and 13) – are primarily responsible for rights violations in areas of limited statehood, such actors can be held accountable by other mechanisms.

As Börzel and Risse suggest, the presence of multiple actors in areas of limited statehood does not mean that the spiral model is irrelevant, just that its mechanisms have to be directed toward actors other than the state or the national government: "If non-state actors such as companies or rebel groups are primarily responsible for human rights violations, the mechanisms of the spiral model including transnational pressure can be directed against them" (p. 83). Individual criminal accountability is another such tool for focusing social mechanisms on specific state and non-state actors under conditions of limited statehood (see above). As for rebel groups, Jo and Bryant argue that the prospect of victory against the state serves to induce rebels and other non-state violent actors to improve compliance with human rights, the Geneva Conventions in this case. In other words, rebel groups and warlords need to become legitimate actors in the eyes of the international community, the closer they get to reaching their goals.

With regard to companies, the literature suggests a variety of functional equivalents to consolidated statehood to induce compliance with human rights. However, as Deitelhoff and Wolf argue in Chapter 12, large-scale violence, which is often experienced in failed states, serves as a "show-stopper" for corporate compliance with human rights (see also Deitelhoff and Wolf 2010). Some minimum degree of effective statehood appears to be essential for inducing companies to implement human rights norms. However, as the examples of both Shell and Nike indicate, the combination of brand names and strong transnational advocacy campaigns served to move both companies toward compliance with human rights in areas of limited statehood where they have been investing. In addition, a transnational corporation's home country seems to matter, too. As Prakash and Potoski argue with regard to ISO 14001, the most commonly used environmental management standard, the number of companies in a firm's home country having committed to the standard is a strong predictor of whether this firm also adopts the standards in their host states (Prakash and Potoski 2007). Similar mechanisms are likely to be at work in the human rights areas. The more awareness about corporate social responsibility including human rights in a company's country of origin, the more likely it should be that the company complies with these norms in areas of limited statehood in which it invests.

Centralized vs. decentralized rule implementation

The degree to which the rule can be implemented by centralized state actors is the second scope condition influencing the ability of targets to comply with human rights norms. Limited statehood as a scope condition that renders human rights compliance more difficult can be regarded as a specific case of decentralized rule implementation. If, for example, governments are willing and capable of centrally enforcing the law, compliance with human rights should not be a problem. However, rule implementation becomes problematic, the more rule targets and rule addressees are distinct, leading to decentralized rule implementation (see Chapter 1). In other words and everything else being equal, decentralized rule implementation constitutes another instance in which the lack of capacity is relevant for compliance. In general then, capacity-building becomes once again a primary mechanism to move actors from commitment to compliance.

Decentralized rule implementation is particularly challenging if rule targets are not only individual citizens, but their "private" behavior requires change in order to comply with human rights norms, as is the case with sexual politics (see Chapter 14). As Brysk argues, in such cases of decentralized rule implementation, coercion or incentives are unlikely to prevent (sexual) violence against women, but a combination of persuasion (in terms of altering culturally embedded practices such as FGM) and capacity-building (institutionalization) are necessary.

Decentralized rule implementation is not only an issue for states, but also for non-state actors who commit to human rights. Transnational corporations, for example, need to enforce compliance along their supply chains which massively complicates rule implementation (see Chapters 11 and 12; see also Thauer 2009). And Jo and Bryant show in Chapter 13 that rebel groups with centralized and hierarchical organizational structures are more likely to comply with the Geneva Conventions than more decentralized groups.

Policy conclusions

The schematic representations of scope conditions above can also be used as tools to think about policy decisions of states, international organizations and advocacy groups. Capacity-building mechanisms will be most effective in states that are willing but unable to implement human rights protections because they have significant areas of limited statehood. Liberalizing and democratizing states that have committed to human rights, but are unable to implement them because of limited statehood, should be the prime candidates for capacity-building measures. This suggests, for example, that Tunisia, Egypt and Libya are at present prime candidates for such mechanisms following the "Arab Spring" (see Chapter 10). Yet, strengthening state institutions alone might lead to adverse consequences in cases of semi-authoritarian regimes with areas of limited statehood (see Chapter 4). In such cases, capacity-building might lead to more, not less, human rights violations (see e.g. Börzel and Pamuk 2012). Capacity-building rather than sanctions and enforcement is a more appropriate policy response mainly in democratic regimes with low degrees of statehood.

The chapters on transnational corporations (Chapters 11 and 12) also suggest target willingness to comply is the most important factor, since companies' compliance records improve if their host governments are committed to human rights, but lack the capacity to effectively implement them. In other words, in cases of democratizing countries whose governments commit to human rights, non-state actors should be more willing to comply and to make up for lack of state capacity. In such cases, strengthening state capacity would also be the right remedy to improve human rights conditions, while social mechanisms such as enforcement, sanctions or even persuasion are unlikely to do the trick.

The situation is different in autocratic regimes with areas of limited statehood. If governments are not even willing to comply, why should companies make up for their lack of capacity? Moreover, simply strengthening the state in areas of limited statehood with autocratic governments (e.g. Yemen, Azerbaijan, Zimbabwe) will have adverse consequences, since it will make regimes more effective in their repressive behavior. In sum, capacity-building as such is no recipe for improving human rights in areas of limited statehood, since its effects strongly depend on regime type. At least, it would have to be accompanied by the other social mechanisms to improve compliance discussed in this volume. The EU, for example, frequently offers material incentives in conjunction with support for capacity-building in its democracy promotion programs (Börzel and Risse 2009).

At the same time, it is also critical for policy-makers to carefully evaluate the degree of issue centralization in any given capacity-building situation. The scope conditions (and the schematic figures above) can be used to think about the level at which capacity-building will be most appropriate. It does not make sense to spend money training judges to abolish FGM if the decisions about implementing change are being taken in families and communities, and the judiciary is rarely involved.

Attention to these scope conditions in any given state or regional-level situation can also assist academic researchers and policy-makers in developing realistic expectations about the general possibility of change and speed with which it might be expected to occur with regard to both specific issues and types of rule targets. Where states are deeply unwilling to bring about change both because they are authoritarian and lack social and material vulnerability, rapid change is unlikely to occur. This does not mean change cannot and should not be promoted. Rather, both scholars and policy-makers should recognize that such change will be difficult and time-consuming.

What these scope conditions and associated data underscore is the fact that the movement toward human rights compliance is a multifactor interactive process. There is no single simple recipe for generic human rights change. The countries most likely to show measurable change in this regard are those with both high ability and high willingness to comply. They also tend to be democratic or democratizing states exhibiting high degrees of statehood that are nevertheless socially or materially vulnerable on any issue where compliance requires a high level of decision-making centralization. In other words, many of the transitional countries that were the subject of the PoHR and the topic of Simmons' (2009) book seem to fall in this category.

This does not mean, as some scholars such as Hafner-Burton and Ron (2009) have concluded, that the various mechanisms and associated processes discussed herein are ineffective for bringing about human rights change and eventual compliance in the great bulk of the world's countries. Rather there are some countries and issues where it will be harder to bring about change than in others and thus more persistence will be required. Because they are harder cases also does not mean they should not be chosen as targets for advocacy. It simply suggests that advocates, both internal and external, should have realistic assumptions about the speed and likelihood of change. For example, groups working on human rights in China or in authoritarian countries with low degrees of statehood should know that change is likely to come slowly and that a high level of persistence will be required.

Finally, attention to these scope conditions should help those engaged in advocacy campaigns to become more strategic in their choice of tactics and mechanisms for encouraging change. The human rights movement has at times been too committed to a small subset of tactics such as naming and shaming – tactics that worked well in initial campaigns but may be less well suited when applied to other issues and in other settings. The tactics and mechanisms should be designed with an eye to taking the full range of relevant scope conditions into account.

However, both Tunisia and Egypt point to a very interesting recent development (see Chapter 10). Some countries that have not been materially and/or socially vulnerable to external pressures in the past and thus have avoided strong international condemnation, have eventually experienced bottom-up pressure which led to dramatic regime change. Moreover, a similar development might eventually be taking place in Russia. There, a formerly quiescent civil society that had benefited from the economic policies of an increasingly authoritarian government has nevertheless started bottom-up protests against electoral fraud. This reminds us once again that ultimately human rights change begins at home with a build-up of domestic pressures. In the final analysis, persistent and sustained human rights change depends on mobilized groups in domestic civil society pressuring for greater democracy, and using the space provided by democratic institutions to vigilantly defend and protect these rights.

The US case reminds us that people concerned with human rights should not be complacent because they live in a democracy. The protection of human rights requires sustained domestic vigilance. International actors can provide invaluable assistance and support for domestic efforts. They can help build capacity, open space for domestic activism, use international tribunals to prosecute major perpetrators, and in the most dire circumstances, actually use military intervention to stop the widespread human rights violations. But the international community cannot create democracy where there is no internal demand or interest for it, nor can it sustain and protect human rights in the absence of internal vigilance. The spiral model starts at home, and eventually ends there as well. Human rights protections, and thus the persistent power of human rights, ultimately depends on both the willingness and capability of domestic actors to demand and sustain these rights.

REFERENCES

Abouharb, M. Rodwan and David L. Cingranelli. 2004. "Human Rights and Structural Adjustment: The Importance of Selection," in Sabine C. Carey and Steven C. Poe (eds.), *Understanding Human Rights Violations: New Systematic Studies.* Aldershot, UK and Burlington, VT: Ashgate, pp. 127–141.

Acharya, Amitav. 2004. "How Ideas Spread: Whose Norms Matter? Norm Localization and Institutional Change in Asian Regionalism," *International Organization* 58 (2): 239–275.

Achvarina, Vera and Simon Reich. 2006. "No Place to Hide: Refugees, Displaced Persons and the Recruitment of Child Soldiers," *International Security* 31 (1): 127–164.

Adam, Heribert and Moodley, Kogila. 1993. *The Opening of the Apartheid Mind.* Berkeley: University of California Press.

Adler, Emanuel. 1997. "Seizing the Middle Ground. Constructivism in World Politics," *European Journal of International Relations* 3 (3): 319–363.

Aeschlimann, Alain. 2005. "Protection of Detainees: ICRC Action behind Bars," *International Review of the Red Cross* 87 (857): 83–122.

African Union. 2005. "The Common African Position on the Proposed Reform of the United Nations: 'The Ezulwini Consensus'," Executive Council, Seventh Extraordinary Session, March 7–8 2005, Addis Ababa, Ethiopia.

Agence France Presse. 1994. "UN Special Envoy Visit to Discuss Timor," Agence France Presse, July 4. Accessed from Lexis-Nexis online database.

Ahl, Björn. 2010. "Exploring Ways of Implementing International Human Rights Treaties in China," *Netherlands Quarterly of Human Rights* 28 (3): 361–403.

Alfredson, Lisa S. 2009. *Creating Human Rights: How Noncitizens Made Sex Persecution Matter to the World.* Philadelphia: Pennsylvania University Press.

Alhargan, Raed A. 2011. "The impact of the UN human rights system and human rights INGOs on the Saudi government with special reference to the spiral model," *The International Journal of Human Rights* 16: 598–623.

Allani, Alaya. 2009. "The Islamists in Tunisia between Confrontation and Participation. 1980–2008," *The Journal of North African Studies* 14 (2): 257–272.

Alston, Philip and James Crawford (eds.) 2000. *The Future of UN Human Rights Treaty Monitoring*. Cambridge University Press.

Amnesty International. 2000. *Amnesty International Report 1999*. London: Amnesty International Publications.

2004. "Amnesty International Report 2004 – Sudan." Accessed September 27, 2010 at www.unhcr.org/refworld/country,,AMNESTY,ANNUALREPORT, SDN,,40b5a2014,0.html.

2006. "Sudan: Crying Out for Safety." Accessed May 10, 2010 at www.amnestyusa. org/document.php?id=ENGAFR540552006&lang=e.

2007. "Darfur: 'When Will They Protect Us?'" Accessed May 10, 2010 at www. amnestyusa.org/document.php?id=ENGAFR540432007.

2011a. *Amnesty International Report 2011. The State of the World's Human Rights*. London.

2011b. *Tunisia in Revolt. State Violence during Anti-government Protests*. London.

Annan, Kofi. 2006. *The United Nations Cannot Stand Still, Because the Threats to Humanity Do Not Stand Still; Address to the Plenary Session of the World Economic Forum at Davos, Switzerland*. New York: United Nations.

Apodaca, Claire. 2001. "Global Economic Patterns and Personal Integrity Rights After the Cold War," *International Studies Quarterly* 45 (4): 587–602.

Arellano, Manuel, and Stephen Bond. 1991. "Some Tests of Specification for Panel Data: Monte Carlo Evidence and an Application to Employment Equations," *The Review of Economic Studies* 58: 277–297.

Arevalo, Jorge A., and Francis T. Fallon. 2008. "Assessing Corporate Responsibility as a Contribution to Global Governance: the Case of the UN Global Compact," *Corporate Governance* 8: 456–470.

Ariely, Dan, Anat Bracha and Stephen Meier. 2009. "Doing Good or Doing Well? Image Motivation and Monetary Incentives in Behaving Prosocially," *American Economic Review* 99: 544–555.

Asante, Samuel. 1989. "The Concept of the Good Corporate Citizen in International Business," *ICSID Review: Foreign Investment Law Journal* 4: 1–38.

Axworthy, Lloyd. 2011. "The Responsibility to Protect," Keynote Address, November 22, 2011, Law School, University of Minnesota.

Ayadi, Rym, Silvia Colombo, Maria Cristina Paciello, and Nathalie Tocci. 2011. *The Tunisian Revolution. An Opportunity for Democratic Transition, IAI Working Papers 11/02*. Rome: Instituto Affari Internazionali.

Baer, Madeline and Alison Brysk. 2009. "New Rights for Private Wrongs: Female Genital Mutilation and Global Framing Dialogues," in Clifford E. Bob (ed.), *The International Struggle for New Human Rights*. Philadelphia: University of Pennsylvania Press, pp. 93–107.

Baker, Philip. 2002. "Human Rights, Europe and the People's Republic of China," *China Quarterly* 169: 45–63.

Baldwin, David A. 2002. "Power and International Relations," in Walter Carlsnaes, Thomas Risse and Beth Simmons (eds.), *Handbook of International Relations.* London: Sage, pp. 177–191.

Ballentine, Karen. 2007. "Promoting Conflict-sensitive Business in Fragile States: Redressing Skewed Issues," in Oli Brown, Mark Halle, Sonia Pena Moreno and Sebastian Winkler (eds.), *Trade, Aid and Security. An Agenda for Peace and Development.* London: Earthscan, pp. 125–157.

Barkemeyer, Ralf. 2009. "Beyond Compliance – Below Expectations? CSR in the Context of International Development," *Business Ethics: A European Review* 18: 273–289.

Barkin, J. Samuel and Bruce Cronin. 1994. "The State and the Nation: Changing Norms and the Rules of Sovereignty in International Relations," *International Organization* 48 (1): 107–130.

Barnett, Michael, and Martha Finnemore. 2005. "The Power of Liberal International Organizations," in Michael Barnett and Raymond Duvall (eds.), *Power in Global Governance.* Cambridge University Press, pp. 161–184.

Barnett, Michael, and Kathryn Sikkink. 2008. "From International Relations to Global Society," in Christian Reus-Smit and Duncan Snidal (eds.), *The Oxford Handbook of International Relations.* Oxford University Press, pp. 62–83.

Barratt, Bethany. 2004. "Aiding or Abetting: British Foreign Aid Decisions and Recipient Country Human Rights," in Sabine C. Carey and Steven C. Poe (eds.), *Understanding Human Rights Violations: New Systematic Studies.* Aldershot, UK and Burlington, VT: Ashgate, pp. 43–62.

BASF. 2010. *Monitoring of Labor and Social Standards at BASF.* Accessed September 5, 2011 at www.basf.com/group/sustainability_en/index.

Baum, Christopher F. 2006. *An Introduction to Modern Econometrics Using Stata.* College Station, TX: Stata Press.

Baum, Richard. 2009. "Politics, Human Rights, and the Beijing Olympics," in David Shambaugh and Gudrun Wacker (eds.), *American and European Relations with China: Advancing Common Agendas, American and European Relations with China.* Berlin: SWP, pp. 31–43.

Baur, Dorothea and Hans Peter Schmitz. 2012. "Corporations and NGOs: When Accountability Leads to Co-optation," *Journal of Business Ethics* 106 (1): 9–21.

Bayefsky, Anne F. 2001. *The UN Human Rights Treaty System: Universality at the Crossroads.* Ardsley, NY: Transnational Publishers.

BBC News. 2010. "Darfur JEM Rebels Sign Deal to Stop Child Soldiers." 21 July. Accessed September 27, 2010 at www.bbc.co.uk/news/world-africa-10710315.

Beittinger-Lee, Verena. 2009. *(Un)Civil Society and Political Change in Indonesia: A Contested Arena.* London: Routledge.

Bellamy, Alex J. 2009. *Responsibility to Protect. The Global Effort to End Mass Atrocities.* Cambridge: Polity Press.

2011. *Global Politics and the Responsibility to Protect*. London: Routledge.

Bénabou, Roland and Jean Tirole. 2006. "Incentives and Pro-social Behavior," *American Economic Review* 96 (5): 1652–1678.

Bennie, Lynn, Patrick Bernhagen and Neil J. Mitchell. 2007. "The Logic of Transnational Action: The Good Corporation and the Global Compact," *Political Studies* 55: 733–753.

Bernhagen, Patrick and Neil J. Mitchell. 2010. "The Private Provision of Public Goods: Corporate Commitments and the United Nations Global Compact," *International Studies Quarterly* 54: 1175–1187.

Bernstein, Richard. 2005. "Rice's Visit: Official Praise, Public Doubts," *New York Times*, December 11, p. 22.

Bertelsmann Stiftung. 2007. *Bertelsmann Transformation Index 2008 – Georgia Country Report*. Gütersloh: Bertelsmann Stiftung.

2009a. *Bertelsmann Transformation Index 2010 – Georgia Country Report*. Gütersloh: Bertelsmann Stiftung.

2009b. *Transformation Index 2010. Political Management in International Comparison*. Gütersloh: Bertelsmann Stiftung.

Black, David. 1999. "The Long and Winding Road: International Norms and Domestic Political Change in South Africa," in Thomas Risse, Stephen C. Ropp and Kathryn Sikkink (eds.), *The Power of Human Rights. International Norms and Domestic Change*. Cambridge University Press, pp. 78–108.

Black, Nicky. 2006. "Business Action on Human Rights – Doing No Harm, Good Works, and Good Business in the Developing World," in Mahad Huniche and Esben Rahbeck Pedersen (eds.), *Corporate Citizenship in Developing Countries. New Partnership Perspectives*. Copenhagen: Copenhagen Business School Press, pp. 57–88.

Blanton, Shannon Lindsey. 2005. "Foreign Policy in Transition? Human Rights, Democracy, and U.S. Arms Exports," *International Studies Quarterly* 49 (4): 647–668.

Blanton, Shannon Lindsey and Robert G. Blanton. 2007. "What Attracts Foreign Investors? An Examination of Human Rights and Foreign Direct Investment," *Journal of Politics* 69 (1): 143–155.

Boda, Jozsef and Kornely Kakachia. 2005. "The Current Status of Police Reform in Georgia." Accessed September 29, 2012 at www.isn.ethz.ch/isn/Digital-Library/Publications/Detail/?ots591=cab359a3-9328-19cc-a1d2-8023e646b22c&lng=en&id=106057.

Boli, John and George M. Thomas. 1999. *Constructing World Culture: International Non-governmental Organizations Since 1875*. Stanford University Press.

Bond, Stephen R. 2002. "Dynamic Panel Data Models: A Guide to Micro Data Methods and Practice," *Portuguese Economic Journal* 1 (2): 141–162.

Bone, Andrew. 2004. "Conflict Diamonds: The De Beers Group and the Kimberley Process," in Alyson Bailes and Isabel Frommelt (eds.), *Business and Security*. Oxford University Press, pp. 129–147.

Börzel, Tanja A. 2002. "Non-State Actors and the Provision of Common Goods. Compliance with International Institutions," in Adrienne Héritier (ed.), *Common Goods. Reinventing European and International Governance.* Lanham: Rowman & Littlefield, pp. 155–178.

Börzel, Tanja A., Adrienne Héritier, Nicole Kranz and Christian Thauer. 2011. "Racing to the Top? Regulatory Competition Among Firms in Areas of Limited Statehood," in Thomas Risse (ed.), *Governance without a State? Policies and Politics in Areas of Limited Statehood.* New York: Columbia University Press, pp. 144–170.

Börzel, Tanja A., Tobias Hofmann, Diana Panke and Carina Sprungk. 2010. "Obstinate and Inefficient: Why Member States Do Not Comply With European Law," *Comparative Political Studies* 43 (11): 1363–1390.

Börzel, Tanja A. and Yasemin Pamuk. 2012. "Pathologies of Europeanization: Fighting Corruption in the Southern Caucasus," *West European Politics* 35 (1): 79–97.

Börzel, Tanja A., Yasemin Pamuk and Andreas Stahn. 2008. "One Size Fits All? How the European Union Promotes Good Governance in Its Near Abroad," *SFB 700 Working Paper* 18, Berlin.

2009. "Democracy or Stability? EU and US Engagement in the Southern Caucasus," in Amichai Magen, Michael McFaul and Thomas Risse (eds.), *Promoting Democracy and the Rule of Law: American and European Strategies,* pp. 150–184. Houndmills, Basingstoke: Palgrave Macmillan.

Börzel, Tanja A. and Thomas Risse. 2009. "Venus Approaching Mars? The European Union's Approaches to Democracy Promotion in Comparative Perspective," in Amichai Magen, Thomas Risse and Michael McFaul (eds.), *Promoting Democracy and the Rule of Law: American and European Strategies,* pp. 34–60. Houndmills, Basingstoke: Palgrave Macmillan.

2010. "Governance without a State: Can it Work?" *Regulation and Governance* 4 (2): 1–22.

Bossuyt, Marc J. 1985. "The Development of Special Procedures of the United Nations Commission on Human Rights," *Human Rights Law Journal* 6: 179–210.

Bowles, Samuel. 2008. "Policies Designed for Self-Interested Citizens May Undermine 'The Moral Sentiments': Evidence from Economic Experiments," *Science* 320 (5883): 1605–1609.

Bowles, Samuel and Herbert Gintis. 2004. "The Evolution of Strong Reciprocity: Cooperation Heterogeneous Populations," *Theoretical Population Biology* 65: 17–28.

Bowles, Samuel and Sung-Ha Hwang. 2008. "Social Preferences and Public Economics: Mechanism Design When Social Preferences Depend on Incentives," *Journal of Public Economics* 92: 1811–1820.

Boyle, Elizabeth H. 2002. *Female Genital Cutting: Cultural Conflict in the Global Community.* Baltimore: Johns Hopkins University Press.

Brahms, Brigadier General David M. 2005. "Military Leaders' Letter to the Senate Judiciary Committee on the Nomination of Alberto Gonzalez to be Attorney

General," January 4. Accessed at www.humanrightsfirst.org/wp-content/uploads/pdf/090108-ETN-jan3-retired-mil-ldrs-ltr-sjc-gonzales.pdf.

Braig, Marianne and Ruth Stanley. 2007. "Die Polizei – (k)ein Freund und Helfer? Die Governance der öffentlichen Sicherheit in Buenos Aires und Mexiko-Stadt," in Thomas Risse and Ursula Lehmkuhl (eds.), *Regieren ohne Staat? Governance in Räumen begrenzter Staatlichkeit.* Baden-Baden: Nomos, pp. 223–243.

Brambor, Thomas, William Roberts Clark and Matt Golder. 2006. "Understanding Interaction Models: Improving Empirical Analyses," *Political Analysis* 14 (1): 63–82.

Brands, Hal. 2010. *Crime, Violence, and the Crisis in Guatemala: A Case Study in the Erosion of the State.* Carlisle, PA: US Army War College, Strategic Studies Institute, May.

Breen, Claire. 2003. "The Role of NGOs in the Formulation of and Compliance with the Optional Protocol to the Convention on the Rights of the Child on Involvement of Children in Armed Conflict," *Human Rights Quarterly* 25 (2): 453–481.

Bremer, Jennifer Ann. 2008. "How Global is the Global Compact?" *Business Ethics: A European Review* 17: 227–244.

Brinkley, Joel. 2005. "U.S. Interrogations are Saving European Lives, Rice Says," *New York Times*, December 6, p. A3.

Broad, Robin, and John Cavanagh. 1997. *The Corporate Accountability Movement: Lessons and Opportunities.* Washington, DC: World Resources Institute.

Brysk, Alison. 1993. "From Above and From Below: Social Movements, the International System, and Human Rights in Argentina," *Comparative Political Studies* 26 (3): 259–285.

　1994. *The Politics of Human Rights in Argentina: Protest, Change, and Democratization.* Stanford University Press.

　1995. "Hearts and Minds: Bringing Symbolic Politics Back In." *Polity XXVII*(4): 559–585.

　2005. *Human Rights and Private Wrongs. Constructing Global Civil Society.* New York and London: Routledge.

　2007. "Making Values Make Sense: The Social Construction of Human Rights Foreign Policy," *Journal For Human Rights [Zeitschrift Für Menschenrechte]* 2: 69–80.

　2009a. "Beyond Framing and Shaming: Human Trafficking, Human Security, and the International Human Rights Regime," *Journal of Human Security* 5 (3): 8–21.

　2009b. "Communicative Action and Human Rights in Colombia," *Colombia Internacional* 69: 36–49.

　2009c. *Global Good Samaritans: Human Rights as Foreign Policy.* Oxford University Press.

　Forthcoming. *Speaking Rights to Power: Constructing Political Will.* Oxford University Press.

Brysk, Alison and Claude Denis. 2010. "Norm Entrepreneurs and Human Rights Promotion," *International Studies Association*, New Orleans, February 17.

Bueno de Mesquita, Bruce and George W. Downs. 2005. "Development and Democracy," *Foreign Affairs* 84 (5): 77–86.

Bueno de Mesquita, Bruce, Feryal Marie Cherif, George W. Downs and Alastair Smith. 2005. "Thinking Inside the Box: A Closer Look at Democracy and Human Rights," *International Studies Quarterly* 49 (3): 439–458.

Burgers, J. Herman and H. Danelius. 1988. *The United Nations Convention against Torture: A Handbook on the Convention against Torture and Other Cruel, Inhuman or Degrading Treatment or Punishment.* Dordrecht: Martinus Nijhoff Publishers.

Byman, Daniel, Peter Chalk, Bruce Hoffman, William Rosenau and David Brannan. 2001. "Trends in Outside Support for Insurgent Movements." RAND Corporation.

CALDH and The International Labor Rights Fund. 2004. *Labor Rights and Legal, Political, Economic, and Cultural Obstacles in Guatemala.* Accessed September 29, 2012 at www.laborrights.org/sites/default/files/publications-and.resources/POLICYGuatemalaLaborLaws.pdf.

Campbell, Patricia J. 2003. "Morocco in Transition. Overcoming the Democratic and Human Rights Legacy of King Hassan II," *African Studies Quarterly* 7 (1): 38–58.

Cardenas, Sonia. 2007. *Conflict and Compliance. State Responses to International Human Rights Pressure.* Philadelphia: University of Pennsylvania Press.

Carey, Sabine C. 2007. "European Aid: Human Rights Versus Bureaucratic Inertia?" *Journal of Peace Research* 44 (4): 447–464.

Cassarino, Jean-Pierre. 2011. *Confidence-building in Tunisia after the Popular Uprising. Strategies and Dilemmas of the Interim Government, IAI Working Papers 11/04, February 2011.* Rome: Instituto Affari Internazionali.

Cassese, Antonio. 1995. *Self-Determination of Peoples: A Legal Appraisal.* Cambridge University Press.

Cavatorta, Francesco. 2009. "'Divided They Stand, Divided They Fail'. Opposition Politics in Morocco," *Democratization* 16 (1): 137–156.

Cetindamar, Dilek and Kristoffer Husoy. 2007. "Corporate Social Responsibility Practices and Environmentally Responsible Behavior: The Case of The United Nations Global Compact," *Journal of Business Ethics* 76: 163–176.

Chandler, Geoffrey. 2003. "The Evolution of the Business and Human Rights Debate," in Rory Sullivan (ed.), *Business and Human Rights: Dilemmas and Solutions.* Sheffield: Greenleaf Publishing, pp. 22–32.

Chase, Anthony T. 2003. "The State and Human Rights: Governance and Sustainable Development in Yemen," *International Journal of Politics* 17 (2): 213–236.

Chayes, Abram, and Antonia Handler Chayes. 1991. "Compliance Without Enforcement: State Behaviour Under Regulatory Treaties," *Negotiation Journal* 7 (July): 311–330.

1993. "On Compliance," *International Organization* 47 (2): 175–205.

1995. *The New Sovereignty. Compliance with International Regulatory Agreements.* Cambridge, MA: Harvard University Press.

Checkel, Jeffrey T. 1998. "The Constructivist Turn in International Relations Theory," *World Politics* 50 (2): 324–348.

2001. "Why Comply? Social Learning and European Identity Change," *International Organization* 55 (3): 553–588.

2005. "International Institutions and Socialization in Europe: Introduction and Framework," *International Organization* 59 (4): 801–826.

Chen, Dingding. 2005. "Explaining China's Changing Discourse on Human Rights 1978–2004," *Asian Perspective* 29 (3): 155–182.

Chen, Guangcheng. 2012. "How China Flouts its Own Laws," *New York Times*, May 29, accessed May 30, 2012, www.nytimes.com/2012/05/30/opinion/how-china-flouts-its-laws.html?_r=2.

Child Soldiers Global Report. Various years. Accessed September 27 2010 at www.childsoldiersglobalreport.org/content/sudan-0.

Chouikha, Larbi. 2006. "Tunisie. Les Chimères Libérales," *Actes Sud* 19: 29–37.

Christmann, Petra and Glen Taylor. 2006. "Firm Self-regulation through International Certifiable Standards: Determinants of Symbolic Versus Substantive Implementation," *Journal of International Business Studies* 37: 863–878.

Chuang, Janie. 2005–2006. "The United States as Global Sheriff: Using Unilateral Sanctions to Combat Human Trafficking," *Michigan Journal of International Law* 27: 437–494.

Cingranelli, David and David L. Richards.1999. "Respect for Human Rights after the End of the Cold War," *Journal of Peace Research* 36 (5): 511–534.

2008a. *The Cingranelli-Richards (CIRI) Human Rights Dataset.* Accessed July 13, 2009 at www.humanrightsdata.org.

2008b. *The Cingranelli-Richards (CIRI) Human Rights Data Project Coding Manual. Version 7.30.08.* Accessed September 7, 2012 at http://ciri.binghamton.edu/documentation/ciri_coding_guide.pdf.

Cizre, Umit. 2001. "The Truth and Fiction about (Turkey's) Human Rights Politics," *Human Rights Review* 3 (1): 55–77.

Clapham, Andrew. 2006. *Human Rights Obligations of Non-State Actors.* Oxford University Press.

Clapp, Jennifer. 2008. "Illegal GMO Releases and Corporate Responsibility: Questioning the Effectiveness of Voluntary Measures," *Ecological Economics* 66: 348–358.

Clark, Ann Marie. 2001. *Diplomacy of Conscience: Amnesty International and Changing Human Rights Norms.* Princeton University Press.

2009. "Human Rights NGOs: Overview," in David P. Forsythe (ed.), *Oxford Encyclopedia of Human Rights.* Oxford University Press, vol. 4, pp. 87–95.

Clark, Ann Marie and Kathryn Sikkink. In press. "Information Effects and Human Rights Data: Is the Good News about Increased Human Rights Information Bad News for Human Rights Measures?" *Human Rights Quarterly.*

Cohen, Cynthia Price. 1990. "The Role of Nongovernmental Organizations in the Drafting of the Convention on the Rights of the Child," *Human Rights Quarterly* 12 (1): 137–147.

Cohen, Roberta. 1987. "People's Republic of China: The Human Rights Exception," *Human Rights Quarterly* 9 (4): 447–549.

Cohen, Stanley. 2001. *States of Denial: Knowing about Atrocities and Suffering.* Cambridge: Polity.

Cole, Wade M. 2005. "Sovereignty Relinquished? Explaining Commitment to the International Human Rights Covenants, 1966–1999," *American Sociological Review* 70 (3): 472–496.

Colombo, Silvia. 2011. *Morocco at the Crossroads: Seizing the Window of Opportunity for Sustainable Development, MEDPRO Technical Report No. 2.* Brussels.

Comprehensive Peace Agreement Between the Government of the Republic of the Sudan and the Sudan People's Liberation Army/Movement. 2005. Accessed May 12, 2010 at www.splamilitary.net/documents/The%20CPA.pdf.

Connor, Michael. 2010. *Nike: Corporate Responsibility at a "Tipping Point".* Accessed August 24, 2010 at http://business-ethics.com/2010/01/24/2154-nike-corpor ate-responsibility-at-a-tipping-point.

Cook, Rebecca (ed.) 1994. *Human Rights of Women: National and International Perspectives.* Philadelphia: University of Pennsylvania Press.

Cortell, Andrew P. and James W. Davis. 2000. "Understanding the Domestic Impact of International Norms: A Research Agenda," *International Studies Review* 2 (1): 65–87.

Council of the European Union. 2001. *Press Release, 2327th Council Meeting – General Affairs: EU-China Dialogue on Human Rights – Council Conclusions* (No. 5279/01). Brussels.

Cross, Frank B. 1999. "The Relevance of Law in Human Rights Protection," *International Review of Law and Economics* 10 (1): 87–98.

Cunningham, David, Kristian Gleditsch and Idean Salehyan. 2009. "It Takes Two: A Dyadic Analysis of Civil War Duration and Outcome," *Journal of Conflict Resolution* 53 (4): 570–597.

Cutler, A. Claire, Virgina Haufler and Tony Porters (eds.) 1999. *Private Authority and International Affairs.* Albany: State University of New York Press.

Dai, Xinyuan. 2002. "Information Systems of Treaty Regimes," *World Politics* 54 (4): 405–436.

 2005. "Why Comply? The Domestic Constituency Mechanism," *International Organization* 59 (2): 363–398.

 2006. "The Conditional Nature of Democratic Compliance," *Journal of Conflict Resolution* 50 (5): 690–713.

 2007. *International Institutions and National Policies.* New York: Cambridge University Press.

Danner, Mark. 2004. *Torture and Truth: America, Abu Ghraib, and the War on Terror.* New York: New York Review Books.

Darbouche, Hakim and Yahia H. Zoubir. 2008. "Conflicting International Policies and the Western Sahara Stalemate," *The International Spectator* 43 (1): 91–105.

Davenport, Christian (ed.) 2000. *Paths to State Repression. Human Rights Violations and Contentious Politics*. Lanham: Rowman & Littlefield.

2007. *State Repression and the Domestic Democratic Peace*. Cambridge University Press.

Davenport, Christian and David A. Armstrong II. 2004. "Democracy and the Violation of Human Rights: A Statistical Analysis from 1976 to 1996," *American Journal of Political Science* 48 (3): 538–554.

Davis, Michael C. 1995. "Chinese Perspectives on Human Rights," in Michael C. Davis (ed.), *Human Rights and Chinese Values: Legal, Philosophical, and Political Perspectives*. Hong Kong: Oxford University Press, pp. 3–24.

1998. "Constitutionalism and Political Culture: The Debate over Human Rights and Asian Values," *Harvard Human Rights Journal* 11: 109–148.

Debiel, Tobias, Rainer Glassner, Conrad Schetter and Ulf Terlinden. 2010. "Local State-Building in Afghanistan and Somaliland," *Peace Review: A Journal of Social Justice* 21: 38–44.

Deci, Edward L. and Richard M. Ryan. 1985. *Intrinsic Motivation and Self-Determination in Human Behavior*. New York: Plenum Press.

2002. *The Handbook of Self-Determination Research*. Rochester: University of Rochester Press.

Deci, Edward L., Richard Koestner and Richard M. Ryan. 1999. "A Meta-analytic Review of Experiments Examining the Effects of Extrinsic Rewards on Intrinsic Motivation," *Psychological Bulletin* 125: 627–668.

Deibert, Michael. 2008–2009. "Guatemala's Death Rattle: Drugs vs. Democracy," *World Policy Journal* 25 (4): 167–175.

Deitelhoff, Nicole. 2006. *Überzeugung in der Politik. Grundzüge einer Diskurstheorie internationalen Regierens*. Frankfurt/Main: Suhrkamp Taschenbuch Wissenschaft.

2009. "The Discursive Process of Legalization: Charting Islands of Persuasion in the ICC Case," *International Organization* 63 (1): 33–65.

Deitelhoff, Nicole and Harald Müller. 2005. "Theoretical Paradise – Empirically Lost? Arguing With Habermas," *Review of International Studies* 31 (1): 167–179.

Deitelhoff, Nicole and Klaus Dieter Wolf (eds.) 2010. *Corporate Security Responsibility? Corporate Governance Contributions to Peace and Security in Zones of Conflict*. Basingstoke: Palgrave Macmillan.

Deitelhoff, Nicole, Moira Feil, Susanne Fischer, Andreas Haidvogl, Klaus Dieter Wolf and Melanie Zimmer. 2010. "Business in Zones of Conflict and Global Security Governance: What has been Learnt and Where to from Here?" in Nicole Deitelhoff and Klaus Dieter Wolf (eds.), *Corporate Security Responsibility? Corporate Governance Contributions to Peace and Security in Zones of Conflict*. Basingstoke: Palgrave Macmillan, pp. 202–226.

Del Sarto, Raffaella A. and Tobias Schumacher. 2011. "From Brussels with Love: Leverage, Benchmarking, and the Action Plans with Jordan and Tunisia in the EU's Democratization Policy," *Democratization* 18 (4): 932–955.

Deng, Francis (ed.) 2010. *New Sudan in the Making?* Trenton: The Red Press, Inc.

Desrues, Thierry and Eduardo Moyano. 2001. "Social Change and Political Transition in Morocco," *Mediterranean Politics* 6 (1): 21–47.

Detainee Abuse and Accountability Project (a joint project of New York University's Center for Human Rights and Global Justice, Human Rights Watch and Human Rights First). 2006. "By the Numbers: Findings of the Detainee Abuse and Accountability Project," Briefing Paper, April.

DeVoe, Debbie. n.d. *Saying "No" to "The Cut" in Kenya.* Accessed August 5, 2009 at http://crs.org/kenya/alternative-rite-of-passage/.

Dezalay, Yves and Bryant Garth. 2006. "From the Cold War to Kosovo: The Rise and Renewal of the Field of International Human Rights," *Annual Review of Law and Social Science* 2 (1): 231–255.

Diamant, Neil Jeffrey, Stanley B. Lubman and Kevin J. O'Brien. 2005. "Law and Society in the People's Republic of China," in Neil Jeffrey Diamant, Stanley B. Lubman and Kevin J. O'Brien (eds.), *Engaging the Law in China: State, Society, and Possibilities for Justice.* Stanford University Press, pp. 3–27.

Diehl, Paul F. 2009. *Correlates of War.* Accessed at www.correlatesofwar.org/.

Dillman, Bradford. 1998. "The Political Economy of Structural Adjustment in Tunisia and Algeria," *The Journal of North African Studies* 3 (3): 1–24.

Donadio, Rachel. 2009. "Italy Convicts 23 Americans for CIA Renditions," *New York Times*, November 4.

Donnelly, Jack. 1998. "Human Rights: A New Standard of Civilization?" *International Affairs* 74 (1): 1–24.

   2003. *Universal Human Rights in Theory and Practice.* 2nd edn. Ithaca: Cornell University Press.

Downs, George W, David M. Rocke and Peter N. Barsoom. 1996. "Is the Good News about Compliance Good News about Cooperation?" *International Organization* 50 (3): 379–406.

Doxey, Margaret P. 1996. *International Sanctions in Contemporary Perspective.* Basingstoke: Palgrave Macmillan.

Durac, Vincent and Francesco Cavatorta. 2009. "Strengthening Authoritarian Rule Through Democracy Promotion? Examining the Paradox of the US and EU Security Strategies: The Case of Bin Ali's Tunisia," *British Journal of Middle Eastern Studies* 36 (1): 3–20.

Eck, Kristine and Lisa Hultman. 2007. "One Sided Violence Against Civilians in Civil War: Insights from New Fatality Dataset," *Journal of Peace Research* 44 (2): 233–246.

Elgström, Ole. 2000. "Norm Negotiation: The Construction of New Norms Regarding Gender and Development in EU Foreign Aid Policy," *Journal of European Public Policy* 7 (3): 457–476.

Elliott, Katja Zvan. 2009. "Reforming the Moroccan Personal Status Code. A Revolution for Whom?" *Mediterranean Politics* 14 (2): 213–227.

Ellmann, Stephen. 1998. "Cause Lawyering in the Third World," in Austin Sarat and Stuart A. Scheingold (eds.), *Cause Lawyering : Political Commitments and Professional Responsibilities*. New York: Oxford University Press, pp. 349–430.

Engert, Stefan. 2010. *EU Enlargement and Socialization: Turkey and Cyprus*. New York: Routledge.

Entelis, John P. 2005. "The Democratic Imperative vs. the Authoritarian Impulse. The Maghrib State between Transition and Terrorism," *The Middle East Journal* 59 (4): 537–558.

Esposito, John L. 2011. "The Muslim Brotherhood and Democracy in Egypt," *CounterPunch*. Accessed September 29, 2012 at www.counterpunch. org/2011/02/07/the-muslim-brotherhood-and-democracy-in-egypt/.

European Commission. 2006. *Commission Staff Working Paper accompanying the Communication from the Commission to the Council and the European Parliament on strengthening the European Neighbourhood Policy. ENP Progress Report. Morocco, SEC(2006) 1511/2, 04.12.2006*. Brussels.

———2007a. *European Neighbourhood and Partnership Instrument. Tunisia Strategy Paper 2007–2013 & National Indicative Programme 2007–2010*. Brussels.

———2007b. *Response Given by Commissioner Benita Ferrero Waldner to Written Question by Vittorio Agnoletto (GUE/NGL) to the Commission. European Parliament Debate 'Defence of Human Rights in China'* (No. E-1285/07). Strasbourg.

Evans, Gareth. 2008. *The Responsibility to Protect: Ending Mass Atrocity Crimes Once And For All*. Washington, DC: Brookings Institution Press.

Ewumbue-Monono, Churchill. 2006. "Respect for International Humanitarian Law by Armed Non-state Actors in Africa," *International Review of the Red Cross* 88 (864): 905–924.

Falk, Armin, Ernst Fehr and Urs Fischbacher. 2008. "Testing Theories of Fairness: Intentions Matter," *Games and Economic Behavior* 62 (1): 287–303.

Farber, Daniel A. 2002. "Rights as Signals," *Journal of Legal Studies* 31 (1): (Part 1) 83–98.

FBI Criminal Justice Information Services. 2003. "E-mail from REDACTED to Gary Bald, Frankie Battle, Arthur Cummings Re: FWD: Impersonating FBI Agents at GITMO," December 5. Accessed August 24, 2011 at www.aclu.org/torture-foia/released/122004.html.

Fehr, Ernst and Armin Falk. 2002. "Joseph Schumpeter Lecture, Psychological Foundations of Incentives," *European Economic Review* 46: 687–724.

Fehr, Ernst and Urs Fischbacher. 2005. "The Economics of Strong Reciprocity," in Herbert Gintis, Samuel Bowles, Robert Boyd and Ernst Fehr (eds.), *Moral Sentiments and Material Interests*. Cambridge, MA: The MIT Press, pp. 151–192.

Fehr, Ernst and Herbert Gintis. 2007. "Human Motivation and Social Cooperation: Experimental and Analytical Foundations," *Annual Review of Sociology* 33: 43–64.

Feil, Moira. 2010. "Here's to Peace! Governance Contributions by Companies in Rwanda and the Democratic Republic of Congo," in Nicole Deitelhoff and Klaus Dieter Wolf (eds.), *Corporate Security Responsibility? Corporate Governance Contributions to Peace and Security in Zones of Conflict*. Basingstoke: Palgrave Macmillan, pp. 26–57.

Feil, Moira, Susanne Fischer, Andreas Haidvogl and Melanie Zimmer. 2008. *Bad Guys, Good Guys, or Something in Between? Corporate Governance Contributions in Zones of Violent Conflict*. Frankfurt am Main: Peace Research Institute Frankfurt.

Feldman-Jacobs, Charlotte and Donna Clifton. 2010. *Female Genital Mutilation/ Cutting: Data and Trends – Update 2010*. Population Reference Bureau.

Felton, John. 2008. "Child Soldiers: Are More Aggressive Efforts Needed to Protect Children?" *CQ Global Researcher* 2 (7): 183–211.

Female Genital Mutilation: A Joint WHO/UNICEF/UNFPA Statement. 1997. Geneva: World Health Organization.

FIDH. 2004. *Les Commissions de Vérité et Réconciliation. L'Expérience Marocaine*. Paris.

2011a. *Maroc. Etat des Lieux du Suivi des Recommandations de l'Instance Equité Réconciliation*. Paris.

2011b. *Tunisie. La Tunisie post Ben Ali Face aux Démons du Passé. Transition Démocratique et Persistance de Violations Graves des Droits de l'Homme*. Paris.

Fields, A. Belden. 2003. *Rethinking Human Rights for the New Millennium*. New York: Palgrave Macmillan.

Fierke, Karen M. 1996. "Multiple Identities, Interfacing Games: The Social Construction of Western Action in Bosnia," *European Journal of International Relations* 2 (4): 467–497.

Fig, David. 1999. "Sanctions and the Nuclear Industry," in Neta Crawford and Audrey Klotz (eds.), *How Sanctions Work: Lessons From South Africa*. London: Palgrave Macmillan, pp. 75–102.

Finnemore, Martha. 1993. "International Organizations as Teachers of Norms: The United Nations Educational, Scientific, and Cultural Organization and Science Policy," *International Organization* 47 (4): 565–597.

2003. *The Purpose of Intervention: Changing Beliefs About the Use of Force*. Ithaca, NY: Cornell University Press.

Finnemore, Martha and Kathryn Sikkink. 1998. "International Norm Dynamics and Political Change," *International Organization* 52 (4): 887–917.

Fisher, Roger. 1981. *Improving Compliance with International Law*. Charlottesville: University of Virginia Press.

Fleay, Caroline. 2005. "The Impact of Internal and External Responses on Human Rights: Practices in China: The Chinese Government and the Spiral Model," PhD Dissertation, Curtin University of Technology, Perth.

Flint, Julie. 2007. "Darfur's Armed Movements," in Alex de Waal (ed.), *War in Darfur*. Cambridge, MA: Global Equity Initiative, Harvard University Press, pp. 140–172.

Flint, Julie and Alex de Waal. 2005. *Darfur: A Short History of a Long War*. London: Zed Books.

Flohr, Annegret, Lothar Rieth, Sandra Schwindenhammer and Klaus Dieter Wolf. 2010. *The Role of Business in Global Governance: Corporations as Norm-Entrepreneurs*. Houndmills, Basingstoke: Palgrave Macmillan.

Foot, Rosemary. 2000. *Rights Beyond Borders: The Global Community and the Struggle over Human Rights in China*. Oxford University Press.

Franklin, James. 1997. "IMF Conditionality, Threat Perception, and Political Repression: A Cross-National Analysis," *Comparative Political Studies* 30: 576–606.

Freedom House. 2011. *Freedom in the World 2011: The Annual Survey of Political Rights and Civil Liberties*. Lanham, MD: Rowman & Littlefield.

Frey, Bruno S. 1997a. "A Constitution for Knaves Crowds out Civic Virtues," *The Economic Journal* 107: 1043–1053.

1997b. *Not Just for the Money: An Economic Theory of Personal Motivation*. Cheltenham: Edward Elgar Publishing.

Frey, Bruno S. and Reto Jegen. 2001. "Motivation Crowding Theory," *Journal of Economic Surveys* 15 (5): 589–611.

Frey, Bruno S. and Alois Stutzer. 2008. "Environmental Morale and Motivation," in Alan Lewis (ed.), *The Cambridge Handbook of Psychology and Economic Behaviour*. Cambridge University Press, pp. 406–428.

Friedman, Elisabeth J., Kathryn Hochstetler and Ann Marie Clark. 2005. *Sovereignty, Democracy, and Global Civil Society: State-society Relations at UN World Conferences, SUNY Series in Global Politics*. Albany: State University of New York Press.

Friedman, Milton. 1970. "The Social Responsibility of Business is to Increase its Profits," *New York Times Magazine*, September 13.

Fu, Hualing and Richard Cullen. 2011. "Climbing the Weiquan Ladder: A Radicalizing Process for Rights-Protection Lawyers," *China Quarterly* 205: 40–59.

Fulmer, Amanda M., Angelina Snodgrass Godoy and Philip Neff. 2008. "Indigenous Rights, Resistance and the Law: Lessons from a Guatemalan Mine," *Latin American Politics and Society* 50 (4): 91–121.

Geisser, Vincent and Eric Gobe. 2004. "Tunisie. Consolidation autoritaire et processus électoraux," *L'Année du Maghreb*: 323–360.

Gellman, Barton. 2008. *Angler: The Cheney Vice Presidency*. New York: The Penguin Press.

Geneva Call. "Signatories to the Deed of Commitment Banning Anti-personnel Landmines." Accessed September 27, 2010 at www.genevacall.org/resources/list-of-signatories/list-of-signatories.htm.

George, Alexander L. and Andrew Bennett. 2005. *Case Studies and Theory Development in the Social Sciences*. Cambridge, MA: MIT Press.

Gerring, John. 2004. "What is a Case Study and What is it Good For?" *American Political Science Review* 98 (2): 341–354.

Gibney, Mark, Linda Cornett and Reed Wood. 2008. *Political Terror Scale, 1980–2006*. Accessed February 24, 2008 at www.politicalterrorscale.org.

Gilbert, Dirk Ulrich. 2010. "The United Nations Global Compact as a Network of Networks," in Andreas Rasche and Georg Kell (eds.), *The United Nations Global Compact: Achievements, Trends and Challenges*. Cambridge University Press, pp. 340–354.

Gillespie, Richard. 2010. "European Union Responses to Conflict in the Western Mediterranean," *The Journal of North African Studies* 15 (1): 85–103.

Global Compact Network Germany. 2011. *Fallbeispiele des Deutschen Global Compact Netzwerks*. Bonn: Global Compact Network Germany.

Global Responsible Investment Network. 2010. *Global 100 Most Sustainable Companies*.

Gneezy, Uri and Aldo Rustichini. 2000a. "A Fine is a Price," *Journal of Legal Studies* 29: 1–17.

2000b. "Pay Enough or Don't Pay At All," *Quarterly Journal of Economics* 115: 791–810.

Goldman, Merle. 2005. *From Comrade to Citizen: The Struggle for Political Rights in China*. Cambridge, MA: Harvard University Press.

Goldsmith, Jack. 2007. *The Terror Presidency: Law and Judgment inside the Bush Administration*. New York: W.W. Norton.

Goldsmith, Jack and Stephen D. Krasner. 2003. "The Limits of Idealism," *Daedalus* 132 (Winter): 47–63.

Goldsmith, Jack L. and Eric A. Posner. 2005. *The Limits of International Law*. New York: Oxford University Press.

Goldstein, Judith L., Miles Kahler, Robert O. Keohane and Anne-Marie Slaughter (eds.) 2000. *Legalization and World Politics. Special Issue of International Organization*. Vol. 54, 3. Cambridge, MA: MIT Press.

Goodliffe, Jay and Darren G. Hawkins. 2006. "Explaining Commitment: States and the Convention against Torture," *The Journal of Politics* 68 (2): 358–371.

Goodman, Ryan. 2009. "The Detention of Civilians in Armed Conflict," *American Journal of International Law* 103 (1): 48–74.

Goodman, Ryan and Derek Jinks. 2003. "Measuring the Effects of Human Rights Treaties," *European Journal of International Law* 13: 171–183.

2004. "How to Influence States: Socialization and International Human Rights Law," *Duke Law Journal* 54: 621–701.

2008. "Incomplete Internalization and Compliance with Human Rights Law," *European Journal of International Law* 19: 725–748.

In press. *Socializing States: Promoting Human Rights Through International Law*. Oxford University Press.

Grami, Amel. 2008. "Gender Equality in Tunisia," *British Journal of Middle Eastern Studies* 35 (3): 349–361.

Gränzer, Sieglinde. 1999. "Changing Discourse: Transnational Advocacy Networks in Tunisia and Morocco," in Thomas Risse, Stephen C. Ropp and Kathryn

Sikkink (eds.), *The Power of Human Rights: International Norms and Domestic Change*. Cambridge University Press, pp. 109–133.

Greenhill, Brian, Layna Mosley and Aseem Prakash. 2009. "Trade-based Diffusion of Labor Rights: A Panel Study, 1986–2002," *American Political Science Review* 103 (4): 669–690.

Guest, Iain. 1992. *Behind the Disappearances*. Philadelphia: University of Pennsylvania Press.

Gurowitz, Amy. 1999. "Mobilizing International Norms: Domestic Actors, Immigrants, and the Japanese State," *World Politics* 51 (3): 413–445.

Haas, Peter. 1992. "Introduction: Epistemic Communities and International Policy Coordination," *International Organization* 46 (1): 1–35.

Hafner-Burton, Emilie M. 2005. "Trading Human Rights: How Preferential Trade Agreements Influence Government Repression," *International Organization* 59 (3): 593–629.

2008. "Sticks and Stones: Naming and Shaming the Human Rights Enforcement Problem," *International Organization* 62 (4): 689–716.

Hafner-Burton, Emilie M. and James Ron. 2009. "Seeing Double: Human Rights Impact through Qualitative and Quantitative Eyes," *World Politics* 6 (2): 360–401.

Hafner-Burton, Emilie and Kiyoteru Tsutsui. 2005. "Human Rights in a Globalizing World: The Paradox of Empty Promises," *American Journal of Sociology* 110 (5): 1373–1411.

2007. "Justice Lost! The Failure of International Human Rights Law to Matter Where Needed Most," *Journal of Peace Research* 44 (4): 407–425.

Hafner-Burton, Emilie M., Kiyoteru Tsutsui and John W. Meyer. 2008. "International Human Rights Law and the Politics of Legitimation: Repressive States and Human Rights Treaties," *International Sociology* 23 (1): 115–141.

Haglund, LaDawn and Rimjhim Aggarwal. 2011. "Test of Our Progress: The Translation of Economic and Social Rights Norms into Practice," *Journal of Human Rights* 10 (4): 494–520.

Hamberg, Stephan. 2010. "Transnational Advocacy Networks, Rebel Groups and Demobilization of Child Soldiers." *Presented at the 2010 APSA Conference, Washington, DC.*

Hand, Keith J. 2006-2007. "Using Law for a Righteous Purpose: The Sun Zhigang Incident and Evolving Forms of Citizen Action in the People's Republic of China," *Columbia Journal of Transnational Law* 45: 114–195.

Hathaway, Oona. 2002. "Do Human Rights Treaties Make a Difference?" *Yale Law Journal* 111 (8): 1935–2042.

2004. "The Promise and Limits of the International Law of Torture," in Sanford Levinson and Alan M. Dershowitz (eds.), *Torture: A Collection*. Oxford and New York: Oxford University Press, pp. 199–212.

2005. "Between Power and Principle: An Integrated Theory of International Law," *University of Chicago Law Review* 72 (2): 469–536.

2007. "Why do Countries Commit to Human Rights Treaties?" *Journal of Conflict Resolution* 51 (4): 588–621.

Haufler, Virginia. 2004. "International Diplomacy and the Privatization of Conflict Prevention," *International Studies Perspectives* 5 (2): 158–163.

Hawkins, Darren G. 2002. *International Human Rights and Authoritarian Rule in Chile*. Lincoln: University of Nebraska Press.

2004. "Explaining Costly International Institutions: Persuasion and Enforceable Human Rights Norms," *International Studies Quarterly* 48 (4): 779–804.

Hawkins, Darren and Jay Goodliffe. 2006. "Explaining Commitment: States and the Convention against Torture," *Journal of Politics* 68 (2): 358–371.

Hayes, Karen and Richard Burge. 2003. *Coltan Mining in the Democratic Republic of Congo: How Tantalum-using Industries Can Commit to the Reconstruction in the DRC, Fauna and Flora International*. Accessed October 25, 2011 at www.gesi.org./LinkClick.aspx?fileticket=PoQTN7xPn4c%3Dandtabid=60.

Heavens, Andrew. 2008. "Up to 6,000 Child Soldiers Recruited in Darfur – UN," *Reuters*, December 23. Accessed September 27, 2010, at www.alertnet.org/thenews/newsdesk/123002956926.htm.

Hedman, Eva-Lotta E. 2000. "State of Siege: Political Violence and Vigilante Mobilization in the Philippines," in Bruce Campbell and Arthur D. Brenner (eds.), *Death Squads in Global Perspective: Murder with Deniability*. New York: St. Martins Press, pp. 125–152.

Helfer, Laurence R. and Anne-Marie Slaughter. 1997. "Toward a Theory of Effective Supranational Adjudication," *Yale Law Journal* 107 (2): 273–391.

Heller, Regina, Martin Kahl and Daniela Pisoiu. 2012. "The 'dark' side of normative argumentation – The case of counterterrorism policy," *Global Constitutionalism* 1(2): 278–312.

Helmchen, Constanze J. 2010. "Running a Global Compact Local Network: Insights from the Experience in Germany," in Andreas Rasche and Georg Kell (eds.), *The United Nations Global Compact: Achievements, Trends and Challenges*. Cambridge: Cambridge University Press, pp. 355–369.

Henckaerts, Jean-Marie. 2002. "Binding Armed Opposition Groups through Humanitarian Treaty Law and Customary Law." *Proceedings of the Bruges Colloquium, Relevance of International Humanitarian Law to Non-State Actors*. October 25–26, 2002, 27 Collegium 123 (Spring 2003).

Henisz, Guillén and Bennett A. Zelner. 2005. "The Worldwide Diffusion of Market-Oriented Infrastructure Reform, 1977–1999," *American Sociological Review* 70 (6): 871–897.

Hiscock, Duncan. 2006. "The Commercialiasation of Post-Soviet Private Security," in Alan Bryden and Marina Caparini (eds.), *Private Actors and Security Governance*. Berlin: Lit-Verlag, pp. 129–148.

Hobe, Stephan. 2008. *Einführung in das Völkerrecht*. Tübingen and Basel: A. Francke Verlag.

Hochstetler, Kathryn, Ann Marie Clark and Elisabeth J. Friedman. 2000. "Sovereignty in the Balance: Claims and Bargains at the UN Conferences on the Environment, Human Rights, and Women," *International Studies Quarterly* 44: 591–614.

Hohnen, Paul. 2010. "The United Nations Global Compact and the Global Reporting Initiative," in Andreas Rasche and Georg Kell (eds.), *The United Nations Global Compact: Achievements, Trends and Challenges.* Cambridge University Press, pp. 293–313.

Hönke, Jana. 2008. "Transnational Mining Business in Areas of Limited Statehood – Patterns of an Extractive Order in the Central African Copperbelt," in Roger Southall and Henning Melber (eds.), *A New Scramble for Africa?* Durban: University of KwaZulu-Natal Press, pp. 274–298.

Horton, Scott. 2010. "The Guantánamo 'Suicides': A Camp Delta Sergeant Blows the Whistle," *Harper's Magazine*, January 18. Accessed at www.harpers.org/archive/2010/01/hbc-90006368.

Hosen, Nadirsyah. 2002. "Human Rights and Freedom of the Press in the Post-Soeharto Era: A Critical Analysis," *Asia-Pacific Journal of Human Rights and the Law* 2: 1–104.

Howe, Marvine. 2000. "Morocco's Democratic Experience," *World Policy Journal* 17 (1): 65–70.

Human Rights Watch. 1998. *Human Rights Watch World Report 1998.* New York: Human Rights Watch.

2005a. *Morocco's Truth Commission. Honoring Past Victims during an Uncertain Present.* New York: Human Rights Watch.

2005b. *Georgia and the European Neighbourhood Policy – Human Rights Watch Briefing Paper.* New York: Human Rights Watch.

2006. *Mexico: The Second Assault. Obstructing Access to Legal Abortion After Rape in Mexico.* New York: Human Rights Watch.

2009a. *Up In Flames Humanitarian Law Violations and Civilian Victims in the Conflict over South Ossetia.* New York: Human Rights Watch.

2009b. "There is No Protection." February 12. Accessed September 27, 2010 at www.hrw.org/en/reports/2009/02/12/there-no-protection.

2010. "UN: Strengthen Civilian Protection in Darfur." July 19. Accessed September 27, 2010 at www.hrw.org/en/news/2010/07/19/un-strengthen-civilian-protection-darfur.

2011. *World Report 2011. Events of 2010.* New York.

Hurd, Ian. 1999. "Legitimacy and Authority in International Politics," *International Organization* 53 (2): 379–408.

Information Office of the State Council of the People's Republic of China. 1991. *Human Rights in China.* Beijing (White Paper of the Chinese Government). Accessed January 29, 2008 at www.china.org.cn/e-white/7/index.htm.

2009. *National Human Rights Action Plan of China (2009–2010).* Beijing. Accessed March 4, 2010 at www.china.org.cn/archive/2009–04/13/content_17595407.htm.

2012. *National Human Rights Action Plan of China (2012–2015).* Beijing.

Innocenti Research Centre/UNICEF. 2010. *The Dynamics of Social Change: Towards the Elimination of Female Genital Mutilation/Cutting in Five African Countries.* UNICEF.

Insel, Ahmed. 2003. "The AKP and Normalizing Democracy in Turkey," *South Atlantic Quarterly* 102 (2–3): 293–308.

International Campaign to Ban Landmines. 2003. *Landmine Monitor Report 2003.* Accessed September 27, 2010 at www.icbl.org/lm.

International Center for Transitional Justice. 2005. *Transitional Justice in Morocco. A Progress Report.* New York.

International Commission on Intervention and State Sovereignty. 2001. *The Responsibility to Protect.* New York: United Nations.

International Committee of the Red Cross. Various Years. *Annual Reports.* Geneva: ICRC Publications.

International Regional Information Network. 2004. "Sudan: SPLA/M Begins Demobilizing Child Soldiers in Upper Nile." Accessed September 27, 2010 at www.irinnews.org/ report.aspx?reportid=48232.

International Service for Human Rights and Meghna Abraham. 2006. "Outcomes of the 1503 and 1235 Procedures (Annex 5.1)," in Eléonore Dziurzynski (ed.), *A New Chapter for Human Rights: A Handbook on Issues of Transition from the Commission on Human Rights to the Human Rights Council.* Geneva, Switzerland: International Service for Human Rights and Friedrich Ebert Stiftung. Accessed July 11, 2006 at www.ishr.ch/handbook/.

Irlenbusch, Bernd and Derk Sliwka. 2005. "Incentives, Decision Frames, and Motivation Crowding Out – An Experimental Investigation," *IZA Discussion Papers, Institute for the Study of Labor* 1758.

Jaffer, Jameel and Amrit Singh. 2007. *Administration of Torture: A Documentary Record from Washington to Abu Ghraib and Beyond.* New York: Columbia University Press.

Jehl, Douglas. 2005. "C.I.A. is Seen as Seeking New Role on Detainees," *New York Times,* February 16.

Jenkins, Rhys. 2005. "Globalization, Corporate Social Responsibility and Poverty," *International Affairs* 81: 525–540.

Jetschke, Anja. 1999. "Linking the Unlinkable? International Norms and Nationalism in Indonesia and the Philippines," in Thomas Risse, Stephen C. Ropp and Kathryn Sikkink (eds.), *The Power of Human Rights: International Norms and Domestic Change.* Cambridge University Press, pp. 134–171.

2010. *Human Rights and State Security: Indonesia and the Philippines.* Philadelphia: University of Pennsylvania Press.

Jo, Hyeran and Catarina Thomson. 2011. "Norm Adherence and Compliance with International Law: Access to Detainees in Civil Conflicts 1991–2006." Working Paper. Texas A&M University.

Joffé, George. 2009. "Morocco's Reform Process. Wider Implications," *Mediterranean Politics* 14 (2): 151–164.

Johnston, Alastair I. 2008. *Social States: China in International Institutions, 1980–2000*. Princeton University Press.

Joyce, James Avery. 1978. *The New Politics of Human Rights*. London: Macmillan.

Justmeans. 2010. *Global 1000 Sustainable Performance Leaders*. Accessed November 3, 2010 at www.justmeans.com/top-global-1000-companies.

Kahan, Dan. 2005. "The Logic of Reciprocity: Trust, Collective Action, and Law," in Herbert Gintis, Samuel Bowles, Robert Boyd and Ernst Fehr (eds.), *Moral Sentiments and Material Interests*. Cambridge, MA: MIT Press, pp. 339–378.

Kalleck, Wolfgang. Personal interview. Berlin, June 6, 2010.

Kamminga, Menno T. 1987. "The Thematic Procedures of the UN Commission on Human Rights," *Netherlands International Law Review* 34: 299–323.

    1992. *Inter-State Accountability for Violations of Human Rights*. Philadelphia: University of Pennsylvania Press.

Katzenstein, Peter J. (ed.) 1996. *The Culture of National Security. Norms and Identity in World Politics*. New York: Columbia University Press.

Kaufmann, Daniel, Aart Kraay and Massimo Mastruzzi. 2010. *The Worldwide Governance Indicators. Methodology and Analytical Issues, World Bank Policy Research Working Paper No. 5430*. The World Bank.

Kausch, Kristina. 2009a. "The European Union and Political Reform in Morocco," *Mediterranean Politics* 14 (2): 165–179.

    2009b. *Tunisia. The Life of Others. Project on Freedom of Association in the Middle East and North Africa, FRIDE Working Paper 85*. Madrid: FRIDE.

Kausikan, Bilahari. 1994. "Human Rights: Asia's Different Standard," *Media Asia* 21 (1): 45–51.

Keck, Margaret E. and Kathryn Sikkink. 1998. *Activists Beyond Borders. Advocacy Networks in International Politics*. Ithaca, NY: Cornell University Press.

Keith, Linda Camp. 1999. "The United Nations International Covenant on Civil and Political Rights: Does It Make a Difference in Human Rights Behavior?" *Journal of Peace Research* 36 (1): 95–118.

Kell, Georg and John G. Ruggie. 1999. "Global Markets and Social Legitimacy: The Case for the Global Compact," *Transnational Corporations* 8: 101–120.

Kent, Ann. 1999. *China, the United Nations, and Human Rights: The Limits of Compliance*. Philadelphia: University of Pennsylvania Press.

Keohane, Robert O. and Joseph S. Nye (eds.) 1971. *Transnational Relations and World Politics*. Cambridge, MA: Harvard University Press.

Kim, Hunjoon and Kathryn Sikkink. 2007. "Do Human Rights Trials Make A Difference?" *Annual Meeting of American Political Science Association, Chicago, IL. August.*

    2010. "Explaining the Deterrence Effect of Human Rights Prosecutions for Transitional Countries," *International Studies Quarterly* 54 (4): 939–963.

King, Gary, Robert Keohane and Sidney Verba. 1994. *Designing Social Inquiry*. Princeton University Press.

Kinzelbach, Katrin. 2010. "The EU's Human Rights Dialogue with China: Constructive Engagement or Failure?" PhD Dissertation, University of Vienna, Vienna.

2012. "Will China's Rise Lead to a New Normative Order? An Analysis of China's Statements on Human Rights at the United Nations 2000–2010," *Netherlands Quarterly of Human Rights* 30 (3): 299–332.

Kolk, Ans and Rob van Tulder. 2005. "Setting New Global Rules? TNCs and Codes of Conduct," *Transnational Corporations* 14: 1–27.

Kollman, Kelly. 2008. "The Regulatory Power of Business Norms: A Call for a New Research Agenda," *International Studies Review* 10 (3): 397–419.

Koo, Jeong-Woo and Francisco O. Ramirez. 2009. "National Incorporation of Global Human Rights: Worldwide Expansion of National Human Rights Institutions, 1966–2004," *Social Forces* 87 (3): 1321–1353.

Koremenos, Barbara, Charles Lipson and Duncan Snidal. 2001. "The Rational Design of International Institutions," *International Organization* 55 (4): 761–799.

Korey, William. 1998. *NGOs and the Universal Declaration of Human Rights: A Curious Grapevine*. New York: St. Martin's Press.

Krasner, Stephen D. 1999. *Sovereignty: Organized Hypocrisy*. Princeton University Press.

Kratochwil, Friedrich. 1989. *Rules, Norms, and Decisions: On the Conditions of Practical and Legal Reasoning in International Relations and Domestic Affairs*. New York: Cambridge University Press.

2000. "How Do Norms Matter?" in Michael Byers (ed.), *The Role of Law in International Politics: Essays in International Relations and International Law*. Oxford University Press, pp. 35–68.

Krebs, Ronald R. and Patrick Thaddeus Jackson. 2007. "Twisting Tongues and Twisting Arms: The Power of Political Rhetoric," *European Journal of International Relations* 13 (1): 35–66.

Landman, Todd. 2005a. *Protecting Human Rights : A Comparative Study, Advancing Human Rights*. Washington, DC: Georgetown University Press.

2005b. "Review Article: The Political Science of Human Rights," *British Journal of Political Science* 35: 549–572.

Langohr, Vicky. 2004. "Too Much Civil Society, Too Little Politics. Egypt and Liberalizing Arab Regimes," *Comparative Politics* 36 (2): 181–204.

La Rosa, Anne-Marie and Carolin Wuerzner. 2008. "Armed Groups, Sanctions and the Implementation of International Humanitarian Law," *International Review of the Red Cross* 90 (870): 327–341.

Laursen, Andreas. 2000. "Israel's Supreme Court and International Human Rights Law: The Judgement on 'Moderate Physical Pressure'," *Nordic Journal of International Law* 69: 413–447.

Lebovic, James H. and Erik Voeten. 2006. "The Politics of Shame: The Condemnation of Country Human Rights Practices in the UNCHR," *International Studies Quarterly* 50: 861–888.

2009. "The Cost of Shame: International Organizations and Foreign Aid in the Punishing of Human Rights Violators," *Journal of Peace Research* 46 (1): 79–97.

Lee, Katie. 2007. "China and the International Covenant on Civil and Political Rights: Prospects and Challenges," *Chinese Journal of International Law* 6 (2): 445–474.

Leibfried, Stephan and Michael Zürn. 2005. *Transformations of the State?* Cambridge University Press.

Lempinen, Miko. 2005. *The United Nations Commission on Human Rights and the Different Treatment of Governments: An Inseparable Part of Promoting and Encouraging Respect for Human Rights?* Turku (Åbo, Finland): Åbo Akademi Press.

Lepper, Mark R. and David Greene. 1978. "Overjustification Research and Beyond: Towards a Means-End Analysis of Intrinsic and Extrinsic Motivation," in Mark R. Lepper and David Greene (eds.), *The Hidden Costs of Reward: New Perspectives on the Psychology of Human Motivation*. Hillsdale, NJ: Lawrence Erlbaum Associates, pp. 109–148.

Lepper, Mark R., Mark Keavney and Michael Drake. 1996. "Intrinsic Motivation and Extrinsic Rewards: A Commentary on Cameron and Pierce's Meta-Analysis," *Review of Educational Research* 66 (1): 5–32.

Levine, Iain. 1997. "Promoting Humanitarian Principles: The Southern Sudan Experience," *Relief and Rehabilitation Network* 21.

Lewis, Margaret K. 2011. "Controlling Abuse to Maintain Control: The Exclusionary Rule in China," *N.Y.U. Journal of International Law and Politics* 43 (3): 629–697.

Lewis, Neil A. 2004. "Red Cross Finds Detainee Abuse in Guatánamo: U.S. Rejects Accusations: Confidential Report Calls Practices Tantamount to Torture," *New York Times*, November 30, pp. A1, A14.

Li, Chenyang. 2003. "Globalizing Cultural Values: International Human Rights Discourse as Moral Persuasion," in Mahmood Monshipouri, Neil Englehart, Andrew J. Nathan and K. Philip (eds.), *Constructing Human Rights in the Age of Globalization*. Armonk: M.E. Sharpe, pp. 288–307.

Li, Yitan and A. Cooper Drury. 2004. "Threatening Sanctions When Engagement Would Be More Effective: Attaining Better Human Rights in China," *International Studies Perspectives* 5 (4): 378–394.

2006. "U.S. Economic Sanction Threats Against China: Failing to Leverage Better Human Rights," *Foreign Policy Analysis* 2: 307–324.

Liese, Andrea. 2006. *Staaten am Pranger. Zur Wirkung Internationaler Regime auf Innerstaatliche Menschenrechtspolitik*. Wiesbaden: VS Verlag für Sozialwissenschaften.

2009. "Exceptional Necessity. How Liberal Democracies Contest the Prohibition of Torture and Ill-treatment When Countering Terrorism," *Journal of International Law and International Relations* 5 (1): 17–47.

Lithwick, Dahlia. 2011. "Damages: An Appeals Court Allows a Suit against Donald Rumsfeld to Go Forward," *Slate*, August 8. Accessed August 19, 2011 at www. slate.com/id/2301176.

Liu, Li. 2005. "Wrongly Jailed Man Freed After 11 Years," *China Daily*, April 14. Accessed January 31, 2010 at www.chinadaily.com.cn/english/doc/2005– 04/14/content_434020.htm.

Lust-Okar, Ellen. 2007. "The Management of Opposition. Formal Structures of Contestation and Informal Political Manipulation in Egypt, Jordan, and Morocco," in Oliver Schlumberger (ed.), *Debating Arab Authoritarianism. Dynamics and Durability in Nondemocratic Regimes*. Stanford University Press, pp. 39–58.

Lutz, Ellen L. and Kathryn Sikkink. 2000. "International Human Rights Law and Practice in Latin America," *International Organization* 54 (3): 633–659.

Lynch, Marc. 2000. "Globalization and International Democracy," *International Studies Review* 2 (3): 91–101.

M2 Presswire. 1997. "UN Commission Urges Human Rights Improvement," April 17. Accessed at Lexis-Nexis online database.

Mackintosh, Kate. 2004. "Note for Humanitarian Organizations on Cooperation with International Tribunals," *International Review of the Red Cross* 86 (853): 131–146.

Magen, Amichai, Thomas Risse and Michael McFaul (eds.) 2009. *Promoting Democracy and the Rule of Law: American and European Strategies*. Houndmills, Basingstoke: Palgrave-Macmillan.

Maghraoui, Driss. 2009. "Introduction. Interpreting Reform in Morocco," *Mediterranean Politics* 14 (2): 143–149.

Majtenyi, Cathy. 2009. *Catholic Church in Kenya Promotes Alternative to Female Circumcision*. Accessed August 5, 2009 at www.voanews.com/english/2009– 07–11-voa22.cfm.

Mantilla, Giovanni. 2009. "Emerging International Human Rights Norms for Transnational Corporations," *Global Governance* 15: 279–298.

March, James G. and Johan P. Olsen. 1998. "The Institutional Dynamics of International Political Orders," *International Organization* 52 (4): 943–969.

Marsh, Christopher and Daniel P. Payne. 2007. "The Globalization of Human Rights and the Socialization of Human Rights Norms," *Brigham Young University Law Review* 3: 665–687.

Marshall, Monty and Keith Jaggers. 2002. *Political Regime Characteristics and Transitions, 1800–2002. Dataset Users Manual*. Center for International Development and Conflict Management (CIDCM), University of Maryland.

2009. *Polity IV Project: Political Regime Characteristics and Transitions, 1800– 2007*. Fairfax, VA: Center for Systemic Peace. Accessed July 9, 2009 at www. systemicpeace.org/polity.

Mayer, Jane. 2005. "Outsourcing Torture," *The New Yorker*, February 14 and 21.

2008. *The Dark Side: The Inside Story of How the War on Terror Turned Into a War on American Ideals*. New York: Anchor Books.

McHugh, Gerard and Manuel Bessler. 2006a. *Guidelines on Humanitarian Negotiation with Armed Groups.* New York: United Nations.

2006b. *Humanitarian Negotiations with Armed Groups: A Manual for Practitioners.* New York: United Nations.

McKinsey & Company. 2004. *Assessing the Global Compact's Impact.* New York: McKinsey & Company.

Médecins Sans Frontières. 1999. *Female Genital Cutting.* Accessed August 5, 2009 at www.msf.org/msfinternational/invoke.cfm?component=articleandobjectid= 7128255C-EC70-11D4-B2010060084A6370andmethod=full_html.

Menkhaus, Ken. 2006/2007. "Governance Without Government in Somalia: Spoilers, State Building, and the Politics of Coping," *International Security* 31 (3): 74–106.

Merkel, Wolfgang and Aurel Croissant. 2000. "Formale und informale Institutionen in defekten Demokratien," *Politische Vierteljahresschrift* 41 (1): 3–30.

Merkel, Wolfgang, Hans-Jürgen Puhle and Aurel Croissant (eds.) 2003–2004. *Defekte Demokratien, 2 vols.* Opladen: VS – Verlag für Sozialwissenschaften.

Metcalf, Cherie. 2008. "Compensation as Discipline in the Justified Limitation of Aboriginal Rights: The Case of Forest Exploitation," *Queen's Law Journal* 33 (2): 385–452.

Meyer, John W., John Boli and George M. Thomas. 1987. "Ontology and Rationalization in the Western Cultural Account," in George M. Thomas, John W. Meyer, Francisco O. Ramirez and John Boli (eds.), *Institutional Structure. Constituting the State, Society, and the Individual.* Newbury Park: Sage, pp. 12–37.

Meyer, John W., John Boli, George M. Thomas and Francisco O. Ramirez. 1997. "World Society and the Nation-State," *American Journal of Sociology* 103 (1): 144–181.

Ministry of Foreign Affairs of Denmark and UNDP Nordic Office. 2010. *Global Compact. Small and Medium-sized Enterprises and their Way Towards Global Responsibility.* Copenhagen: Ministry of Foreign Affairs of Denmark.

Mitchell, Ronald B. 1994. "Regime Design Matters: Intentional Oil Pollution and Treaty Compliance," *International Organization* 48 (3): 425–458.

Moore, David H. 2003. "A Signaling Theory of Human Rights Compliance," *Northwestern University Law Review* 97 (2): 879–910.

Moravcsik, Andrew. 2000. "The Origins of Human Rights Regimes: Democratic Delegation in Postwar Europe," *International Organization* 54 (2): 217–252.

MSCI. 2011. *Global Compact Plus.* Accessed October 1, 2011 at www.msci.com/ products/esg/research/global_compact_plus/.

Müller, Harald. 2004. "Arguing, Bargaining, and All That: Communicative Action, Rationalist Theory and the Logic of Appropriateness in International Relations," *European Journal of International Relations* 10 (3): 395–435.

Muñoz, Alejandro. 2009. "Transnational and Domestic Processes in the Definition of Human Rights Policies in Mexico," *Human Rights Quarterly* 1: 35–58.

Murdie, Amanda and David R. Davis. 2012. "Shaming and Blaming: Using Event Data to Assess the Impact of Human Rights INGOs," *International Studies Quarterly*: 56(1): 1–16.

Murphy, Emma C. 2011. "The Tunisian Uprising and the Precarious Path to Democracy," *Mediterranean Politics* 16 (2): 299–305.

Nadelmann, Ethan. 1990. "Global Prohibition Regimes: The Evolution of Norms in International Society," *International Organization* 44 (4): 479–526.

Nagin, Daniel S. 1998. "Criminal Deterrence Research at the Outset of the Twenty-First Century," *Crime and Justice: A Review of Research* 23: 1–42.

Najem, Tom Pierre. 2003. "State Power and Democratization in North Africa. Developments in Morocco, Algeria, Tunisia, and Libya," in Amin Saikal and Albrecht Schnabel (eds.), *Democratization in the Middle East. Experiences, Struggles, Challenges*. Tokyo: United Nations University Press, pp. 183–201.

Neumayer, Eric. 2005. "Do International Human Rights Treaties Improve Respect for Human Rights?" *Journal of Conflict Resolution* 49 (6): 925–953.

Nielsen, Rich and Beth A. Simmons. 2009. "Rewards for Rights Ratification? Testing for Tangible and Intangible Benefits of Human Rights Treaty Ratification," in *Annual Meeting of the American Political Science Association*. Toronto. Accessed September 11, 2012 at http://ssrn.com/abstract=1451630.

Nifosi, Ingrid. 2005. *The UN Special Procedures in the Field of Human Rights*. Antwerp and Oxford: Intersentia.

Nike, Inc. 2010. *Corporate Sustainability Report FY07–09*. Accessed August 23, 2010 at www.nikebiz.com/crreport/content/pdf/documents/en-US/full-report.pdf.

Nodia, Ghia. 1995. "Georgia's Identity Crisis," *Journal of Democracy* 6 (1): 104–116.

Nye, Joseph S. Jr. 2004. *Soft Power. The Means to Succeed in World Politics*. New York: PublicAffairs Press.

Oberholzer-Gee, Felix and Howard Kunreuther. 2005. "Social Pressures in Siting Conflicts: A Case Study of Siting a Radioactive Waste Repository in Pennsylvania," in S. Hayden Lesbirel and Daigee Shaw (eds.), *Managing Conflict in Facility Siting*. Northampton, MA: Edward Elgar Publishing, pp. 85–108.

Office for Democratic Institutions and Human Rights. 2008a. *Human Rights in the War-Affected Areas Following the Conflict in Georgia*. Warsaw: OSCE.

2008b. *OSCE-ODIHR Election Observation Mission Final Report*. Warsaw: OSCE.

Olsen, Tricia D., Leigh A. Payne and Andrew G. Reiter. 2010. *Transitional Justice in the Balance: Comparing Processes, Weighing Efficacy*. Washington, DC: USIP Press.

Orford, Anne. 2011. *International Authority and the Responsibility to Protect*. Cambridge University Press.

Ostrom, Elinor. 2005. "Policies that Crowd Out Reciprocity and Collective Action," in Herbert Gintis, Samuel Bowles, Robert Boyd and Ernst Fehr (eds.), *Moral Sentiments and Material Interests: The Foundations of Cooperation in Economic Life*. Cambridge, MA: MIT Press, pp. 253–275.

Ottaway, Marina. 2011. *The New Moroccan Constitution. Real Change or More of the Same? Commentary, 20 June 2011*. Washington, DC: Carnegie Endowment.

Oud, Malin. 2009. "A Lot of Thunder but Little Rain? The 'Human Rights-Based Approach' to Development Cooperation with China." Thesis, Melbourne University.

Oxfam. 2010. *So What's the Problem with Nike?* Accessed August 24, 2010 at www.oxfam.org.au/explore/workers-rights/nike.

Paciello, Maria Cristina. 2011. *Tunisia. Changes and Challenges of Political Transition, MEDPRO Technical Report No. 3*. Brussels.

Pan, Philip P. 2008. *Out of Mao's Shadow: The Struggle for the Soul of a New China*. New York: Simon & Schuster.

Payne, Rodger A. 2001. "Persuasion, Frames and Norm Construction," *European Journal of International Relations* 7 (1): 37–61.

Pearlstein, Deborah and Priti Patel. 2005. *Behind the Wire: An Update to Ending Secret Detentions*. New York: Human Rights First, March.

Peerenboom, Randall P. 2007. *China Modernizes: Threat to the West or Model for the Rest?* Oxford and New York: Oxford University Press.

People's Republic of China. 2004. *Constitution of the People's Republic of China Approved by the 10th National People's Congress at its 2nd Session (as amended)*. Beijing.

Pils, Eva. 2006–2007. "Asking the Tiger for His Skin: Rights Activism in China," *Fordham International Law Journal* 30: 1209–1287.

⎯⎯ 2009. "The Dislocation of the Chinese Human Rights Movement," in Stacy Mosher and Patrick Poon (eds.), *A Sword and a Shield: China's Human Rights Lawyers*. Hong Kong: China Human Rights Lawyers Concern Group, pp. 141–159.

Poe, Steven C. and Neal C. Tate. 1994. "Repression of Human Rights to Personal Integrity in the 1980s: A Global Analysis," *American Political Science Review* 88: 853–871.

Poe, Steven C., Neal C. Tate and Linda Camp Keith. 1999. "Repression of the Human Right to Personal Integrity Revisited: A Global Crossnational Study Covering the Years 1976–1993," *International Studies Quarterly* 43: 291–315.

Polillo, Simone and Mauro Guillén. 2005. "Globalization Pressures and the State: The Worldwide Spread of Central Bank Independence," *American Journal of Sociology* 110 (6): 1764–1802.

Prakash, Aseem and Matthew Potoski. 2007. "Investing Up: FDI and the Cross-Country Diffusion of ISO 14001 Management Systems," *International Studies Quarterly* 51 (3): 723–744.

Prentice, Deborah A. 2012. "The Psychology of Social Norms and the Promotion of Human Rights," in Ryan Goodman, Derek Jinks and Andrew K. Woods (eds.), *Understanding Social Action, Promoting Human Rights*. New York: Oxford University Press, pp. 23–34.

Presidency-in-Office of the Council of the European Union, Netherlands. 2004. *EU-China Human Rights Dialogue (1995–2004): Evaluation by the Presidency* (No. CFSP/PRES/HAG/1021/04; CFSP/COM/370/04). The Hague.

Price, Richard. 1998. "Reversing the Gun Sights: Transnational Civil Society Targets Land Mines," *International Organization* 52 (3): 613–644.

Probst, Marc. 2007. "Human Security and Business – A Contradiction in Terms?" in Benjamin Leisinger and Marc Probst (eds.), *Human Security and Business*. Zürich: rüffer & rüb, pp. 20–43.

Putnam, Robert. 1988. "Diplomacy and Domestic Politics. The Logic of Two-Level Games," *International Organization* 42 (2): 427–460.

Rahman, Anika and Nahid Toubia (eds.) 2000. *Female Genital Mutilation: A Guide to Laws and Policies Worldwide*. New York: St. Martin's Press.

Ramcharan, Bertie G. 2009. *The Protection Roles of UN Human Rights Special Procedures*. Leiden: Martinus Nijhoff.

Rasche, Andreas. 2009. "'A Necessary Supplement': What the United Nations Global Compact Is and Is Not," *Business and Society* 48: 511–537.

Ratner, Michael. 2010. Personal interview. New York City, May 12.

Ratner, Steven R. 2001. "Corporations and Human Rights: A Theory of Legal Responsibility," *The Yale Law Review* 111: 443–545.

Raustiala, Kal and Anne-Marie Slaughter. 2002. "International Law, International Relations, and Compliance," in Walter Carlsnaes, Beth Simmons and Thomas Risse (eds.), *Handbook of International Relations*. London: Sage, pp. 538–558.

Rieth, Lothar and Oliver Glindemann. 2010. *Deutsche Unternehmen im Global Compact. Kontinuität oder Fortschritt? COP-Projekte IV and V*. Darmstadt: Technische Universität Darmstadt.

Rieth, Lothar and Melanie Zimmer. 2004. *Transnational Corporations and Conflict Prevention: The Impact of Norms on Private Actors*. Tübingen: Universität Tübingen.

Rieth, Lothar, Melanie Zimmer, Ralph Hamann and Jon Hank. 2007. "The UN Global Compact in Sub-Saharan Africa: Decentralisation and Effectiveness," *Journal of Corporate Citizenship* 28: 99–112.

Risse, Thomas. 2000. "'Let's Argue!' Communicative Action in International Relations," *International Organization* 54 (1): 1–39.

2011a. "Governance in Areas of Limited Statehood: Introduction and Overview," in Thomas Risse (ed.), *Governance Without a State? Policies and Politics in Areas of Limited Statehood*. New York: Columbia University Press, pp. 1–38.

(ed.) 2011b. *Governance Without a State? Policies and Politics in Areas of Limited Statehood*. New York: Columbia University Press.

Risse, Thomas and Ursula Lehmkuhl (eds.) 2007. *Regieren ohne Staat? Governance in Räumen begrenzter Staatlichkeit, Schriften zur Governance-Forschung*. Baden-Baden: Nomos.

Risse, Thomas and Stephen C. Ropp. 1999. "The Socialization of Human Rights Norms into Domestic Practices: Conclusion," in Thomas Risse, Stephen C. Ropp and Kathryn Sikkink (eds.), *The Power of Human Rights. International Norms and Domestic Change*. Cambridge, MA: Cambridge University Press, pp. 234–278.

Risse, Thomas, and Kathryn Sikkink. 1999. "The Socialization of Human Rights Norms into Domestic Practices: Introduction," in Thomas Risse, Stephen C. Ropp and Kathryn Sikkink (eds.), *The Power of Human Rights. International Norms and Domestic Change*. Cambridge, MA: Cambridge University Press, pp. 1–38.

Risse, Thomas, Anja Jetschke and Hans Peter Schmitz. 2002. *Die Macht der Menschenrechte. Internationale Normen, kommunikatives Handeln und politischer Wandel in den Ländern des Südens*. Baden-Baden: Nomos.

Risse, Thomas, Stephen C. Ropp and Kathryn Sikkink (eds.) 1999. *The Power of Human Rights: International Norms and Domestic Change*. Cambridge University Press.

Robinson, Geoffrey. 2010. *If You Leave Us Here, We Will Die: How Genocide Was Stopped in East Timor*. Princeton University Press.

Rodley, Nigel. 2003. "United Nations Human Rights Treaty Bodies and Special Procedures of the Commission on Human Rights – Complementarity or Competition?" *Human Rights Quarterly* 25: 882–908.

Ron, James. 1997. "Varying Methods of State Violence," *International Organization* 51 (2): 275–300.

Roodman, D. 2009. "How to Do Xtabond2: An Introduction to Difference and System GMM in Stata," *Stata Journal* 9 (1): 86–136.

Ropp, Stephen C. and Kathryn Sikkink. 1999. "International Norms and Domestic Politics in Chile and Guatemala," in Thomas Risse, Stephen C. Ropp and Kathryn Sikkink (eds.), *The Power of Human Rights. International Norms and Domestic Change*. Cambridge University Press, pp. 172–204.

Rotberg, Robert I. (ed.) 2003. *State Failure and State Weakness in a Time of Terror*. Washington, DC: Brookings Institution Press.

2004. *When States Fail. Causes and Consequences*. Princeton University Press.

Ruggie, John G. 2002. "The Theory and Practice of Learning Networks: Corporate Social Responsibility and the Global Compact," *Journal of Corporate Citizenship* 5: 27–36.

2006. *Human Rights Policies and Management Practices of Fortune 500 Firms: Results of a Survey*. Harvard University. Accessed September 29, 2012 at www. humanrights.ch/upload/pdf/070706/Ruggie-survey-Fortune-Global-500. pdf.

2007. "Business and Human Rights: Mapping International Standards of Responsibility and Accountablity for Corporate Acts," in Benjamin Leisinger and Marc Probst (eds.), *Human Security and Business*. Zürich: rüffer & rüb, pp. 230–257.

2009. *Promotion of all Human Rights, Civil, Political, Economic, Social and Cultural Rights, including the Right to Development. Business and Human Rights: Towards Operationalizing the 'Protect, Respect and Remedy' Framework*. United Nations, General Assembly, Human Rights Council, New York, April 22.

Rumford, Chris. 2001. "Human Rights and Democratization in Turkey in the Context of EU Candidature," *Journal of European Area Studies* 9 (1): 93–105.

Runhaar, Hens and Helene Lafferty. 2009. "Governing Corporate Social Responsibility: An Assessment of the Contribution of the UN Global Compact to CSR Strategies in the Telecommunications Industry," *Journal of Business Ethics* 84: 479–495.

Ryan, Richard M. and Edward L. Deci. 2000. "Self-determination Theory and the Facilitation of Intrinsic Motivation, Social Development, and Well-being," *American Psychologist* 55 (1): 68–78.

Sadiki, Larbi. 2002a. "Political Liberalization in Bin Ali's Tunisia. Façade Democracy," *Democratization* 9 (4): 122–141.

2002b. "The Search for Citizenship in Bin Ali's Tunisia. Democracy versus Unity," *Political Studies* 50 (3): 497–513.

Sagafi-Nejad, Tagi. 2005. "Should Global Rules Have Legal Teeth? Policing (WHO Framework Convention on Tobacco Control) vs. Good Citizenship (UN Global Compact)," *International Journal of Business* 10: 363–382.

Sambanis, Nicholas. 2004. "Using Case Studies to Expand Economic Models of Civil War," *Perspectives on Politics* 2 (2): 259–279.

Schapper, Andrea. 2010. "Global Child Rights and Local Change. Evidence from Bangladesh," *Journal of Human Security* 6 (1): 3–21.

Schimmelfennig, Frank, Stefan Engert and Heiko Knobel. 2003. "Costs, Commitment, and Compliance. The Impact of EU Democratic Conditionality on Latvia, Slovakia, and Turkey," *Journal of Common Market Studies* 41 (3): 495–517.

Schmidt, Markus. 2003. "The Follow-up Activities by the UN Human Rights Treaty Bodies and the OHCHR, Contribution by the Office of the UN High Commissioner on Human Rights," conference paper, in *Meeting on the Impact of the Work of UN Human Rights Treaty Bodies on National Courts and Tribunals*. Turku (Åbo, Finland): Institute for Human Rights, Åbo Akademi University. Accessed May 21, 2009 at http://web.abo.fi/instut/imr/.

Schmitt, Eric. 2005. "Exception Sought in Detainee Abuse Ban: White House Wants More Leeway for C.I.A. on Interrogations," *New York Times*, October 25, p. A17.

Schmitz, Hans Peter. 1999. "Transnational Activism and Political Change in Kenya and Uganda," in Thomas Risse, Stephen C. Ropp and Kathryn Sikkink (eds.), *The Power of Human Rights: International Norms and Domestic Change*. Cambridge University Press, pp. 39–77.

Schneckener, Ulrich (ed.) 2004. *States at Risk. Fragile Staaten als Sicherheits- und Entwicklungsproblem*. Berlin: Stiftung Wissenschaft und Politik.

Schraeder, Peter J. and Hamadi Redissi. 2011. "Ben Ali's Fall," *Journal of Democracy* 22 (3): 5–19.

Schroeder, Miriam. 2008. "The Construction of China's Climate Politics: Transnational NGOs and the Spiral Model of International Relations," *Cambridge Review of International Affairs* 21 (4): 505–525.

Schwarz, Rolf. 2004a. "The Paradox of Sovereignty, Regime Type and Human Rights Compliance," *International Journal of Human Rights* 8 (2): 199–215.

———. 2004b. "Sovereign Claims: Recent Contributions to the Debate on Sovereignty in the Light of Intervention Policies in the Third World," *Cooperation and Conflict* 39 (1): 77–88.

Scott, Marvin B., and Stanford M. Lyman. 1968. "Accounts," *American Sociological Review* 33 (1): 46–62.

Sharp, Jeremy M. 2010. *U.S. Foreign Assistance to the Middle East. Historical Background, Recent Trends, and the FY2011 Request, CRS Report for Congress*. Washington, DC: Congressional Research Service.

Shell. 2009. *Shell Nigeria and the Environment, Shell*. Accessed July 8, 2009 at www.shell.com/home/content2/nigeria/society_environment/sust_dev/env.html.

Shelton, Dinah. 2000. *Commitment and Compliance: The Role of Non-binding Norms in the International Legal System*. Oxford University Press.

Shor, Eran. 2008. "Conflict, Terrorism, and the Socialization of Human Rights Norms: The Spiral Model Revisited," *Social Problems* 55 (1): 117–138.

Sifton, John. 2010a. "The Get Out of Jail Free Card for Torture: It's Called a Declination; Just Ask the CIA," *Slate*, March 29. Accessed August 19, 2011 at www.slate.com/id/2249126.

———. 2010b. Personal interview. New York City, May 13.

Sikkink, Kathryn. 1993. "Human Rights, Principled Issue Networks, and Sovereignty in Latin America," *International Organization* 47: 411–441.

———. 2004. *Mixed Signals. U.S. Human Rights Policy and Latin America*. Ithaca, NY: Cornell University Press.

———. 2011. *The Justice Cascade: Human Rights Prosecutions and World Politics*. New York: W.W. Norton.

Simmons, Beth. 1998. "Compliance with International Agreements," *The Annual Review of Political Science* 1: 75–93.

———. 2009. *Mobilizing for Human Rights: International Law in Domestic Politics*. New York: Cambridge University Press.

———. 2010. "Treaty Compliance and Violation," *Annual Review of Political Science* 13: 273–296.

Simmons, Beth A., Frank Dobbin and Geoffrey Garrett. 2008. *The Global Diffusion of Markets and Democracy*. Cambridge University Press.

Sivakumaran, Sandesh. 2006. "Binding Armed Opposition Groups," *International and Comparative Law Quarterly* 55 (2): 369–394.

Skaine, Rosemarie. 2005. *Female Genital Mutilation: Legal, Cultural and Medical Issues*. Jefferson, NC: McFarland and Company, Inc.

Sliwka, Dirk. 2003. "On the Hidden Costs of Incentive Schemes," *IZA Discussion Papers, Institute for the Study of Labor* No. 844.

———. 2007. "Trust as a Signal of a Social Norm and the Hidden Costs of Incentive Schemes," *American Economic Review* 97 (3): 999–1012.

Sly, Liz. 2011. "Unrest in Syria Threatens Regional Stability," *Washington Post*, May 2.

Smillie, Ian, Lansana Gberie and Ralph Hazleton. 2000. *The Heart of the Matter. Sierra Leone, Diamonds and Human Security*. Ottawa: Partnership Africa Canada.

Smith, R. Jeffrey. 2006. "Detainee Abuse Charges Feared," *Washington Post*, July 28, p. A1.

Snow, David A. and Robert D. Benford. 1988. "Ideology, Frame Resonance, and Participant Mobilization," in Bert Klandermans, Hanspeter Kriesi and Sidney Tarrow (eds.), *International Social Movement Research. A Research Annual. From Structure to Action: Comparing Social Movement Research across Cultures*. Greenwich, CT: JAI Press Inc., pp. 197–217.

Snyder, Jack and Leslie Vinjamuri. 2004. "Trials and Errors: Principle and Pragmatism in Strategies of International Justice," *International Security* 28 (3): 5–44.

Spar, Deborah, and Lane La Mure. 2003. "The Power of Activism. Assessing the Impact of NGOs on Global Business," *California Management Review* 45 (3): 78–101.

Spataro, Armando. 2008. Personal Interview. Rome, October 14.

SPLM Political Secretariat. 1998. *The Fifteen-Point Programme of the SPLM*. March. Accessed May 21, 2010 at www.splmtoday.com/index.php?option=com_content &view=article&id=15&Itemid=35.

Stachursky, Benjamin. 2010. "The Promise and Perils of Transnationalisation. A Critical Assessment of the Role of NGO Activism in the Socialisation of Women's Human Rights in Egypt and Iran," PhD Dissertation. University of Potsdam, Potsdam.

Steiner, Henry, Philip Alston and Ryan Goodman. 2008. *International Human Rights in Context: Law, Politics, Morals*. 3rd edn. Oxford University Press.

Stephenson, Matthew. 2006. "A Trojan Horse in China?" in Thomas Carothers (ed.), *Promoting the Rule of Law Abroad: In Search of Knowledge*. Washington, DC: Carnegie Endowment for International Peace, pp. 191–215.

Steyn, Johan. 2008. "Guantanamo Bay: The Legal Black Hole," *International and Comparative Law Quarterly* 53: 1–15.

Stoker, Gerry. 1998. "Governance as Theory: Five Propositions," *International Social Science Journal* 50 (155): 17–28.

Sudan Human Security Baseline Assessment, Small Arms Survey. 2011a. "Justice and Equality Movement (JEM)." Accessed January 30, 2011 at www.smallarmssurvey-sudan.org/pdfs/facts-figures/armed-groups/darfur/HSBA-Armed-Groups-JEM.pdf.

———— 2011b. "Sudan Liberation Army – Minni Minawi (SLA-MM)." Accessed January 30, 2011 at www.smallarmssurveysudan.org/ pdfs/ facts-figures/ armed-groups/darfur/HSBA-Armed-Groups-SLA-MM.pdf.

Sudan People's Liberation Movement. July 31, 1983. *Manifesto*. Accessed May 10, 2010 at http://thelinowuorabeyifoundation.org/SPLAMANIFESTO1983.doc.

Sunstein, Cass R. 1996. "The Expressive Function of Law," *University of Pennsylvania Law Review* 144 (5): 2021–2053.

Svensson, Marina. 2002. *Debating Human Rights in China: A Conceptual and Political History*. Lanham, MD: Rowman & Littlefield.

Tallberg, Jonas. 2002. "Paths to Compliance. Enforcement, Management, and the European Union," *International Organization* 56 (3): 609–643.

Tashman, Peter and Jorge Rivera. 2010. "Are Members of Business for Social Responsibility More Socially Responsible?," *Policy Studies Journal* 38: 487–514.

Thakur, Ramesh. 2011. *The Responsibility to Protect: Norms, Laws and the Use of Force in International Politics*. London and New York: Routledge.

Thauer, Christian. 2009. "Corporate Social Responsibility in the Regulatory Void: Does the Promise Hold? Self-Regulation by Business in South Africa and China," PhD Dissertation, Social and Political Science Department, European University Institute, Florence.

Thérien, Jean-Philippe and Vincent Pouliot. 2006. "The Global Compact: Shifting the Politics of International Development?" *Global Governance* 12: 55–75.

Thimm, Johannes. 2009. "Understanding US Unilateralism. American Foreign Policy and Multilateral Treaties," PhD Dissertation, Department of Social and Political Science, Freie Universität Berlin, Berlin.

Thomas, Daniel C. 1999. "The Helsinki Accords and Political Change in Eastern Europe," in Thomas Risse, Stephen C. Ropp and Kathryn Sikkink (eds.), *The Power of Human Rights: International Norms and Domestic Change*. Cambridge University Press, pp. 205–233.

Thompson, Mark R. 2001. "Whatever Happened to 'Asian Values'?" *Journal of Democracy* 12 (4): 154–165.

Two Tomorrows. 2010. *Tomorrow's Value Rating*. Accessed November 13, 2010 at www.tomorrowsvaluerating.com/.

Ulbert, Cornelia and Thomas Risse. 2005. "Deliberately Changing the Discourse: What Does Make Arguing Effective?" *Acta Politica* 40: 351–367.

Uma, Julius. 2010. "SPLA to Demobilize All Child Soldiers by End of the Year," *Sudan Tribune*, August 30. Accessed September 27, 2010 at www.sudantribune.com/spip.php? article36125.

UN Convention Against Torture Observations. 2006. Accessed at www.human-rightsfirst.org/us_law/etn/cat/blog/post-050906-rona.asp.

UNCCPR. 2007. *Concluding Observations of the Human Rights Committee. Georgia. UN International Convenant on Civil and Political Rights*, October 21, 2010.

United Nations. n.d. *UN Treaty Collection. United Nations*. Accessed April 16, 2009 at http://treaties.un.org.

    1966. *International Covenant on Civil and Political Rights*. (GA res. 2200A (XXI), 21 UN GAOR Supp. (No. 16) at 52, UN Doc. A/6316 (1966), 999 UNTS 171), entered into Force March 23, 1976.

    1968. *United Nations Conference on Human Rights, Proclamation of Tehran, 22 April to 13 May, 1968. (A/CONF. 32/41)*. Reproduced in "United

Nations Conference on Human Rights, Tehran, 22 April to 13 May, 1968: Proclamation of Tehran," *American Journal of International Law* 63 (3): 674–677.

1984. *Convention against Torture and Other Cruel, Inhuman or Degrading Treatment or Punishment.* (GA res. 39/46, annex, 39 UN GAOR Supp. (No. 51) at 197, UN Doc. A/39/51 (1984)), entered into force June 26, 1987.

1996. *Beijing Declaration and Platform for Action.* Accessed August 5, 2009, at www.un.org/womenwatch/daw/beijing/platform/.

United Nations, Committee against Torture. 2008. *Convention Against Torture and Other Cruel, Inhuman or Degrading Treatment or Punishment: General Comment No. 2.* (CAT/C/GC/2). Geneva.

United Nations Development Programme Sudan. "Mine Action Capacity Building and Programme Development." Accessed September 27, 2010 at www.sd.undp.org/projects/ mine.htm.

United Nations Economic and Social Council. 1967. *Res. 1235 (XLII) of 6 June 1967.* (UN Doc. No. E/Res/1235 (XLII)).

1970. *Res. 1503 (XLVIII) of 27 May 1970.* (UN Doc. No. E/Res/1503 (XLVIII)).

United Nations Economic and Social Council, Sub-Commission on Prevention of Discrimination and Protection of Minorities. 1971. *Sub-Commission Resolution 1 (XXIV) of 13 August 1971.*

United Nations, General Assembly. 2005. "2005 World Summit Outcome," September 15. A/60/L.1.

United Nations General Assembly, Human Rights Council. 2008. *Report of the Special Rapporteur on Torture and Other Cruel, Inhuman or Degrading Treatment or Punishment, Manfred Nowak: Addendum, Mission to Indonesia.* (UN Doc. A/HRC/3/Add.7). March 10.

United Nations Global Compact Office. 2010a. *The Ten Principles.* Accessed August 12, 2011 at www.unglobalcompact.org/AboutTheGC/TheTenPrinciples/index.html.

2010b. *UN Global Compact Bulletin December 2010.* New York: UN Global Compact.

2010c. *United Nations Global Compact Local Network Report 2010.* New York: UN Global Compact.

2010d. *What is a Global Compact Local Network?* Accessed March 11, 2011 at www.unglobalcompact.org/NetworksAroundTheWorld/Guidelines_and_Recommendations.html.

2011. *United Nations Global Compact Local Network Report 2011.* New York: United Nations Global Compact.

United Nations Office of the High Commissioner for Human Rights. n.d. *The Revised 1503 Procedure.* Geneva. Accessed April 16, 2009 at www.unhchr.ch/html/menu2/8/1503.htm.

United Nations Office of the High Commissioner for Human Rights. Committee Against Torture. 2001. *Concluding Observations: Indonesia* (UN Doc.

A/57/44). Accessed September 29, 2010 at www2.ohchr.org/english/bodies/cat/cats27.htm.

2008. *Concluding Observations of the Committee Against Torture: Indonesia.* Accessed September 29, 2010 at www.ohchr.org/english/bodies/cat/cats40.htm.

United Nations Special Rapporteur on the Right to Education. 2003. *Report Submitted by the Special Rapporteur, Katarina Tomaševski. Addendum. Mission to China: Commission on Human Rights, 16th session* (No. E/CN.4/2004/45/Add.1). Geneva.

US Department of Justice, Office of Legal Counsel, Office of the Assistant Attorney General. 2002. "Memorandum for Alberto R. Gonzales, Re: Standards of Conduct for Interrogation under 18 USC. 2340–2340A," August 1.

2004. "Memorandum for James B. Comey, Deputy Attorney General, Re: Legal Standards Applicable Under 18 USC. 2340–2340A," December 30.

US Department of State. 2010. "2010 Human Rights Report: Sudan." Accessed September 12, 2011 at www.state.gov/g/drl/rls/hrrpt/2010/af/154371.htm.

2011. *2010 Country Reports on Human Rights Practices.* Washington, DC.

Vairel, Frédéric. 2008. "Morocco. From Mobilizations to Reconciliation?" *Mediterranean Politics* 13 (2): 229–241.

Valentino, Benjamin, Paul Huth and Dylan Balch-Lindsay. 2004. "'Draining the Sea': Mass Killing and Guerrilla Warfare," *International Organization* 58 (2): 375–407.

Van Hüllen, Vera. 2012. "Europeanization Through Cooperation? EU Democracy Promotion in Morocco and Tunisia," *West European Politics* 35 (1): 117–134.

Van Hüllen, Vera and Andreas Stahn. 2009. "Comparing EU and US Democracy Promotion in the Mediterranean and the Newly Independent States," in Amichai Magen, Thomas Risse and Michael McFaul (eds.), *Promoting Democracy and the Rule of Law. American and European Strategies.* Houndmills, Basingstoke: Palgrave Macmillan, pp. 118–149.

Venzke, Ingo. 2009. "Legal Contestation about 'Enemy Combatants': On the Exercise of Power in Legal Interpretation," *Journal of International Law and International Relations* 5 (1): 155–184.

Veuthey, Michel. 1983. "Guerrilla Warfare and Humanitarian Law," *International Review of the Red Cross* 23: 115–138.

Vreeland, James Raymond. 2008. "Political Institutions and Human Rights: Why Dictatorships Enter into the United Nations Convention Against Torture," *International Organization* 62 (1): 65–101.

Wachman, Alan M. 2001. "Does the Diplomacy of Shame Promote Human Rights in China?" *Third World Quarterly* 22 (2): 257–281.

Waddock, Sandra. 2005. "What Will it Take to Create a Tipping Point for Corporate Responsibility?" in Marc J. Epstein and Kirk O. Hanson (eds.), *The Accountable Corporation.* Greenfield, CT: Praeger, pp. 75–96.

Waldmeir, Patti. 1998. *Anatomy of a Miracle: The End of Apartheid and the Birth of the New South Africa.* New York: W.W. Norton.

Wallbott, Linda. 2010. "Calling on Peace: The International ICT Sector and the Conflict in the Democratic Republic of Congo," in Nicole Deitelhoff and Klaus Dieter Wolf (eds.), *Corporate Security Responsibility? Corporate Governance Contributions to Peace and Security in Zones of Conflict.* Houndmills, Basingstoke: Palgrave Macmillan, pp. 85–105.

Wa Mutua, Makau. 2000. "Politics and Human Rights: An Essential Symbiosis," in Michael Byers (ed.), *The Role of Law in International Politics. Essays in International Relations and International Law.* Oxford University Press, pp. 149–175.

Wan, Ming. 2001. *Human Rights in Chinese Foreign Relations: Defining and Defending National Interests.* Philadelphia: University of Pennsylvania Press.

    2007. "Human Rights Lawmaking in China: Domestic Politics, International Law, and International Politics," *Human Rights Quarterly* 29: 727–753.

Watchlist on Children in Armed Conflict. 2007. "Sudan's Children at a Crossroads: An Urgent Need for Protection." April. Accessed September 27, 2010 at www.watchlist.org/reports/pdf/sudan_07_final.pdf.

Weatherley, Robert. 1999. *The Discourse of Human Rights in China: Historical and Ideological Perspectives.* Houndmills, Basingstoke: Palgrave Macmillan.

Weber, Max. 1921/1980. *Wirtschaft und Gesellschaft.* 5th edn. Tübingen: J. C. B. Mohr.

Weinstein, Jeremy. 2007. *Inside Rebellion: The Politics of Insurgent Violence.* Cambridge University Press.

Weiss, Edith Brown and Jacobson, Harold K. (eds.) 1998. *Engaging Countries: Strengthening Compliance with International Environmental Accords.* Cambridge, MA: MIT Press.

Weiss, Thomas. 2005. *Military-Civilian Interactions: Humanitarian Crises and the Responsibility to Protect.* 2nd edn. Lanham, MD: Rowman & Littlefield.

Weissbrodt, David S. 1986. "The Three 'Theme' Special Rapporteurs of the UN Commission on Human Rights," *American Journal of International Law* 80: 685–699.

Weissbrodt, David S. and Wendy Mahling. n.d. "Highlights of the 46th Session of the Sub-Commission [1994]," *Minneapolis: University of Minnesota Human Rights Library.* Accessed September 29, 2010 at www1.umn.edu/humanrts/demo/subrept.htm.

Weissbrodt, David S., Joan Fitzpatrick and Frank C. Newman. 2001. *International Human Rights: Law, Policy, Process.* Cincinnati: Anderson.

Wendt, Alexander. 1992. "Anarchy Is What States Make of It: The Social Construction of Power Politics," *International Organization* 88 (2): 384–396.

    1999. *Social Theory of International Politics.* Cambridge University Press.

    2001. "Driving with the Rearview Mirror: On the Rational Science of Institutional Design," *International Organization* 55: 1019–1049.

Whelan, Nessa. 2010. "Building the United Nations Global Compact Local Network Model: History and Insights," in Andreas Rasche and Georg Kell (eds.), *The United Nations Global Compact: Achievements, Trends and Challenges*. Cambridge University Press, pp. 317–339.

Whitehouse, Lisa. 2003. "Corporate Social Responsibility, Corporate Citizenship and the Global Compact: A New Approach to Regulating Corporate Social Power?" *Global Social Policy* 3: 299–318.

Wiener, Antje. 2009. "Enacting Meaning-in-Use. Qualitative Research on Norms and International Relations," *Review of International Studies* 35 (1): 175–193.

Willis, Michael J. 2006. "Containing Radicalism through the Political Process in North Africa," *Mediterranean Politics* 11 (2): 137–150.

2009. "Conclusion. The Dynamics of Reform in Morocco," *Mediterranean Politics* 14 (2): 229–237.

Willis, Michael J. and Nizar Messari. 2005. "Analyzing Moroccan Foreign Policy and Relations with Europe," in Gerd Nonneman (ed.), *Analysing Middle East Foreign Policies. The Relationship with Europe*. London: Routledge, pp. 43–63.

Wolf, Klaus Dieter, Nicole Deitelhoff and Stefan Engert. 2007. "Corporate Security Responsibility: Towards a Conceptual Framework for a Comparative Research Agenda," *Cooperation and Conflict* 42 (3): 294–320.

Woodman, Sophia. 2007. "Driving without a Map: Implementing Legal Projects in China Aimed at Improving Human Rights," in Daniel A. Bell and Jean-Marc Coicaud (eds.), *Ethics in Action: The Ethical Challenges of International Human Rights Nongovernmental Organizations*. New York: Cambridge University Press, pp. 132–150.

World Bank Group. 2009. *World Development Indicators Online. World Bank Group*. Accessed November 9, 2009 at http://data.worldbank.org/indicator.

World Health Organization. 1999. *Female Genital Mutilation: Programmes to Date: What Works and What Doesn't. A Review*. Accessed August 5, 2009, at www. who.int/reproductivehealth/publications/fgm/en/index.html.

2000. *Female Genital Mutilation: A Handbook for Frontline Workers*. Accessed August 5, 2009, at www.who.int/reproductivehealth/publications/fgm/en/index.html.

2001a. *Female Genital Mutilation: Integrating the Prevention and the Management of the Health Complications into the Curricula of Nursing and Midwifery. A Student's Guide*. Accessed August 5, 2009, at www.who.int/reproductive-health/publications/fgm/en/index.html.

2001b. *Female Genital Mutilation: Integrating the Prevention and the Management of the Health Complications into the Curricula of Nursing and Midwifery. A Teacher's Guide*. Accessed August 5, 2009, at www.who.int/reproductive-health/publications/fgm/en/index.html.

2001c. *Female Genital Mutilation: The Prevention and the Management of the Health Complications. Policy Guidelines for Nurses and Midwives*. Accessed

August 5, 2009 at www.who.int/reproductivehealth/publications/fgm/en/index.html.

2006. "Female Genital Mutilation and Obstetric Outcome: WHO Collaborative Prospective Study in Six African Countries," *The Lancet 367*: 1835–1841.

2008. *Eliminating Female Genital Mutilation: An Interagency Statement – OHCHR, UNAIDS, UNDP, UNECA, UNESCO, UNFPA, UNHCR, UNICEF, UNIFEM, WHO.* Accessed August 5, 2009, at www.who.int/reproductivehealth/publications/fgm/9789241596442/en/.

World Medical Association. 1993. *Policy: The World Medical Association Statement on Female Genital Mutilation, adopted by the 45th World Medical Assembly, Budapest, Hungary, October 1993.* Accessed August 5, 2009, at www.wma.net/e/policy/c10.htm.

1997. *Female Circumcision (2).* Accessed August 5, 2009, at www.wma.net/e/press/1997_11.htm.

2003. *New WMA President Condemns Ill Treatment of Children.* Accessed August 5, 2009 at www.wma.net/e/press/2003_17.htm.

Wotipka, Christine Min and Francisco O. Ramirez. 2008. "World Society and Human Rights: An Event History Analysis of the Convention on the Elimination of all forms of Discrimination Against Women," in Beth A. Simmons, Frank Dobbin and Geoffrey Garrett (eds.), *The Global Diffusion of Markets and Democracy.* New York: Cambridge University Press, pp. 303–343.

Young, John. 2008. "Sudan: The Incomplete Transition from the SPLA to the SPLM," in Jeroen de Zeeuw (eds.), *From Soldiers to Politicians: Transforming Rebel Movements After Civil War.* Boulder, CO: Lynne Rienner, pp. 157–178.

Young, Oran R. 1979. *Compliance and Public Authority: A Theory with International Applications.* Baltimore: Johns Hopkins University Press.

Zacher, Mark W. 2001. "The Territorial Integrity Norm: International Boundaries and the Use of Force," *International Organization* 55 (2): 215–250.

Zadek, Simon. 2004. "The Path to Corporate Responsibility," *Harvard Business Review* 48 (12): 125–132.

Zald, Mayer. 1996. "Culture, Ideology, and Strategic Framing," in Doug McAdam, John McCarthy and Mayer Zald (eds.), *Comparative Perspectives on Social Movements. Political Opportunities, Mobilizing Structures, and Cultural Framings.* Cambridge University Press, pp. 259–274.

Zegveld, Liesbeth. 2002. *Accountability of Armed Opposition Groups in International Law.* Cambridge University Press.

Zernike, Kate. 2004. "New Released Reports Show Early Concern on Prison Abuse," *New York Times*, January 6, p. A18.

Zhao, Ling. 2005. "The Unjust Murder Case of Nie Shubin Still Hangs Undecided," *Nanfang Zhoumo* 16.03.2005. Translation by D. Owen Young. Accessed January 31, 2010 at www.pressinterpreter.org/index.php?q=node/120.

Zimmer, Melanie. 2010. "Oil Companies in Nigeria: Emerging Good Practice or Still Fueling Conflict?" in Nicole Deitelhoff and Klaus Dieter Wolf (eds.), *Corporate*

Security Responsibility? Corporate Governance Contributions to Peace and Security in Zones of Conflict. Houndmills, Basingstoke: Palgrave Macmillan, pp. 58–84.

Zimmern, Alfred Eckhard. 1939. *The League of Nations and the Rule of Law, 1918–1935.* London: Macmillan.

Zürn, Michael. 2002. "Politik in der postnationalen Konstellation. Über das Elend des methodologischen Nationalismus," in Christine Landfried (ed.), *Politik in einer entgrenzten Welt. 21. Wissenschaftlicher Kongress der Deutschen Vereinigung für Politische Wissenschaft.* Köln: Verlag Wissenschaft und Politik, pp. 181–203.

INDEX

CAMBRIDGE STUDIES IN INTERNATIONAL RELATIONS

Printed in Great Britain
by Amazon.co.uk, Ltd.,
Marston Gate.